The End of Communist Power

Europe and the International Order

Series Editor: Joel Krieger

The dramatic events of 1989, perestroika and post-perestroika developments in the Soviet Union, the apparent end of the Cold War, European integration, and the aftermath of the War in the Persian Gulf mark a period of extraordinary volatility in Europe. This series considers the causes, dimensions, and consequences of these new transitions in European politics. It includes books which transcend the divisions of East and West, challenge narrow disciplinary approaches, and examine the connections between international and domestic politics.

Published

Forthcoming

The End of Communist Power

Anti-Corruption Campaigns and Legitimation Crisis

Leslie Holmes

Oxford University Press • New York
1993

Oxford University Press

Copyright © Leslie Holmes 1993

First published in 1993 by Polity Press
in association with Blackwell Publishers

First published in North America by Oxford University Press, Inc.,
200 Madison Avenue, New York 10016

Oxford is a registered trademark of Oxford University Press

A CIP catalogue record for this book is available
from the Library of Congress

ISBN 0-19-521013-1
ISBN 0-19-521014-X (pbk.)

Printing (last digit): 9 8 7 6 5 4 3 2 1

Printed in Great Britain.

For Cate, my slozhnaya cariad

Contents

Preface

By almost any criteria, 1989 represented what was to become the most eventful period in the communist world since the 1940s – far more so even than 1956. At the beginning of the year, the Soviets completed their military withdrawal from Afghanistan; this was a highly significant symbol of the reversal of their earlier expansionism. In April, the People's Republic of Kampuchea symbolically began a process of renouncing communism by renaming itself the State of Cambodia; by September, the last of the occupying Vietnamese troops had withdrawn from the country. Beginning in April 1989, Chinese students protested against the authorities, then occupied the world's largest square, Tiananmen; in June, many of those still demonstrating in Beijing were viciously massacred. But none of the events in communist Asia was as momentous as those occurring in Eastern Europe. After four decades of communist rule, the six countries of Eastern Europe still within the Soviet sphere of influence – those that, collectively, had often been referred to as the 'Soviet external empire' – underwent what can only be described as revolutionary transformations. By the end of the year, the communists were no longer dominant in the governments of Czechoslovakia, Poland and – arguably – Hungary, while their hold on power in the GDR and Bulgaria was tenuous; they looked set to – and did – lose power in those countries in 1990.[1] Symbolically, at least, the Berlin Wall came down in November 1989. Even in the most authoritarian and seemingly immutable of all the Soviet-bloc countries of the region, Romania, the quarter-century dictatorship of Nicolae and Elena Ceauşescu had collapsed – unfortunately, at considerable human cost. There, as in other East European countries, the constitutional guarantee of the 'leading role' of the communist party had by the year's end been abolished, and the country was no longer officially described as a 'Socialist Republic'. Moving beyond the

Soviet bloc, Yugoslavia was clearly in crisis; not only was the ideology of Marxism–Leninism apparently about to be officially abandoned, but the country itself was in real danger of disintegration.

But perhaps the most powerful sign of the crisis of communism was in the home of Marxism–Leninism itself, the USSR. The policies of the man whom *Time* magazine in December 1989 named 'Man of the Decade', Mikhail Gorbachev, looked increasingly endangered. *Perestroika* (restructuring) was not only not improving the economic situation in the USSR, but appeared to be making matters worse; at the same time, *glasnost* (public openness or honesty) was leading to ever more radical demands being made of the communist authorities. As in Yugoslavia, not only was Marxism-Leninism in danger, but there were signs that the federation itself might disintegrate. Leading Georgian and Baltic politicians had publicly declared that their republics would attempt to exercise their formal right to secede, while leaders in several other republics looked set to follow suit. When Gorbachev had himself appointed to the new post of chair of the Russia Buro of the Central Committee in December – a post akin to one which had been established under Khrushchev and abolished in 1966 – it did not seem too fanciful or cold-warlike to infer that he might be preparing for the break-up of the USSR itself (that is, if the USSR and hence the Communist Party of the Soviet Union in its existing format were to be either dismantled or else reduced in scope, Gorbachev could by this new measure at least hope to maintain control over the largest republic of the USSR, the RSFSR).

By the end of 1991, the processes that had so dominated the world's media during the latter months of 1989 had largely crystallized. The Soviet 'external empire' clearly had collapsed; even Comecon and the Warsaw Treaty Organization had ceased to exist. But, even more dramatically, the Soviet 'internal empire' – the USSR itself – had also disintegrated. Following the failed coup attempt in Moscow in August 1991, the threat from 'the right' (that is, from those that many Russians themselves call the 'fundamentalist' communists, plus sections of the state's coercive agencies) that had been growing for some time had, at least for the time being, been removed. In the aftermath of this fiasco, the transition towards post-communism in the USSR[2] took two giant steps. First, communist power was essentially ended when Gorbachev resigned as General Secretary of the Central Committee of the Communist Party of the Soviet Union and the party itself was *de facto* banned; Gorbachev's own ambitions to stay on as the Russian leader had also been frustrated by the end of the year. Second, the USSR ceased to exist.

This process started when the Russian authorities recognized the sovereignty of the Baltic states; subsequently – in December 1991 – Russian President Boris Yeltsin and a number of other Republican leaders declared the USSR dead, and established a new Commonwealth of Independent States on the basis of eleven former republics (Georgia and the Baltic states were not part of this as of January 1992). The final collapse of communism in most parts of what had been Yugoslavia, and the disintegration of the Yugoslav state itself, had also occurred by the end of 1991.

By December 1991, there were several indications that post-communism, too, was in crisis. But this crisis was itself largely an outcome of the crisis and collapse of communism – so that an understanding of these new crises requires as deep an understanding of the crises that preceded them as possible.

The events of 1989–91 can be described as the *double rejective revolution*. The first rejection was of the communist power system. The second was of what was perceived to be external domination – by the USSR in the case of most of Eastern Europe, mainly by the Russians in the USSR, largely by the Serbs in the case of Yugoslavia. The two rejections were intimately linked; what particularly irritated many of the revolutionary forces was not simply the domination itself, but the fact that the dominator's own system had largely failed, with all sorts of negative ramifications for the dominated. Controversially, perhaps, I would argue that domination by an economically dynamic and successful country or ethnic group would have been far more tolerable to many in the dominated countries/ regions.

The double rejective revolution also meant that the debates that had taken place among Western political scientists during the 1980s on whether or not communism was moving towards a crisis situation had become redundant. There could no longer be any doubt whatsoever that communism as a system of power had not only entered a crisis period, but had largely collapsed; by the end of 1991, the few remaining pockets of communism in the world (mostly in East Asia) looked distinctly fragile. This crisis and collapse of communism acts as a backcloth to the present study. Although the bulk of the book is concerned with official corruption in what has by now almost become an historical phenomenon – the communist world – the campaigns against such corruption are taken as one major symbol of the overall dynamics of communist politics that resulted in the 1989–91 crisis and collapse. The book elaborates a general theory of this dynamism, and analyses factors other than anti-corruption campaigns that reveal and exemplify it. Let us now consider more closely the genesis and *raison d'être* of this book, and the relationship between anti-corruption campaigns and the developing crisis of communism.

Like many books, this one was conceived almost by accident. During the Andropov era of Soviet politics (1982–4), I was struck by the energy with which the new Soviet leader was attacking all sorts of social problems – including corruption, which was suddenly being officially described as one of the most serious problem-areas in society. Shortly after my interest in Soviet corruption had been kindled, I was reading a collection of Castro's speeches, and found that he had been highly critical of corruption in Cuba in the same year as Andropov had started his campaign. My interest whetted, I looked to China – only to discover that the Chinese Communist Party had launched a major campaign against corruption in 1982! Was this coincidence? Had similar campaigns been happening elsewhere at about the same time? Eventually I discovered that some of the East European regimes, notably Bulgaria, Czechoslovakia, Hungary and Poland, had also launched anti-corruption campaigns in the early to mid-1980s, while Vietnam had been intensifying its fight against corruption. But *why* had so many leaderships apparently been 'washing their dirty linen in public' or, worse still, 'shooting themselves in the foot'? Was this connected with increasing signs of crisis in many parts of the communist world? To someone who in recent years has preferred to work on comparative communism than to specialize in just one country, this topic looked ripe for analysis. Was there a concerted, perhaps Soviet-led policy in the communist world to combat corruption? Given the range of countries, this was likely to be at most only partially true; China could hardly be seen as a puppet of the USSR, and Cuba was asserting its autonomy far more in the 1980s than it had been in the 1960s and 1970s. In any case, the campaigns in China, Cuba and Poland appeared to *pre-date* the Soviet one. Moreover, some of the countries often seen as being very close allies of the USSR – notably the GDR – did *not* at that stage seem to be having anti-corruption campaigns. Nor did North Korea. One of the features both the former GDR and the DPRK had in common was that, being separate parts of what many at that time still saw as a larger whole (this still pertains in the case of the DPRK), they had particular legitimation problems of a sort not experienced by most other communist countries – Vietnam until 1975, South Yemen until 1990, and to a very limited extent China being possible exceptions. Could there be a connection here, and if so, what was it?

At the same time as I was pondering this issue, I published a textbook on comparative communism (Holmes, 1986a) that was, to my relief, generally well received. But some reviewers of that book, and other scholars who had attended various seminars I had been giving at that time, justifiably argued that I was keeping my own views on communism too much to myself. Some of them urged me to reveal my own theoretical perspectives on the nature and dynamism of communist politics; the links I thought I saw developing between the reporting of corruption (which could be researched empirically) and both legitimation and crisis began to look like a way of simultaneously adhering to my preference for detailed research and satisfying those who wanted an elaboration of my own theoretical perspective. It must be acknowledged that by the time I had finished the book – at a time of recent or ongoing revolution in most parts of the communist world – I was far more excited by the large theoretical questions I had been tackling than in the more empirical material; readers will have to judge for themselves my success in blending the two.

This, in a nutshell, is what led me to research corruption in the communist world, and to locate that empirical study in a theoretical framework based primarily on legitimation and the concept of crisis.

The central argument of this study arose initially very much as a reaction to two views, widely held among writers on comparative communism during the 1970s and 1980s, about legitimation in the communist world. The first was that communist leaderships are or should be far more concerned with legitimating themselves and the political system to their bureaucracies (staffs) than to the public (masses); the latter's attitudes had been treated by some observers as if they were of essentially marginal significance. The second was that the dominant mode of legitimation in the communist world is the goal-rational. An alternative argument – the central thesis of this book – can be briefly summarized in terms of seven interrelated and progressive propositions (for a fuller exposition of these, see pp. 41–4). First, communist leaderships typically attempt to move over time from predominantly coercion-based to predominantly legitimation-based power; as they do so, they focus initially on their staffs, subsequently on the masses – whose values and attitudes *are* of significance. The argument here is *not* that the masses' views are *more* important than those of the staffs, but that there emerges a growing, dynamic interaction between the two sets, so that any view focusing exclusively or predominantly on the leaders and/or the leader–staff nexus is being inappropriately reductionist. Second, the tendency over time in terms of mass legitimation is towards the eudaemonic (in essence, performance-based) mode. Third, the eudaemonic mode can, however, become problematic for leaderships, especially if it is dependent upon economic reform that negatively affects the interests of the staffs. Fourth, in order to resolve this problem, leaderships may well mobilize mass opinion against the staffs; recent anti-corruption campaigns can be seen partially in this light. Given the problem of eudaemonic legitimation, this involvement of the masses typically takes place in the context of a general move in the direction of the legal-rational mode. Fifth, the notion of appealing to the masses over the heads of the staffs can be dangerous to the leaders; if the moves fail to achieve the desired effect, they can backfire, leaving both an alienated staff and a frustrated citizenry. This constitutes a particularly dangerous political situation. Sixth, it is possible in some circumstances for the tactics described in the fourth proposition to be effective in the short to medium term; leaders may temporarily succeed in shifting away from imperfect legal-rationality back towards eudaemonism. However, this tactic of shifting between legitimation modes – especially between eudaemonism and legal-rationality – cannot be employed indefinitely. Finally, eudaemonism sooner or later proves inadequate, and demands for more permanent moves deeper into legal-rationality increase. But the further communist leaderships move into legal-rationality, the more they find themselves in a *contradictory transition* – a concept that is particularly useful in explaining the revolutions of 1989–91. In general, the argument is that a *fundamental* contradiction exists between the 'rule of law' (a basic tenet of legal-rationality) and communism as a system of power; this contradiction eventually results in the collapse of a communist system – although there might in some circumstances be a *temporary* return to coercion as the dominant form of power, prior to the *subsequent* collapse of the system.

One of the many problems that arises in writing on communism and post-communism at the beginning of the 1990s is that different countries are at different stages of transition. At one end of the spectrum, the DPRK was still – as of December 1991 – essentially an unreconstructed communist system, and Cuba had only just begun officially to acknowledge the need for significant reform. At the other end of the spectrum were the trailblazers into post-communism, such as Hungary and Poland – while in between were countries/regions such as China, Vietnam and parts of Yugoslavia that were at various stages of transition from communism but could not yet be said to have reached post-communism. In short, one is writing about a moving target. One implication of this is that it is not always obvious which tense of a verb should be used; for some countries the present would be appropriate, for others the past – while for a third group, the future (possibly conditional) would be the correct form. During January 1992, I attempted to rewrite virtually the whole book in the past tense, on the grounds that the vast majority of the 23 states that could be classified at the beginning of 1989 as 'communist' were by then either already at the stage of post-communism or else well on the way to it. Eventually, however, I abandoned this project, partly because the conversion of much of the material on corruption read more awkwardly – less elegantly – in the past tense than in the present. Instead, the general policy I have adopted is to use the past (imperfect) tense, mostly, for past events in specific countries; to use the past tense in most cases when discussing actual developments in the communist world; to use the present or perfect tense, mostly, when analysing general aspects of communist systems (because I am at those points considering a type of system, essentially isolated from its historical context); to use the present tense, mostly, for the general analysis of corruption (as distinct from the analysis of specific cases of corruption); and, connected with the last point, to use the present tense when discussing general phenomena that do not necessarily relate only to communism. While this is not a perfect solution, I believe it to be the optimal one in the circumstances. Of course, readers who would prefer to change tenses for themselves as they read are very welcome to do so. They should bear in mind, however, that more than a billion people still – as of early 1992 – live under communist rule in East Asia, South East Asia and Cuba, so that to put everything in the past tense might appear to be excessively Eurocentric.

The reference system used in this book is basically the Harvard one. However, where articles from the popular press (both dailies and weeklies) are cited, full reference details are provided in the text. The principal reason for this is to keep the bibliography within manageable proportions.

My thanks are due both to institutions and to individuals. I would like to express my gratitude to the Australian Research Grants Scheme (ARGS) and to the University of Melbourne for their generous financial support of this research project over a three-year period. This enabled me to acquire the services of a full-time co-researcher, Dr Keith Forster (until recently of the Contemporary China Centre at the Australian National University) and two part-time research assistants, Vera Butler and Karin von Strokirch; I was also lucky enough to have had access to the data-processing skills of Tony Clayworth. The grants enabled me as well to visit eight of the countries included here, where I conducted interviews – on a very haphazard basis (communist states were for the most part not prepared to allow systematic investigation by Westerners of their more serious problems) – and, in some cases, experienced corruption

first-hand. In addition to visiting these eight, however, I have been
fortunate enough to discuss corruption over the past few years with a
number of visitors from communist states and with severel émigrés
from these countries. My thanks to all these people – researchers,
interviewees, visitors, etc. – for their help.

I would also like to thank a number of individuals who were
generous enough with their time to read and comment upon various
drafts of part or all of this book; they are, in alphabetical order, Ruth
Abbey, John Cash, Michael Dutton, Graeme Gill, David McLellan
and Tony Phillips. Thanks, too, to the numerous people who
attended and made comments at seminars I have given relating to the
content-matter of this book – in Washington DC, Palmerston
North, Oxford, Canterbury (England), Taipei, Beijing, Leiden,
Montreal, Armidale, Brisbane and Melbourne.

I am deeply indebted to Jan Souter, Vanda Arfi and Rita Corelli,
both for typing the manuscript and for keeping remarkably sweet-
tempered (*most* of the time) when faced either with page after page of
my appalling handwriting or else with worn-out tapes for use in
their dictaphones. Samm kindly lent me her 'study', while Bill and
Joan generously let me use their cabin when I needed somewhere
quiet and 'away from it all' to put the finishing touches to this book.
And I am very grateful to St Antony's College, Oxford – in
particular, to Professor Archie Brown – for granting me Senior
Associate Membership in the Michaelmas Term 1987; it was at St
Antony's that the original, full-length draft of this book was written.

Unfortunately, and as the reader might correctly infer from the
last sentence, the 'final polish' of this book took far longer than it
should have done. There were two main reasons for this. First, I was
– for my sins – elected head of department in 1988; during my first
two years in office, learning the ropes of the new job left me with
very little time for research and writing. Second, and more significantly, the crisis that serves as the focal point of the book really burst
into the open in 1989, and for a long time it was all most analysts –
myself included – could do simply to keep abreast of developments,
let alone sit back and contemplate them from a broader perspective. I
preferred not to publish while everything was still very much in flux,
since the book *might* then have been all but redundant virtually from
the moment of publication. Fortunately, I feel that the 'legitimation
crisis' theory that permeates the book – and which, in essentially
similar form, I first publicly articulated in 1988 (Holmes, 1988) –
stood the test of time reasonably well (the main flaw in the original
version was that I had underestimated the level of tension and
contradiction between Marxism-Leninism and legal-rationality). But

one could not have been certain that this would be the case, given the quite extraordinary and unprecedented events of the past three years. With the abandonment of communism in the USSR and the break-up – or at least revamping – of the country, however, I feel that an appropriate juncture has been reached from which to consider the 1989–91 revolution from a deeper analytical perspective. In all events, my final thanks are to my publisher, Tony Giddens, and my publishing manager at Polity Press, Debbie Seymour, for their incredible patience and understanding; I can only hope that, despite its numerous weaknesses, they agree with me that the book is better for the delay, since I have had longer to ponder and refine my original ideas.

L.T.H.
Ocean Grove

NOTES

1   It is debatable whether or not it is legitimate to claim that the communists lost power in Hungary by the end of 1989 and in Bulgaria during 1990, since the dominant forces in Hungary until the March–April 1990 elections and in Bulgaria until the October 1991 elections were 'socialists' who were for the most part former communists. However, in that these people consciously renamed their parties (in October 1989 in the case of Hungary, April 1990 in the case of Bulgaria) and explicitly rejected – both in theory and in practice – so many basic tenets of communism, I have opted to suggest here that the communists had lost power. See too note 11, Chapter 8.

2   Although the USSR *de facto* ceased to exist in December 1991 – much of it to be replaced by the CIS – the vast majority of the analysis in this book deals with events that occurred prior to that date, so that the terms 'USSR', 'Soviet Union' and 'Soviet' are used in most cases. The term 'CIS' – which itself might relatively soon be redundant – is used only when referring to present (early 1992) and future situations.

Abbreviations

ALP	Albanian Labour Party
AR	Autonomous Region
BCP	Bulgarian Communist Party
BR	*Beijing Review*
CCP	Chinese Communist Party
CD	*China Daily*
CDIC	Central Discipline Inspection Commission
CDSP	*Current Digest of the Soviet Press*
CIS	Commonwealth of Independent States
CMEA	Council for Mutual Economic Assistance
Comecon	(same as CMEA)
COPWE	Commission for Organizing the Party of the Working People of Ethiopia
CP	Communist Party
CPC	Communist Party of Cuba
CPCS	Communist Party of Czechoslovakia
CPK	Communist Party of Kampuchea
CPSU	Communist Party of the Soviet Union
DIC	Discipline Inspection Commission
DPRK	Democratic People's Republic of Korea
E(E)C	European (Economic) Community
EIU	Economist Intelligence Unit
FBIS	Foreign Broadcast Information Service
FEER	*Far Eastern Economic Review*
FNLA	(National Front for the Liberation of Angola)
Frelimo	(Front for the Liberation of Mozambique)
FRG	Federal Republic of Germany
GDR	German Democratic Republic
GPCR	Great Proletarian Cultural Revolution
HSWP	Hungarian Socialist Workers' Party

IB	*Information Bulletin – Documents of the Communist and Workers' Parties, Articles and Speeches*
KCA	*Keesing's Contemporary Archives*
KGB	(Committee of State Security)
Komsomol	(Communist Youth League)
KRWE	*Keesing's Record of World Events*
LCY	League of Communists of Yugoslavia
LPRP	Lao People's Revolutionary Party
MFN	Most Favoured Nation
MN	*Moscow News*
MPLA	(Popular Movement for the Liberation of Angola)
MPRP	Mongolian People's Revolutionary Party
NIE	Newly Industrializing Economy
NT	*New Times*
PDPA	People's Democratic Party of Afghanistan
PDRY	People's Democratic Republic of Yemen
PDS	Party of Democratic Socialism
PLA	People's Liberation Army
PRC	People's Republic of China
PUWP	Polish United Workers' Party
QER	*Quarterly Economic Review*
RFE	Radio Free Europe
RMRB	*Renmin Ribao*
ROK	Republic of Korea
RSFSR	Russian Soviet Federal Socialist Republic
SED	(Socialist Unity Party of Germany)
SFRY	Socialist Federal Republic of Yugoslavia
SWB	*Summary of World Broadcasts*
UDBa	(State Security Administration)
UN	United Nations
UNITA	(National Union for the Total Independence of Angola)
US(A)	United States (of America)
USSR	Union of Soviet Socialist Republics
VCP	Vietnamese Communist Party
WTO	Warsaw Treaty Organization
YICA	*Yearbook on International Communist Affairs*
YL	*Yugoslav Life*
YSP	Yemeni Socialist Party

1

Theoretical Framework

We must complete the creation of the socialist legal state.
>   Mikhail Gorbachev in *Pravda*, 11 May 1988

Socialist democracy is inseparable from a socialist legal system
. . . through reform, we should gradually establish a legal framework
for our socialist democracy and institutionalise it. This is a fundamental
guarantee against a recurrence of the 'cultural revolution' and for lasting
political stability in the country.
>   Zhao Ziyang at the 13th Congress of the CCP, October 1987

1989 was a watershed year in the history of communism. Mass
unrest in Beijing and other Chinese cities was suppressed in June; the
communists were able to retain power for the time being – primarily
through brute force (martial law in Beijing was only formally lifted
in January 1990). But in Eastern Europe,[1] mass unrest was on one
level and at least partially responsible for the overthrow of existing
communist regimes in Bulgaria, Czechoslovakia, the GDR and
Romania. The same is true of Poland, which many see as the cradle
of the recent East European revolution. While it would be overly
reductionist to identify any one event or process as *the* starting point
of this revolution, the establishment of Solidarity in September 1980
should certainly be taken as *one* of the key longer-term events in the
build-up to 1989. Solidarity was the first large-scale unofficial workers' organization in the communist world to be more or less recognized by the authorities; at its peak, its membership was some three
or four times larger than that of the Polish communist party
(PUWP). Although it was suppressed following the imposition of
martial law in December 1981, Solidarity never completely collapsed. By 1988, with mounting economic and other problems in
Poland, the masses began to reassert themselves. A wave of strikes in
August led to negotiations between the communists and the still

illegal trade union organization; these resulted not only in the legalization of Solidarity in April 1989, but also in 'semi-free' elections
(this term is used by Frentzel-Zagorska, 1989) in June and eventually
– in September – in a coalition government dominated by members
of Solidarity. It was also in September that a survey of PUWP
members revealed that the majority wanted the party to change both
its name and nature at the next party congress, scheduled for early
1990. When this congress took place in January 1990, the PUWP
split into two new parties – both claiming to be social democratic;
communism as a system of power in Poland was dead. The situation
in Hungary was somewhat different from that in the other East
European countries already mentioned. There, the revolution was in
many ways and more overtly set in train by the communists themselves, in a manner not dissimilar from what had happened in
Czechoslovakia during the so-called Prague Spring of 1968. The
Hungarian process became very visible in 1988, with the relatively
gentle removal of the leader, Kádár, and his replacement by a
radically reformist team. By the end of 1989, the communist party
(HSWP) had changed its name, structure and image. But none of this
was sufficient to save it. When the masses were given the opportun-
ity to show whether or not they supported the dramatically
revamped communist party – during the general election of March–
April 1990 – they revealed that they were no more willing to support
such an organization than were the masses in the other East European countries referred to. In Hungary, too, communism as a system
of power was dead. In Yugoslavia, not only was Marxism-Leninism
and the LCY (federal communist party) increasingly under threat by
1989, but there were signs that the federal system itself might
collapse; for instance, in September the Slovene Assembly declared
the republic's right to secede. The LCY congress collapsed in January
1990, and by November the LCY itself had been replaced by the
'League of Communists – Movement for Yugoslavia' – in which the
military was prominent. During the course of 1990, moreover, four
of the six republics (Slovenia, Croatia, Bosnia-Hercegovina and
Macedonia) of Yugoslavia had replaced their communist governments with non-communist ones. Divisions and tensions were
deepening, and Yugoslavia appeared to be at an advanced stage in a
bumpy transition from communism to post-communism. This
became even more obvious in mid-1991, when fighting erupted
between, most notably, the Yugoslav army and Croatian nationalists; by the end of the year, Yugoslavia as the world had come to
know it had ceased to exist. By the beginning of the new decade,
there were even signs that the only East European communist state

that until then had appeared to have avoided the 1989–90 revolution – Albania – might be set to join its neighbours; by June 1991, it too had joined the ranks of what Brzezinski (1989, esp. pp. 252–8) and others have called 'post-communism'.

The anti-communist revolution that began to emerge in 1989, though most developed and visible in Eastern Europe, had by the early 1990s become evident in many other parts of the communist world. In Benin, for example, the minister for planning and statistics appealed in July 1989 for a multi-party system. In January 1990, members of the newly formed Mongolian Democratic Federation and other demonstrators in Ulan Bator called for an end to the political monopoly of the Mongolian communist party; this was followed by the establishment of several political parties in the first months of 1990, legalization of multi-party competitive elections in May 1990, and a genuinely contested election during July and August. Although the communist party (MPRP) won the most seats at this, the concept of a legal opposition and an end to the communist political monopoly had been officially accepted. Basically similar changes were beginning to occur in Angola, Congo, Mozambique and elsewhere by 1990, too, whilst the communist system in Ethiopia essentially collapsed in 1991.

But probably most significant of all was the threat to the existing power system in the home of communism, the USSR. Throughout 1989, there were signs that the radical reform policies of Mikhail Gorbachev were in serious trouble. Early in January 1990, Gorbachev's statements to the Lithuanians gave the impression that the Soviet leader might at last be publicly accepting for the Soviet Union what he had apparently been recently urging East European communist leaders to accept – viz that the concept of the leading or vanguard role of the communist party would have to be abandoned, and that communists would have to compete with others in genuinely contested elections. These radical ideas were adopted *de facto* in 1990, even if the constitutional position on a genuine multi-party system was still not entirely clear (on the development of the multi-party system in the USSR see Tolz, 1990; for the October 1990 law on social organizations see *Vedomosti Verkhovnogo Soveta*, No. 42, 1990, pp. 1024–35). Even more dramatically, Gorbachev appeared to many observers to be entertaining the possibility of an eventual break-up of the Russians' 'internal empire', the USSR itself. Although he seemed to be changing his position on this by late 1990, it was far from clear that Gorbachev – or anyone else (including Ligachev or the military) – would be able to prevent such a dissolution in the medium term. Following the failed coup attempt of

August 1991, it became clear once and for all that a radical restructuring and at least partial dismemberment of the Soviet Union was underway. The post-coup government almost immediately recognized the sovereignty of three of the fifteen republics (the Baltic states of Estonia, Latvia and Lithuania), while a number of other republics, such as Georgia, reiterated their claims that they were now sovereign states. By December 1991, the USSR had ceased to exist, and eleven of the former fifteen republics had re-formed themselves into the CIS. The other most significant development in the aftermath of the August 1991 coup was Gorbachev's resignation as head of the Communist Party of the Soviet Union and the party's subsequent collapse. Thus, by December 1991, both the USSR and communist power in that country were essentially finished; whatever changes occur in the future – even the return of a form of communism in the CIS – nothing can ever be the same again in that part of the world. During the present decade, it seems highly probable that other communist states, too – including Vietnam, Cuba, China and even North Korea – will undergo transformations radical enough to warrant the term 'revolution'. The recent prognoses of writers such as Brzezinski (1989) about the collapse of communist power as we know it have proven largely correct.

Two questions that must now be addressed by social scientists are how (and why) such an anti-communist revolution came about, and how what we had come to know as 'the communist world' – but what is now increasingly the post-communist world – might look in the 1990s and the twenty-first century. On the latter question, for instance, can we accept at face value Brzezinski's argument (1989, p. 258) that the next century is likely to be dominated by democracy rather than communism? Is such a dichotomy too simple? It is not the primary aim of this book to provide comprehensive or definitive answers to these two basic – and enormous – questions. It is highly questionable that anyone could provide an answer to the first that would be acceptable to most, while the second involves futurology and is likely to cause even more controversy. Nevertheless, it *is* an aim of this book to provide one interpretation of the dynamism that led up to the events of 1989–91 and, by projecting the logic of the argument forward, to speculate in a limited way on future possibilities.

In attempting to describe 'the' dynamism of communism – which is, of course, postulated on the subjective hypothesis that such a dynamism both exists and can be analysed – I have focused in this book on one particular symbol of the growing crisis, anti-corruption campaigns, and of how both corruption itself and these campaigns were symptomatic of legitimation problems that eventually became a general crisis that resulted in system-collapse. Thus, the approach adopted here is to concentrate on a specific phenomenon as a symbol or manifestation of something much bigger and more complex. However, since I was interested in the general as much as the particular, several other 'particulars' – the component parts of the general – are briefly elaborated in order to demonstrate the confluence and interaction of several variables that simultaneously contributed to and were reflective of the general crisis and, in so many countries, the collapse of communism. The basic argument is a relatively simple one, and focuses on the growing *identity crisis* of communism as its own internal dynamic took it increasingly into a situation of *contradictory transition*. The argument can be expressed simply and briefly; a more detailed exposition will unfold in the following pages. In an endeavour to overcome numerous problems, especially economic and legitimation ones, communist leaderships began to adopt policies and practices that from some perspectives made their systems look increasingly similar to those of their traditional ideological enemy, the West; this development was thus in direct contradiction to former basic tenets of the official ideology. However, as this process unfolded, it appeared to many citizens and even officials in the communist world that they were being increasingly subjected to all the negative aspects of both capitalism and communism (such as inflation, unemployment, bankruptcies, crime; the virtual monopoly of political power, shortages of goods, etc.) at the same time as the positive aspects of both (such as high levels of freedom of speech and belief, freedom to travel, high-quality consumer goods; low levels of stratification and alienation, high levels of security, etc.) seemed in many cases at least as distant as they had ever been. In short, communism was changing dramatically, but appeared more and more to represent the worst of all worlds, rather than the best. While Marxism-Leninism can be, should be and has been a highly flexible ideology, the point at which communism becomes virtually indistinguishable from capitalism and liberal democracy in anything but a disadvantageous light is the limit of the ideology's flexibility – a point of identity crisis. Within this framework of identity crisis and contradictory transition, anti-corruption campaigns are taken as one concrete symbol of the general phenomenon, while the concept of changing modes of legitimation serves as the basis for understanding the dynamics of the transition.

The reader may be forgiven for assuming that the author is foolhardy not only for analysing one phenomenon (the actual or potential collapse of communist power and the emergence of post-communism) that is still very much ongoing, but also for attempting to write a book about two other phenomena, corruption and legitimation, that are notoriously difficult to define and to research, and about a part of the world which, despite growing *glasnost* in many parts of it, was still at the end of the 1980s *relatively* difficult to research, certainly in comparison with the liberal-democratic world. Corruption is also such a complex phenomenon that one could and ideally should look at it from the perspective of the political scientist *and* the economist *and* the criminologist *and* the sociologist *and* the psychologist *and* the social theorist *and* the anthropologist. One wonders whether such a person exists; the author certainly makes no claim to such Renaissance qualities. It would be easy enough, and in some senses justifiable, to use these several and very real difficulties as an excuse not even to try to understand either corruption or legitimation in the communist world. On the other hand, it is clear that communists in many countries themselves made a major issue out of corruption in recent years, and perceived it – or at least said they perceived it – as a very serious problem. To cite just four of innumerable quotations to this effect that could be given, Politburo member Lê Duc Tho wrote in the main Vietnamese newspaper, *Nhân Dân*, in May 1986:

> in this second stage [since April 1975], the challenge is material temptation, bourgeois lifestyle, money, beautiful girls and commodities . . . It causes the qualities and ethics of a revolutionary to gradually dissipate. It secretly destroys the strength of our contingent . . . Ideologically speaking, complex developments are being noted among cadres and party members . . . Some popular phenomena among cadres and party members are corruption, bribery, smuggling, enrichment, dissolute and depraved living, feasting and open bribery with presents . . . This situation exists everywhere and at every echelon. It has caused great wastage in production and people's lives, caused cadres and party to become degenerate and diminished the public's confidence. It may be said that in our party there has not previously been a degeneration of virtues and the way of living as is the case now. *This is a major, very serious issue.* (*SWB*, FE/8257/B/3 – emphasis added)

while the General Secretary of the Yemeni Socialist Party, Ali Salem al-Bidh, stated at the party conference convened by the YSP Central Committee in June 1987 that:

> The right-wing opportunistic deviation produced such negative phenomena as an inflation of state apparatus staffs, *corruption of a part of the administrative apparatus*, negligence, indiscipline, bureaucratic practi-

ces, *the squandering of state funds*, neglect of official instructions and internal regulations, *bribe-taking* and the infiltration of the organs of state power by hostile class elements. *It is now an urgent task to combat these phenomena.* (*IB*, Vol. 25, No. 19, 1987, p. 39 – emphasis added)

In January 1988, at a plenary meeting of the Central Committee of the Communist Party of Slovakia, the then Czechoslovak General Secretary Milos Jakeš argued that:

> Leading the drive for renewal means being in the forefront of struggle with reprehensible things in our society like corruption, illicit personal enrichment, embezzlement of socialist property, abuse of power . . . The conflict between one's words and actions has unfavourable ideological, moral and political repercussions and generates distrust not only of state and economic bodies, but also of the party and socialism generally . . . Therefore, what the party, its bodies and organisations and every Communist should do in the first place is to consistently and uncompromisingly battle against such behaviour, which is incompatible with socialist moral values . . . whoever the person concerned and whatever their post. No one is above public control and legitimate criticism. (from *Rudé Právo*, 15 January 1988 – translated in *IB*, Vol. 26, No. 7, 1988, p. 45)

And at the 13th Congress of the CCP (October–November 1987), the then General Secretary Zhao Ziyang made the following observations:

> The people complain a great deal now that a small number of Party members, particularly leading cadres, have abused their power for private gain at the expense of the people's interests, hindering the smooth progress of the reform and implementation of the open policy and damaging the Party's prestige. *This is a grave problem which we must take seriously and tackle in earnest* . . . The inner-Party struggle against corruption is unavoidable when we are carrying out reform and the open policy. If we tolerate decadent elements in the Party, the whole Party will decline. (Chinese Communist Party, 1987, pp. 65–6 – emphasis added)

It should be obvious even from these four examples that corruption has not only existed but *has publicly been perceived by communist leaders as a serious problem.* It could *inter alia* reflect badly on communist socialization processes and the progress towards the creation of a society of 'new socialist persons' (on this see Volgyes, 1975; see too *Pravda*, 10 August 1983, p. 3). Indeed, in some countries the problem was even before 1989 *said* to have been threatening the very existence of the system; by now it seems clear that this was indeed the case in some countries. In this context, it is interesting to note that when the student protestors started their demonstration in Tiananmen Square in April 1989, an end to official corruption was one of their principal demands (see, for example, *BR*, Vol. 32, No. 18, p. 9; *BR*, Vol. 32, No. 19, p. 5; *Time*, 29 May 1989, p. 23). Since then, the charges of corruption against ousted communist leaders such as Honecker (GDR) and Zhivkov (Bulgaria) are on one level an indication of the way in which new leaderships will sometimes attempt to gain or enhance their own legitimacy by focusing on an aspect of their predecessors about which they believe the masses feel particularly aggrieved. It is thus clearly important at least to attempt to study corruption and both its effects on legitimacy and its contribution to the crisis and collapse of communism; definitional and methodological problems notwithstanding, it would be even more foolhardy not even to attempt to analyse the phenomenon than it is to seek at least partially and imperfectly to comprehend it.

The significance of corruption both to communists themselves and to the citizens of communist states is not the sole reason for analysing it. Anyone seeking ways to improve their own society should at least consider other types of system – whether it be to learn how a given situation might be improved upon by adopting an approach used successfully elsewhere or, equally, to identify the sorts of difficulty that can arise in the practice of implementing what *a priori* seemed like a sensible solution to a problem. Although this book is overwhelmingly concerned with analysing corruption in *communist* systems, a number of comparisons are made with other types of system – especially liberal democracies – at appropriate junctures, since it is a secondary concern of the author to see to what extent certain phenomena are correlated with particular types of politico-socio-economic system.

Since the 'inner core' of this book is the issue of official corruption, the whole of the next chapter has been devoted to its definition and to an analysis of the various forms it can assume. Hence this is not the point at which to consider the meaning of the term. But it is appropriate to consider here definitions and approaches to legitimacy, legitimation and crisis, and to elaborate the theoretical approach adopted in the present study.

On Legitimacy, Legitimation and Crisis

As relatively recently as 1982, one of the leading scholars in the field of comparative communism, T.H. Rigby, was properly able to claim that the book he and Ferenc Fehér had just edited was 'the first ever to focus on political legitimation in the communist countries' (p. 9). Much has been written since that time, and there were certainly a number of articles, papers, and sections of books before the Rigby and Fehér collection (such as Gitelman, 1970; Gilison, 1972; Baylis, 1972 and 1974; Rothschild, 1979; Ludz, 1979; Lane, 1979). There now exists an interesting and fairly extensive literature on legitimacy and legitimation in communist states – a lot of it emanating from Australia. Much of this is pitched at an abstract level, however, and deals with questions such as 'What is legitimacy?', 'What is legitimation?', 'To which group in society is it most important to legitimise the political system?', etc. There is still relatively little empirically based analysis of legitimacy in communist states.[2] One major reason for this is that there is not even a widely held view, let alone a dominant one, on how the degree of legitimacy could actually be measured or investigated, even in a hypothetical – far less a concrete – sense (for example, one might postulate that surveys of citizens' or officials' attitudes should be conducted, which would not in practice have been feasible up to 1989, and may still not be in those few communist states that survive in the 1990s). This inability to devise a methodology for measuring legitimacy is a very serious one, and there is considerable validity to Alfred Meyer's comment (1972, p. 67) to the effect that we only *really* know that a communist state is illegitimate (or close to it) when we see it collapse or in overt danger of collapsing. In this context, it is difficult to envisage a convincing counter-argument to the notion that all of the communist systems of Eastern Europe had by 1989 become, or were rapidly becoming, essentially illegitimate. But what the events of 1989 do *not* tell us is whether or not some or all of the European communist states *ever* enjoyed a degree of legitimacy; if so, how much; among which social groups they enjoyed a degree of legitimacy and among which they enjoyed little or none; and what led to the general, overt crisis of 1989. The present study does not – indeed *cannot* – claim to have devised methods for answering all these questions. Rather, the argument is that we can study an actual phenomenon in the communist world – in this case corruption – and formulate hypotheses on the relationship of this observable and observed phenomenon to the legitimacy, legitimation and crisis of communist states. There is no way many of the hypotheses can be proven conclusively; but it is argued that they cannot be disproven or empirically falsified either. If any progress in the empirical analysis of legitimacy is to be made, we must begin by making well-reasoned arguments about possible relationships between it and observed phenomena.

At this juncture, it is appropriate to state the first basic assumption of the book, since it serves as a driving force through the somewhat complex argument that follows. This assumption is that *recent leadership concerns about and reactions to official corruption in so many communist states, and the notable increase in the reporting of corruption in the official media, were neither fortuitous nor necessarily simply reflective of a growing incidence of corruption in these societies. Rather, they reflected, at least to some extent, a change in the leaders' perception of their own and their system's legitimacy and an attempt to alter the balance between different modes of legitimation – especially popular legitimation. More specifically, they reflected a trend observable in several parts of the communist world in the 1980s towards the legal-rational as the dominant mode of legitimation.* Expressed crudely, it is hypothesized that communist leaderships wanted publicly to demonstrate their concern about official corruption and that there was a connection between this concern and their perception of legitimation problems. The question of whether this move towards legal-rationality represented a step in the direction of what is sometimes called a 'legitimation crisis', or, conversely, away from such a crisis – or whether it makes any difference – is one that is more appropriately addressed later in the study. At this point, some of the terms just used – such as legitimacy, legitimation, legal-rationality and crisis – need to be examined.

In some senses, the concept of legitimacy can be found in the Greek classics of political thought. Plato and Aristotle were concerned *inter alia* with obligation, obedience and authority, and thus with many of the issues that relate to a modern analysis of legitimacy. The term itself derives from Latin (and hence Ancient Rome), with *legitimus* meaning 'lawful' or 'legal'. But the term 'legitimate' is not always seen nowadays as being synonymous with 'lawful' or 'legal'; although the three terms are used in many contexts interchangeably, there are occasions on which it is important to distinguish the latter two from the former. An everyday situation will exemplify this. Parking is forbidden on the main street of a small town between 6.00 a.m. and 12.00 midnight. However, everyone knows that there is little traffic on the street in the evening, especially during the early part of the week, and it is so broad anyway that parked vehicles are in no real sense hindering the traffic flow. The law says I may not park my car outside the restaurant I am visiting on Main Street at 9.00 p.m. on a Tuesday – but both citizens and police officers turn a blind eye in a way they would not during the evening rush-hour three or four hours earlier. The law here is quite explicit, so that police officers who do not issue me with a parking ticket are not simply interpreting an ambiguous law in a 'sensible' way. Rather, the rule has illegitimacy *in certain circumstances*. Thus, despite recognizing some overlap, most contemporary conceptions of legality and legitimacy treat them as discrete concepts; this is how they are treated here.

Jan Pakulski has defined legitimacy as 'the normative validity of an order', and emphasizes that it is 'a matter of belief' (hence normative) by the 'participants-actors' (Pakulski, 1986, p. 35). This definition is quite acceptable as far as it goes, but it constitutes only an introduction to the concept of legitimacy. For instance, there is no discussion of what is meant by an 'order'. T.H. Rigby provides a more explicit definition, when he argues that the legitimacy of political power and authority refers to:

> The expectation of political authorities that people will comply with their demands . . . not only [because of] such considerations as the latter's fear of punishment, hope of reward, habit or apathy, but also on the notion that they have the right to make such demands. This notion both inheres, explicitly or implicitly, in the claims of the authorities, and is reciprocated, to a greater or lesser extent, in the minds of those of whom compliance is demanded. (1982, p. 1)

Such a definition contains many of the key elements that must be incorporated into any conceptualization of legitimacy. It distinguishes, for instance, between 'political authorities' and 'the people', and allows for *degrees* of legitimacy in the reference to 'a greater or lesser extent'. Furthermore, Rigby later (1982, p. 4) points out that the person who most clearly put the issue of legitimacy on the twentieth-century social scientist's agenda, Max Weber, discusses legitimacy with reference to two kinds of order. On the one hand, there is the total 'social' order; on the other, there is the political order or 'system of rule', which is a sub-system of the total social order. Not only is Rigby's approach more specific than Pakulski's, but it also takes a very definite – Weberian – position, namely that legitimacy is primarily something that exists (or not, as the case may be) in the minds of 'political authorities' and only secondarily in the minds of citizens ('people').[3]

Two points that emerge from the above are that legitimacy involves normative orientations, and that, in analysing it, we must distinguish at least between rulers and ruled, and between social and political orders. Heller, summarizing and concurring with Weber's views on this, argues that a social order is legitimate if:

 i. 'at least one part of the population acknowledges the order as exemplary and binding'

and　ii.　'the other part does not confront the existing social order
　　　　with the image of an alternative one as equally exemplary'
　　　　(Fehér, Heller and Márkus, 1984, p. 137).

The part acknowledging the order as exemplary and binding can be a
small minority, possibly just the rulers, and Heller argues that this is
sufficient for the system to be legitimate if the non-legitimating
masses 'are merely dissatisfied'. If, on the other hand, the majority of
the population actually wants an alternative order and has a reasonably clear image of it then, in Heller's view (pp. 137–8), there is a
legitimation crisis, a fundamental tension between the rulers who
believe in the legitimacy of the order and the masses who not only do
not but *in addition* want something else. I shall return to this part of
her argument later.

The bifurcated (rulers and ruled) approach to legitimacy has been
seen by many commentators on communist states as inadequate. The
majority had by the 1980s adopted a version of Weber's own *three-
fold* division of a given society's total population, into what Rigby
(1982, pp. 14, 17) calls 'the ruling group/rulers', 'the administrative
staff' and 'the population at large/subjects'. Similar tripartite distinctions have been drawn by Lewis (1984a, p. 6), who referred to 'the
central or higher elite', 'the intermediate cadres' and 'the public'; by
Pakulski (1986, p. 36), who referred to 'the rulers', 'their executive
staff' and 'the ruled masses'; and by Teiwes (1984, esp. pp. 44–5)
who, while also adopting a trifurcated approach, focused specifically
on one person – the leader – at the top, and distinguished this person
from the CCP elite and from the public. There has been a fairly high
level of agreement among both many of the writers on legitimacy in
communist states (see, for example, Bialer, 1980, pp. 194–5) and
others (see, for example, Skocpol, 1979, p. 32) that in terms of the
relationship between the legitimacy of a political order and its
stability, what is critically important are the beliefs, normative values
– the political culture – of the rulers and their staffs rather than the
beliefs and values of the masses; this is in line with the Weberian/
Rigby position referred to above. Pakulski (1986, p. 35), for instance, argued that in Soviet-type societies, 'the concept of legitimacy
is not appropriate for the analysis of mass compliance', and that the
stability (or its absence) of an order is better understood in terms of
'conditional tolerance'. This view shares some similarities with that
of commentators who identified a 'social contract' (sometimes called
a 'social compact') in Eastern European communist states, although
Pakulski's approach is broader. Part of the argument of the 'social
contract' theorists was that for there to be a *stable* system, there is a

need for legitimacy in the eyes of the rulers and their staffs, but that other factors, most notably improvements in living standards, can serve just as well as mass support (*popular* legitimacy) for maintaining stability among the bulk of the citizenry. Expressed simply, in the social contract picture, citizens will forego substantial political change in return for economic (including social welfare) improvements. Pakulski's analysis – which is in many ways more convincing – took essentially the same view *vis à vis* legitimacy, but argued that the masses' 'tolerance' may be based as much on an essentially pragmatic cost-benefit analysis of the likely outcome of protest as on living standards. Before proceeding with this part of the argument, let us temporarily abandon the problem of who is legitimating what, and instead focus for the present on *how* legitimacy may be acquired – in other words, on *legitimation*.

In Weber's classic treatment of this issue, three ideal types (or 'pure' types) of legitimation are recognized:

1   *Traditional* – defined as 'an established belief in the sanctity of immemorial traditions and the legitimacy of those exercising authority under them' (Weber, 1947, p. 328). Here the emphasis is on a continuity of existing patterns, such as the long-established and widely accepted 'divine right of monarchs' or the somewhat similar – though not identical – 'mandate of heaven' (on the latter concept, and the way in which it differs from the former, see Pye, 1968, pp. 17–18).

2   *Charismatic* – defined as based on 'devotion to the exceptional sanctity, heroism or exemplary character of an individual person and of the normative patterns of order revealed or ordained by him' (Weber, 1947, p. 328). In this case – which Weber saw as the least stable form of legitimation – legitimacy is based on the charisma of a leader. According to Weber, this is perceived by others as 'a certain quality of an individual personality by virtue of which he is set apart from ordinary men and treated as endowed with supernatural, superhuman, or at least specifically exceptional powers or qualities.' (Quoted in Teiwes, 1984, p. 46. For a comparative analysis of Stalin and Mao as charismatic leaders, see Gill, 1982.)[4]

3   *Legal-rational* – based on a belief in 'the legality of patterns of normative rules and the right of those elevated to authority under such rules to issue commands' (Weber, 1947, p. 328). Here, the emphasis is on what are held to be 'objective',

impersonal rules and a legal order that gives those in authority the right to rule. One rule might be that rulers are
subject to the same laws as everyone else. Another might be
that people only have the right to rule if they have been
accorded this in elections run on the further rules of universal, equal, free and direct suffrage, and competition between
candidates. One of the salient aspects of legitimacy based on
legal–rational legitimation, according to Weber, is that obedience is given to *norms* rather than to persons (Weber,
1968, p. 954).

Weber was fully aware that all three 'pure' types overlap both
conceptually and in the practice of 'the real world'. Legal-rational
modes of legitimation often become a tradition over time, for
instance, and kings or queens can certainly be legitimated simultaneously by tradition and charisma. Thus Weber does acknowledge
the real possibility of 'highly complex variations, transitions, and
combinations' (Weber, 1918, p. 79) of the three pure types.

However, Rigby has argued that the rational mode of legitimation
does not necessarily have to be based on rules and legality. It can,
instead, focus on a *telos* – or 'goal', as Rigby would prefer to call it.
Indeed, Rigby has seen this *goal-rationality* as the dominant form of
legitimation in many communist societies. Since his argument has
been so influential in the field of communist studies, it is important
to convey it as accurately as possible – and two quotations are
probably the best way to do this. Thus Rigby writes:

There are three main points I would like to argue in summarising my
own position:
1. The Soviet type of socio-political order[5] consists of a complex
   pattern of command-structures (or 'bureaucracies') bound together
   into a single all-embracing structure by the communist party
   machine: it is a mono-organisational society.
2. The predominant orientation of these command-structures is
   towards goal-achievement, rather than towards the application of
   rules, which Weber correctly identifies as the predominant orientation of the public bureaucracies of Western 'capitalist' societies.
3. Consonant with this, the legitimacy claimed for the commands
   issuing from this sytem and for those holding office under it is
   framed in terms of 'goal-rationality' rather than the formal-legal
   rationality of Western 'capitalist' systems. (1982, p. 10)

and

the legitimacy claims of the political system, of those holding office
under it, and of the latter's commands, are validated in terms of the
final goal ('communism'). (1982, p. 12)

Rigby's line seems reasonably clear; the rulers seek legitimacy now
not by reference to tradition or to charisma or even to a legal
framework but rather in terms of the end-goal. Bureaucracies are
geared more to the achieving of (micro-)goals – themselves directed
towards the macro-goal of communism – than to the just application
of laws and other kinds of rules. This is legitimation in terms of
'goal-rationality' (for a recent – though pre-Tiananmen – argument
that the PRC is legitimated primarily in terms of goal-rationality see
Hannan, 1988, p. 12).

While the notion that goal-rational legitimation is the dominant
mode in many communist systems *may* have been true at certain
periods in the past (though Heller, 1982, p. 51 raises doubts about
this), I would argue that the situation was clearly changing by the
1980s. For one thing, in the recent past many communists in power
sought legitimacy from the masses as well as from their staffs, and
they did this primarily in terms of their own effectiveness, especially
in running the economy; the numerous economic reforms there were
in the communist world from the 1960s, starting with the GDR's
'New Economic System' of 1963, should be interpreted partially
from this perspective. Rootes (1983, esp. pp. 9–10) has argued
convincingly that Lipset's distinction between 'legitimacy' and
'effectiveness' (for this see Lipset 1960, esp. pp. 77–83, and 1981, pp.
88–92) is unsound, and that economic and social-welfare performance can itself be effective as a mode of legitimation. This essentially
performance-related or instrumental mode of legitimation, geared as
it is to satisfying and to some extent directing the growing material
aspirations of the masses, is often referred to as *social eudaemonic*
legitimation and is recognized by some writers on communism as a
legitimation mode (see, for example, Tökés, 1972; Gill, 1986, p. 249;
S. White, 1986). There is an important difference between the 'social
contract' approach and the notion of eudaemonic legitimation; the
former does not imply any normative relationship (other than
mutual regard for the contract) between rulers and masses, whereas
the latter holds that the order's ability to mould and meet the masses'
economic and social-welfare demands can have a legitimating effect
for that order. It is argued here that satisfactory economic perform-

ance can indeed encourage citizens to reassess an order and actually start to become more supportive of it.[6]

All modes of legitimation can become problematic – that is, can lose their putative legitimating force. For instance, the eudaemonic mode of legitimation can become problematic when, for whatever reason, an economy falters. Many communist states certainly encountered major economic problems in recent years, some severe enough even before the end of the 1980s to have been labelled 'crisis' by Western observers (see, for example, Drewnoski, 1982; Goldman, 1983; Csapo, 1988). The reasons for this were several and complex. One was the communist world's *de facto* increasing integration into the world (capitalist) market, with its booms and recessions (for further elaboration of this see Comisso and D'Andrea Tyson, 1986). Another, according to some versions of modernization theory, was the alleged inability of communists to pursue economic reform beyond a given limit because of the political reforms that appear necessary at a certain stage of economic reform if the latter is to continue; if communist leaderships baulked at the political reforms, the economic reforms were bound to falter too. A third, which is closely related to the second, was the conservatism of parts of the staff/bureaucracy, whose interests were often threatened by the economic reforms; this is more appropriately examined later in the argument. Then there were the growing ramifications of structural imbalances typical of a communist economy – often the result of a conscious policy of sectoral privileging – which could result in a shortage of consumer goods, both durable and non-durable, at the same time as consumer aspirations increased; this imbalance could negatively affect labour productivity – workers could not be adequately motivated – with knock-on effects for the whole economy. Natural disasters – flood, drought, forest fires, etc. – can also contribute to economic problems. Many other factors can lead to economic difficulties; the point here is not to elaborate them all, but to show that they can and have result(ed) in a relative or absolute decline in economic performance. When eudaemonic legitimation begins to break down, a leadership has to seek yet other modes of legitimation. It might move to a form of 'traditional' legitimation – in this context, not by reference to 'the divine right of monarchs', but rather to the much newer, communist tradition of the leading role of the vanguard party, etc.; this can be called *'new traditional'* legitimation (Heller – in Fehér, Heller and Márkus, 1984, p. 151 – uses this term, but not in quite the same way as here). Gorbachev's frequent references in the late 1980s to the similarities between his own approach and policies and those of Lenin constituted a good example of such 'new traditional' legitimation (on this see Smart, 1990). If it was feasible, leaders might also or instead have attempted to move to a form of charismatic legitimation, perhaps by developing a personality cult (there were signs of one emerging around Deng – as well as signs of 'new traditional' legitimation – following the June 1989 massacre). Or they might have tried *returning* to goal-rational legitimation; in view of the alternative definition of 'traditional' just given, it should be clear that 'goal-rational'/teleological legitimation is in this situation at least as close to the 'traditional' mode of legitimation as it is to the 'legal-rational' mode. For this reason, I would argue that Rigby's approach to goal-rational legitimation, in which the version of Weber's three-fold categorization of legitimation to which it most closely approximates – the legal-rational – cannot be universalized; sometimes, goal-rational legitimation has been closer to other modes than to the legal-rational. But yet another possibility was that the particular communist leadership would attempt to move away from eudaemonic legitimation not in the direction of 'new traditional', charismatic or goal-rational/teleological legitimation, but rather in one or both of two other directions.

The first of these was *official nationalism*, in which leaders might, for instance, seek the right to rule by locating themselves in a tradition of national hero-leaders (the former Romanian leader Ceauşescu did this on a grand scale). Or, to take another example, the leadership might pursue a strongly xenophobic line (Albania did this). A third example is leadership emphasis on the fact that they or the country are/is recognized and/or admired by other states (for example, the GDR being admitted to the UN in 1973; Gorbachev's image as an international statesperson). This mode of legitimation often has connections both with the two possible forms of traditional legitimation already identified and with charismatic legitimation.

The second possible direction is the *legal-rational*. According to Gianfranco Poggi (1978, pp. 101 and 132), this is the only mode of legitimation appropriate to the modern state;[7] this is an argument to which we shall be returning in the concluding chapter. For now, the foregoing can be summarized and restructured to provide the classification of domestic/internal (see below on external) legitimation modes used in this study:

1 *'Old' traditional* – 'divine right of monarchs', etc.;
2 *Charismatic*;
3 *Goal-rational/teleological*;
4 *Eudaemonic*;

5   *Official nationalist*;
6   *'New' traditional*;
7   *Legal-rational*.

There is some rationale to the above ordering, in that it is assumed that the typical pattern of the dynamic of communist legitimation ran in sequence from 1 (clearly pre-communist) through to 3 and that 7 was in most cases chronologically the last form to emerge; the order in which types 4–6 became salient seems to me to have varied considerably. Not all modes will be found in analysing the history of a given communist state; charismatic legitimation, for instance, tended to be more obvious in countries in which native communists took power largely through their own efforts than in countries in which communism was virtually imposed from outside. Moreover, *there is no suggestion at all that each stage will be discrete* – in the real world, there will almost always be a blurring of stages and the simultaneous coexistence of two, three or even more modes. On this point, the argument here is in complete agreement with Weber's. This said, I do argue that a maximum of two modes, and frequently one mode, will be *dominant* at any particular point in time (for an analysis of changes over time in dominant modes of legitimation in the USSR see Heller, 1982 – while Pakulski, 1986, pp. 51–4, provides an analysis of the stages of 'mass compliance' in Eastern Europe).

We turn now to focus on the question of what is being legitimated. Few would dispute that legitimation attempts in the communist world were primarily concerned with what was earlier referred to as the political order. This term has deliberately been used to this point because it is vague; shortly it will be necessary to become more precise. In order to reach that point of the argument, however, it is necessary to return to the issue of how many and which groups in society confer legitimacy on an order. It has been shown that there is universal agreement on *at least* a two-fold distinction between rulers and ruled, and that many now accept that legitimacy is more a matter of the former believing in what they are doing than of the latter believing this. It has further been demonstrated that many believe that the distinction between rulers and ruled is too simple, and that the concept of the 'rulers' or 'power elite' needs to be further subdivided into what Weber himself called 'chiefs' and 'staffs'. If the chiefs believe in their own right to rule but the staffs do not believe in this, then many analysts argue that there is a serious legitimation problem, which some would call a crisis. Where does this leave the masses?

For the sake of analysis – these categories are not as distinct in the real world as here – we can *start* by suggesting that ordinary citizens more or less closely approximate to one of three stances:

1   Clearly believe the rulers have the right to rule;
2   Clearly believe the rulers do not have the right to rule;
3   Do not think and/or do not care much – if at all – about this issue; the predominant mood here is apathy, but not active hostility.

Obviously, if the majority of the population falls into category 1, and the rulers (both chiefs and staffs) believe in their own legitimacy, then an order is legitimate. If most citizens fall into category 3, and the rulers (both chiefs and staffs) believe in their own legitimacy, then most commentators would agree with Weber that the order is legitimate. If, on the other hand, most citizens fall into category 2, there can be a serious legitimation problem, even a 'crisis'. This could be argued to depend on:

1   The extent to which *both* chiefs and staff believe in the legitimacy of the order; and
2   The extent to which the rulers are able to control the masses, either through coercion and/or short-term contract.[8]

From this, it follows that an order can enjoy a degree of legitimacy *and* be highly coercive.[9] If the rulers – both chiefs and staff – believe they have the right to rule and are able to keep the masses under control through coercion (actual or threatened) or contract, then an order is legitimate.

Or is it? Are we here falling into the common trap of confusing 'stability' and 'legitimacy'? The longer one thinks about the above proposition, the more questionable – intuitively – it begins to sound. On the basis of Heller's (and Weber's) argument, it could be argued that an order would become illegitimate only if at least part of the population *not only* does not support the order *but also* has a vision of an alternative order. But is this distinction between having and not having an alternative vision convincing? I might generally be aware that 'there must be something better than this', but not have any clear image of this better order. Yet if someone urges me to be more precise, I *can* say that I want the powers of the secret police drastically reduced, I want more say in choosing my representatives, I want my country to be recognized as a fully sovereign entity, etc. As long as I can identify what displeases me about the existing system, I can form some picture of an alternative. This may be little more than an essentially vague nationalism based on romantic images of pre-communist traditions, of a sort that has recently become far more overt in many East European states and (former) Soviet republics. It is not *necessary* for me to have a detailed knowledge of alternative actually existing systems – liberal democracies, for instance. My alternative vision does not, in short, have to be inductive or coherent or complete – it can be deductive and incoherent and incomplete.

Before reaching conclusions about the people in category 2 in our discussion of legitimacy, it is necessary to examine those in category 3. We need to ask why they do not think or care much about the order in which they live. To argue that many people simply do not think about politics anyway is not really satisfactory; they may not think about the fine points of party programmes, but virtually everyone is aware to some extent of power relations (in the family, at work) and has views on these. These views may not be detailed or coherent, but they exist. If people do in fact think 'politically' in this broad sense, but claim they do not think or care about the political order, it is just as possible that such an attitude is a result of, for instance, pragmatism as of genuine indifference or 'false conscious-ness'. It may be that people *fear* thinking too much about the order – because of the possibility of external intervention, the overt or covert coercion of the domestic rulers, etc. By covert, I do not only mean implicitly threatened coercion (although this can, of course, be a form of covert coercion) but also the feeling that one is powerless to change the order, and that therefore one is only confusing and frustrating oneself even to *attempt* to change it. The 'covert' coercion here, then, is internalized self-control created by the purposive socialization process, one's own experiences, and the interaction of these two. Some analysts of compliance by the masses in Western societies have suggested that in addition to or instead of this prag-matism, the masses have been indoctrinated with the values and beliefs of the rulers – or 'ruling class' – in such a way that they accept their subordinate position; if this explanation applied in communist societies too, I would argue that the order could not be described as illegitimate, assuming the rulers saw it as legitimate. It does not matter in a practical – as distinct from an ethical – sense how the masses acquire their values; if they believe that an order is the 'natural' or 'proper' one – if, in short, they accept it – then it has some degree of legitimacy.

Michael Mann (1970, p. 436), examining mass attitudes in liberal democracies, has argued that socialization by the rulers does not always work to bind the masses to the order, but rather to *divide* the masses on what they might do about changing it. Rootes summarizes this argument well: 'The political passivity of the working class, then, rests upon its lack of ability to conceptualise radical alternatives to the roles it now pragmatically accepts' (1983, p. 2). This goes beyond the Heller/Weber argument – and is more convincing. It is not simply a matter of having an alternative *vision of society*, but, more specifically, a belief that there is a *realistic possibility of attaining it*. If – because of coercion and/or socialization and/or 'pragmatic calculation' – the masses do not envisage a realizable path to an alternative order, then, assuming the chiefs and staffs hold it so to be, by most of the definitions so far cited an order is legitimate. Heller does not go this far, of course, since she believes that it is simply a matter of the masses having an alternative view of an order; partially for this reason she has argued of the communist period that 'Eastern European societies, and in particular the three just mentioned above [Czechoslovakia, Poland and Hungary], continue to exist in a permanent legitimation crisis' (Fehér, Heller and Márkus, 1984, p. 138). For her, the USSR – in contrast to the East European systems – was not suffering a legitimation crisis at the time she was writing, precisely because the masses had no vision of an alternative order. It should be clear from the argument above concerning the specificity of the vision that I do not hold this to be a convincing position, on one level because it is unclear at what point desire for change becomes a vision of an alternative society and vice versa. It is appropriate at this point to unpack and develop the critique of Heller's argument, particularly since the events of 1989–91 may at first sight appear to have endorsed her view on permanent legitimation crisis.

As indicated above, a major flaw in Heller's argument is that it concentrates on alternative visions rather than on realistic possibilities of attaining change. In my view, 1989 revealed convincingly that, as far as the masses were concerned, it was indeed the realistic possibility of attaining change (Gorbachev's unambiguous abandonment of the Brezhnev Doctrine), not the emergence of an alternative vision, that triggered the crisis. In fact, one point that became very clear from the middle of 1989 was that most of the demonstrators, opposition groups, etc. had only a very hazy vision of an alternative social order at the time they challenged the communist power system, a fact that became even more obvious during the 1990 elections. In short, 1989 was far more a symbol of *rejection* by the masses – of the elitism, hypocrisy, corruption, sycophancy and poor performance of the communists; of Soviet domination in the case of most of the East European countries – than a symbol of their alternative vision. It was the *double rejective revolution*.

A second – related – problem with Heller's argument is that it would have been difficult to use it to predict the circumstances under which an overt crisis would be likely to arise in a particular communist system. It became clear in 1989 not only that most of the East European states were in crisis, but also that the USSR itself was – a situation one could hardly have foreseen on the basis of Heller's argument. Even allowing for the fact that the USSR had not – yet – undergone as radical a political transformation as many of the East European countries experienced, it seems to me that if essentially similar phenomena (such as mass unrest, demands for an end to the communist party monopoly, etc.) occur at about the same time, in very similar ways, and for basically similar reasons (in this case, the implications of Gorbachev's policies of *perestroika, glasnost* and *demokratisatsiya*), then it is unclear how it can convincingly be argued that, prior to these developments, country A was in a 'permanent legitimation crisis' while country B was not.

It might be objected that the last point is unfair to Heller's argument, in that it was precisely the emergence of a 'legitimation crisis' within the USSR that created the conditions necessary for the emergence of overt general crisis in Eastern Europe. Even allowing for such an interpretation – which in my view is not inherent in Heller's argument – there are still serious problems with her position. These can be subsumed under two main – and related – headings, viz insensitivity and a lack of dynamism. Both these points require elaboration.

To talk of a 'permanent legitimation crisis' in Eastern Europe without *essentially* allowing for the real differences that existed in attitudes towards, for instance, the 'normalization' regime in Czechoslovakia after 1969, Ceauşescu's Romania and Kádár's Hungary (notwithstanding the concession Heller makes about Hungary – see below) is in my view insufficiently sensitive. To refer to *permanent* crisis is surely oxymoronic and devalues the term 'crisis'. Moreover, it does not inherently allow for substantial differences in the *degree* and *type* of legitimacy. It would be inadequate in any serious, scholarly analysis to argue in a blanket fashion merely that communist power in Eastern Europe began to collapse in 1989; it needs also to be borne in mind, and explained, that the nature of the transformation was very different in, for instance, Hungary and Romania. Another insensitivity of the blanket notion of permanent legitimation crisis is that Heller is not, apparently, taking sufficient heed of her own point about one part of the population acknowledging the order as exemplary and binding. To use the same term (legitimation crisis) for at least two situations – on the one hand, one in which the masses do have some alternative vision but the leaders and staffs believe in the legitimacy of the order; on the other hand, one in which not only the masses but also the leaders and staffs have lost faith – is confusing, and insufficiently alert to important differences. Expressing this another way, *a clear distinction should be drawn between a 'legitimation crisis' and a 'severe legitimacy deficit'*. The term 'legitimation crisis' should, logically, be applied only when those who would normally be expected to attempt to legitimate the order are no longer able and/or willing to do so. This situation is conceptually quite distinct from one in which the official ideologists, etc., *do* have new ideas for legitimation and a belief in what they are doing, but appear to be limited in their success at legitimating the order to the masses. This might be interpreted as implying that the attitudes of the masses are irrelevant or of only marginal significance, and would thus appear to contradict what I have earlier argued (that is, that the views of the masses *are* significant in explaining the emergence of legitimation crises). But this is not, in fact, a contradictory position. One needs to ask *why* the ideologists lose faith in what they are doing. Twentieth-century leaders and staffs do not live in a vacuum, totally divorced from the masses. If there is perceived to be a severe deficit of popular legitimacy – if those charged with legitimating the system to the masses both feel that they are badly failing in their task and are concerned about this – then they may lose faith in themselves, which can result in a legitimation crisis. It is worth reminding ourselves here that the ideologists may reach such a critical juncture and then successfully emerge from it by moving to a new dominant mode or modes of legitimation. If they believe that such a move will, or even only may, increase the order's popular legitimacy, then there is no longer a legitimation crisis, whether or not the new dominant mode(s) actually do(es) result in more positive popular evaluations of the political order. In short, and *ceteris paribus*, the very fact of moving from one dominant mode of legitimation to another may of itself help to avoid or overcome a legitimation crisis.

The last point necessarily involves change and reaction – in short, *dynamism*. It has already been suggested that the very fact of changing dominant legitimation modes may give new faith to the legitimators (ideologists in a broad sense). It may also lead to increased popular legitimacy – or, at the very least, new hopes among the citizenry that perhaps things really will improve this time. The process can thus 'buy time', and can be called the *legitimating effect of legitimation shifts*. If, however, the new dominant mode(s) of legitimation prove(s) over time to be no more successful in gaining popular support than its/their predecessor(s), then a new legitimation crisis can arise. This issue of dynamism is crucial, and insufficient attention to it is in my view another weakness of Heller's position on communist Eastern Europe; although she did allow for some dynamism in legitimation there, her view of attitudes was relatively static. For her argument to be convincing, it would have to be successfully demonstrated that political attitudes in Eastern Europe in the early 1980s were essentially the same as in the previous three and a half decades – and, presumably, in 1989. The 'attitudes' referred to here are not only those of the masses – it would not be too difficult to argue persuasively, though not prove conclusively, that *some* of these had been relatively constant for decades – but *also* those of the chiefs and staffs.

Another aspect of dynamism that helps to explain the 1989 crisis of communism relates to the point briefly referred to earlier concerning a 'legitimation crisis' within the USSR. Many popular analyses of the 1989 events suggest that Eastern European communism 'collapsed' because of the withdrawal of Soviet support. There are at least two ways of interpreting such 'support'. The first focuses on the notion that the East European rulers believed they could call on the Soviets/ WTO for military support if their populations became too restless. If power really had been exercised in this way in Eastern Europe, then most of the Soviet-bloc systems – Romania being an exception – would have been operating mainly on what might be called 'vicarious' or *external coercion*; attempts at legitimation would have played a minor role in such a scenario, so that the use of the term 'legitimation crisis' would – in our way of using it – be inappropriate anyway. But it is argued here that most of the communist states of Eastern Europe did make serious attempts to move away from the coercion-dominated exercise of power towards a situation in which, although coercion – implicit or explicit, internal or external – was still clearly present to a far higher level than in most liberal democracies, legitimation played a more significant role than hitherto. In many cases – Poland during the early to mid-1980s, Czechoslovakia for some years after 1969 – the attempted transition proved to be a difficult one. Nevertheless, attempts to shift from one dominant mode of the exercise of power to the other were made. The all-important change in 1989 was that the East European legitimators, who were already finding it very difficult to reconcile legal-rationality and the communist style of power, *lost their role-model*; the leaders of the first and at that time still dominant communist state were by now questioning, and in some areas abandoning, long-held basic tenets of the communist system. It was this blend of internal contradictions and the collapse of this very particular type of '*external*' *legitimation* (a form of support) that resulted in the near-universal crisis of communism in Eastern Europe in 1989.[10] Expressing this another way, there was a profound *change* by 1989; the incompatibilities of communist power and legal-rationality became all too obvious to many communist legitimators – *including* the Soviet leaders, so that the USSR could no longer serve as a role-model. It was this that constituted the full-blown legitimation crisis, as distinct from the severe deficit of legitimacy that, in my view, Heller is principally discussing.

There is yet another important point arising from Heller's argument, and this is that the masses might actually look *to their rulers* to change the order. This seems to have happened in Hungary where, as pointed out earlier, the 1989 revolution took a very different form from that in, most notably, Romania. Given these differences, and Heller's particular interest in Hungary, let us briefly consider aspects of her argument on this more closely. At one point in her essay, Heller argued that there was a legitimation crisis in Hungary *even though* the Kádár government was popular: 'Legitimation means not so much the legitimation of government as a form of domination, and relative popular support is given to the government precisely because it practises the otherwise rejected Hungarian form of domination in a more tolerable fashion than is the case in other countries' (Fehér, Heller and Márkus, 1984, p. 138). At first sight, it may appear absurd to argue that a relatively popular government can be in a legitimation crisis. In attempting to resolve this dilemma, we have now reached the point at which it is appropriate to draw a sharp distinction between two components of what has so far only been referred to in a blanket sense as 'the political order'. These two components are *the system* and *the regime*.[11] In theory, a citizen might generally be in favour of several aspects of a communist country's political *system* and *goals* – the vanguard concept of the party, democratic centralism, a commitment to state inculcation of the values of the new socialist person, a commitment to state provision of welfare broadly understood, etc. – but disapprove of the particular leadership team (the *regime*) that is currently running the system.[12] In the Hungarian case cited by Heller, in contrast, the people are held to have been more supportive of the regime (what she calls 'government') than of the system. Here, then, is a case where the masses might actually look to their rulers rather than among themselves for change.[13] The notion that citizens either believe or do not believe that the rulers have a right to rule begins to look too simple; we have to distinguish between 'system legitimacy' and 'regime legitimacy'.

How can this argument be applied to Heller's view of what she calls a 'legitimation crisis' in Hungary?

In order to answer this, it is necessary to start by reminding ourselves once again that societies are *dynamic*. Bearing this in mind, it initially seems reasonable to infer that there is a limit to how long and how far a regime can continue to attack the very system it is supposed to manage and represent before it undermines any legitimacy that system may have. Indeed, if the regime becomes popular by attacking the system, then what is the basis of the latter's legitimacy? It is precisely this problem that has led several commentators on legitimacy in communist countries to argue that legitimacy is more about what the rulers – both chiefs and staffs – believe than what the masses believe. If the rulers, in attempting to increase their popularity, find they have to attack what they are supposed to represent and defend, then, it is argued, they are in a dilemma that can become a legitimation crisis.

But one cannot help feeling that there is a fatal flaw in the argument that a regime – a government – can actually be in *more* of a legitimation crisis through becoming more popular; intuitively, this seems nonsensical. I would argue that – *to a certain point* – there is a solution to this particular aspect of the problem. The solution is to *limit* the distinction drawn between 'system' and 'regime', and to see them as being in a dynamic, dialectical relationship. Viewing them in this way, it becomes feasible that a regime actually *remoulds* a system, changes salient aspects of it, and in doing so increases support for both itself *and* the system. At this point, two caveats need to be made. First, this is not a *necessary* scenario; the regime – or part of it, such as the staff – may indeed lose faith in itself in the process of trying to popularize itself. But it is a perfectly feasible scenario. Second, it is not a scenario that can continue indefinitely. Just as water heats up to a point where it becomes steam, so this interactive dynamic eventually reaches a point at which change is not merely quantitative but fundamentally qualitative; until that point, however, the water is still water, even though it is changing by becoming warmer. In sum, the events of 1989 do not necessarily endorse the concept of a permanent legitimation crisis in Eastern Europe since the 1940s – at least as convincing counter-arguments can be made.

There are other, more general criticisms to be made of the notion of legitimation crisis. But these are more appropriately dealt with below; for now, and bearing the above argument in mind, a possible dynamic scenario of legitimation in a communist state can be suggested. In the formative years of a new political order – following a revolutionary change – it is often difficult to distinguish clearly between system and regime, since the latter is in any case probably deciding what the former will be. There might be a constituent assembly, or its equivalent, for instance. The relationship then is very fluid, as indeed is the political and social order generally. This stage is often followed by major and rapid structural change directed from above (such as collectivization or communization, socialization of the means of production, industrialization and urbanization, etc.). Legitimation is often of relatively little importance at this stage;[14] power in any system is exercised primarily through coercion or through legitimation, and in this case the former is the salient mode.[15] Over time, this situation changes. The system crystallizes, and the people running it are no longer the people who created it. The initial 'revolution from above' is nearing completion. Chiefs increasingly realize the importance of legitimating themselves to their staffs, especially as coercion as a whole declines. With this decline, chiefs also begin to place a growing emphasis on *mass* support, wanting it for *both* components (system and regime) – although it is unlikely in the real world that if politicians have to choose between legitimating themselves and legitimating the system they will choose the latter rather than the former. Indeed, as suggested above, they will change – overtly or covertly, fully or only partially consciously – the system in an endeavour to legitimate their own rule, whether this be at this stage principally to the masses or to the staffs/intermediate cadres. In doing so they may make both elements – themselves and the system – more popular in the short to medium term. According to this line of argument, therefore, Heller's statement about Hungary would be put in question and/or have to be modified – though it would not, of course, be proven incorrect; it would simply mean that there would have to be both a more detailed argument and more empirical evidence to support her case.

If we need to distinguish between system and regime in terms of legitimacy – while also seeing them as inextricably linked – which is it of these that can face the legitimation crisis? The answer, in line with an earlier part of the argument, is that either can, or *both* might simultaneously. The latter case would be the worst form of legitimation crisis – using the earlier analogy, the point at which water might become steam. Conversely, a 'legitimation crisis' for a regime only must be treated as a minor crisis. At this juncture, it is necessary to focus more specifically on the concepts of crisis and legitimation crisis.

In recent years, there has been a lively debate among Western political and social theorists on the question of legitimation and legitimacy crisis in Western societies. Debate has been conducted among non-Marxists, among Marxists and between these two groups, and is traceable in its recent wave at least to the 1960s. Few would dispute that the German theorist Jürgen Habermas has dominated the debate, at least on legitimation crisis. Many have seen Habermas' book *Legitimationsprobleme im Spätkapitalismus* (the title has been loosely translated as *Legitimation Crisis* in the English version – a more accurate rendering would be *Legitimation Problems in Late Capitalism*) as his most important work (until recently, at least – see McLellan, 1979, p. 273) and his ideas on this as being at the very centre of contemporary debates on legitimation and legitimacy crisis in advanced capitalist societies (Connolly, 1984b, p. 11). As the German title suggests, Habermas' book is explicitly and primarily concerned with advanced industrial society organized along pre-dominantly capitalist lines. However, it is also marginally concerned with communist states – at least the industrially developed ones[16] – and in any case provides a useful starting point and framework for this part of our analysis.

Although Habermas' work has been seen as seminal, many commen-tators have either implicitly or explicitly suggested that several basic aspects of it, including definitions, need to be more precisely formu-lated before one can proceed with the argument itself (for critiques see, for example, McCarthy, 1981; Thompson and Held, 1982). Most notably for our purposes, despite his professed aim of finding a 'social-scientific concept of the term', Habermas never fully satisfac-torily defines the word 'crisis'. As is evident from the opening sentence of *Legitimation Crisis*, he can give the impression of inter-changing the terms 'contradictions' and 'crisis'. His attempts at defining crisis both early in his book (pp. 1–4) and in his 1973 article on legitimation crisis (1973, pp. 134–5) are largely metaphorical/ analogical. However, he does come close to a definition when he writes, 'We therefore associate with crises the idea of an objective force that deprives a subject of some part of its normal sovereignty' (1976, p. 1). Later on, we learn that crises arise from 'unresolved steering problems', and that, in 'liberal capitalism' (Habermas' term', 'crises appear *in the form* of unresolved *economic* steering problems' (1976, p. 24 – emphasis added to 'economic'; see too p. 4). There are always problems in economics, whether 'liberal capitalist' or 'state socialist', and the point at which problems reach crisis proportions is not clear in Habermas' analysis. Habermas recognizes this himself when he argues that 'It is not easy to determine empiri-cally the probability of boundary conditions under which the *possible* crisis tendencies *actually* set in and prevail. The empirical indicators we have at our disposal are as yet inadequate' (1976, p. 33 – original emphasis). Hence we often cannot be sure whether a given state is in crisis or not, according to Habermas, and he provides few indications of how one would set about determining this empirically. He therefore calls for more empirical work to be done on the topic without in any very clear sense suggesting how one should set about this. The 'legitimation crisis' is thus primarily a deduced rather than empirically induced concept for Habermas. Indeed, this applies to most conceptions of legitimation crisis, largely because of the nature of the beast; ultimately, whether one accepts or rejects the very concept of legitimation crisis depends to some extent on one's epistemological position. Reference has already been made to Meyer's 'ultimate test' of legitimacy and proof of crisis; beyond this, it is unclear how one could empirically test the level of legitimacy of a given political order with any precision, just as it is often unclear whether or not that order is close to or even in a legitimation crisis.

The above all said, it will be argued below that some indications of legitimation problems – and potential crisis – *were* discernible in the communist world pre-1989. Moreover, just because we cannot fully satisfactorily test a phenomenon does not render it unimportant. If greater understanding of any phenomenon is sought, it must be accepted that some parts of one's understanding will at times have to be deductive. With this point in mind, this brief analysis of Habermas' conception of crisis can proceed.

In capitalist states, the potential crisis is seen as a complex one, involving four major stages:

1   An economic crisis;
2   A crisis of rationality;
3   A crisis of legitimation;
4   A crisis of motivation, defined as 'a discrepancy between the need for motives declared by the state, the educational system and the occupational system on the one hand and the motivation supplied by the socio-cultural system on the other' (Habermas, 1976, p. 75).

Since Habermas devotes most of his attention to the capitalist state, we need not consider his argument in detail; rather, I shall merely attempt to apply the main components of the argument to the communist world, though elaborating these where it seems necessary for those readers not familiar with them.

The first point is to remind the reader that since Habermas is primarily concerned with advanced capitalist states, the argument was likely to have been more applicable to the economically more advanced communist states such as the USSR or several of the East European states than to the less-developed communist states of Asia or Africa. This is not to argue that the latter could not or cannot be subject to legitimation crises too, but rather that, if they are, the nature of such crises will be different and less severe. In many of them, it must be borne in mind, communist power was, until it collapsed, tenuous and/or exercised primarily in its coercive form, with popular legitimation being of less concern than in the more developed states. Since the argument here is that a full-blown legitimation crisis can occur only where the rulers are attempting to exercise power primarily through legitimation, it becomes obvious why 'legitimation crises' generally assume a different level of significance and nature in less well-established communist states. On the other hand, it is argued here that although the details of policy will change from country to country according to political culture, the international situation, etc., there has been a broad similarity in the way most communist countries developed, and that universal features such as the deepening division of labour, rising educational levels, the lengthening of the period of communist rule – plus the general commitment to a Marxist-Leninist system – were likely to lead to similar problems and patterns emerging in most consolidated communist countries over time. With this caveat in mind, let us now examine the four types of crisis as they might have affected communist systems and regimes.

For a number of reasons – some of which were cited above – communist states often faced severe economic problems, even crisis. By the late 1980s, for instance, the Soviet leadership not only argued that the USSR was in a pre-crisis situation in the late 1970s/early 1980s (see Gorbachev, 1987), but had begun explicitly to recognize that the USSR was now in an even worse situation, which it was prepared to describe as an economic crisis. One major reason for this economic crisis was that the USSR had competed with the West militarily. There can be little doubt that one of the straws that broke the camel's (the Soviet Union's) back in the 1980s was the USA's determination to proceed with the Strategic Defence Initiative ('Star Wars'). The USSR had neither the technological nor the pecuniary wherewithal to move to this new stage of the arms race. As this fact became obvious to Gorbachev and other Soviet leaders, so they came to accept that they had now lost the decades-long competition with capitalism. This must be seen as a major factor explaining the Soviet leadership's loss of faith in itself. In all events, such economic problems and/or crises could result in very visible popular dissatisfaction. Thus many of the pre-1989 outbursts of mass unrest in the communist world (for example, in the GDR 1953; the USSR 1962; Poland 1970–1, 1976, 1980–1; Romania 1977, 1987; etc.) were triggered by economic discontent relating to structural imbalances (in some countries connected to the emphasis on heavy industry and/ or defence), centrally planned pricing, poor distribution, declining growth rates, etc.

In Habermas' analysis, economic crises in capitalism can lead to rationality crises; this argument requires unpacking. Habermas maintains that the contemporary capitalist state seeks either to avoid or else to overcome economic, social, environmental and other crises that might arise by intervening in the economy. Although it might thus succeed in avoiding or reducing the impact of the economic and economy-related crises, the modern capitalist state is seen simultaneously to undermine its own position. The traditional capitalist state espouses an ideology of minimal involvement in the economy, in line with classical liberal political theory; in the new conditions, there is increasing planning and intervention – and the state rapidly moves away from its erstwhile minimalist approach. In doing so, it begins to lose its rationale in terms of the original tenets. If this continues, there emerges a crisis of rationality. This tension between theory and practice is not necessarily of great significance to most citizens if the economy is performing well. But if the system simultaneously has shaky theoretical underpinnings and cannot compensate for this via sound economic performance, leaders and/or staffs can lose faith in their own policies and even in their right to rule, which in turn exacerbates whatever delegitimizing process has been occurring among the citizenry. Legitimacy declines, and the rulers have no new source of legitimacy. In short, there arises a major legitimation crisis. Habermas' theory can certainly be questioned *vis-à-vis* capitalist states – but that is well beyond the scope of the present study.

At first sight, it might appear 'obvious' that communist states were innately more prone to rationality and subsequently legitimation crises than capitalist states precisely because of their all-embracing nature (this point seems to be implied by Lovenduski and Woodall in their 1987 book, p. 432). The moves taken by Western states towards greater intervention in the economy were taken much more rapidly and comprehensively in communist systems. The vanguard party and the party–state complex initially made claims to virtual omniscience (in the guise of 'scientific socialism') and omni-competence, and assumed overwhelming responsibility for the economy. As already argued, they either started out or else very soon became committed to social ownership of the means of production, long-term central planning, rational-synoptic decision-making, etc. This meant that 'the rulers' could take even more credit than Western leaders can when the economy was performing well – but conversely that they had less of an excuse when things went wrong. Although they might have attempted, as Stalin did in the 1930s, to attribute problems to the treachery of other leaders or insubordinate and inefficient 'staffs', this proved less useful over time than recourse to Adam Smith's 'invisible hand' of the market, or, more likely in recent years, 'international economic forces'. But the rationality crisis – and the potential for a subsequent legitimation crisis – did not in fact develop quite in this way; this is a Western-centric argument. Since communist ideology did attempt to legitimate party–state involvement in the economy from early on, it was not growing but rather *declining* involvement in the economy that caused a rationality crisis for communist systems; in this sense, there is a basic difference between capitalist and communist states, and the 'obvious' notion that *because* communist states were more involved in the economy they were more prone to legitimation crises is cast in doubt. Instead, it would be more accurate to argue that communist states – like capitalist states – could fall into a rationality crisis as a result of economic crisis; this is a subtly but significantly different argument from the one just cited.

According to this argument, something very similar to what happens in capitalist states – that is, a tension between original principles and current practice – could and did arise in communist states when leaderships sought to overcome economic problems. Since the ideological tenets of communist states were so different from those in capitalist liberal democracies, the direction and details of the change were radically different, indeed almost diametrically opposed. Unfortunately, as has already been shown, communists did not in practice prove to be as able to control and steer the economy as they would have preferred, so that they too felt compelled to move away from their original tenets. Some communist states (such as Yugoslavia, China, Vietnam) began overtly to acknowledge and accept unemployment;[17] many came to acknowledge inflation; some (such as Poland, Yugoslavia, China and more recently the USSR) allowed decollectivization or the breakdown of communes;[18] some entered into joint ventures with capitalist countries or even allowed foreign capitalist firms to establish plants within their borders; and most both allowed the private sector to increase in significance within the economy and reduced – or claimed they would –

the significance of central planning in the economy. In sum, policy changes cumulatively appeared to represent a move away from original tenets, from faith in the omniscience and omnipotence of the party and the plan, towards the acknowledgement of limitation and fallibility. Once again, this might have been of relatively minor consequence if the economy had thus prospered. But this did not typically happen, and communists found themselves in a somewhat similar situation to that of their capitalist counterparts, facing major problems of legitimation and increasing legitimacy deficits. It is appropriate to conclude this discussion of the second and third stages by noting that, inasmuch as the recent economic practices of many communist states not only conflicted with their original ideological tenets but also brought them closer to capitalist practices, there is considerable overlap between the Habermasian conception of rationality crisis as applied to communism and our own conception of identity crisis.[19]

In the fourth stage, according to Habermas, the rulers find it difficult to motivate the masses or, ultimately, even themselves. If everyone loses faith in what the political order is doing and motivation declines, economic problems will increase, which has a knock-on effect for the other three types of crisis. The problem intensifies and becomes self-perpetuating. Habermas does not actually specify what happens at this point. However, he does argue that there is no neat progression (regression?) from type 1 to type 4; contemporary capitalist states often shift around between the four types. Let us now apply such arguments explicitly to communist states.

Certainly there is no inherent reason why, if capitalist states can – at least in the short to medium term – overcome their economic crises and modify their ideologies so that the new versions become more or less acceptable (as with Keynesianism), this could not also have applied to communist states in the short to medium term. However, the reader is reminded of the water-to-steam analogy, which implies that there is a limit to how far this process can continue in the communist world. The problem really begins to become serious if there is simultaneous economic and rationality crisis – if, in terms of the modes referred to earlier in the analysis, eudaemonic *and* teleological *and* new traditional legitimation all fail at about the same time. At this juncture, communists need some other mode of legitimation, or to revert to coercion; alternatively they may lose power altogether (that is, the crisis becomes a general crisis of power, which in turn becomes system-collapse, as began to emerge in 1989).

In concluding this section on the applicability of Habermas' conception of legitimation crisis to the communist world, two additional but related points need to be made.

First, precisely because communists traditionally emphasized the close interrelatedness of the economy and polity, an economic crisis was – *ceteris paribus* – worse for a communist system than for a liberal-democratic capitalist one, since there was very limited scope for recourse to 'external' and/or 'uncontrollable' scapegoats. The more communists referred to external forces, the more they had to deal with a growing rationality problem – an internal inconsistency in the ideology of 'scientific socialism'. Communists themselves stressed 'politics in command' over economics, in a manner that was clearly at odds with classical Marxism; thus they had to live with the consequences of their own excessive voluntarism.

Second, and connected with the first point, the sequence in which eudaemonism and legal-rationality became dominant modes of legitimation was the reverse in communist states of that in liberal democracies; in the latter, legal-rationality generally precedes eudaemonism, which renders them more resistant. The ability to fall back on 'the rule of law', impersonal politics, competitive politics (including regularized regime changes), etc. – at least within the parameters of reasonable expectation – in times of economic crisis provides the liberal democracies with greater strength and durability than the communist systems enjoyed.

It is appropriate at this point of the argument to return briefly to corruption and its relationship to legitimacy, legitimation and crisis. The second, follow-on assumption of this book is that *as the recent anti-corruption campaigns in the communist world developed – in most countries in the context of a deteriorating economic situation and, in the case of many states, declining Soviet influence – so many leaderships became increasingly aware of the fundamental contradictions between their existing values and legal-rationality. In many cases, the campaigns became ever more dysfunctional, as – beyond a certain point – they began to exert a negative influence on both regime and system legitimacy. This delegitimizing process contributed to and was part of the general crisis – of rationality, identity, legitimation and power – observable in so many communist states by the end of the 1980s.* It should be noted that it is *not* being argued here that an increase in the reporting of corruption in a given country invariably reflects a major legitimation crisis, at least in the short term. Rather, it is argued that such reporting may signify a tendency towards legitimation or general crisis, or it may help to avert such crises temporarily by establishing a new rationale for the regime (initially) and the system (subsequently). In any attempt at deciding whether a particular campaign is being functional or dysfunctional to legitimacy, it must be contextualized. The analyst needs to decide whether it is occurring at the same time as the economic situation is perceptibly improving or deteriorating, for instance. Among the many additional contextual variables to be considered are the political culture (including attitudes towards corruption); who the targets are and their role in the system; and whether or not a particular campaign appears to be reflective of a general dynamic that, logically and *ceteris paribus*, should either lead to rationality and identity crises or else deepen crises that have already begun to emerge.

Before concluding this section on legitimation, there are still three closely interrelated aspects of the argument that must be more fully explored; all have been referred to but not yet finalized.

First, what is meant by a crisis in the rest of *this* study, and how can one be identified? We have seen that Habermas' definition is problematic. In fact, it is not possible to produce a definition that is totally satisfactory for general social science purposes (though for a useful overview of attempts, with particular reference to Eastern Europe, see Lewis, 1984a, esp. pp. 6–15). For now, a crisis can be defined – in only slightly circular fashion – as a critical juncture or watershed, a point at which a system and/or regime is uncertain about its future direction and/or is seriously threatened, either by external forces or through its own internal contradictions or – as frequently happens – an interaction of these.[20] It is important to note that a crisis – even a general crisis of power – is not synonymous with 'collapse' (breakdown), which is one possible outcome of a crisis. It is to no small extent precisely because of this difference between 'crisis' and 'collapse' that the identification of a crisis is so often necessarily a highly subjective judgement. Few would dispute the notion that if the masses protest in the streets against a regime and/or system, then there is a crisis, often reflecting a legitimation crisis and certainly a severe legitimacy deficit (one must bear in mind, however, that a protest merely against a particular policy or one aspect of a regime/system does not of itself constitute the same sort of threat). But what if there is an absence of such overt manifestations? For our purposes, explicit references to crisis by leaders or others considered 'authoritative' living in a country are accepted as evidence that some important political actors perceive the possibility or actual existence of crisis and are acting, or demanding action, to avert this (Gorbachev is by no means the only communist leader to have spoken of crisis or pre-crisis in his country before the 1989 events[21] – for the Czechoslovak leadership doing this see *IB*, Vol. 25, No. 9, 1987, p. 30; for the Polish leadership doing it see *IB*, Vol. 25,

No. 10, 1987, p. 47, and Vol. 27, No. 3, 1989, p. 62; for the Yugoslav leadership doing it see *IB*, Vol. 27, No. 4, 1989, p. 19). In other words, it is not necessary to provide a precise definition or set of criteria for identifying a crisis; the *perception* by some of the actors involved that there either *is* a crisis or that a country is moving *towards* one is taken – with one minor reservation[22] – as sufficient evidence of either of these cases.[23]

Moreover, and independent of the last point, it is quite proper for the purposes of analysis and argument to suggest a tendency, derived from deductive reasoning, *towards* or *away from* a given phenomenon – in this case crisis – even though that phenomenon cannot be precisely defined or identified. For instance, de-emphasizing one mode of legitimation and emphasizing another can be taken as strong evidence that a leadership perceives a problem in the legitimating effect of the first mode. It is, ultimately, a highly subjective decision as to whether this problem should be called a 'crisis' or not, and one's answer largely depends on the precise circumstances. If it is still possible for rulers to shift to a new dominant mode of legitimation (because it has not relatively recently been tried and rejected), then Gorbachev's term 'pre-crisis' will often be an appropriate one, depending on the stage at which the shift occurs. In the pre-crisis situation, the leadership has perceived a potentially serious problem with the existing dominant mode, but believes there is, or might be, a solution. This said, since it is accepted here both that legal-rationality is the ultimate form of system-legitimation,[24] and that communist power is incompatible with full legal-rationality, it follows that the more a communist system attempts to legitimate itself in the legal-rational mode, the clearer are the signs of fundamental legitimation crisis. Finally, when a regime moves back to coercion as the dominant mode of exercising power (as did Jaruzelski's in December 1981, Husák's in 1969, Deng's in 1989, and as both Gorbachev's and Marković's appeared to be about to in late 1990 and early 1991), there can be no question that this represents a concrete sign of full-blown legitimation crisis, in that the leadership no longer feels able to place more emphasis on legitimation than on coercion. On the basis of these relatively concrete manifestations of crisis, it is argued here that there were signs of both pre-crisis and crisis in the communist world on various occasions prior to 1989, at the same time as the notion of a *permanent* legitimation crisis is rejected.

Second, how can legitimacy be measured? To reiterate, this cannot be done in any satisfactory and/or empirical way. It has already been argued that we need to distinguish at least between rulers, staffs and the masses; in the real world, there will always be sub-divisions within each of these – a distinction between non-staff intellectuals and the rest of the citizenry is often appropriate, for instance (see He Baogang, 1989) – cross-cutting cleavages and coherences, etc. There will also be varying strengths of opinion; some people (among rulers, staffs and masses) will be mildly or strongly supportive of the order, some mildly or strongly opposed to it, and some will appear not to care. In the case of the communist countries, as indicated earlier, outsiders were not generally permitted to go in and conduct opinion surveys anyway, so that it was not possible to measure in any even quasi-quantitative way attitudes towards legitimacy. In one sense, it might appear that we are unable to proceed beyond the argument that all we can really know is that a regime/system is illegitimate if the masses rebel and the leadership/staff cannot control them as a result of their own divisions and doubts. But once again perceptions – and intuition, which must play a significant role in social science – are important. As argued above, if leaders and others perceive there to be legitimacy problems – or, worse, a legitimation crisis – then we accept this as reflective of actual problems of legitimacy and legitimation.

Third, although it is not possible to measure legitimacy in a quantitative way, we can at least talk *deductively* about degrees of legitimacy, and draw together the strands of the earlier discussion. In the abstract, four degrees of legitimacy can be distinguished:

1   *High*. In this situation, the leaders believe in what they are doing and their own right to rule, staffs are loyal to the leaders, and the masses for the most party positively support the regime and system.

2   *Medium*. Here, the leaders believe in what they are doing and their right to rule, staff are basically loyal to the leaders, and the masses for the most part accept the regime and system.

3   *Low*. In this case, the leaders more or less believe in what they are doing and their right to rule; staffs have some doubts, but these are insufficient to threaten the leaders' position. The masses do not generally support the regime (their attitudes towards the system are often ambivalent), and may or may not have an alternative vision of society. Whether they do or not, they believe that there is no realistic possibility of overthrowing the existing order. The masses comply with the regime not because they basically believe in or even accept it – that is, not because it has real legitimacy from their, as distinct from the leaders', perspec-

tive – but primarily because of coercion (overt and/or covert, domestic and/or external, actual and/or threatened).
4   *Very low to none.* In this situation, the leaders lose faith in what they are doing and then in their right to rule; staffs and/or the masses have little or no faith in the leaders (and perhaps the system). If staffs and/or the masses are in addition prepared to act on their beliefs, to attempt to overthrow the regime or even system, there is an overt crisis; this will be followed by collapse if, as is quite possible, there is insufficient residual commitment among the staff to resist such a challenge. In this type of crisis, therefore, there will be observable manifestations of unrest, probably leading to collapse and a temporary situation of no legitimacy.

It should be immediately obvious that the above typology is far from exhaustive of every possible configuration. Since each of the three groups can adopt a number of positions and one should in one sense analyse each of them (for example, *vis à vis* regime and system separately), a comprehensive listing would be long and detailed. If it were worth the effort, then such a listing would be elaborated here (for a more disaggregated approach see Rose, 1969). But since legitimacy is such a rubbery concept anyway, the detailed listing would be pseudo-science. The above list does seem to provide enough ideal-types for what must after all be a largely subjective exercise. Given that they are ideal-types, it should be self-evident that even if we were able precisely to gauge the degree of legitimacy of a given order (and we never can), we can acknowledge that this might well fall between categories, just as in the real world orders often move between categories over time.

This section can now be summarized and concluded in terms of two sets of propositions. The first relates generally to legitimacy, legitimation and crisis. The second pertains more specifically to the communist world and the relationships between legitimacy, legitimation, corruption and crisis in that world.

First Set of Propositions

1   Legitimacy is a vague concept, but relates to normative values/ beliefs concerning who has the authority to make decisions about society (for example, about the distribution of power or wealth)

on behalf of society that are binding on society – in short, it is about the right to rule.

2 The process whereby legitimacy is acquired – legitimation – can occur via a number of channels. At least seven modes of internal (domestic) legitimation can be identified – old traditional, charismatic, goal-rational or teleological, eudaemonic, official nationalist, new traditional, legal-rational. Usually, one or two of these modes is/are dominant in a given society at a given point in time. Some modes cannot be *dominant* simultaneously with other dominant modes (for example, charismatic and legal-rational); in this very specific and limited sense, there are certain incompatibilities between some legitimation modes.

3 In addition to internal legitimation modes, there are various forms of external legitimation. In terms of popular legitimacy, the latter are less significant than the former.

4 The level of legitimacy of a given order can vary. In trying to decide how much legitimacy an order has, it is necessary to distinguish the values and beliefs of *at least* three groups – leaders, their staffs, the masses. In practice, further disaggregation is usually necessary. For instance, 'the masses' should in many cases be sub-divided, into 'non-staff intellectuals' and 'others'.

5 Legitimacy is not merely about mass/popular attitudes towards a regime and/or system. Nor is it merely concerned with the beliefs of the leaders and/or the staffs. It is about *all* of these.

6 Different groups in society may accord a degree of legitimacy to the system and/or regime on the basis of different legitimation modes or sub-divisions of a legitimation mode.

7 Although all systems operate on the basis of a mixture of coercion and legitimation, leaders and staffs exercise power over the masses primarily through one or the other. Where the emphasis is on legitimation, the leadership's perception of the success of that process – that is, the acquisition of popular (mass) legitimacy – acts as a major determinant of the level of coercion in society.

8 For an order that has very little popular legitimacy to maintain or acquire stability there must be relatively high levels of coercion, either realized or threatened, and/or a 'social contract' (at least in the short term). Coercion can be overt or covert. Overt coercion can come either from the domestic coercive agencies (what Althusser, 1971, esp. pp. 137–86, calls the 'repressive state apparatuses', such as the police, security police, military) and/or from external agents of coercion (such as a foreign army); covert coercion can take the form of internalized self-limitation by citizens, who acquire their subjective orientations largely through

their experience of and interaction with what Althusser calls the 'ideological state apparatuses' (such as the media, the educational system).

9   It is inappropriate to refer to a major 'legitimation crisis' in a system in which power over the citizenry is exercised primarily through coercion, except in the extreme case where those exercising power lose faith in their own right and ability to rule. If the latter occurs, the system will rapidly fall into general crisis and probably collapse. In systems in which power is exercised primarily through an emphasis on legitimation, three forms of legitimation crisis – two minor and one major – can be identified. In the first (minor) form, those running a system lose faith in the capacity of a given dominant legitimation mode to acquire what they perceive to be adequate popular legitimacy. This form of crisis – or, often, pre-crisis – can be overcome if those responsible for legitimating the system believe they can enhance popular legitimacy by switching to (an) alternative dominant legitimation mode(s); this solution can be described as 'the legitimating effect of legitimation shifts'. In the second (minor) form, a particular regime loses faith in itself, but there are others with enough faith in the basics of the system to form a new regime and to continue running the system, possibly with modifications. The major form of legitimation crisis occurs when a system falls into an apparently irreversible identity crisis – with *fundamental* contradictions – and the regime (and any subsequent regime) loses faith not merely in itself but also in the system and its capacity to shift successfully to (an) alternative mode(s) of legitimation. This form of legitimation crisis results in general, overt systemic crisis and, frequently, collapse – especially if the staffs and/or the masses have *some* vision of an alternative order *and* of how to achieve this. However, a new regime – possibly including many members of the former regime – may overcome such a major legitimation crisis on a short-term basis by switching from legitimation to coercion as the dominant mode of exercising power. This is possible if at least *some* of the leaders and staffs have sufficient will to maintain power even in the face of fundamental contradictions (that is, in the absence of a viable system-model), and if the masses and the other members of the staffs and leadership have little in the way of a vision both of an alternative order and of how to achieve this. But the identity crisis that led to the major legitimation crisis in the first place does not totally disappear in such a scenario, and a general crisis of power will re-emerge. Thus the life-span of such a regime is limited.

10   Partially on the basis of some of the arguments in the

previous point, the concept of a *permanent* legitimation crisis is rejected. However, it is accepted that a system and/or regime can survive for *relatively* long periods with a severe legitimacy deficit, here meaning that the system/regime enjoys very limited popular legitimacy.

11   The vision of an alternative order referred to in point 9 can be incomplete and incoherent, such as a form of nationalism that provides few indications of how the post-revolutionary (that is, post-system-collapse) economic system should be either structured or constructed. Nevertheless such an essentially vague vision can be sufficient both to stimulate the staffs and/or masses to bring about the collapse of an existing system and also to act as a form of social cement in the early stages following such a collapse. Eventually, however, its inadequacies become both obvious and dysfunctional, and a more complete system-model has to emerge if a new, stable system is to crystallize. The absence of such a model will sooner or later result in new crises.

Second Set of Propositions

1   Communist states were dynamic, and there was a shift over time in most communist countries from a predominance of coercive forms of power towards attempts at popular (mass) legitimation. Although the 'chiefs' may at earlier stages of the total legitimation process have sought legitimacy – both for themselves and in the eyes of their staffs – primarily in terms of goal-rationality, and although this *may* (as Rigby maintained – though see point 3 below) have remained the dominant mode *vis à vis* the staffs, such teleological legitimation could not last indefinitely as the dominant mode of legitimation to the masses.

2   At a certain point in this process of mass legitimation, eudaemonic legitimation became a – perhaps the – dominant mode in many countries; the emphasis various communist leaderships placed on economic reform and its positive ramifications for the consumer from the 1960s and 1970s is the best example of such eudaemonic legitimation. Although the masses may have been cynical and did not necessarily afford the regime (or system) much legitimacy in the early stages, they were prepared to enter into a social contract – conditionally to tolerate – the regime in return for improving living standards. But this social contract arrangement

was not static; the regime (and perhaps also the system) could have increased its legitimacy, had the system performed well.

3　However, communist experience revealed that the eudaemonic mode could also become problematical to the leadership and to the legitimation process. In addition to the reasons cited above (p. 16), one major factor was that better economic performance typically involved a reform of the economic system which – in practice – was often resisted by at least sections of the staffs. These people saw their powers and privileges threatened by 'economic' reform – which *always* implies *some* political reform, if only in the sense of a redistribution of decision-making powers within the industrial hierarchy – and so became obstructionist. This obstructionism may itself have been symptomatic of problems of legitimating at least the regime – and possibly the system – to the staffs in terms of goal-rationality.

4　In trying to overcome the problems of eudaemonic legitimation, leaderships had to choose between legitimating themselves principally to their staffs or to the masses. The choice was a relative, not an absolute one. This is to say that it was not a matter of leaders choosing to attempt to legitimate themselves *either* to the masses *or* to the staffs, but rather of placing more emphasis than hitherto on popular legitimation and less on staff legitimation. Typically, the decision was to focus more on popular legitimation. One method of doing this was to mobilize mass opinion against certain aspects of the staff, including corruption among its membership. Such mobilization was expected to be most effective if part of a package representing a move towards the legal-rational mode of legitimation.

5　Although problems (even the perception of a 'pre-crisis' or crisis situation) compelled chiefs towards mass legitimation, there were risks in moving from more staff-oriented legitimation towards mass-oriented legitimation, especially if the latter involved attacks on the staff. First, the process could engender growing hostility among the staff towards the regime. Both Weber and many of the analysts of legitimacy in communist systems cited in this chapter have argued that legitimation of the political order to the staffs is typically of critical importance; an alienated staff can become a source of instability and possibly regime- (or even system) collapse. This danger is compounded by the fact that the staffs generally interact more frequently and directly with the public than does the leadership, and can thus at least hinder and possibly even counteract the latter's attempts at legitimation. Second, the dynamism of the movement towards the legal-rational mode was difficult for leaderships to control, with the masses often expecting more radical and/or extensive reforms than the chiefs were prepared to tolerate. If there was *both* an alienated staff *and* a frustrated citizenry, and if the regime had moved away from more coercion-based forms of power towards more normative- (legitimacy-) based forms, there existed a very real danger of political instability and overt crisis.

6 Such crises were not *bound* to arise, however, in the short to medium term. If the measures taken to weaken, or at least change, the staff (for example, to make it less corrupt and/or more receptive to reform) in the context of moves towards the legal-rational mode had been successful, then economic reform itself could have been more successful. In turn, there could have been a move away from the legal-rational and back towards the eudaemonic as the dominant mode of mass legitimation – at least on a temporary basis. Such a move could for a time have both satisfied the consumerist aspirations of citizens, and appeared to be less threatening to the staffs than several ramifications of the moves towards legal-rational legitimation. In short, there could have been, and in the case of the still-existing communist states there can be, a series of dynamic, interactive relationships – between two modes of legitimation, between chiefs and staffs, between chiefs and masses, between staffs and masses – which could have led/lead to temporary stability and increasing legitimacy just as much as they led/lead to a major legitimation and general crisis. Whether a crisis – including a major legitimation crisis – arises in a given communist country at a particular time depends largely on the specific developments in that country and its neighbours, and it is not possible to generalize on the short-term outcomes.

7 In the longer term, however, eudaemonism was inadequate, and pressures again increased for a move towards legal-rationality. However, the further a communist regime felt compelled to move into legal-rational legitimation, the more obvious became the fundamental contradictions between this norm-oriented mode of legitimation and the very nature of communist power. Sooner or later, communism was bound to move into a situation of contradictory transition from which it could not save itself. The 'rule of law' is ultimately incompatible with communist power as the latter has actually been implemented; in practice, all communist systems have been voluntaristic and personalized – not necessarily in one person, but at least to a relatively small elite (the one possible exception to this was Yugoslavia in the 1980s; but this

state was so unstable that it can hardly be taken as an example of the compatibility of communism and legal-rationality). Communists could attempt to resolve this fundamental contradiction only in one or other of two basic ways – both of which involved crisis.

In the first, they attempted to move away from legal-rationality. If they could, they preferred to move towards some other mode of legitimation; this process represented a minor legitimation crisis. However, the possibilities for resolving the contradiction by this method were reduced over time, as other legitimation modes were tried and proved inadequate. If moves to other modes of popular legitimation were not feasible, leaders could resort to coercion as the dominant mode of exercising power; in terms of the present analysis, this represented a major legitimation crisis. Moreover, moves back to coercion ultimately had a destabilizing effect on staffs, who in many cases were able to recall the negative effects on themselves or their colleagues/ predecessors of previous coercive phases. This new phase of coercion also had even less rationale than earlier phases, notably the first 'revolution from above'. The latter often inspired many members of both staffs and the citizenry; at the same time, it could in no sense be confused with the style and policies of capitalist liberal democracy. The earlier coercive phases were thus not occurring within the context of the identity crisis that the later phase did. For these reasons, this new coercive phase was inherently more dangerous to communist systems than earlier phases. Such a form of communist rule – which became visible in China in 1989 and in late 1990/early 1991 appeared to be a real possibility both for Yugoslavia and for the USSR – thus contains the seeds of its own destruction.

The second basic 'solution' for communists was for them to attempt to move even closer to full legal-rationality. In doing so, however, they were obliged to abandon so many of the basic tenets of Marxism-Leninism that communism as a distinctive system of power disappeared altogether. Even where this transition process was initially controlled by the communists and occurred relatively peacefully, as was the case in Hungary 1988–90, the eventual disappearance (collapse) of the existing power system must be seen as the inevitable outcome of this attempt to resolve the most extreme form of crisis for communist systems.

Hypotheses Concerning Corruption

Although the relationship between corruption and both legitimation and legitimacy are the principal theoretical concerns of this study, there are a number of secondary ones. These mostly relate to various assumptions and hypotheses about corruption in communist states that have appeared in political science literature, although a few are either my own *a priori* assumptions or assumptions that have been made verbally to me. In the abstract, four types of assumption can be identified. The first are those that can be tested against the empirical findings of this study. A second group does not require the empirical evidence of this study, but can be questioned either in terms of existing knowledge and/or in terms of deductive reasoning. A third group is in theory testable, but is not in practice because of current data deficits. The final group cannot be tested either empirically or deductively; but they can be identified as untestable and therefore subject to doubt. Unfortunately, although it would be desirable for the sake of clarity to categorize all the hypotheses in terms of these four headings, in practice many writers' hypotheses are complex ones that straddle categories. For this reason, the only division here is between hypotheses that will be addressed in the concluding chapter and those that can be adequately dealt with in this chapter and on which this study is unlikely to shed any new light.

Assumptions to be Addressed in the Concluding Chapter

The anti-corruption drive under Andropov (USSR) was a temporary phenomenon In what is unquestionably one of the more interesting and imaginative approaches to corruption in the USSR, F.J.M. Feldbrugge argues that the anti-corruption moves taken by Soviet General Secretary Yurii Andropov in his brief tenure (November 1982–February 1984) were only an 'incidental organizational adaptation' (1984, p. 542). Feldbrugge's article was published when Chernenko (Andropov's successor, February 1984–March 1985) was in power, and his perception was almost certainly influenced by the apparent return to many Brezhnevian policies and approaches under Chernenko. We shall see if it does appear to be the case that the toleration of corruption (or at least the leadership perception that corruption was not a serious threat to the system) did increase under Chernenko, and whether this growing tolerance by the leadership – if it existed – survived Chernenko.

Campaigns against corruption are never sustained and decisive   David
Law (1974, pp. 106–7) has argued that Soviet anti-corruption campaigns are explicable primarily in terms of conflict between the self-
interest of central elites and the self-interest of local elites (a view
similar to one part of the argument of the present study). He goes on
to argue that too deep and systematic an examination of the corruption of local elites by the central elite would put the latter's own
legitimacy in question, so that examinations and campaigns remain
'at the level of the particular, the accidental and the superficial' and
are 'never sustained and decisive'. At the time Law was writing, his
argument seemed valid; it can now be tested against subsequent
developments.

*Anti-Corruption drives are often associated with new leaderships, but new
leaderships do not always mount such drives*   In the final part of this
chapter, details are provided on the scope of the study; from this it
becomes clear that since the primary empirical focus is on two
communist countries – the USSR and the PRC – for only a relatively
short period, there will be insufficient evidence in terms of leadership
changes to draw very firm conclusions on this issue. On the other
hand, there have been some successions in this period in the two
most populous communist states; by using a mixture of our own
primary research and others' research on other communist states, a
tentative answer will be possible. Moreover, suggestions as to why
some leaderships did not mount anti-corruption drives will be made.

*Corruption increases or decreases according to levels of economic develop-
ment*   A number of analysts – not only Westerners, such as McMullan (1961), LaPalombara (1963b) and Levine (1975), but also communists such as Deng Xiaoping (1984, 1985) – have argued that the
nature and scale of corruption is related to levels of economic
development. Some have argued that corruption is particularly
appropriate – functional – to a country undergoing rapid economic
modernization. On the one hand, there are often both severe shortages and bottlenecks at this stage and, on the other hand, some
problems have to be overcome – a machine has to be oiled – if the
development is to maintain its momentum. Corruption is frequently
one of the 'lubricants'. At later stages, as a country moves into the
developed stage, corruption is held to become increasingly dysfunctional and unnecessary. According to Werner (1983, pp. 146–7), the
logic of some functionalists who have studied developing countries
would lead them to conclude that corruption *disappears* once an
economy has a highly developed infrastructure, enough goods, etc.,

and that therefore Western countries are not corrupt. This argument is so obviously flawed that it does not merit further consideration.[25] But the notion that the scale and nature of corruption change markedly at different levels of economic development is an interesting one. Writing on China, Milton Yeh (1987, p. 11) has argued that the number of cases of corruption reported there since the modernization programme began in 1978 has increased dramatically, as has happened in many Third World countries once they have seriously embarked upon an economic modernization programme. And T.H. Rigby (1985, p. 12) has referred to the fairly common view that political corruption is typical of earlier stages of modernization but tends to decline at later stages (a view he does not share, it should be noted).

Unfortunately, major problems arise in attempting to define and measure levels of economic development. Clearly the GDR had a developed economy, whereas Benin does not. But what about North Korea or Romania? Both could be seen to have developing economies, but it is difficult to decide which variables should dominate in any attempt at deciding which is the more developed, and in particular in any attempt at locating them on a *scale* of development. As of 1991, the USSR had a developed economy, and it did not have one in 1925. But what about 1950? Was 1953 as clearly an economic watershed – from developing to developed economy – as it was a political one? There are no fully satisfactory solutions to these problems. One way in which the problem of comparing developing with developed countries could be *partially* overcome would be to compare a number of what are widely agreed to be economically developing countries with an equal number of clearly highly developed countries. One difficulty with such a methodology, however, is that it would be impossible to know how much weight should be attributed to *cultural* differences. To overcome this problem, it would be more useful to compare a number of countries individually over time, and then to analyse the findings in aggregate; given the problem mentioned above of identifying 'break-points' in development, it would be sensible to compare three-year periods, say 15–20 years apart, in various countries that are generally perceived to have been already modernizing in the earliest period and at a high level of development in the latest. Unfortunately, not only is such an exercise beyond the scope of the present study, but of anyone attempting to assess the scale or extent of corruption in any given country. Much corruption is by its very nature clandestine, and the corrupt official typically attempts to hide his/her activities from the outside world. The most we can hope to discover is how much corruption has been revealed by the authorities, which may or may not be related to the scale of the phenomenon. But it is not possible to produce an adequate, let alone complete, picture of the reporting of corruption in the communist world here; both conceptual problems (different classification methods) and inadequate resources for carrying out such an enormous research task preclude this. Given these problems – both general ones relating to any country, and particular ones relating to communist countries – it is not possible to reach any firm, empirically based conclusions on this hypothesis. Nevertheless, a few comments on this issue will be possible in the concluding chapter.

Some forms of corruption are peculiar to communist countries Writers such as Forster (1985, p. 5) have suggested that some forms of corruption relate specifically to the nature of communist systems; this can be tested, *inter alia*, by comparing findings of this study with others' findings on corruption in non-communist systems.

Corruption is more destructive in communist countries than elsewhere Although this assumption cannot be empirically tested in a satisfactory way, some speculation on its validity will be appropriate after the phenomenon of corruption in communist countries has been analysed.

Assumptions Considered Here

Corruption cannot be eradicated Yeh (1987, p. 15) has argued that 'the systematic sharing of bribes between cadres at different levels of responsibility has made it hopeless to fight corruption in mainland China'. The reference to 'hopeless' implies that corruption cannot be eradicated. While the evidence from all parts of the world makes it impossible to argue on the basis of any inductive reasoning that corruption can be totally eradicated, two features of Yeh's statement should be commented upon. The first is that just because a phenomenon cannot be *totally* eradicated does not mean that it cannot be brought under control. The second can be seen to derive from the first; in not acknowledging the difference between a phenomenon being either out of control or controllable (though not eradicable), Yeh's position could be interpreted as wishful thinking and politically loaded. Even if the problem is as serious as Yeh implies – and our own findings suggest it might well be in China – there is no obvious reason why the leadership should give up its struggle against it. Indeed, given the connection being suggested in this study between legitimacy and corruption, it can sometimes – depending on the overall situation in a country – be worse not to fight official corruption than to continue the struggle against it, even if the results are by many criteria disappointing.

Corruption can be eradicated Another assumption made by several commentators is that corruption could be solved by changing the system. Some feel it is the political system in particular that has to be changed, others – such as Deng (1985, p. 59) – just the economic system. Although writers who have argued for changes in the political system (for example, Simis, 1982, pp. 299–300; Lampert, 1984, p. 384; Schöpflin, 1984, p. 400) also made the point that it was at least unlikely if not apparently impossible that the existing communist *political* system could be fundamentally changed from within, I would take issue with the notion that such a change, assuming it were possible (and recent developments in several countries prove it is), would of itself be sufficient to cure corruption. As already pointed out, some corruption exists in *all* existing (political) systems, so that there is no reason to suppose that changing one type of elite and system for another will lead to the elimination of corruption. Whereas a given type of power system may exacerbate or reduce the problem of corruption, the phenomenon is caused by so many factors (see chapters 5 and 6) that a single change, albeit a major one, in existing power relationships will be insufficient to secure the elimination of corruption. If it is the case that one of the many factors leading to corruption is perception of inequalities and/or shortages, then it is very difficult, it not impossible, to envisage a situation in the real world in which such perceptions could be fully eradicated. The concept of shortage is closely related to the concept of need, and need is a socially determined rather than an absolute concept; what a Russian or Hungarian (let alone Australian or American) urban white-collar worker thinks of as the minimum legitimate expectations of any working person will not be as basic as the expectations of a Vietnamese or Ethiopian peasant. Expressing this differently, shortages are not manifested only in queues outside shops; in one sense, material expectations that exceed actual material wealth can lead to perceptions of shortages and, consequently, corrupt practices as a way of reaching the 'legitimate' (that is, justified by the corrupt individual to him/herself) levels of consumption. In short, although it is accepted here that corruption rates vary and that they may and do alter with changing circumstances, and although it is accepted that corruption may be more or less under control or out of control, the notion that it can ever be eradicated is rejected.

Professor   Katsenelinboigen's   hypotheses   In   a   controversial   and
thought-provoking article on corruption in the USSR, A. Katsenelinboigen (1983) listed three 'laws' that in my view need to be
questioned. The first is that 'the higher the level of the person in
society, the greater the percentage of bribes in his total income' (p.
233). Unfortunately, it is not possible to test this empirically at
present, since reliable data even on *official* incomes, let alone unofficial ones, of senior bureaucrats in communist states has been and
may well continue to be notoriously difficult – in many cases
impossible – to obtain.

Katsenelinboigen's second law (p. 234) is that 'the less tyrannical
authoritarian leadership, the more it uses corruption of lower-level
employees as a method to increase its own power'. Certainly,
corruption of lower-level officials has occurred in even the most
tyrannical of communist regimes (Pol Pot's – see Vickery, 1984, p.
158), although this does not in itself invalidate Katsenelinboigen's
point, which is concerned with *relative* levels of corruption. Again,
this hypothesis cannot really be either confirmed or disproven on the
basis of the currently available information. However, certain questions about the validity of the hypothesis can and should be raised. If
there appears to be widespread corruption among lower-level cadres
in a relatively non-tyrannical regime, it could at least as plausibly be
the case that the corruption is self-motivated among those officials
rather than initiated and/or encouraged from above, simply because
the officials are less fearful of the consequences of being discovered
and are therefore more likely to take risks. In short, there is no
obvious reason to assume that the leadership is using lower-level
corruption for its own ends. Second, the assumption fits poorly with
many of the individual case-studies of corruption that have already
been conducted, since these suggest that it is often the leadership that
initiates investigations of and proceedings against corrupt lower-
level officials. If Katsenelinboigen's hypothesis is correct, there
would be the very real danger that those lower-level officials not
caught in the leadership's net would resent the hypocrisy of the
leadership, which in turn would undermine morale and support for
the leadership. Precisely because the regime is 'less tyrannical', the
chances are greater that these negative attitudes among officials will
lead to a widespread questioning of the leadership of that regime – at
least among the 'staffs', and probably even among the masses –
which is hardly conducive to an increase in power (and legitimacy).
In short, by pursuing such practices the leadership could well *reduce*
its power rather than increase it.

Katsenelinboigen's third law (p. 234) is that 'the lower the ratio of the population's legal income to its semi-legal and illegal income, the higher the amount of corruption'. Intuitively, this seems to be a reasonable assumption, although it should be noted that the term 'amount of corruption' needs to be defined (for example, is one talking about sums of money or numbers of officials?). In connection with this argument, Katsenelinboigen compares the Baltic states (which had high incomes until their incorporation into the USSR in 1940 and consequently, according to Katsenelinboigen, had to be paid highly by the central authorities in order to placate potential political unrest) with the RSFSR, where there was allegedly much more semi-legal and illegal activity, which in turn led to the corruption of the controlling agencies that 'cover up' such activities. Once again, the hypothesis cannot be satisfactorily tested because of data deficiencies. However, it can at least be pointed out that there are other equally plausible reasons for the apparently lower levels of corruption in the Baltic states. One is that the central Soviet authorities felt that levels of hostility towards themselves were still so high that greater legal incomes for Balts would have been insufficient on their own to keep potential political unrest in check; for this reason, they both investigated and reported on corruption less in the Baltic states and in other areas in which they felt that the advantages of exposing cases of corruption outweighed the disadvantages. Another possible explanation is the cultural one; it is sometimes suggested that Balts are traditionally less corrupt than Georgians, for example. Connected with the cultural explanation is the possibility – suggested to me by a leading Estonian social scientist – that a high level of hostility to the central Soviet authorities on the part of many Balts could manifest itself in a form of pride, whereby Balts would not sully themselves with corruption because they might then – if caught and sent to trial – have been subject to humiliation by the very central authorities they despised; better poorer but nobler!

Summary and Conclusions

Much of this chapter has been concerned with questions of legitimacy and legitimation in communist states, and with the possible connection between these and public campaigns against official corruption. It has been argued that one of the major problems with writing on legitimacy in communist states (and more generally) is that writers do not usually distinguish clearly between political system and regime; one of the major tenets of the present argument is that an awareness of this distinction is vital both in understanding legitimacy in the communist world generally, and in understanding the particular relationship between the reporting of corruption and legitimacy. It is further suggested that the recent leadership focus on corruption in so many communist states can be understood on one level in the context of the *dynamism* of both legitimation and power. Many communists in power attempted to move away from predominantly coercive towards more legitimate power, and from teleological towards other forms of legitimation; but some of these – eudaemonic legitimation, official nationalist legitimation, etc. – became increasingly problematic for communist leaderships. Thus eudaemonic legitimation can become a hindrance if citizen expectations exceed economic performance, while official nationalism can inspire unofficial (counter-hegemonic) nationalism, which is clearly dysfunctional to both regime and system. Partially for these reasons, several moves towards a more legal-rational mode of legitimation were taken in the communist world in recent years. It is argued in this study that anti-corruption drives were in themselves not only insufficient to legitimate modern communist states in the legal-rational mode, but that they could lead to a backlash, causing serious legitimation problems or even crisis. This fits well with the broader argument that, beyond a certain point, the fundamental contradictions between the communist system of power and legal-rationality become very visible; this is a major part of the explanation for the crises and revolutions in so many communist countries at the end of the 1980s/beginning of the 1990s.

Without further elaboration of the theoretical bases of this study, the chapter can be concluded by focusing in more detail on the scope, methodology, reasons for and layout of this book.

Despite the severe problems involved in researching corruption, the phenomenon was perceived as widespread and serious in many communist countries and deserves to be studied, however imperfectly. At the beginning of this chapter, I noted the various types of specialist that might bring their expertise to bear on a study of corruption; at this point, my own very real limitations must be acknowledged. I am neither a sociologist nor a criminologist nor a psychologist nor an anthropologist, although I have read a little from each of these disciplines. Rather, I have trained as a political scientist with a particular interest in communist economic policy; it is principally from this perspective that I have approached corruption, although I have tried to incorporate at least some of the approaches the other specialists might adopt, since the intention is to analyse corruption from as many angles as possible.

The study is concerned with the nature, scale, causes, treatment, functions and dysfunctions of corruption and its reporting – based on primary, secondary and what in chapter 4 are called 'intermediate' sources – in states that, at least until 1989, were claiming to be building or to have built socialism and having communism as their professed end-goal. Such states have been identified by their adoption of Marxism-Leninism as their official ideology, a polity constructed according to the organizational principles of democratic centralism, and by their commitment – at least until recently – to a wholly or predominantly socialized and planned economy. The absence of any of these factors will disqualify a given state, so that some of the 'socialist' states that have not adopted Marxism-Leninism – such as Burma (also known as Myanmar), Tanzania or Libya – are explicitly excluded. Using these criteria, 23 countries were identified for investigation through to 1989; listed alphabetically they are Afghanistan, Albania, Angola, Benin, Bulgaria, Cambodia (Kampuchea 1979–1989), China (PRC), Congo (Brazzaville), Cuba, Czechoslovakia, East Germany (GDR), Ethiopia, Hungary, Laos, Mongolia, Mozambique, North Korea (DPRK), Poland, Romania, Soviet Union (USSR), Vietnam, South Yemen (PDRY), Yugoslavia.

Although these could be all classified until 1989 as communist states, their levels of economic development, their economic policies and structures, their political cultures and the length of time they had been under communist rule varied considerably. Albania and the DPRK, for instance, (have) had highly socialized and centralized planned economies in comparison with the *relatively* mixed, decentralized and *laissez-faire* economies of communist Hungary, Yugoslavia or even the PRC. The twentieth-century history of Czechoslovakia, with its tradition of liberal democracy in the inter-war years and its relatively highly developed economy at the time of communist consolidation of power (1948), is clearly very different from that of a country such as Mozambique, which was an economically underdeveloped colony of Portugal with a relatively poorly developed sense of national consciousness or democracy at the time of the communists' accession to power (1975). A predominantly Moslem state, such as Afghanistan or South Yemen, presented the communists with different traditions to deal with in building socialism to those of a state in which Catholicism (for example, Poland) or Confucianism (PRC, North Korea) had been the dominant belief-system.

In an ideal world – of teams of researchers having a deep knowledge of the cultures, languages and systems of each of the 23 countries; of access to the kind of data one can realistically hope to obtain on corruption for each country; of data-bases sufficiently hard, detailed and rank-orderable to be able to run complex regression analyses; etc. – one would be able to produce a far more sophisticated and thorough analysis of the complex relationships between different types of culture, levels of development, levels of centralization, etc., than can be done here. The aim of this study is far more modest. On several points, one must be satisfied with impressions rather than rigorous analysis. Only two countries have been systematically analysed to a reasonable depth, viz the USSR and the PRC; the reasons for this choice, and the possible problems associated with it, are elaborated in chapter 4. Even though they have been studied more systematically and in considerably more depth than all the other states, sometimes severe problems of data collection and interpretation have arisen, and the conclusions drawn in chapter 4 on the basis of an analysis of even these two countries must be treated with extreme caution. This said, extensive use has been made of a wide range of intermediate and secondary literature – and *some* use of primary sources – from the vast majority of the countries specified. Subject to these real limitations and caveats, this study is offered as a comparative one.

One point that will become increasingly obvious as the study progresses is that the following statement, from one of the classic comparative studies of corruption, was by the 1980s no longer valid (in fact, it is questionable that it was even at the time it was made): 'The material on the socialist bloc is sparse and concerns mainly the informal economic arrangements designed to circumvent the snarls of central planning, which may seem inadequate for a general discussion of corruption in such systems' (J.C. Scott, 1972, p. x). The material is no longer sparse; indeed it is rich and often fascinating, while the ingenuity and gall of some corrupt officials is sometimes hard to believe. There is also a much greater variety of forms of corruption than is implied in Scott's statement, and much of this is by now well documented. Indeed, the present situation on secondary material, while still far from satisfactory, is basically encouraging. Among the many articles and books on corruption and the second economy (see chapter 2 for the distinction) in the USSR that have been published since the early 1970s are those by Staats (1972), Law (1974), Katsenelinboigen (1977 and 1983), Kramer (1977), Schwartz (1979), Simis (1982), Lampert (1983, 1984, 1985) and Teague (1988, pp. 261–90). With the exception of China, the rest of the communist world is far less well served, though there is some material. On the individual countries of Eastern Europe, for instance, there are analyses by Kenedi (1981 – on Hungary) Łos (1982 – on Poland), Sampson

(1983 – on Romania), Ghermani (1983 – also on Romania) and Simecka (1984 – on Czechoslovakia). Alan Liu (1983), Keith Forster (1985), C. Stubb-Ostergaard (1986), Milton Yeh (1987), Lynn White (1988), Jean Oi (1989) and James Myers (1989) are among those who have published articles on corruption in the PRC.

Although the amount of material being published in the West on corruption in communist states is increasing – and may well accelerate as post-communist states reveal more information on their predecessors – some countries still await even an article-length analysis, and genuinely comparative analyses are rare (though see Schöpflin, 1984 – on Eastern Europe; Harris, 1986 – on the USSR and the PRC; Tarkowski, 1989 – on the USSR and Poland; Łos, 1990 – on the second economy in several communist states). This is in some ways surprising given that most studies of corruption define the phenomenon in terms of the tension between public interests and resources on the one hand and private interests on the other; their purposive socialization programmes notwithstanding, the emphasis communist systems placed on public ownership of the means of production and state involvement in virtually all areas of society, added to the relatively low level of answerability of public officials to the citizenry (whatever happened to the classical Marxist admiration for the Paris Commune?), means that, *a priori* at least, communist states were among the most susceptible to the phenomenon of corruption. A detailed, comparative analysis is thus at least due – if not already overdue.

As is necessary for the sake of analysis – while acknowledging that the real world is never so tidy – the book is divided into sections that consider different aspects of corruption. In the next chapter, a number of others' definitions of corruption are considered, plus explanations of why no definition can satisfy all; the definition used for this study is also provided. The chapter concludes with a taxonomy – a list of the various guises corruption can assume. In the following chapter, examples of corruption from most of the 23 countries are given, classified according to the taxonomy in chapter 2. The focus of chapter 4 is explicitly on the reporting of corruption in the two countries analysed in most depth for this study, the USSR and the PRC. In the first part, I outline the numerous methodological difficulties encountered in researching corruption in those two countries, explain and justify the solutions adopted, and emphasize the limitations and tentative nature of the findings that follow. The second part of chapter 4 deals with patterns of corruption (for example, in terms of regional distribution, functional distribution, hierarchical levels, etc.) – at least as these are suggested by patterns of reporting. Chapters 5 and 6 consider the reasons for corruption from a number of perspectives; chapter 5 focuses on the factors that lead those engaging in corruption to do so, whereas chapter 6 is concerned with the reasons why it can in some circumstances be useful – in other circumstances detrimental – to a regime or system to investigate and report corruption, and why communist regimes do or do not encourage investigation into and reporting of corruption. In the following chapter (7), I consider the general reactions of the authorities to corruption – in terms of official policy statements, campaigns, legislation and actual punishments.

The concluding chapter starts with a narrow focus, then broadens out. The first part addresses the first six hypotheses on corruption outlined in this chapter. This is followed by an analysis of the evidence on the steps taken towards legal-rationality in various communist countries during the 1970s and, particularly, the 1980s, plus a consideration of why it is maintained in this book that teleological legitimation was not the dominant form of legitimation in recent years. The third section considers the transition from communism to post-communism in a number of countries, while the fourth part locates recent change in the communist/post-communist world within the broader debates on modernity and post-modernity. This part of the discussion is both brief and superficial; it is included primarily in a bid to ensure that the communist/post-communist world is included on the agenda of future debates on modernity and post-modernity, rather than to provide a comprehensive and/or definitive set of answers to the various issues raised.

NOTES

1   I am sympathetic to the argument many Poles, Hungarians, Czechs, Slovaks and others are now making that their countries should be seen as part of *Central* rather than Eastern Europe. However, I have opted here for the latter term – primarily because it is still in much wider usage and is more readily understood than the term 'Central Europe'. Moreover, I wish to use a term that explicitly includes the Balkan states, and 'Central Europe' is usually interpreted as excluding these.

2   For an explicit statement that thorough empirical examinations of real legitimacy in communist countries 'are prevented by obvious serious difficulties' see Brunner, 1982, p. 27. Nevertheless, for innovative – if necessarily limited, and methodologically questionable – attempts at measurement see, for example, Hart and Keeri-Santo (1978), Shafir (1987) and Ziolkowski (1988).

3   It should be noted that Pakulski (1986, p. 56) also starts from a Weberian position, but concentrates on what he sees as a less familiar dimension of Weber's argument – viz those aspects of his analysis that 'are devoted to forms of domination and control based not on authoritative commands and voluntary submission but on the manipulation of circumstances that affect the very premises of (rational) calculation'. Rigby's argument focuses on the better-known Weberian arguments on legitimacy.

4   The reader should note the distinction between charismatic legitimation and charismatic legitimacy. Many have argued that personality cults that have been created around individual communist leaders have in many cases been artificial, and did not represent evidence of genuine charismatic legitimacy. While I have much sympathy for such an argument (though also some reservations), my primary concern here is with ways in which leaderships might seek to obtain charismatic legitimacy, not with the separate question of whether or not they succeed in these attempts.

5   Like many writers on comparative communism, Rigby has often assumed that the Soviet Union served as a role-model for most other communist systems, even though each communist country had some distinctive features. Although there have certainly been significant exceptions to this generalization – Yugoslavia and Pol Pot's Kampuchea being two – I would agree with Rigby's assumption.

6   Although it is often claimed that instrumental popular support – or even 'tolerance' – is not to be equated with the more normatively based concept of mass legitimacy (see, for example, Mayntz, 1975, *passim*; Pakulski, 1987, esp. pp. 134–7 – while Rothschild, 1979, esp. p. 38, draws a distinction between 'utilitarian' and 'normative' techniques of rule), it is argued here that such distinctions are for most *practical* purposes over-rigid and unconvincing. To begin with, we need to ask where 'values' and 'norms' come from in the first place; the obvious answer is that they are largely a function of socialization. Our ancestors' respect for 'the divine right of monarchs' – to the extent that this really was an effective legitimating mechanism – was in no sense innate; they were socialized into accepting this as a mode of legitimation. Once this point is acknowledged, it becomes clearer that the distinction that is sometimes drawn between effectiveness and legitimacy, or between instrumental and substantive legitimation, is much hazier than is often assumed. If we are *socialized* into *evaluating* a political order at least partially in terms of its economic and social-welfare performance, then such performance becomes part of the legitimation process and *may* enhance legitimacy. The main point here is that there can be a dialectical or interactive dynamic relationship between 'basic' values and current assessments, with many citizens seeking to resolve tensions here by becoming more positively oriented towards a system (cf. the debates in psychology about 'cognitive dissonance'). Thus, while the distinctions drawn above by others are of some use in an abstract, definitional sense, they run the real danger of focusing on relationships too statically or synchronically, rather than in an ultimately more revealing diachronic way. One final point here is that even 'legal-rationality' is in the real world not as objective and substantive a form of legitimation as is often maintained.

7   Rothschild was arguing in the late 1970s (see 1979 – which is in fact a reprint of a 1977 article – p. 38) that legal-rational legitimation already typified the communist states of Eastern Europe. If he was correct in this, it is certainly the case that the process became much deeper and more visible in the late 1980s.

8   The term 'short-term' is used to emphasize the fact that I do not accept the notion of an *ongoing* 'social compact' or 'social contract' arrangement that is divorced from the concepts of either legitimacy or coercion.

9   Indeed, it is surely the case that no system can exist for any length of time without *any* legitimacy, since someone must believe in what s/he is doing. Thus, just as no state can continue without a degree of coercion, so no state can survive without a degree of legitimacy.

10 The question of *external* legitimation has in my view been inadequately considered in most of the literature on legitimation in communist states. While it is difficult to reach firm conclusions on the reasons for this, they *might* relate to the fact that much of this writing takes as its starting point Western analyses of legitimation in First World states, in which external legitimation has generally played less role than in the ex-colonies and other 'marginalized' countries of the so-called Second and Third Worlds. As already argued in the text, the reference here to external legitimation is not to be equated with the impact of the threat or actual use of external *coercion* (for example, invasion by the USSR or the WTO); this is conceptually quite distinct from the notion of legitimation, even if, as with domestic coercion and legitimation, *both* elements coexist in a changing balance in the actual exercise of power. External legitimation relates to the fact that *no* state – not even Albania or North Korea – exists in total isolation, and that no government can survive without reference to the outside world. It is argued here that *domestic* (or *internal*) legitimation is ultimately the top priority of a communist leadership attempting to exercise power more through legitimation than through coercion. Nevertheless, the question of external support for the exercise of power cannot and must not be overlooked; this was especially true of the East European communist states, although even the USSR was affected by it. For the sake of analysis, at least three versions of such external legitimation can be identified. The first is the rather obvious legal or quasi-legal form, in which a substantial number of foreign states and international organizations (notably the UN) recognize a particular government of a country as 'legitimate', possibly quite independently of the normative orientations of the majority of citizens of that country. As indicated earlier, this form of external legitimation has often been used by communist leaderships as part of the attempt at internal popular legitimation through the official nationalist mode. Less obvious is the self-legitimation a leader like Gorbachev experiences via the international community; expressed crudely, a leader may retain faith in what s/he is doing and represents – despite internal criticism and low popularity – because of such external support. The third version is close to the second, but is discrete. The focus here is on an external agent not as an overt legitimator or support, but rather – as argued in the text – as a role-model, whether self-conciously or not. If a given leadership is experiencing problems in legitimating itself at home, but still basically believes in itself and its actions because it is emulating an external role-model in which it also still believes, then it can acquire – at least in its own mind – a form of legitimacy. This phenomenon can be called the *'third face'* of external legitimation, and is the 'particular type' referred to in the text. Thus, a distinction is drawn here between a situation in which Gorbachev retains faith in what he is doing because the West believes in him – even though his ultimate goal may only partially resemble whatever 'the Western model' might be – and one in which a Jakeš or a Zhivkov continued to believe that, despite their many and serious problems, the Soviets still basically knew where they were heading.

This is why it it so important *not* to underestimate the symbolic significance of the Soviet withdrawal from Afghanistan at about the same time as the USSR was both tolerating the Polish and Hungarian experiments of 1988–9 (all of which revealed in a very tangible way the abandonment of the Brezhnev Doctrine) and so dramatically expanding the scope of its own *glasnost, perestroika* and *demokratisatsiya* that these were rapidly getting out of control; all this happening simultaneously was a clear indication that the USSR was in crisis and had lost its direction. Once this became clear, it was only a matter of time and circumstance before the leaders of Eastern Europe – many of whom had until then still believed in the possibility of a radical reform communism – threw in the towel.

11 Meyer (1972, pp. 49–50) was one of the first analysts of communist politics to touch on this distinction, but did not develop the point at that stage.

12 Pakulski (1987, p. 132) points out that many surveys of Polish mass attitudes over the years indicated widespread support for the general idea of socialism; *if* these findings can be accepted, they would constitute a form of evidence for the argument put forward here.

13 There were signs of something similar happening in Lithuania in late 1989/early 1990, with many Lithuanian citizens strongly supporting their *communist* leader, Brazauskas, in his conflict with Moscow. Although the nationalist group Sajudis won the Lithuanian election in February 1990, Brazauskas himself did very well. His problem was that he did not have a *team* that impressed the Lithuanian electorate sufficiently, so that – in a situation not dissimilar from Ortega's in Nicaragua – the popularity of the individual leader proved insufficient to win an election for that leader's party (on all this see Senn, 1990). Election results in Bulgaria, Romania, Mongolia, Hungary (where former communist leader Németh proved to be the single most popular candidate) and parts of the USSR and Yugoslavia in 1990 would also endorse the argument that communist regimes and/or individual members of such regimes can enjoy widespread popular support, even though it is maintained here that communists and quasi-communists in most – possibly all – of these countries/republics will lose power in the 1990s.

14 During this 'revolution from above' stage, the legitimation attempts made by communist leaderships tended to be mainly of the charismatic or teleological sort, though elements of official nationalism were also often discernible.

15 Some maintain that there is a third major way in which power can be exercised, namely material reward (see, for example, Dallin and Breslauer, 1970, p. 2). This mode is treated very much as a secondary form in the present study; three main arguments for this can be adduced:

   1 If citizens have no real option but to work for the state in order to survive, the state can be seen to be exercising a form of dominance and coercion over them. In this situation, then, 'material power' is in fact subordinate to coercive power.

   2 Conversely, it could be argued that most citizens in communist systems do not directly relate their material rewards to the state. Even if they are ultimately paid by the state, citizen perceptions will typically focus on the place of work, and will perceive little if any connection between their material situation and the state's exercise of power (for example, the expectation of citizen obedience).

   3 To the extent that there *is* recognition by citizens that they obey the

state in return for material rewards, the point about dynamic interaction pertains. By this I mean that material reward can be seen as a method by which those exercising power hope to acquire greater legitimacy over time. In other words, material rewards/incentives can be seen as a component of eudaemonic legitimation. This said, the argument in this chapter should make it quite clear that no inferences are being made about the level of success of such attempts at eudaemonic legitimation; less ambitiously, the argument here is that those exercising power hope that the recipients of material rewards will not only obey, but will also over time develop some loyalty to, those providing the goodies. Thus in this interpretation, the material-based exercise of power can be treated – controversially – as essentially an element of the legitimation-based exercise of power.

It could be objected that types 1, 2 and 3 above are mutually incompatible. On one level this does not matter, in that any one of them can explain why the reward-based conception of power is not treated as a primary one in this study. Conversely, it can be retorted that one or other type is salient for different sections of the population, so that the three arguments *can* coexist.

16 Commentators such as Arato (1982, pp. 196–201, esp. p. 199) have argued that it can be inferred that Habermas has also been interested in state socialist societies; in fact, Habermas' interest is rather more explicit than such writers acknowledge. The very first sentence of Habermas' book reads, 'To use the expression "late capitalism" is to put forward the hypothesis that *even in state-regulated capitalism*, social developments involve contradictions or crises' (p. 1 – emphasis added). There are many Western marxists (such as Binns, Hallas, Cliff) who long argued that the communist states, at least the USSR and Eastern Europe, were 'state capitalist'; the developments since 1978 in China have been seen by some (such as Chossudovsky, 1986) to have added weight to this general argument. But even here we are still making inferences about what Habermas intends to include in his analysis, and this is not strictly necessary. Habermas himself (1976, p. 17) refers to 'state socialist societies', and describes them as 'post-capitalist class societies'. Following this he argues that 'The interest behind the examination of crisis tendencies in late- *and post-capitalist class societies* is in exploring the possibilities of a "post-modern" society' (1976, p. 17 – emphasis added). In sum, although Arato and others are quite correct in arguing that Habermas does not *focus* on communist states, Habermas does claim that his analysis refers to them, or at least some of them; whether or not such states should ever have been described as post-capitalist is a moot point, but one that should not distract us at this juncture. It is appropriate to note here that the relationships between communism, post-communism, modernity and post-modernity are considered in a very introductory way in chapter 8 of this book.

17 It should be noted that other communist states had by the late 1980s argued the need for unemployment (there were discussions between Solidarity and the Polish government on this issue as early as the 1980–1 period). The leading Soviet proponent of unemployment in recent years was N. Shmelev – see, for example, his 1987 article, esp. pp. 148–9; Shmelev's calls for unemployment were initially rejected by Gorbachev (see *Pravda*, 22 June 1987, p. 1). However, it is testimony to the rapid pace of change in the former USSR that the first unemployment exchanges were officially opened there in July 1991.

18   It is not argued here that decollectivisation/decommunisation is exclusively the result of economic problems; but it is maintained that this is often part of the reason for the change of policy.

19   Habermas himself, however, sometimes draws an explicit distinction between 'rationality crisis' and 'identity crisis' (for example, 1976, p. 45), without – in my view – adequately explaining the reasons for this.

20   This definition is close to and basically compatible with that provided by Alexander Motyl: 'crises are best defined as immediately life-threatening conditions upon whose successful resolution systemic survival depends' (1989, p. 278). Motyl goes on (p. 279) to provide an interesting and persuasive analysis of the relationship between crisis and radical reform. The main reason why I have not used Motyl's definition for the present study is because the reference to 'systematic' is too limited for my purposes. It implicitly excludes both the concept of regime crisis and the distinction I draw later in this chapter between minor and major forms of crisis, particularly with reference to legitimation crisis.

21   In an interesting – if brief – analysis of the distinction between 'pre-crisis' and 'crisis' in the USSR, Alexander Lebedev (in *NT*, No. 6, 1989, p. 9) wrote the following:

> Did people then understand that the country was in a pre-crisis situation, as it was afterwards defined? I think that most people understood that, and many would have used a stronger word – crisis – had it not been associated with such phenomena 'alien' to our society as class conflict, unemployment, inflation, bankruptices, the closing down of factories, strikes, human tragedies and the decline of morals.

In short, Lebedev was arguing that the Soviets only avoided the use of the term crisis to describe their own situation because the term had become virtually synonymous with the phrase 'crisis of capitalism'. Although this term may once have been inappropriate to their situation, Soviets were by 1990 clearly acknowledging that their country *was* experiencing most of the phenomena listed by Lebedev.

22   The reservation is that, under certain circumstances, a leadership may publicly claim that there is a crisis or pre-crisis situation, even though it does not fully believe this itself. It does this in the expectation that it will be able to 'overcome' the 'crisis', thereby enhancing its own legitimacy through its successful resolution of a major problem. In a sense, then, one could identify this as yet another mode of legitimation – 'crisis management'. However, it is argued here that such a form of legitimation is too marginal to be included in our main list. There are several reasons for this. First, it can *per se* serve to legitimate only a regime, not a system, and in this sense is only partial. Second, if it is to be effective, it can operate only on a very short-term basis. Third, given the various ramifications of Leninist voluntarism, communist leaderships could hardly avoid much – probably most – of the blame for the crisis or pre-crisis situation. This meant not only that such a form of 'legitimation' was usually available only to a new (incoming) regime, but also that – even then – the new leadership was endangering whatever popular legitimacy the system itself may have had by focusing on crisis within that system. Consequently, it made little sense for communist leaders to refer to a crisis (or pre-crisis) situation unless they really believed there was one. This is not to deny, however, that commun-

ist leaderships did not always act on such rational premises – which is why references to crisis (pre-crisis) by communist leaders should be used with a degree of caution.

23   There is some similarity between the approach to the meaning of crisis adopted here and Giddens' concept of the 'double hermeneutic', in that I am allowing for the interaction of social science terminology and ordinary language – see Giddens, 1977, p. 12.

24   The reference to 'system' here relates primarily to the state in its broad sense (see Holmes, 1986a, pp. 174–6) and its relationship to society; it thus assumes a perceptible distinction between the 'state' and 'society'. The crisis of the state *per se* – as distinct from the crisis of a particular *type* of state – is a major concern in debates on post-modernity, and must be high on the agenda for analysts of contemporary politics. However – and unfortunately – this crucial issue lies beyond the relatively precise and modest parameters of the present study, although it is again touched upon in chapter 8.

25   The reader might well infer from Werner's wording that Nye (1967) exemplifies this approach. In fact, despite a move in this direction on p. 418, the very first sentence of Nye's article seems to contradict such an inference, and the rest of the article gives no clear indication that Nye does not see corruption as a feature of all systems. Hence it would be interesting to know which functionalist(s) Werner has in mind.

2

Towards a Definition and Taxonomy of Corruption

A major problem of comparing corruption in different countries – even if these are all communist, let alone if they have fundamentally different systems – is that the term 'corruption' can have different meanings in different countries. In fact, not only do different cultures and ethnic groups define and interpret corruption differently, but even *within* a given culture, different groups – legal specialists, party *apparatchiki*, workers, etc. – may perceive corruption differently. As will shortly be demonstrated – and despite Lynn White's implication to the contrary (1988, p. 50) – a glance at even a few Western analyses of corruption by scholars from essentially rather similar backgrounds will reveal important differences in approach; in other words, there can be differences even *within* a given group. Thus it must be strongly emphasized at the outset that it is not possible for *anyone* to provide a universally applicable or universally acceptable definition of corruption. However, to say that it can mean different things should not blind us to the fact that some actions are seen as corrupt in most if not all societies, just as the concept of murder has an essentially similar meaning in almost all societies; there is, in short, much common ground. Hence, while the comparativist must always be alert to the dangers of excessive generalization, s/he should only yield to the country-specialist's claim that 'my country is unique' or 'my country is different' if and when this case is proven. There are times when it makes sense to distinguish whites from yellows from blacks, men from women, old people from young people, blue-collar from white-collar workers, etc.; at other times, it makes more sense to talk of humans as a collective entity, to distinguish them from wombats or parrots or rhododendrons – all of which can, collectively, be distinguished from inanimate objects. Moreover, if even the people *within* one country are not fully in agreement about the meaning of corruption, then the argument of the Sinologist,

Sovietologist or whoever about cultural uniqueness and the inappropriateness of the comparative approach becomes unconvincing; the 'specialist' and the comparativist are talking – whether wittingly or not – about quantitative rather than qualitative differences in their respective approaches. In sum, it would be absurd to suggest that we should always look either at the trees or at the wood – both exercises are valid in different contexts and for different purposes.

The above helps to put the present chapter into context. The expression 'towards a definition' has been used very consciously, to emphasize the fact that there cannot be a totally satisfactory definition of corruption for comparative – or, indeed, any other – purposes, precisely because, at the edges, different cultures and even individuals perceive corruption differently. Conversely, it does seem both possible and desirable to identify the problems of definition and to seek to overcome these to the extent that this is intellectually respectable and necessary if we are to make comparisons.

The chapter divides into two main parts. In the first, I shall consider several possible meanings of the term 'corruption', and demonstrate in what ways and to what extent the concept overlaps with and/or is distinguished from related concepts such as 'second economy' and 'economic crime'; at the end of this section, the definition of corruption used in this study is provided. The second part provides a listing – a taxonomy – of the different forms corruption can take, and a brief explanation of each form; this serves as a framework for the following chapter.

What is Corruption?

An opening point to be made about the term 'corruption' is that even if we focus only on its use in social science literature, it can have a number of figurative meanings. An example of figurative use in a serious work of social theory can be found in *Dictatorship Over Needs*, where the authors write: 'We have no doubt that Cuba, in an ignominious *corruption* of the genuinely radical hopes raised by its revolution all over the world, has become a particularly nasty police state' (Fehér, Heller and Márkus, 1984, p. x – emphasis added). Such usage can in some circumstances be confusing; in *this* study, the term is used only in a literal, not in any figurative, sense.

A definition cited by Leslie Palmier (1983, p. 207)[1] is a useful one with which to start, in that it represents one of the most popular basic approaches. According to this definition, corruption is:

the use of public office for private advantage

– the latter term being understood not only in a pecuniary sense but also in terms of status and influence.[2]

However, as Friedrich (1966, pp. 74–5) – among others – has pointed out, the use of public office for private advantage is not always widely perceived in a given society to be corrupt. Particularly if an individual making personal gains is simultaneously making a positive contribution to the society – and, as any advocate of an entrepreneurial economy will readily appreciate, there is no *necessary* contradiction between private advantage and contributing to the general good – many citizens will see such actions as at least accept-able and sometimes even 'just reward'. Thus, although corruption *usually* implies a form of betrayal of public confidence, even an approach based on this criterion cannot be universally applied. Because of the clash that can arise between an abstract definition of corruption and its application to a complex real world, some writers have distinguished between what can crudely be called 'good', 'bad' and 'ambiguous' corruption. For instance, Katsenelinboigen (1983, p. 236) identifies two basic types of corruption:

1   Actions whose harmful effects on society are questionable. Acccording to Katsenelinboigen, this form of corruption involves redesigning the system and legalizing the appropri-ate actions of people in it.[3]
2   Actions that unambiguously harm society. Such acts should be treated as corrupt and criminal.

Another bifurcated approach is that between 'grass-eaters' and 'meat-eaters' (see, for example, Clarke, 1983b, pp. xiii–xiv; accord-ing to Nas, Price and Weber, 1986, p. 109, the terms derive from the Knapp Commission's report on police corruption in New York City). Grass-eaters are public officials who accept bribes or favours offered, but do not actively solicit them; meat-eaters, on the other hand, consciously seek favours and will not perform certain public duties unless they receive what they perceive to be adequate additio-nal recompense, usually from the citizen wanting something pro-vided by the state (goods, permits, etc.). Whereas meat-eaters are almost universally condemned, attitudes towards grass-eaters vary considerably from culture to culture and even within a given coun-try.

In his pioneering comparative study of corruption, Arnold Heidenheimer (1970b, esp. pp. 26–7) goes one further and identifies *three* basic categories of corruption – black, white and grey – depending on the level of commonality of perception of a given act by public officials and citizens. 'Black' acts of corruption are perceived as wrong by both officials and citizens, 'white' acts are more or less accepted by both groups (for example, there is general acceptance that some corruption is useful to the smooth functioning of the economy which, on balance, is in the general interest), whereas 'grey' acts are those about which both officials and citizens disagree. It is interesting to note here that communists themselves often overtly recognize that there is a 'hierarchy' of corruption. This can be inferred from the wide range of punishments that are meted out for different kinds of economic crime, for instance. The Soviets clearly felt that bribery and embezzlement on whatever scale were worse forms of corruption than small-scale use of public resources for private ends (such as using workers to do private jobs in enterprise time – see Lampert, 1984, p. 371); this is in line with the distinction drawn between various forms of corruption in many communist criminal codes and the different penalties applied for engaging in them (for further details, see chapter 7). However, communists are often even more explicit than this in their recognition that some forms of corruption are more tolerable than others. The Chinese, for instance, officially distinguish between – in ascending order of seriousness – 'mistakes at work', 'unsavoury tendencies', 'unhealthy tendencies' and actual crimes (Forster, 1985, pp. 5–6). On occasions, cadres, specialists and citizens argue in the communist press that the state should make explicit distinctions between more and less evil forms of corruption. In 1986, for instance, writers to the Chinese Communist Party journal *Hongqi* suggested that the authorities should take the motive for various forms of economic crime into consideration when dealing with corrupt officials, arguing that there is, for instance, a difference between someone who commits a given crime because of pure greed and someone who commits the *same* crime because of imperfections in the existing regulations and system. Similarly, writers in *Guangming Ribao* argued in 1986 that society should draw a clearer distinction between overt violations of the law and discipline on the one hand and 'necessary social intercourse in the management of an enterprise' on the other, or between measures of expediency and actual resistance to reform policies (details from Yeh, 1987, p. 23). The Chinese leadership has responded to such questioning and comments, and has attempted to incorporate such distinctions into their approach to corruption. This is revealed in the following quotation – made at the end of June 1986 – from Hu Yaobang:

> Contradictions are antagonistic in nature between the Party and those Party members who *seriously* violate the law and Party discipline, abuse their authority to seek selfish gains or advance the small-group interests of their own units or departments at the expense of the interests of the Party and the people. This is a very important line of demarcation. Only by bearing this in mind can we distinguish *antagonistic contradictions* from those arising from *different views and mistakes* in ideological consciousness and work. (Yeh, 1987, p. 24 – emphasis added)

Approaching the problem of how to distinguish various forms and levels of corruption from a different perspective, Peters and Welch (1978, pp. 976–8) have suggested an approach that focuses on both the actors and the actions involved. For them, there are two basic actors (donor, recipient) and two basic actions (favour, pay-off). However, while the actors can usually be identified reasonably straightforwardly, the designation of specific actions in the real world can be problematic (in the sense of subject to differing interpretations). Ultimately, the Peters and Welch approach is primarily concerned with separating a specific act of corruption into its component parts rather than classifying different types of corruption, which is a subsequent process. Thus it is neither a substitute for nor an improvement on the classifications considered above, but rather a way of analysing a given act or series of acts of corruption prior to any rank-ordering of them.

The more one thinks about different taxonomies of corruption – whether grass-eating/meat-eating; or black, white and grey; or whatever – the more obvious it becomes that ultimately, as with many other concepts in political science, conceptions of corruption depend very much on *perception*. Attempting to assess a given group's perception of a specific act is difficult enough in Western liberal democracies; it is considerably more difficult in the case of communist states. We cannot conduct independent surveys of attitudes, for instance – even assuming we could agree on the interpretation of the data generated by such surveys.[4] But all is not lost. While recognizing the very real limitations on our present ability to use a conception of corruption that depends heavily on the participants' perceptions, it should also be appreciated that it is possible to obtain *some* information on perceptions of what is and is not acceptable in a given society. One of the most obvious sources is *laws and formal rules*; the study of these as a method for making inferences about societal perceptions has become very popular in recent years. If we are to use laws and formal rules to make inferences about perceptions and, on the basis of these, to reach a definition of corruption that is appropriate – in the sense of practically applicable – to communist states, then J.C. Scott's definition (1972, p. 4 – which is very close to Nye's, 1967, p. 416 – itself derived from Banfield, 1961, p. 315) might seem to be a suitable one: 'behaviour [which for Scott very sensibly includes *non*-actions] which deviates from the *formal* duties of a public role (elective or appointive) because of private-regarding (personal, close family, private clique) wealth or status gains: or violates rules against the exercise of certain types of private-regarding influence' (emphasis added). This definition is a useful one – but it, too, has its limitations. If we want to argue that the sort of nepotism that has been so rife and visible in Romania, Cuba, Bulgaria, etc., is one form of corruption – and I *do* wish to argue this – then, in the absence of *formal* rules concerning this kind of behaviour, the definition can be seen to be deficient. J.C. Scott (1972, pp. 3–5) argues forcefully that a practically applicable definition of corruption must stress the formal rules of office, since this is more easily analysed than abstract 'perceptions'. But this is surely being unnecessarily self-limiting.

At the opposite end of the spectrum of approaches and definitions is that of Simcha Werner (1983, p. 147) who maintains that corruption, like beauty, 'lies in the eyes of the beholder'. Despite having a certain attraction, such a definition in some respects goes too far. Certainly it could not be satisfactorily operationalized for research into communist states, precisely because of the problems involved in conducting surveys of people's attitudes.

For these reasons, it would seem that the most useful kind of definition would incorporate a mixture of 'hard' and 'soft' components. By 'hard' components I mean unambiguous, concrete signs that given phenomena are considered illegitimate – by the authorities (officialdom) at least. The most common form of such 'hard' components is indeed laws and regulations. However, even the existence of laws is not invariably unambiguous evidence that specific acts are perceived as illegitimate. Quite apart from the fact that officials and citizens may disagree on whether a given act should be treated as illegitimate or not, there is the point that not all laws in any society are rigorously enforced anyway. One reason for this is that a distinction sometimes has to be drawn between illegality and illegitimacy; this point was elaborated in chapter 1, in the example of the parked car. This distinction between illegality and illegitimacy means that allegedly unambiguous, narrow and 'hard' approaches to the study of corruption, based as so many are on *formal* rules, are more problematic than some of their proponents acknowledge.

On the assumption that illegitimacy is not only a broader but also a more useful concept than illegality – while acknowledging that illegality often implies illegitimacy – we can now focus on the 'soft' components of our definition. One of the most significant of these is what Palmier (1983, p. 208) calls 'moral condemnation'. A given act may not clearly be illegal, but if there is evidence that many people see it as improper (illegitimate), then such evidence is to be included in the present analysis of corruption. Two of the most obvious and useful sources of such moral condemnation in the communist world are speeches by politicians (for example, at party congresses) and both articles and letters in the press.

Although nepotism was openly condemned in some communist states for decades (see, for example, *Izvestiya*, 22 February 1966, p. 3) and in others only more recently (for a relatively recent Chinese condemnation that also reveals differences of opinion on nepotism see *BR*, 3 March 1986, pp. 5–6), there were in the 1980s some countries which – no doubt at least partially because of the level and scope of it in them – did not generally discuss this issue publicly. Romania was probably the best example until the end of 1989. Partially for this reason, it makes sense to include in any conception of corruption an explicitly normative component. By this I mean that certain phenomena that are widely seen as corrupt in Western societies but which, because of censorship and other limitations, are unlikely to be discussed openly in at least some communist countries should be included. This is particularly so if the phenomena were also condemned by the two men whose ideas putatively underlie the political activity of communist states, viz Marx and Lenin.[5] At present, nepotism is the principal phenomenon included in this category. Of course, in the absence of any hard data on perceptions in the communist world, it cannot be conclusively proven that nepotism *is* (or *was*) seen as corrupt in all countries. However, almost everyone I questioned on this in private conversations in the communist world, including in Romania, said *either* that they did perceive nepotism as a form of corruption *or*, less forcefully, that it was not clearly *not* corrupt. Moreover, as long as the point is made explicitly in any study of corruption that certain assumptions have been based on a combination of Western values, the ideas of Marx and Lenin, and informal conversations with citizens from communist states – plus, if possible, formal policy in *some* communist states – then it seems to me that it is not only acceptable but actually desirable to include this normative 'soft' component; were it to be excluded, we would be throwing the baby out with the bathwater.

Before reaching a working definition, two additional problems need to be addressed. First, it was mentioned in the introduction that the economies in communist states either have been or else were to have become largely or wholly socialized; despite the rejection of this now in most parts of what was the communist world, the general point still pertains as a salient feature of 'model' communist states, and was applicable until very recently even in those countries that have now abandoned communism. For this reason, Western definitions of corruption that focus on public and private interests can be very misleading when applied to communist states. For instance, several definitions that emphasize the difference between 'private' and 'public' would explicitly exclude as examples of corruption acts in which a senior person bends or clearly breaks rules for personal gain within a privately owned company. Moreover, whereas nepotism in the public sector is seen by most commentators as corrupt, it is acceptable to some if it occurs in the private sector. Thus Robert Williams (1982, pp. 1–2) argues:

> Specifically, it [corruption] involves relationships which seek to use the resources of public offices for improper ends. In all cases, the notion of public office is crucial because the essence of corruption is the conflation of public and private purposes. The owner manager of a private company has a property right which justifies the appointment of family members to the board of directors. The imitation of this practice by public officials produces the charge of nepotism because family ties and personal feelings are not accepted as legitimate qualifications for recruitment to modern bureaucracies.

It should be noted that not all commentators would necessarily accept this line of argument. Susan Rose-Ackermann (1978, p. 1), for instance, refers to 'the corruption of public *and private* officials' (emphasis added); however, Rose-Ackermann's approach is a minority one, and I shall focus on the difficulties raised by the more common one.

One problem that arises with Williams' type of approach is that corruption could, *ceteris paribus*, appear to be more widespread in the communist world than in liberal democracies *simply because of differences in the economic systems and the systems of property rights*. This is a serious problem, particularly if we want to examine the similarities and differences between corruption in the liberal democracies and the communist countries.[6] In order to highlight – if not fully overcome –

this problem, it was decided to use here a definition of corruption that avoids any reference to 'private' and 'public' purposes. Instead, the terms 'individual' and 'collective' are used, although it is acknowledged that this solution is not watertight.

One problem that arises is that the individual may appear to be contrasted with *all* aggregations of individuals, from a small group to society at large. As Lampert (1984, p. 370) has argued of the USSR: 'it is appropriate to interpret some typical abuses as "organisational" rather than "individual"; the purpose of illegal practices is to further the overall aims of the organisation, not the personal interests of individuals within it', while Harris (1986, pp. 20, 24–8) has argued that *group* corruption is very much a feature of corrupt activity in the USSR and the PRC. Lampert himself subsequently acknowledges, however, that the distinction between the organization and the individual can become blurred, both because organizational success will often lead to status and/or material rewards to the individual, and because *individual* offences may be rationalized in terms of 'the good of the organization'. In this, Lampert is absolutely correct. But he also maintains that there are times when it is *still* important to distinguish *organizational* corruption – or 'abuse of office' as he prefers to call it[7] – from individual corruption. It is not clear to me that this distinction is necessary, for two reasons. First, individuals become involved in 'organizational' corruption for *ultimately* personal motivation – for instance because of fear, as well as the material and status rewards Lampert identifies. Second, it is usually *part* of an organization that is corrupt rather than the whole of it; even if *all* the party secretaries were to help *all* the managers of an enterprise to obtain supplies through questionable means (an unlikely scenario), it is improbable that most let alone all members of the organization – workers, secretaries, etc. – would be involved in any meaningful sense, even if they were to benefit by it. In the light of this, I would argue that reference to 'groups of individuals' is less problematic than a reference to 'organizational' corruption – and that the slight change of *terminology* in no way conflicts with the *phenomenon* very rightly identified by Lampert.

It should be noted that the private/public dichotomy can suffer from the same insensitivity to the individual/group/society distinction of which the individual/collective dichotomy can be accused, so that there is no obvious advantage to the private/public distinction from this angle. Moreover, not only does the use of 'individual' and 'collective' for the study of communist societies mean different terms are being employed to reflect somewhat different circumstances (that is, in terms of ownership of the means of production), but the words themselves are reminiscent of the political language of communism – while also being perfectly acceptable in the language of Western political theory – and thus particularly apt.

The distinction just drawn between 'individual' and 'collective' interests is only a necessary, not a sufficient amendment to definitions that are derived primarily from market economies; this would still not distinguish an enterprise manager engaged in economic crime from a local party secretary acting in a similar fashion, for instance. Since directors of major enterprises were usually on the party *nomenklatura* in communist states (there is still too little on this in the literature relative to its importance – but see Harasymiw, 1969; Löwenhardt, 1984; Holmes, 1986a, pp. 134–9; Burns, 1987; Rigby, 1988), a definition based on these lists would also be inappropriate; that is, too broad. Given these problems, and the fact that for both comparative purposes (to compare like with like to the maximum extent possible) and practical purposes (to set parameters for what would otherwise be an enormous data-base), it makes sense to focus as clearly as possible on those posts that would be considered 'public' in non-communist systems. Thus it was decided to analyse corruption among only six groups of people:

1   Party *apparatchiki* and members of party committees;
2   Elected representatives to state representative bodies (such as soviets in the USSR, local people's congresses in the PRC);
3   State bureaucrats (including ministry officials other than those concerned with law enforcement; local council officers);
4   Officers of the law (broadly understood to include judges, regular and security police officers, customs officials, ministry officials concerned with law enforcement);
5   Military officers;
6   Those not covered in 1–5 who are in most societies expected to 'set an example' and are relatively senior (such as diplomats, university rectors, heads of trade union movements, heads of communist youth leagues, etc.).

The last category is, of course, vague, and it has to be acknowledged that on some occasions, decisions on whether to include a given person or group of persons for the purposes of analysis have to be, if not entirely arbitrary, then at least intuitive. Such cases are, fortunately, relatively rare. Both in order to avoid undue repetition and to emphasize the narrow conception of corruption deliberately used in this study, people included in any of the six categories will often be referred to simply as 'officials'.

One other 'boundary' point to consider here concerns members of an official's family or close friends. During the course of the research for this book, several cases were discovered in which members of an official's family would, for instance, use the official's name to curry favour with or threaten others in the individual interests of those family members. Should such cases be treated as corruption or not? After deliberation, it was decided that such cases would only be treated as corruption if the official him/herself were involved. Like-wise, if a *group* was engaged in economic crime, for example, its activities would be considered corrupt only if one or more members of the group were officials.

The second point relates to the distinctions to be drawn between corruption and a number of terms and concepts that are closely related both to it and to each other – viz second economy, unplanned economy, unofficial economy, unregistered economy, the parallel market, the counter-economy, the shadow economy, the fictitious economy, the black economy and the black market. There is some confusion and disagreement in the literature about these terms, mostly revolving around different notions of 'legality' and 'private'. Gregory Grossman (1977, p. 25), for instance, points out that the term 'second economy', when applied to communist states by some scholars, refers to all production and exchange activity that fulfills at least one of two criteria:

1 Being directly for private gain;
2 Being in some significant respect in knowing contravention of existing law.

One problem with such an approach is that the term 'private gain' is ambiguous. It could be argued that anyone who earns wages or a salary (and, in most communist states, production- and/or productivity-related bonuses) is working for 'private gain' at least as much as for the good of society or a large collective. This is especially true as long as reward is intentionally unequal and exchange is conducted primarily in money. The focus should surely be not on the gain itself but on *how* it is acquired; the most important factor is whether the means of production involved in the 'private gain' are totally/largely privately owned or not. However, even this argument is deficient – although 'private' taxi-drivers might own their cabs, or the peasants own everything used on their private plots, what of the teacher who offers 'private' tuition? It would be stretching a point to absurdity to argue that the teacher is earning money through private ownership of the means of production. In sum, the reference to 'private' is problematical.

Another potential problem – at least for those who tend to interchange 'corruption' and 'the second economy' – is that it follows from the definition cited by Grossman that since only one criterion needs to be met, and since this can be point 1 (that is, it does not specifically have to be point 2), then much perfectly legal and legitimate economic activity – the private plot in agriculture, small-scale businesses in the service sector, etc. – is included. Hence, the term as defined here may blur the very real distinction the communist states themselves draw between legitimate and illegitimate economic activities. For this reason, Feldbrugge's (1984, p. 529) definition of the second economy – 'those economic activities which for some reason escape control of the state. The cardinal criterion in this definition is control' – is an improvement on that cited by Grossman. But it, too, is not fully satisfactory, since Feldbrugge *also* explicitly rejects the notion that a distinction should be drawn between legal and illegal activity.

Following on from this, Feldbrugge argues against those who wish to talk of the 'shadow economy' in terms of legality and illegality. This seems to me to be unnecessary; if we accept the notion that the second economy is that part of the economy over which the state has minimal control (in terms of pricing, awareness of its existence, incorporation into plans, etc.), then we can further *sub-divide* this into legitimate and illegitimate second economy activity. Since the terms 'shadow' and 'black' literally have sinister overtones, it would seem sensible to use the terms 'shadow economy' and 'black economy' only for the illegitimate parts of the 'second economy', rather than see them as essentially synonymous with it as Feldbrugge does.[8] Although the terms 'shadow' and 'black' can be and often are used interchangeably, a fine distinction can be drawn between them; whereas 'black' economic activity is clearly illegal and illegitimate, 'shadow' activity is less unambiguously illegitimate and sometimes also less unambiguously illegal. The *black market* can be seen largely as a sub-division of the black economy, referring – strictly speaking – only to illegal *trade* in goods, currency, services, etc. (that is, it does not refer to production itself, which *can* be included under the terms 'shadow' or 'black' economy). I use the term 'largely' since the black market can also trade in goods manufactured legally in the first economy; but the black market is not in any sense part of – as distinct from closely linked to – the first economy in such cases, since it is beyond the control of the state authorities and thus wholly part of the second economy.

With the above distinctions in mind, we can define the *first* economy, in crude terms, as that part of the total economy:

i) That is more or less planned and controlled by a state agency outside and above the individual or small group of individuals (such as a family); *and*
ii) In which all or most of the means of production are owned either by the state and/or a large collective (such as a collective farm, an industrial enterprise).

In contrast, the *second* economy is that part of the total economy:

a) That is not to any meaningful extent planned or controlled by an agency outside and above the individual or small group of individuals; *and/or*
b) In which the means of production are owned wholly or largely by an individual or a small group of individuals.

It should be noted that whereas in the definition of the first economy, *both* criteria are necessary, this is not true of the definition of the second economy. This allows for uncontrolled activity by individuals who do *not* own the means of production (other than their own labour) – whether their activity be legal or illegal. Of course, economic activity in the second economy can be legal or illegal even when *both* criteria are met.

With the above points in mind, we can now consider the terms listed earlier that have not yet been discussed. The 'unplanned' economy is synonymous with criterion 'a' and might – but does not have to – correlate with criterion 'b'; since the definition of the second economy adopted here *may* relate only to criterion 'b', it follows that the 'unplanned' and the 'second' economy are close but not synonymous. The term 'unofficial economy', in contrast, can be interchanged with the term 'second economy', since it can apply either to what is not under official control or what is not under state or collective ownership. The 'unregistered economy' is, strictly speaking, narrower than everything that can be included under the 'second economy', since much legal, private economic activity would in a formal sense be registered. The 'parallel market' should really be applied only to trading activity over which the state has limited control; it makes sense to apply this only to legal, uncontrolled activity – to distinguish it from the black market. The 'counter-economy' connotes something in opposition to the state-run economy, and therefore should only be applied to those economic activities not sanctioned by the state; in this sense, it is narrower than the 'second economy' and, despite having a different *image* from the terms 'shadow economy' and 'black economy', is *conceptually* indistinguishable. Finally, the term 'fictitious economy', which was introduced into Soviet discussions by V. Yanishevskaya, has been defined as 'the production, marketing and delivery of poor-quality goods which nobody wants and which may even be a health hazard' (*NT*, No. 42, October 1989, p. 33). According to Yanishevskaya (ibid., p. 32), the only illegal practice involved in this is the upward distortion of output statistics. Thus, while the 'fictitious economy' relates to some of the phenomena analysed above, it does so only marginally, being more a reflection of problems that seem to be inherent in centrally planned economies.

In parenthesis, it can be remarked that the term 'third economy' sometimes appears in Western literature on communist states. It most commonly refers to the goods and services to which middle-ranking and senior officials have nearly or totally exclusive access (that is, which are not normally and legitimately available to 'ordinary citizens'), such as foreign consumer goods, special shops, exclusive hospitals, etc.[9]

Having separated these various terms from one another, let us now consider how the term 'corruption' relates to them. By now it should be clear that corruption is *narrower* than most of the terms defined above, though it may form *part* of some of them. Most corruption is illegal and illegitimate, so that there is overlap with definitions that focus on these aspects of economic activity. But since *some* corruption is seen as 'white' and is not only not clearly illegal but possibly not even clearly illegitimate (merely more or less improper), the rigid boundaries between legal and illegal (or legitimate and illegitimate) economic activity do not fully pertain. If we add to this the focus on officials, and the fact that not all corruption is of a clearly economic nature, it follows that corruption is close to and/or overlaps with and/or is part of all the above terms, but is fully synonymous with none of them.

Another term that is sometimes interchanged with corruption is 'economic crime'. This is the principal 'key term' a researcher will look for in scanning the Chinese press for examples of corruption, for instance, since it overlaps to a large extent with corruption and is much more frequently used in the Chinese media than the normal Chinese terms for corruption (*tanwu, fubai*); according to Forster (1985, p. 5), this is largely because the words for corruption are considered to be more vague, more moralistic and less objective than the term 'economic crime', so that the currently preferred term can be seen to be in line with the present policy of increasing legal codification and making the system appear more institutionalized and less subjective than it was in the Mao era. Given that many cases of improper economic activity do not involve officials, and that some cases of corruption are not clearly economic in nature, it becomes obvious why the terms corruption and 'economic crime' cannot invariably be used interchangeably. A less obvious reason why they often cannot be interchanged relates to the range of definitions given by communists to the term 'economic crime'. Many communists will see *lack of economic discipline* as economic crime, for instance. An example from Czechoslovakia exemplifies this. In March 1987, five men were handed down relatively harsh sentences (at least one of 18 months' imprisonment) in Ostrava for allowing – through their negligence – the escape of almost 80 tonnes of heating oil into three local rivers in December 1986. The Prague radio announcer who reported this case both gave the pecuniary value (at least one million crowns) of the damage caused and referred to the serious environmental implications. There was no suggestion that the negligence was in any sense related to the personal or individual interests of the five men; rather, they had failed to observe all the precautions specified in the regulations (details of this case from *SWB*/EE/8528/B/3, 28 March 1987). Despite the fact that the *result* of these people's negligence was a major expense to the state and society, few in the West would see it as economic crime; in the absence of some private-regarding interest as a motive for negligence, such activity should certainly not be seen as corruption. In conclusion, some cases of corruption can also be called economic crimes, just as some cases of economic crime are cases of corruption – but the two terms are not fully interchangeable.

One other term that occurs in the literature is 'conspiracy'. This implies working *with* others; while many examples of corruption involve conspiracy, some only involve one person working alone. Hence not all acts of corruption involve conspiracy – while conspiracy can also occur among non-officials, and thus be beyond the parameters of corruption specified in this study.

In view of the above arguments, the definition of corruption to be used in this study is as follows:

> Actions or non-actions – by an individual or small group of individuals occupying (an) official (party and/or state and/or legal and/or military and/or socially responsible) elective or appointed position(s) – that are perceived, by at least some criteria, to be improper and illegitimate in the particular sense of being seen as simultaneously against the collective (societal) interest and in the official's (officials') individual (self-regarding) interests.

Although acts will be identified as corrupt or not on the basis of the above definition, it is acknowledged that there are varying degrees of impropriety of action, and specific acts of corruption will be judged on a scale of acceptability rather than in simple, bi-polar terms.

A Taxonomy of Forms of Corruption

It is evident from the above discussion that there is a wide range of corrupt acts. A number of authors have produced their own taxonomies, and the citing of just three of these will reveal how diverse and complex they can be.

In one of his studies of 'abuse of office' in the USSR, Lampert (1985, pp. 269–70) identifies six basic types. His taxonomy is based on the distinctions made in Soviet criminal law, within the categories 'crimes against socialist property', 'economic crimes' and 'official crimes'. The six types are embezzlement of socialist property (for example, officials selling in their own interest goods that have been allocated to state and cooperative enterprises); false reporting (such as *pripiski* – designed to *overstate* the performance of an organization in order to gain illicit rewards for its members; or else *understating* the quantity of materials or output of goods so as to cover up for theft or spoilage); forging of documents (similar to the previous type, but covering a different range of activities and types of organization); the acceptance or offering of bribes; deception of customers (for example, overcharging for goods or cheating on the weighing of goods); the use of state or cooperative property as a base for illegal forms of production.

Using the indigenous media for determining the sorts of act that were perceived as corrupt in the PRC in the period 1977–80, Alan Liu (1983, pp. 603–6) came up with no less than sixteen discrete types of corruption (housing irregularity; illegitimate feasting; embezzlement; bribe or extortion; appropriation of public goods; hiring irregularity; sexual abuse of women; illegal imprisonment and torture; obstruction of justice; reprisal against informers; cheating on school examinations; false models; feudal rites; irregularity in residence permits; illegal trade of public goods; irregularity in party membership). In any comparative analysis, some of these categories could be collapsed (for example, housing irregularity could be subsumed under forging of documents, accepting bribes, etc., according to the individual case). Nevertheless, it is interesting to see just how many different types of corruption Liu could identify from the

Chinese press. Indeed, contemporary Mandarin has a very extensive and colourful range of terms for the various kinds of corruption, including *dachi dahe* (excessive eating and drinking at public expense), *qishang manxia* (deceiving superiors and hoodwinking subordinates) and *qingke songli* (giving dinners and sending gifts in order to curry favour).

Using yet another approach, Schöpflin (1984, pp. 394–9) has identified three major 'patterns of corruption'; what he is ultimately identifying here are the actual *outcomes* of corruption. The first, 'patron–client networks', sub-divides into 'traditional extended family networks' (particularly common in the Balkans, especially Montenegro, Kosovo, Albania and Romania); 'shared experience' networks (for example, partisans in Yugoslavia); and the most common form, the 'mutual interest network', in which 'members are bound to each other by their ability to control some, but not all of the power accorded them by their positions in the system, by their readiness to extend their power as a "unit of account" and the readiness to achieve their aims by trading favours with other members of the bureaucracy similarly inclined'. In this third form of patron–client network, the unit of account is power rather than financial advantage. Schöpflin's second manifestation of corruption is 'bureaucratism', by which, atypically, he means the *irregular functioning* of the bureaucracy. He links this to the imperfections – and imperfectability – of a centrally planned economy, which leads to distortions, misreporting of performance, etc. Since individuals and discrete groups within the system can never survey the whole of the system – and hence appreciate the 'general interest' – they will often pursue individual and/or small group interests which appear to conflict, and are perceived by outsiders as conflicting, with the collective (that is, societal) interest. The third and final ramification of corruption for Schöpflin is the 'secondary' (that is, second) economy.

On the basis of these and others' taxonomies and our own research, a taxonomy of 20 different forms of corruption can be produced. It should be noted when considering the following list *that two or more forms of corruption may well be involved in a single act* (for example, an official may forge a document in return for a bribe), so that not all forms can be seen as fully discrete. Moreover, the taxonomy should not be taken as rank-ordered. In the early stages of research, it looked as if the treatment of various forms of corruption suggested in criminal legislation would yield a rank-ordered listing of misdemeanours (cf. the point made earlier that embezzlement and bribery are usually seen as being more serious than illegal use of socialized property). This subsequently proved not to be possible, for three main reasons. First, some forms identified are not officially recognized in many countries, and are included on the list because they are considered forms of corruption under our 'third approach' (that is, Western normative and/or Marxist and Leninist normative, with endorsement by some citizens in communist countries and *possibly* official condemnation in some communist states). Second, the rank-ordering does not stay constant over time and/or across countries. Finally, an empirical examination of the punishments meted out for various forms of corruption reveals that even the rank-orderings based on criminal codes could be misleading, in that, for example, cases of embezzlement and bribery do not invariably incur stiffer penalties than cases of illegal use of socialist property; although the former *generally* lead to harsher sentences, individual cases often relate to the pecuniary value involved and/or the type of official engaged in the activity, and the number of exceptions to the general rule is sufficient for the rank-ordering to be considered potentially misleading. Although there is no precise rank-ordering in the following taxonomy, there is *some* structure to it. Where a number of forms of corruption are closely related to each other, they have been bunched together – partially to highlight groupings of similar forms, and partially so that the fine distinctions between some outwardly very similar forms become more obvious through close comparison.

At one stage, an attempt was made to classify different forms of corruption according to whether they were necessarily interactive (that is, they had to involve donor and recipient, though only one of these has to be an official) or not necessarily interactive (that is, where an individual or group of individuals could engage in surreptitious activities that do not necessarily involve others at all); this produced an overly complex and somewhat repetitious taxonomy, especially since the interactive forms were further sub-divided into 'donor's perspective' and 'recipient's perspective'. On the latter point, nepotism was sub-divided into 'patron (or donor's) perspective' and 'client (or recipient)'s perspective', for example; since one of the main purposes of the taxonomy was to provide a framework for looking at actual examples of corruption in the next chapter, and since it makes little sense to divide real-world cases of – in this case – nepotism into 'donor's perspective' and 'recipient's perspective', this attempt was abandoned. Instead, at various appropriate points, reference is made to 'interactive' or 'non-interactive' forms, and to donor or recipient perspectives in the case of interactive forms.

Deliberate Dereliction of Duties, Inaction and Obstruction

1 Turning a blind eye An official is aware that something improper and falling under his/her jurisdiction is occurring, but does nothing or too little about it because of individual interest.

2 Refusal to investigate/charge, and/or obstructing investigation An official responsible for exercising a supervisory role in some form or another has reason to believe that something improper is occurring, but, for reasons of personal interest, refuses to mount an investigation despite external pressure to do so. Such deliberate non-action ranges from a refusal to investigate suspected cheating in the examination hall to a refusal to investigate charges of serious crimes among subordinates. In some cases, investigations have been carried out, but no charges laid – for reasons that are not obvious to all observers. Closely related to these activities is the deliberate obstruction of an investigation by third parties – again for reasons of individual interest.

3 Avoidance of specified procedures Since this book is about corruption, we exclude cases where an official does not 'go by the book' simply because everyone knows that the formally stipulated method is unnecessarily detailed and actually inefficient. Rather, the assumption is that there are more sinister reasons for non-compliance with the regulations, mainly relating to the personal vested interests of the official.

Improper Filling of Office – Patronage

In patron–client relations, someone already in public office (the patron) promotes another (the client) less because of the client's merit and formal suitability – in terms of qualifications and/or experience – than because of some interest common to both parties and, very often, assumed future advantage at least by the patron.

All cases of patronage are interactive, although the focus is primarily on the donor rather than the recipient; the latter may not be an official anyway (certainly prior to promotion), and in most cases of patronage, it is the patron who is seen as the prime abuser of office. Three major forms of patronage can be discerned:

4 Nepotism In this context, nepotism is the granting of public office on the basis of family ties. Originally, the term referred to special favours shown to a pope's nephew, but in its current usage it refers to 'unfair preferment of nephews *or relatives* to other qualified persons' (*Compact Edition of the Oxford English Dictionary* – emphasis added).

As already indicated, this is a good example of a point where different cultures have very different attitudes towards some forms of corruption, since many Western observers agree that nepotism does not have the negative connotation for many East Asians, for example, that it does for many Westerners. For instance, Dennis Bloodworth has written: 'no one could understand politics in Laos if they don't understand the importance and significance of family connections' (*Asia Magazine*, 28 June 1987, p. 54), and argues that many citizens actually expect officials to help members of their own family through promotion. But given that the ruling communist party itself formally forbids this – in addition to our 'third, normative' approach to corruption – nepotism is nevertheless treated as a form of corruption even in these countries (for a recent Soviet example of formal condemnation of nepotism and 'selecting personnel on the basis of kinship' see *Pravda*, 24 October 1986, p. 3; for an official Mozambican condemnation see *IB*, Vol. 27, No. 2, 1989, p. 26).

5 Shared experiences (cronyism)   Here, the patron and client have usually worked together in the past and are on good terms, and the patron promotes or has promoted the client on the basis of these past experiences and warm relationship.

6 Shared interests   In this case, the patron does not have common experiences with someone s/he wishes to promote, but rather a common interest (for example, they both come from the same republic and/or are of the same ethnic group; they both favour a large increase in defence expenditure, in contrast to what others want; they are of the same gender, etc.).

Deliberate Deception

Many of the acts included in this section are forms of *fraud*, which is usually defined in terms of deliberate deception. However, the term 'fraud' normally refers explicitly to *criminal* deception; since some of the manifestations of deception here are considered improper but not necessarily criminal, it was decided to use a broader term (that is, 'deliberate deception') rather than 'fraud'. Where specific cases are treated as crimes, the term 'fraud' can be applied.

7 False reporting – overstatement   An official dishonestly, and for reasons ultimately connected with individual interest, claims that something – most frequently output – has been higher than is actually the case. An alternative common term for this is 'report-padding'. It should be noted that false reporting for pecuniary gain is sometimes described by communist authorities as 'embezzlement'; this is thus an example of the fuzziness that can exist between the 'discrete' categories identified in this study.

8 False reporting – understatement An official dishonestly, and for reasons ultimately connected with individual interest, claims that something – most frequently output – has been lower than is actually the case.

Whereas overstatements are commonly intended to cover up inefficiences and/or to lead to higher bonuses, understatements may be made so that a proportion of output – that which is not reported – can be 'creamed off' and sold on the black market. Alternatively, understatements may be made because the officials filing the reports believe it will be more difficult in the following plan-period to reach the targets actually achieved in the current period, and do not wish to be accused of underfulfilment in the future.

Both under- and overstatements may relate to tax evasion, whether corporate or personal – although it should be borne in mind that personal income tax has played a far less significant role in the communist world than in liberal democracies (or, it can be noted, in the post-communist world).

9 Deception of supplicants Whereas types 7 and 8 are examples of officials trying to deceive the state and/or superiors, there is a related phenomenon in which officials are principally deceiving people who are in some sense 'subordinates' – though not necessarily in any work hierarchy – and who have requested something of the officials. A local elected representative might promise a constituent a new flat within three months (perhaps in return for a bribe), knowing full well that it will be at least a year before such a flat becomes available.

10 Forging of documents An official deliberately falsifies information for personal gain and/or to help someone else, in such a way that it is not only dishonest but against the collective interest.

Other Interactive, Gain-Based Forms of Corruption

11 Accepting bribes The *Shorter Oxford English Dictionary* defines a bribe as: 'a reward given to pervert the judgement or corrupt the conduct'. If an official accepts a bribe, s/he is clearly a recipient. The mere *acceptance* of a bribe (as distinct from a *demand* for one) is a form of 'grass–eating' corruption. The main forms of bribe identified in the research were:

1   Material benefit – money, goods, services; and
2   Status (often *implicitly* suggesting material) benefit – notably promotion to a higher post.

In addition, however, we should note:

3   Sexual favours. In the research, we discovered no clear cases of this. Liu (1983, *passim*) refers in a generalized way to cases of this in the PRC, but he may well be referring to the few cases of *rape* that we encountered. In that these are demanded, rather than accepted; might well not be related to any exchange; and may or may not relate to the rapist's public office, I have opted not to include such cases here. It should be noted that the acceptance by an official of sexual favours was in recent years no longer seen as bribe-taking in the USSR, though it once was (Grossman, 1977, p. 27 – citing Chalidze, 1977, p. 238); it is still seen as bribe-taking in the PRC, however.

One final point is that, in practice, there can sometimes arise a problem in distinguishing a 'bribe' from a (reasonably legitimate) 'gift'. To some extent, this is another example of cultural differences of interpretation. But one Soviet writer (M. Smirnova in *Sovetskaya Kultura*, 8 April 1975 – in *CDSP*, Vol. 27, No. 21, pp. 10 and 24) has argued convincingly that one way of distinguishing these is to see how openly the money/item is given and/or accepted. Thus, if there are signs that the transaction is in any way clandestine, then the donor and/or recipient can be argued to be aware of the possible (or even clear-cut) impropriety of the act. While there will be some instances in which an official will accept a gift openly and without any sense of impropriety, only to be accused later of corruption, Smirnova's distinction is useful in most situations of this type (the reader interested in following a Soviet debate on the problem of distinguishing 'gifts' from 'bribes' will find one in the pages of *Literaturnaya Gazeta* during 1976 and 1977 – see, for example, the issue of 5 January 1977, p. 13).

12 Offering bribes   Here, an official offers a bribe to some individual or group in anticipation of some reciprocated personal or group gain. The focus is now on the donor, and this is, of course, an interactive form of impropriety. Bribes will be primarily in the form of:

1   Material benefit – money, goods, services; or
2   Status (often *implicitly* suggesting material) benefit – notably promotion to a higher post.

Although an official could, in theory, offer sexual favours to someone else, we have not found any concrete references to such a form of corruption.

13 Extortion   According to *The Oxford English Dictionary*, extortion is:

> the art or practice of extorting [defined as '*either* to wrest or wring from a person, extract by torture *or* to obtain from a reluctant person by violence, torture, intimidation, or abuse of legal or official authority, or – in a weaker sense – by importunity, overwhelming arguments, or any powerful influence'] or wresting anything, especially money, from a person by force or by undue exercise of authority or power.

While this form of activity has much in common with the accepting of bribes, it is clearly a 'meat-eating' form of corruption, in which the official's approach towards someone wanting something of him/her is far more aggressive than in the case of the official who merely *accepts* a bribe; often, we are dealing here with the *soliciting* of bribes.

Controversially perhaps, I have also included in this section examples of *rape* in which a male official has used the powers of his office to force sexual favours from a female supplicant.

14 Blackmail   This is closely related to extortion, but here explicitly involves a threat by an official to reveal some misdemeanour, committed by the individual being blackmailed, to the authorities, spouse, etc., unless that individual agrees to pay off the blackmailer. Although this form of corruption appears to have occurred infrequently in the communist world, it is not unknown.

Possibly Non-Interactive, Gain-Based Forms of Corruption

In the following forms of corruption, an official may well operate individually, although s/he may also work in a group and may even be working interactively with other officials (for example, one official may engage in smuggling, and bribes other officials to turn a blind eye).

15 Not earning one's salary   In this situation, officials are paid to perform certain duties, but either do not perform them at all or else do so very inadequately – in all cases because of personal interest.

The reason is often that they are 'saving themselves' for other work. The term 'salary' is used rather than wages because the study is concerned with officials rather than ordinary workers. The clumsy phrase 'not earning one's salary' is consciously used in preference to the more common term 'unearned' income. One reason is that not all 'unearned' income is acquired illegally or illegitimately; as one *Izvestiya* correspondent noted in 1986 (2 June, p. 3), lottery winnings are not earned income but they are perfectly legal; in this study, we are concerned only with illegally or improperly acquired unearned income. Second, the term 'improperly acquired unearned income' is no more elegant than the term used here. Moreover, it can be applied to various forms of improper pecuniary gain, and is not sufficiently distinct from several other forms of corruption considered in this study.

16 Improper use of socialized property   In this situation – which is in most cases seen as one of the milder forms of corruption – officials take advantage of their position for reasons that may or may not be related to *direct* personal gain. For instance, a party secretary may use the weight of office to ensure that his/her own office in an enterprise is larger than even the works canteen (and be criticized by others as selfish in doing so) or may borrow a works' car at the weekend, contrary to regulations; both of these cases are clearly for the personal benefit of the official. On the other hand, officials may be accused of wasting public money on a sumptuous banquet for a visiting trade delegation. In this case, the officials can be accused of wasting public money, but may not have done so for primarily selfish reasons – *possible* long-term benefits, in terms of promotion if a deal materializes, being too indirect to include in the same category as the case of the car that disappears at weekends. Because the *motives* are very different in the two cases – which can have repercussions for the punishment meted out, for instance – it makes sense to distinguish them in some way as categories:

1   Improper use of socialized property primarily for direct and immediate personal benefit;
2   Improper use of socialized property primarily for motives other than direct and immediate personal benefit but for reasons that may relate to long-term individual advantage.

For the purposes of the present study – notably for the empirical analysis in chapter 4 – only cases that clearly or almost certainly fit the first category are treated as examples of this form of corruption; this somewhat narrow approach has been adopted because the second category is not fully compatible with the definition of corruption used here.

A final note in this sub-section is that the word 'improper' has been used, rather than 'illegal' or 'illegitimate'. Illegal would be over-restrictive in this context – many examples fall into the 'grey' area of the law and regulations (in many cases simply not being mentioned at all in proscriptive documents). 'Illegitimate' is also too precise; many citizens, for instance, would see nothing wrong in the party secretary borrowing the works' car for a weekend (for evidence of Soviet confusion over the distinction between 'temporary use' and 'theft', see *Izvestiya*, 19 August 1966, p. 3, translated in *CDSP*, Vol. 18, No. 33, 7 September 1966, p. 21). 'Improper' is a vaguer term – and is more suitable precisely for that reason.

17 *Embezzlement*   The act of embezzlement can mean:

1   Fraudulent appropriation of property entrusted to one; or
2   To carry off secretly for one's own use; or
3   To mutilate, tamper with a document; or
4   Diverting to one's own use in violation of trust or official duty. (*Shorter Oxford English Dictionary*).

Clearly, definitions 1, 2 and 4 are closely related to the previous category, especially definition 1 in category 16; however, definition 1 there refers either to a temporary phenomenon (the car is returned by Monday morning) or to something which the official is not seriously attempting to hide. Embezzlement, in contrast, refers to a permanent (or intended as permanent) appropriation of social property and a consciously deceptive mode of operating.

Definition 3 is of a very different nature, and the research for this book revealed that such activities were not normally defined in the communist world as embezzlement; since this type of activity is included in the section above on deliberate deception, this particular meaning of 'embezzlement' is not used in this study.

18 *Speculation*   Speculation is the action or practice of buying or selling goods, land, stocks and shares, etc. in order to profit by the rise or fall in the 'market value' (*Compact Edition of the Oxford English Dictionary*). The emphasis in speculation is on risk-taking and unusual profit-making; in almost all communist countries, private speculation is – or was until very recently – forbidden. But the fact that it is forbidden does not, of course, mean it does not occur. One common version is for officials to sell goods and/or foreign currency they have acquired by various means – through the third economy,

on overseas trips, through confiscation, etc. – on the black market.
19 Smuggling   Smuggling is defined as 'the illegal and clandestine conveyance of goods (broadly understood) into or out of a country in order to avoid payment of dues' (adapted from the *Shorter Oxford English Dictionary*). In practice, this is often linked with speculation, in that officials will in some way be involved in the smuggling in of foreign goods in order to profit by their sale on the black market. But the two acts are conceptually distinct and are sometimes so in practice (for example, an official might smuggle in goods for his/her personal use); it thus makes sense to separate them here.
20 Treason   Not all cases of treason – defined as a serious violation by a citizen of his/her allegiance to the state – are corrupt acts. For the purposes of this study, we are only concerned with acts of serious disloyalty to one's state, often by illegal communication of classified information to an external authority or power, by an official (as distinct from an ordinary citizen) for reasons of personal gain. Such cases are very rare, but do occur.

Conclusions

It should by now be clear that there are a number of ways of defining corruption, and that the term itself overlaps with a number of others. While being constantly aware of the difficulties of definition and that alternative terms – 'abuse of office', etc. – have their attractions, the traditional term 'corruption' seems to me to be no less satisfactory than any alternative, and better than most. Peter Harris (1986), for instance, prefers to use the term 'graft'; but since 'graft' refers fairly explicitly to pecuniary gain (the *Shorter Oxford English Dictionary* defines it as 'a means of making illicit profit; dishonest gains or illicit profits, especially in connexion with political or municipal business'), it is too narrow a concept to cover the range of activities included here. The term 'corruption' cannot be defined satisfactorily, but I have sought in the definition provided here to minimize problem-areas and to maximize its applicability to all societies.

Similarly, it is not possible to provide a taxonomy that is suitable for all. Part of the problem is that it is sometimes difficult to disentangle the general from the specific, to agree on whether a particular example of corruption one encounters is a form in its own right or a sub-division of a broader category. Again, there cannot be total agreement on this – what one observer perceives as a generic type is a particular example to another. This all said, the taxonomy provided here does, I would argue, allow for all forms of corruption as defined in this study, even if parts of it are either more or less aggregated than others would have preferred.

In a very sensitive and sensible approach to the definition of corruption, R. Williams (1987, p. 19) has summarized neatly much of what needs to be said in concluding this discussion:

> it is necessary, if slightly invidious, to suggest that the importance of defining the term has perhaps been either misunderstood or exaggerated. One possible source of difficulty lies in the apparent presumption that a specific and irrevocable choice needs to be made about which meaning of corruption to employ. Yet no all-purpose definition is available. How corruption is defined is partly a function of the kinds of questions analysts pose and what it is they wish to understand. It is, of course, important to be clear about what we mean, but it is not compulsory, and may not be desirable, to adhere rigidly to only one meaning. What is more important is that we are clear about which meaning is being used at any particular point in our analysis.

Expressing this slightly differently, since corruption itself is a somewhat imprecise phenomenon – it has a hard core about which virtually everyone can agree, but soft edges that are disputed – the definition employed should also have a hard core but some greyness at the edges; obviously, the definition opted for has direct implications for the taxonomy. We cannot be over-rigid in defining corruption, yet we must have sufficient precision to be able to proceed with an analysis of what is clearly an important phenomenon. This chapter at least provides a framework for analysing the wide range of corrupt acts that has existed in the communist world, and to which we now turn.

NOTES

1   It should be noted that Palmier's own preferred definition (p. 208) is 'the acquisition of forbidden benefits by officials or employees, so bringing into question their loyalty to their employers'. This is a broad approach, and has certain merits for a comparative analysis. However, it could be applied to many ordinary blue-collar workers who steal on the job – whether in a capitalist or a socialist enterprise. It is thus *too* broad by most criteria, and certainly – as shall become obvious – for the present study.

2   The definition cited by Palmier is, in abbreviated form, close to that provided by Soviet specialist M.A. Krutogolov (1973, p. 216): 'a crime involving the direct use by an official [*dolzhnostnym litsom*] of the rights accorded him/her by virtue of his/her office for the purpose of personal enrichment'.

3   It can be noted that, in line with his point cited earlier, Carl Friedrich went even further and argued that if questionable actions – whatever they may be – result in public benefit, then they should be described only as *devious*, not corrupt.

4   As intimated in chapter 1, survey data on communist states do exist. However, these are overwhelmingly either data generated from surveys by communists themselves, or else based on Western interviews of émigrés. For a good, reasonably up-to-date example of the latter type of survey, based on Soviet émigrés, see Millar, 1987; unfortunately, this does not focus on corruption.

5   Although Marx did not write extensively on corruption, he was certainly critical of it – see, for example, Marx and Engels, 1980a, pp. 189–93, and 1980b, pp. 526–31. For Lenin's condemnations see, for example, Lenin, 1964, pp. 47, 73 and 106.

6   Some commentators are at least partially aware of this problem and wish to compare like with like – see Lampert, 1984, p. 369.

7   Lampert is not in fact considering exactly the same area of activity as I am, since he rejects the use of the term 'corruption', preferring 'abuse of office'. He defines this as 'an umbrella term to refer to a number of managerial and official practices that are prohibited in Soviet criminal law' (1984, p. 366). This reveals that he is analysing a broader range of individuals than I am (n.b. his reference to 'managerial'), but a narrower range of misdemeanours (only actions prohibited in 'criminal law').

8   It is accepted here that there *is* some ambiguity in the use of the term 'shadow economy'. This ambiguity is reflected in a recent Soviet definition: 'entrepreneurial activity beyond the control of government statistical, planning and fiscal agencies, practised clandestinely' (*NT*, No. 42, October 1989, p. 32). However, although the author (N. Andreyev) avoids any reference to illegality or illegitimacy in this definition, the fact that the activity is 'practised clandestinely' strongly suggests that those engaging in it are aware that it either is or else might be illegal and/or perceived by others as illegitimate. In this sense, even this 'ambiguous' definition does not go far enough to support Feldbrugge's argument. It can be noted that Andreyev refers in his article to other Soviet analysts who do see the shadow economy as a *clearly* illegal phenomenon (ibid., pp. 32–4).

9   Although the way the term 'third economy' is used in this study is common in the Western world, it is not a universally accepted definition. Many Hungarians, for example, have seen the 'second economy' as the legal private economy and the 'third economy' as the illegal economy – see *SWB/EE/7963/B/2* 29 May 1985.

3

Examples of Corruption

The aim of this chapter is to provide the reader with some idea of the range and nature of corruption in the communist world. Examples have been classified in terms of the taxonomy provided in the last chapter. It should be noted, however, that reports on corruption often reveal that one individual or group of individuals has engaged in more than one form of the impropriety; in such cases, examples have been classified by what appears to be the main form of corruption or, where this is unclear, arbitrarily in one of the appropriate 'slots'. Although the USSR and the PRC are the only two countries analysed reasonably systematically in this study, data for this and other chapter(s) have been gathered for all 23 countries identified in chapter 1 as being or having been 'communist'. Given the absence of systematic research for most countries, no serious attempt is made here to suggest that a particular type of corruption is peculiar to a given country – although some comments on this are made as appropriate. Just as there is no rationale for the choice of examples – other than that there are far more from the USSR and the PRC than from anywhere else, and that at least one example is taken from most countries – so there is no clear rationale to the choice of functional groups cited other than a desire to provide examples of corruption by all six groups of 'officials' identified in chapter 2. I have also sought to include examples from different levels of officialdom.

1 Turning a Blind Eye

Cuba

One of the examples of corruption cited by Fidel Castro in an April 1982 speech on corruption related to 'Operation Crocodile', whereby thugs used to intimidate people queueing for goods in short supply. They were thereby able to queue-jump – often several times over in the same queue – and thus to obtain far more of the goods than would have been the case had they waited their turn like everyone else. Apparently, various officials received complaints about this, but turned a blind eye to it in return for bribes from the thugs (Castro, 1983, p. 348).

Laos

Although most of it is circumstantial, there is considerable evidence that Laotian officials – and possibly even the government itself – have for many years turned a blind eye to much of the smuggling of drugs (mostly opium) from Laos to Thailand (though see p. 106 below). An investigation by John McBeth for the *Far Eastern Economic Review* (5 September 1980, pp. 36–42) is persuasive that the government might well be consciously tolerating the trafficking, which helps to bring additional hard currency – illegally – into the system (for similar charges of Albanian state involvement in smuggling see Zanga, 1988b).

The DPRK

Cases of corruption are very rarely publicized in North Korea. However, an example of North Korean security officials turning a blind eye – in return for a bribe – was published in South Korea early in 1987. In February of that year, 11 North Koreans arrived in Seoul; they had defected from the DPRK in January, and had reached the ROK via Japan and Taiwan. The leader of the group – a doctor by the name of Kim Man Chol – told journalists of how he had bribed guards at a North Korean port with wine and cigarettes so that they would turn a blind eye while his family and friends boarded a boat to flee the country. Interestingly, Kim also revealed that he had bribed an (unspecified) city official with medicine so that he could see the political dossier on his (Kim's) family (all details from *EIU Country Report – China, North Korea*, No. 1, 1987, p. 33).

2 Refusal to Investigate/Charge, and/or Obstructing Investigation

The PRC

A report that was broadcast by a Southern Chinese radio station in 1985 (Guangdong Provincial Service – in *SWB*/FE/8053/BII/13) provides a good example of how officials can obstruct an investigation because of their own vested interests. Huang Shezhen (secretary of the Zongtang District Committee of the CCP) and Xie Zicai (governor of the same district) attempted to block an investigation by public security personnel into a pornographic tapes operation. The police confiscated equipment at a showing of pornographic films, following which Huang and Xie claimed that this was not an issue for the police to handle. Huang convened a meeting of the district committee and got it to endorse a resolution cancelling bonuses for local police officers on the grounds that the latters' reports were at variance with the facts. It was subsequently revealed that Huang and Xie were themselves ring-leaders of the pornography operation.

There are a number of reasons *why* legal agencies and/or individual officials responsible for doing so do not in fact carry out their investigations, but one interesting insight provided by two articles that appeared in the Soviet press in mid-1987 (*Pravda*, 15 June, p. 3, and 24 August, p. 4) is that local party and state officials and elected representatives can pressure officers of the law into dropping investigations:

> The use by individual party committees of various forms of pressure on court and prosecutor's office officials – in response to their principled position in their fight against illegal actions committed by Volyn Province party leaders – is by no means an isolated phenomenon . . . Trials in recent years of plunderers and bribe-takers holding high office show that in almost every case the prosecutor's office had long had sufficient grounds for bringing criminal charges but that, under heavy pressure from local authorities, it had played a sort of 'good samaritan' role, refusing, on formal pretexts, to institute criminal proceedings in response to justified complaints from citizens. (*Pravda*, 24 August 1987, p. 4)

3 Avoidance of Specified Procedures

The USSR

In October 1985, it was revealed that the Soviet deputy minister for agricultural machinery, V.I. Vishnyakov, had been sentenced to 15 years' imprisonment for having distributed apartments, motor cars, residence permits and jobs in return for private pecuniary advantage (on all this see *Izvestiya*, 9 October 1985, p. 6). At his trial – along with several others – before the Criminal Cases Collegium of the USSR Supreme Court, it was revealed that Vishnyakov had acquired about 100,000 rubles in bribes alone (in addition to over 100,000 rubles from speculation in motor vehicles). Like so many cases of corruption, Vishnyakov's involves a variety of forms of corruption, including an extraordinary case of 'avoidance of specified procedures'. At the trial, it was revealed that Vishnyakov had succeeded in bringing a woman to Moscow; there was a hint he was having an affair with her, although this point is not made explicitly. The story is so bizarre that it warrants citing verbatim from *Izvestiya*:

> When he [Vishnyakov] moved to Moscow, he very much wanted a particular person to move there from Rostov. The job was assigned to the loyal Seryezha Slovutskii. He said it would be impossible to obtain a residence permit. That is difficult to do in the capital. 'But is it difficult even for me?'. Vishnyakov had long since become convinced that some norms were not for him. 'Here's what I want you to do, Seryezha. Find me a single fellow. I'll put him in a decent job, give him an apartment, and even get him a Volga [a Russian brand of motor-car] without him having to be on a waiting list. Just one thing will be required of him: a false marriage with . . . [*Izvestiya* breaks off at this point]. 'Well I never!' – exclaimed Seryezha. 'Were I in a position, on those terms, Viktor Ivanovich – it's a pity I'm married.' – 'Then get divorced . . .' And so it was, Sergei Slovutskii told the court, that he discussed it with his wife Lilya, who agreed to a divorce, how they got divorced, how he obtained the post of head of the supplies department, and then acquired a Volga without going on the waiting list, how he had 'wangled' a flat, how he had registered his marriage to a woman he had seen for the first time at the door of the registry office.

4 Nepotism

Examples of nepotism can be found in most communist countries, although, as was pointed out in the last chapter, the very nature of nepotism in relatively closed societies is such that it is not always possible to distinguish 'proper' from 'improper' promotion of relatives to high office. If the media or other leaders explicitly refer to the impropriety of a given promotion, for instance, then we are justified in seeing this as corruption. If, on the other hand, there are apparently no criticisms of a given promotion as in one sense or another improper, then we have to make more subjective judgements. The latter are perfectly permissible as long as it is made clear that a given action is treated as corrupt on the basis of our own values and/or classical Marxism and Leninism.

The DPRK

One of the best examples of the latter kind of problem can be seen in the leadership succession arrangements of the DPR Korea. In what many observers – not only in the West, but also in several communist countries other than North Korea – have seen as the world's first communist dynasty, the man who has led North Korea since the mid-1940s, Kim Il Sung, is to be succeeded as 'the leader' (in terms of offices, this means general secretary of the Korean Workers' Party and probably head of state) by his only son Kim Jong Il. According to North Korean sources, this nomination came not from Kim Il Sung himself but from the KWP (specifically the Central Committee, at the Sixth Congress in October 1980) – although many Korean and pro-Korean books on the subject refer vaguely to 'the Korean people' having chosen Kim Jong Il (quite how they did this is not spelt out: see, for example, Inoue, 1984, esp. pp. 111–25). Although North Korea has its own ideology – 'Juche' – it has not (yet?) abandoned its commitment to Marxism-Leninism[1]; by virtually any interpretation of Marxism and/or Leninism, such a transfer of power would be seen as corrupt. In this case, then, the nomination is not only nepotistic by most liberal-democratic criteria, but also within the terms of Marxism-Leninism. And yet there are not, apparently, any North Korean sources that raise doubts about this method of transferring power. There is certainly a formal ban on political nepotism, as revealed in article 45 of the KWP Statute; but where the

Central Committee (or the party generally) has made a nomination, *for whatever reason(s)*, this does not count as nepotism.

It might be objected that it is not so much a liberal-democratic as a European conception of propriety that is critical of such practice. Marx and Lenin were, after all, Europeans. As pointed out in the last chapter, there certainly is a cultural dimension to the question of family connections in politics, with most East Asian cultures traditionally being seen as more tolerant of family ties than most European. But the point just made about a formal commitment to Marxism-Leninism overrides this argument. Where there *is* room for differing interpretations of the succession is on the question of whether this form of corruption is black or white or grey in Heidenheimer's terms. A case can be made – and is, by many North Korean officials – that the DPRK is in a very fragile position, and is under constant threat of attack from the South. For this reason, it is argued, it is in the citizens' interests that the leadership succession be as smooth as possible, since a succession crisis could be exploited by enemies of the system. It is a moot point as to whether the majority of the population of North Korea actually do want a continuation of their present type of system. Assuming (against my own judgement) for the present that they do, one can cite North Vietnam in the late 1960s as a case of another East Asian communist state under very real threat, which managed a non-nepotistic transfer of power when Ho Chi Minh died in 1969. In this case, some have argued that it was precisely *because* of the external threat, and even some internal threats, that the leadership succession went so smoothly; certainly this case shows that a smooth leadership succession can be achieved without nepotism.

One final point about the DPRK is that Kim Jong Il's position is not the only example of Kim Il Sung's nepotism. 'The Great Leader's older brother, Kim Yang Joo, and his second wife have also occupied very high office, as have various cousins, nephews, in-laws and other relatives (for details see *FEER*, 16 May 1975, pp. 28–32) – primarily, it seems, on the basis of their family connections.

Cuba

In a manner similar to Kim Il Sung's, Castro has nominated a relative – in this case his younger brother Raúl – to succeed him. While most would accept that Raúl really has done a great deal for Cuba since 1959 – certainly more than Kim Jong Il has done for North Korea – the nomination is not defensible in terms of classical Marxism-

Leninism. Although there may be doubts about Castro's propensity
to nepotism on the basis of Raúl's position, defenders of Castro still
need to explain the fact that when a new Politburo was elected at the
end of the Third CPC Congress in 1986, one of the new full
members was Raúl's wife, Vilma Espín Guillois. Perhaps it was
Castro's growing sensitivity to charges of nepotism, however, that
led to Ms Espín being dropped from the Politburo in October 1991.

The Balkan Communist States

Nepotism was for many years rife in the Balkan communist states.
In *Bulgaria*, for instance, the leader from 1954 to 1989, Todor
Zhivkov, had his daughter Lyudmila appointed to various posts in
the 1970s. In 1976, for example, she was promoted straight to full
membership of the Central Committee (without having served the
usual probationary or 'candidature' period). She became a full member of the politburo in July 1979 at what was, by communist
standards, the remarkably young age of 36. In 1980, continuing a
meteoric rise since 1971 in the cultural establishment, she was put in
charge of the politburo's Committee for Science, Education and
Culture; this was in addition to being head of the State Committee
on Culture. By 1981, some Western commentators saw Zhivkova as
the second most powerful person in Bulgaria (see, for example, *QER
Rumania, Bulgaria, Albania*, No. 1, 1980, p. 11) and she might have
been destined for the same fate – nomination as successor to a close
relative – as Raúl Castro and Kim Jong Il, had she not died suddenly
and unexpectedly of a brain haemorrhage in July 1981.

The ex-Bulgarian leader continued to involve various members of
his family in political affairs after his daughter's death – and on
occasions may have been embarrassed by his own actions. Thus,
when he visited China in May 1987 there was a discrepancy between
the Chinese and Bulgarian official lists of guests; the former included
his 20-year-old granddaughter, Evgenia Zhivkova, while the latter
made no reference to her. At least one analyst (*Eastern Europe Newslet-
ter*, Vol. 1, No. 1, 3 June 1987, p. 8) has inferred that Zhivkov was
trying to hide her presence from the Bulgarian citizenry – although
one must allow for the possibility that there was a last-minute change
of plan or even a genuine error.

Albania under Hoxha (in power 1944–85) also witnessed a great
deal of nepotism, although not just in terms of the Hoxha family.
For example, of the 53 people elected to the ALP's Central Committee by the Fourth Congress (1961), almost one half were related to

each other, either by blood or through marriage (Pano, 1984, p. 226). And no less than five married couples (including Hoxha and his wife, Prime Minister Mehmet Shehu and his wife) were elected to the Central Committee by the Seventh Congress in 1976 (Szajkowski, 1981, p. 45).

Of all the communist countries, few would dispute that *Romania* was, until Ceauşescu's fall in December 1989, the most nepotistic. This led to a number of witty comments about the Romanian political system. For instance, various commentators (such as P. Moore, 1984, p. 199) have described the Romanian communist system as 'socialism in one family' (this term is derived from the Stalinist policy of 'socialism in one country' – for a brief analysis of some of the clan see de Flers, 1984). According to another (Sampson, 1983, p. 55), there was a bitter popular joke in Romania that the acronym 'PRC', which officially referred to the Romanian Communist Party (in Romanian) actually stood for (the Romanian words for) 'connections, acquaintances and relations'. The list of Ceauşescu's family in senior positions within the Romanian power elite was by the 1980s so long that it is inappropriate to go into details here – even if this were possible (Shafir, 1985, p. 78 claims that the list was so complex that it would have been impossible to provide a complete one). Suffice it to make three points instead. First, Ceauşescu all but named his youngest son (Nicu) as his official heir – in a manner not unlike Kim Il Sung's and Fidel Castro's (see Tismaneanu, 1986, esp. p. 69). Second, and following on from this, at least one Western specialist on Romania claims that Ceauşescu first had the idea of a communist dynasty during a visit to North Korea in 1971 (see Jowitt, 1974, pp. 133–5). Third, Ceauşescu showed himself willing to sacrifice (symbolically!) relatives if this appeared to be politically advantageous. In the early 1980s, for instance, his putative nephew Corneliu Burtica was demoted from his ministerial position and expelled from both the Central Committee and the Political Executive Committee (a sort of extended politburo), largely as a scapegoat for various economic problems the country was experiencing. Ceauşescu's alleged brother-in-law Ilie Verdet also suffered career-wise in the early 1980s, although this setback was in his case relatively short-lived (on all this see Shafir, 1985, pp. 78–9).

The GDR

Yet another example that is sometimes cited as communist nepotism is that of Erich and Margot Honecker in the GDR. This is, in fact, a much more ambiguous example than most, in that Margot Honecker – who was East German minister for education from 1963 to 1989 – was already making her own political career at the time she married Erich. Moreover, she was appointed to her ministerial post some eight years before Honecker became general secretary and retained it after the couple's alleged estrangement.

This last example leads to an important issue relating (sic) to nepotism – if it is improper to promote unqualified (broadly understood) members of one's family to high office, it could be argued that it is equally improper to disadvantage family members who are well suited to a particular job.[2] In theory, this must surely be the case. In practice, it is often difficult to determine whether a given individual is occupying high office *primarily* because of his/her own qualities or because of family connections. The solution to this perception problem should surely be to allow *others* (outside of the family and inner elite) to decide, preferably the citizenry at large. In the absence of such a public control mechanism, there is some justification in perceiving a given promotion or occupancy as 'corrupt'. In short, the onus of proof is on those who promote/nominate members of their own family.

From even these few examples of nepotism in the communist world, it becomes clear that this form of corruption has not only been widespread but has, unlike most other forms of corruption, been particularly noticeable at the *top* of the political system. Among the many communist leaders not already mentioned whose wives and/or children and/or other relatives have been promoted to high office are Brezhnev, Mao and Gorbachev.

5 Shared Experiences (Cronyism)

In the real world, there is often some overlap in cases of patronage between 'shared experiences' and the next category, 'shared interests'.

The PRC

One such case – which must be included somewhere in this chapter to give an impression of the range of forms corruption can take – was commented upon by Deng in his major anti-corruption speech of April 1982. Deng referred to recent events in Feixiang county (Hebei

Province), where a group of like-minded party officials used the occasion of the election of the leading party organ of a new party committee at the county level to remove committee members of whose line they disapproved and replace them with what Deng called 'a factionalist group'. Deng described the method of installing the new members thus: 'they did [this] by establishing illicit secret contacts among themselves and employing other reprehensible tactics common during the "Cultural Revolution" '. In this particular case, Deng said that the leading body should be dissolved and a new one established (all from Deng, 1984, p. 382). Of course, the practice of superior party organs directly – and in a strict sense (that is, according to party statutes) improperly – being involved in so-called 'elections' has been common enough in communist parties *generally*, and relates to the vanguard concept, democratic centralism and the *nomenklatura* system. However, it seems that it was not a matter of superior organs in this case – in addition to which Deng implied that *he* saw this as corrupt, even if many others perceived it more as sour grapes on the part of the Dengists at that level, who lost out. This is a classic example of a case that is only corrupt by some criteria and from some perspectives – but not by/from others. In Heidenheimer's terms, it would be a case of 'grey' corruption.

The USSR

One of the best examples of patronage on the basis of shared experiences occurred during the Khrushchev era, when many people were alleged to have been promoted to senior political office on the basis of having worked together with Khrushchev in the Ukraine; among these people were A.I. Kirichenko, A.P. Kirilenko, A.S. Shevchenko and L.I. Brezhnev (for further details see Frankland, 1966, p. 142; Linden, 1966, *passim*, esp. pp. 232–5; Medvedev and Medvedev, 1977, pp. 136–7). Something similar occurred under Brezhnev, and commentators such as Zhores Medvedev (1983, p. 60) have referred to this phenomenon as the 'Dnepropetrovsk mafia'.

6 Shared Interests

The USSR

Even when someone had died, the long arm of the Soviet investigative machinery could in some ways still reach them. Perhaps the best example of this is that of Sh. Rashidov, who was the first party secretary of Uzbekistan from 1959 until his death in 1983 (he was also a candidate member of the Politburo from 1961 to 1983). In December 1983, Rashidov was posthumously honoured by the Central Committee and the Council of Ministers. But this was rescinded in May 1986 on the grounds that Rashidov was: 'to a considerable extent personally to blame for flagrant deviations from Leninist norms of party life, widespread bribe-taking, fraud and report-padding and serious violations of socialist legality' (*Pravda Vostoka*, 7 June 1986, p. 1 – here *CDSP*, Vol. 38, No. 23, 9 July 1986, p. 12). In addition to all these crimes, Rashidov was accused of various forms of patronage and promotions 'on the basis of kinship, *common place of origin*, personal loyalty and servility – and frequently for reasons of personal gain' (ibid. – emphasis added).

7 False Reporting – Overstatement

The USSR

The majority of reports on cases of report-padding have related only to the individual production unit. But bodies above this have frequently been more or less aware of what is happening, and the ramifications of report-padding can spread far and wide. A good example of just how far up it could reach is provided by the major cotton-growing (or, more precisely, *not*-growing) scandal that burst in the USSR in mid-1986. In August of that year, the former minister of the cotton-processing industry of Uzbekistan, V. Usmanov – together with a number of other senior officials in the branch forming what *Izvestiya* (5 September 1986, p. 6, and 6 September 1986, p. 3) described as a crime syndicate (which even required 'protection' money) – was tried by the USSR Supreme Court's Judicial Collegium for report-padding on cotton-fibre production, as well as for accepting large bribes and protecting thieves (for a brief, official announcement of this see *Pravda*, 28 August 1986, p. 6). Usmanov and the officials covered up shortfalls in cotton production of between 500,000 and 900,000 tonnes every year – yet allowed cotton-growing farms to receive central state funds (that is, procurement payments) for this 'air' (as *Izvestiya* put it). Investigations revealed that between 1978 and 1983 alone, some 4.5 million tonnes of raw cotton were produced on paper only, costing the state 'hundreds of millions of rubles' per annum. According to *Izvestiya*:

Of course, this money never actually reached those who were 'plod-
ding away' in the fields; it was withdrawn *en route*, with the aid of
fictitious work orders, pay-rolls and persons, creating in advance a
'cash box' for funding future bribes at the reception-centres. Thus
arose a vicious circle of report-padding – misappropriation – bribes. (5
September 1986, p. 6)

Of particular interest is the fact that both the former minister of light
industry for the USSR, N. Tarasov, and the former chairperson of
the Uzbek Council of Ministers, N. Khudaiberdiyev, acknowledged
that the report-padding was 'an open secret' and that they had
known about it for several years.

The *Izvestiya* reports also pointed to one of the most serious
implications of corruption:

The paradox was that all of them had a secret vested interest in
aggravating the difficulties involved in the procurement of cotton.
The worse the situation became, the better it was for them. The more
unrealistic the plan and the greater the practical impossibility of
fulfilling it through honest labour, the more report-padding there
was, giving rise to a chain reaction of embezzlement. (6 September
1986, p. 3)

In other words, here is an example of communist acknowledgement
of the dangers of the 'knock-on' effects of one form of corruption.

As a result of his crimes, Usmanov acquired money and goods to
the value of 'several hundred thousand rubles'. The property he had
acquired illegally was confiscated by the state, and Usmanov was
executed. In this particular case, the death sentence was more likely
to have been for the scale of his bribe-taking and the losses to the
state than for the report-padding, which in itself was not generally
treated as one of the more serious forms of corruption in the USSR.

Hungary

One of the many cases of corruption reported in the Hungarian press
in 1988 illustrates well the ultimate form of 'overstatement' – stating
there is production when there is in fact none at all. A fraud
investigation in Debrecen revealed that the local party chief, György
Sikula, had been involved in a scheme whereby a number of Debrecen officials obtained millions of forints from Budapest to subsidize a
goose farm which did not actually exist (all details from *The Independent*, 1 November 1988).

Vietnam

Most cases of false reporting involve over- or understatements connected with production. But there are other forms of false reporting connected with individual interests. One case of corruption that was reported in the Vietnamese media in November 1984 is a classic example of how one person can simultaneously engage in several of the forms of corruption identified in this study – and a good example of this alternative notion of 'false reporting'.

The director of the public security service in Dong Nai province, Nguyên Huu Gioc, engaged in various kinds of corrupt activity in the period 1979–83. He released 'reactionaries' from re-education centres, and then found them posts in government offices – all in return for bribes. He secured the release of a former adviser to President Thieu when the man was arrested – again in return for a bribe. He extorted gold and money from ethnic Chinese (Hoa) fleeing Vietnam. He distributed state property to close relatives and accomplices. He directed a cross-border smuggling racket. Various officials knew of Nguyên's activities, and tried to expose him. Nguyên's response was to draw up false reports on his accusers (that is, 'report' things they had not done – in this sense 'overstatement') and have them arrested.

Nguyên Huu Gioc was tried, found guilty, and sentenced to death in November 1984; various accomplices received prison sentences ranging from five to fifteen years (from *Vietnam News Agency*, 9 November 1984, and *Nhân Dân*, 9 November 1984, in *SWB*/FE/ 7797/B/6–7 and *SWB*/FE/7806/B/3–4).

8 False Reporting – Understatement

The PRC

Two articles in *Renmin Ribao* – the main newspaper in the PRC – that were published in 1982 (*RMRB* 11 March, 22 April) reported on the director and party secretary of an electronics import-export corporation in Shenzhen, one Zhou Zhirong, who was engaged throughout most of the previous year not only in smuggling, but also in the deliberate misrepresentation of the nature of the goods his company was importing. He did this in order that excise duty on the imports would be lower than it should have been – and he did so in return for bribes from the exporters. The state was deprived of more than two million yuan worth of duty because of the activities of Zhou and his accomplice in Shenzhen, Xu Zhiliang. The two were expelled from the CCP, dismissed from their posts and arrested (we have not discovered what subsequently happened); the party committee Zhou had headed was also considered corrupt, and was therefore dissolved.

This is an interesting example of understatement; it was not – apparently – the *number* of goods that was misrepresented, but rather the *type*. However, the effect was to deceive the state and to deprive it of large sums of money for reasons of personal gain. In this sense, this is a classic case of corrupt understatement.

9 Deception of Supplicants

There have been numerous reports in the communist media of, for instance, shop assistants who cheat customers by giving them less of a particular product than has been paid for. However – surprisingly – I have been unable to discover unambiguous published reports of officials acting in an essentially similar manner. This said, examples of this type of official corruption have been cited to me verbally by a number of interviewees. For this reason, the category has been included here in the knowledge that it has existed and on the assumption that reports will become available.

10 Forging of Documents

The USSR

Although the Baltic states have a reputation for being less subject to economic crime than some more southerly parts of the former USSR, they have certainly not been devoid of corruption. One good example was reported in *Pravda* in the mid-1970s (11 April 1974, p. 6). An inspector in the social security department under the Executive Committee of the Paide District (Estonia) Soviet, one L. Lemberg, forged various documents, in return for bribes, authorizing the payment of (or increases in) pensions and various kinds of benefit. She was tried in 1974, and found guilty of forging documents in over forty cases, causing losses to the state amounting to almost 50,000 rubles. All her property was confiscated, and she was sentenced to 11 years' imprisonment.

11 Accepting Bribes

Romania

One of the most blatant examples I ever personally experienced of an official accepting a bribe occurred on a visit to Romania in August 1986. Arriving at Bucharest (Otopeni) International Airport, I was standing behind three young men from the Middle East in a queue at passport control. They were experiencing difficulties in gaining entry to Romania, and had been arguing with the passport control officer for several minutes. Eventually, one of them offered the officer US $30.00 and a carton of Kent cigarettes (an invaluable currency when visiting Romania); this was accepted, and the passports were stamped immediately.

Mozambique

In 1983, a Mozambican businessman was arrested for having regularly smuggled up to 15 tonnes of prawns at a time to Swaziland. In order to ensure smooth passage of his cargo, he had been giving large bribes to customs officials. He was tried in camera, found guilty, and executed; the customs officials' fate is unclear.

Although our primary focus is on the officials rather than the businessman, it should be noted that the latter's execution revealed both how seriously the Mozambican leaders viewed this kind and scale of economic crime, and also that the conception of the rule of law prevalent in the West is not necessarily adopted elsewhere. Until this case, the death penalty had not been specified in the statute books as a possible punishment for this sort of crime, the senior leadership having preferred a re-education approach. But in the light of this case, legislation was rushed through the Permanent Commission of the People's Assembly in March 1983, *after* the businessman had already been arrested, and became effective while he was in custody (details from R. Williams, 1987, esp. pp. 94–5, and *YICA*, 1984, p. 50). In this young communist state, at least, the concept of legal-rationality was still a long way off.

Angola

In 1984, a gang of diamond smugglers and dealers was arrested by the police in Luanda. They too had been bribing officials at various levels, and the government estimated the loss to the state coffers at nearly 300 million dollars between 1981 and 1983. The ring leaders were executed (*YICA*, 1985, p. 6); Angola, too, believed in the death penalty for serious economic crime.

Poland

Early in 1985, the former deputy mayor of Zory, S. Tatarczyk, was formally charged by the provincial prosecutor's office in Katowice of accepting bribes from ten people in the period 1980–4. The value of the bribes was at least 134,700 złoty. He was accused of accepting the bribes in return for approving the improper allocation of various building sites, for granting building permits, and for suspending an eviction order from a flat that was being occupied illegally (details from *SWB* EE/7872/B/6 11 February 1985).

Laos

In August 1988, between 47 and 50 defendants – 14 of them Lao nationals – were tried in Vientiane on various charges relating to the production and smuggling of heroin. Late in 1987, two Chinese of Thai citizenship set about establishing two heroin-processing plants in Oudomsai Province. One part of the operation involved bribing local officials to turn a blind eye or indeed ensure protection of the plants, according to the particular official's position. The plants started processing heroin in March 1988, but the project was discovered by the authorities in June. Among the 14 Lao were a police officer, a soldier, a local state functionary – and the secretary of the Oudomsai Province Party Committee and member of the LPRP Central Committee, Sompheng Keobounhouan. The secretary was found guilty and sentenced to seven years' imprisonment (all information from *FBIS Daily Report – East Asia*, No. 156, 12 August 1988, pp. 45–6, No. 157, 15 August 1988, pp. 56–7, and No. 159, 17 August 1988, pp. 35–6).

The GDR

Although the GDR did not publish many articles on corruption until the end of the 1980s, cases did occasionally find their way into the press. Thus in September 1982, a Potsdam newspaper reported that the departmental head of a local housing office had been sentenced to 14 months' imprisonment and an 8,000-mark fine for having accepted bribes on a number of occasions. For example, he had 'sold' three complete heating systems to private citizens in return for bribes amounting to 6,250 marks. The citizens who had offered him the bribes were only fined (*SWB* EE/7146/B/4 2 October 1982).

Sexual Favours

As mentioned in chapter 2, I have been unable to find any hard evidence on accepting sexual favours as a form of bribe-acceptance. There are several reasons why such a form of corruption is rarely, if ever, reported on. The first is that this may simply reflect the actuality of the situation; that is, it really is a rare form of corruption. Second, it may reflect the taboo on public discussion of sexual matters in many communist states. It may also reflect the fact that it is against the interests of many of those who offer sex 'voluntarily' – although of course they would presumably not do so if there were easier ways of acquiring permits, etc. – to report it. Finally, unlike economically based corruption that can be revealed through close auditing and/or sudden changes in consumption patterns, there is comparatively little evidence of sexual favours – although cases of sexually transmitted disease and pregnancies could lead to questions being asked and this form of bribery being revealed.[3]

12 Offering Bribes

The PRC

A sordid case of one official offering a bribe to others was reported in the Chinese press in August 1980 (*RMRB*, 26 August 1980, p. 4). In 1977, the director and party secretary of a coal-mine capital construction unit in Hunan discovered that his son had been arrested for raping a woman in the local county hospital. The father (together with his wife, the rapist's mother) encouraged colleagues to provide a banquet for the deputy head of the county court and the head of the county public security bureau – two officials directly involved in the investigation and trial of the son. At the banquet, the two officials were offered no less than 43 jobs for people of their naming – in return for clemency. The young man was originally to have been sentenced to three years' imprisonment – instead of which it was reduced to two. But in the event, even this sentence was not formally pronounced. After the jobs had been allocated – as promised by the rapist's father – in January 1978, the official verdict was changed to 'exempt from criminal sanctions – released for education'. When news of this leaked out, a number of incensed citizens wrote and complained to the media. The county and district party committees sent in investigative teams no less than three times, but on each occasion met a wall of resistance and silence. Indeed, it later transpired that some members of the investigative bodies were themselves supporting and protecting the wrongdoers – as a result of which the investigations made no progress for two years. The details of the case were finally uncovered in 1980 by the recently formed Hunan Discipline Inspection Commission. The father, who had offered the bribes, was dismissed from all his posts. The mother lost her job (as head of the education section in the company) and was put on two years' probation. The deputy head of the court received a stern warning and was dismissed from his job, while the public security chief came off lightly, with a warning.

13 Extortion

The PRC

In March 1985, Chinese foreign trade official Li Huiquan led a delegation to Japan, and conducted talks and business on behalf of Tianjin's foreign trade administration. While in Japan, he decided to purchase a sophisticated hi-fi system. He very soon realized he would be unable to purchase this on his Chinese salary – so he insisted that his Japanese host company 'present' him with the money (some 300,000 yen) to buy one. As if this were not enough, he then demanded that his host company fork out another 130,000 yen to cover the costs of his excess baggage on the flight back to China. The Japanese company wrote to the Chinese government complaining about Li's behaviour. He was found guilty by a Tianjin court of extorting money from a company abroad, and was sentenced to eight years' imprisonment. Moreover, the items he had acquired through extortion were confiscated. According to the Chinese newspaper that first reported the case (*Economic Daily*), 'practices such as Li's were not rare among staff at units dealing with foreign trade affairs' (cited in *CD*, 14 July 1987).

Cuba

Castro has criticized the practice whereby town planners sometimes extort money from citizens for drawing up small plans (Castro, 1983, p. 341). Apparently some Cuban citizens have arrived at town halls wanting to make repairs or alterations to their houses, and are told that permission can only be granted if they submit a plan. The official also offers to produce the plan, implying that this will ensure that the required permit is forthcoming. But the charge for the plan is not a state-imposed one – it goes straight into the pocket of the planner who, conversely, may well refuse to grant a permit if s/he has not been paid to supply the plan.

Benin

Shortly after the People's Republic of Benin was proclaimed (1975), the authorities launched a major anti-witchcraft campaign as part of a general clampdown on fetishist religion. Various analysts of Beninois politics have claimed that the range of permits required during this period (1976–7), and the dangers faced if one were to be identified as a witch, led to corruption among officials. One of the main forms of corruption involved extorting money from frightened women in return for not denouncing them as witches (from Allen, 1988, pp. 65–6).

The PRC (Rape)

A deputy director – and deputy secretary of the party committee – of a Jiangxi plate-glass factory was dismissed from his post and expelled from the CCP in 1978 for engaging in numerous forms of corruption. Among the charges laid against him was the 'raping and duping' of no less than six women (*RMRB*, 4 December 1978, p. 1). It is to be inferred – and hoped – that he subsequently received harsher penalties, although we were unable to find any references to this.

Details of another interesting case that is most appropriately classified as 'extortion' were published in the Chinese press in late 1980 (*RMRB*, 4 October 1980, p. 1). Chen Mingzhu – the director of the Xiyang County Party Committee's Department of Propaganda – had, with the help of his influential father, ascended the political ladder relatively quickly. As he did so, he tired of his wife. One sign of this was that he raped several women. But another was that he divorced his first wife and then forced a subordinate to break off his engagement so that he – Chen – could take the man's former fiancée as his own second wife!

14 Blackmail

The USSR

An article that appeared in *Pravda* at the end of August 1987 provides one of the few examples encountered of blackmail; the blackmailers were two police officers. A worker at the Kiev Motorcycle Plant, Dubrovskii, used to steal spare parts – which were in even shorter supply in many parts of the communist world than were finished products – from work, and then sell them at three times the official price. A fitter called Lurye found out about Dubrovskii's activities and decided that he could partake of Dubrovskii's earnings. He approached two police officers, Major Vorobyev and Second Lieutenant Luginya, and the three worked out a blackmail plan. The two officers stopped Dubrovskii one evening as he was driving his car and found it to be full of stolen wares. A blackmail demand of 20,000 rubles was made – otherwise, the police officers threatened, they would arrest him, and he would face up to 15 years' imprisonment. Eventually the two sides settled on 16,000 rubles. But Dubrovskii was most unhappy at having to hand over so much of his ill-gotten gains – so much so that eventually, after more than two years, he went to the police himself and told them what had happened. Lurye, as the ring-leader, was tried and sentenced to 10 years' imprisonment; Vorobyev and Luginya were sentenced to six and seven years' respectively. Dubrovskii himself received the relatively light sentence of three years' 'deprivation of freedom' (*Pravda*, 31 August 1987, p. 8).

15 Not Earning One's Salary

Albania

In 1967, a number of articles in the Albanian press referred to various forms of economic crime and corruption. One form that was particularly criticized was the practice of various state officials who 'rested' by day – when they were paid by the state to perform various functions – in order to conserve energy, ready for doing illegal work of various kinds at night. Clearly this problem was not solved, since further criticism of exactly the same practice appeared in 1975 (details from Schnytzer, 1982, pp. 48 and 57).

16 Improper Use of Socialized Property

The PRC

One of the most bizarre cases of corruption encountered in the research for this book occurred in Heilongjiang Province in May 1987. At that time, there were serious forest fires in the North-East of China, and the deputy director of the Firefighting Section of Mohe County Public Security Bureau, Qin Baoshan, was charged with protecting, among other places, his own village of Xilinji. He was under orders to instruct his firefighters to protect various public buildings in the village – instead of which, he used them to protect his own house. Three of the five fire engines under his command were loaded with furniture from the home he and his family shared with the county magistrate and driven to safety. Following this, Qin summoned two bulldozers, and then instructed their drivers to demolish two houses next to his so as to create a firebreak. The fire swept through the village within a few hours, killing 51 people, injuring a further 68, leaving 15,000 homeless and destroying 3,600 houses. Only one building survived the fire – Qin's house. He was charged with 'neglect of duty' – a surprisingly minor charge given the facts of the case (all details from *CD*, 16 July 1987); it was announced in July 1988 (*BR*, Vol. 31, No. 27, p. 7) that Qin had been sentenced to four years' imprisonment – and had lodged an appeal. One must question not only the morality, but also the judgement – and perhaps even the sanity – of a person who could believe they were likely to get away with such a crime.

Vietnam

One of the features that will emerge from the next chapter is that both China and the USSR (have) published very little on corruption within the military. My impression is that this is typical of many communist states. It is therefore interesting that a case of military officers misusing socialized property was published in Ho Chi Minh City early in 1988. Senior Captain Phan Van Thanh and a number of accomplices from the 28th Convalescence Group used military vehicles (ambulances?) to help hundreds of people escape Vietnam. In return, they received 20 taels of gold. Phan was tried by a military tribunal and sentenced to 12 years' imprisonment. His accomplices received sentences ranging from a three-year suspended prison sentence to 11 years (*Saigon Giai Phong*, 10 January 1988; in *SWB* FE/0058/B/1 26 January 1988). It may be that publication of this case was part of a campaign designed to bring the Vietnamese military under greater control (on this see, for example, *SWB* FE/0063/B/4, 1 February 1988, and *SWB* FE/0069/B/3, 8 February 1988, for a Defence Ministry criticism of military personnel who use military vehicles for their own use) – a campaign that the military did not take lying down (see *SWB* FE/067/B/1–2, 5 February 1988, and FE/0084/B/3, 25 February 1988, for examples of military writers complaining about corruption among *civilian* party and state cadres).

17 Embezzlement

Bulgaria

In 1982, Bulgaria witnessed the so-called 'Popov Affair', in which the deputy foreign minister and Central Committee candidate Zhivko Popov was dismissed from office and tried for embezzlement. He had been using state funds allocated for the purchase of art works overseas (as part of Lyudmila Zhivkova's plan to construct an art gallery of international reputation in Sofia) for his own personal ends. Popov received a 20-year prison sentence, had all his property confiscated, and was deprived of the right ever again to hold an official post or live in Sofia. A number of other Bulgarian officials were implicated in the affair (*YICA* 1983, pp. 251–2; *QER Rumania, Bulgaria, Albania*, No. 2, 1982, p. 18, and No. 3, 1982, p. 14).

The PRC

Although the vast majority of cases of corruption reported relate to men, female officials can, of course, also be corrupt and are also sometimes caught. Wang Shouxin, who was not only a manager of an energy company in Heilongjiang Province but also party secretary, embezzled over 500,000 yuan in both cash and goods over the years 1971–8. As in many cases of corruption, this particular one involved several forms. Thus Wang Shouxin also operated a number of 'underground' farms and workshops, in which goods were produced that were then used as bribes to other officials – for instance, to assist the children of cadres close to her to obtain jobs or enter university. Wang Shouxin is also one of the very few females in the communist world to have received the highest possible penalty – execution – for her corruption (details from Forster, 1985, pp. 3–4).

Czechoslovakia

A major trial of ten defendants took place in Bratislava, 23 March–30 June 1987, and was widely publicized; indeed the Czechoslovak politburo (Presidium of the Central Committee) announced publicly on 3 July 1987 that all ten defendants had been expelled from the CPCS. Not only were all the defendants party members, but two of them – J. Murin and P. Kyman – were clearly officials as defined in this study (chairperson of the Dolny Kubin District National Committee and first secretary of the Dolny Kubin District Party Committee respectively). The charges were theft, embezzlement and unlawful handling of state funds. Sentences ranged from one to fourteen and a half years.

The case has become known as the Babinsky Affair, after the leader of the group of ten. Babinsky had been head of a catering establishment in Dolny Kubin, and was said to have supplied a substantial number of party and state officials from both Bratislava and Prague with money, goods, services and entertainment (including prostitutes). The crimes took place between 1975 and 1984, when Babinsky was arrested; investigations and the preparation of the trial lasted some three years. According to Western sources, at his trial Babinsky apparently named a number of very senior Czechoslovak officials who, he claimed, had enjoyed his illegal goods and services. These included General J. Kovac (former first deputy minister of internal affairs), B. Chňoupek (foreign minister) and P. Colotka (deputy premier and politburo member). It must be noted that these names were *not* made public at the time the affair was reported. However, in February 1988, the party daily *Rudé Právo* did list many of the senior officials Babinsky had named, stating that although their activities were not strictly illegal, in accepting cheap goods and services, they had not fulfilled their 'moral responsibility'. General Kovac and a former head of a department of the Slovak CP's Central Committee, S. Dudasek, were expelled from the CPCS. Five officials were given an official party 'reprimand with warning', while another eleven (including two federal ministers) received an official party reprimand. No mention was made of Chňoupek or Colotka, who *may* have been unfairly accused by Babinsky. It could be, however, that the latter two were considered *too* senior and well known to be publicly acknowledged as involved in such a scandal (all details from Kusin, 1988).

Cuba

In July 1987, Castro personally ordered the arrest of a ministerial-level official, Luis Orlando Domínguez, for the alleged embezzlement of several hundred thousand pesos of public funds. Orlando was at that stage head of the Civil Aeronautics Institute, and a member of the CPC Central Committee; he had previously been secretary of the Communist Youth League. According to Castro, Orlando had distributed public funds to family and friends, built a mansion on a beach outside Havana, used state-owned foreign exchange to purchase electronic equipment and electrical appliances overseas, and had large sums of money stashed away in two of his homes. He was tried, found guilty, and sentenced to 20 years' imprisonment. Castro seems to have been particularly angry and disappointed about the Orlando case, since Orlando had been publicly heralded as a model 'new socialist person', and the sort of individual young people should emulate; in the leader's words, 'It makes one ponder when one sees a new cadre like Luis Orlando, who supposedly represents the promise of the future, turning corrupt.' Castro also made it clear that Orlando's was just one of several cases of corruption among officials that had recently been uncovered (all details from *YICA 1988*, p. 68).

Mongolia

In 1981, at the 18th MPRP Congress, General Secretary Tsedenbal called for a clampdown on corruption and promised to root out 'weeds of all kinds' from the party. In the following January, the MPRP's Central Committee accused Professor B. Shirendev of having embezzled 'hundreds of thousands' of dollars; allegedly, the money had been used for throwing lavish parties and for the acquisition of various luxury items for Professor Shirendev's own use. Shirendev was a leading official; not only had he been the president of the Mongolian Academy of Sciences for 22 years, but he was also a member of the MPRP's Central Committee and a deputy chairperson of the Great Khural (the Mongolian legislature). It should be noted that politico-ideological charges were also laid against Shirendev, in particular that he had either ignored or else been rude to various Soviet scholars; it is not clear whether he was being punished more for his economic or his political misdemeanours (details from *Index on Censorship*, Vol. 11, No. 4, August 1982, p. 37).

18 Speculation

Hungary

Late in 1988, the Hungarian media carried details of what would have been a spectacularly successful example of speculation – had the speculator not been discovered. The man who had led the city council in the southern city of Szeged since 1973, Gyula Papp, purchased some land very cheaply in areas that he knew – because of his position – would later be required for development. When he came to sell the land, he realized a 13,000-per-cent profit (some two and a half million forints' worth).

Early in 1988, Papp realized that others had discovered his impropriety, and he apparently agreed to take early retirement. However, he later learnt that there was to be a full judicial inquiry. Presumably in order to help his own position, Papp then 'spilt the beans' on others. He claimed, most notably, that the new HSWP headquarters in Szeged had been built largely with money officially allocated by the city council for public housing. The city party committee convened an emergency meeting to discuss the charges, and admitted that the HSWP itself, which should have entirely funded the new headquarters, had in fact covered less than half the total costs. The rest – nearly 54 million forints' worth – had indeed been diverted from the housing fund. Papp did eventually retire, even though the judicial enquiry resolved that his actions had been ethically highly questionable but not technically illegal. The whole affair caused a great deal of political embarrassment, both for the Szeged City Council (which in December passed a vote of no confidence in its own executive committee and its secretary) and for the Szeged City Party Committee (all details from *SWB* EE/0290/B/2, 24 October 1988; *SWB* EE/0294/B/7, 28 October 1988; *SWB* EE/0322/B/3, 30 November 1988; *SWB* EE/0328/B/6, 7 December

1988; *SWB* EE/0322/B/6, 12 December 1988; and *The Independent*, 1 November 1988).

It has been claimed by some Westerners that this and other cases of corruption publicized in the Hungarian media in the late 1980s were part of a campaign by Kádár's successors to discredit senior members of their predecessor's government. In this particular case, for inst-ance, the HSWP project had been authorized in 1982 by Politburo member Károly Németh. Whether Németh himself was involved or not in the corruption is unclear; it would be ironic if he were, since he had strongly criticized 'abuse of power' by party members at the March 1979 plenum of the HSWP Central Committee (*YICA*, 1980, p. 42). Moreover, Németh was appointed Hungarian premier in November 1988, which casts further doubt on this particular hypothesis. Németh's own case might be an exception, however, and *if* the general claim is accurate, the campaign would constitute a good example of a new regime attempting to bolster its own legitimacy by criticizing and distancing itself from its predecessor. It must not be overlooked, however, that there were major corruption scandals in the Kádár era, too – perhaps the best-known one involv-ing the deputy minister of justice and Central Committee member Ádám Bonifert towards the end of 1983 (see *KCA*, 1984, p. 32940, for details of this and other cases of official corruption). At least one commentator has seen this as part of a drive against corruption in the HSWP (see *YICA*, 1985, pp. 296–7).[4]

Albania

In late 1988, the Albanian media carried criticisms of the practice whereby various party and state officials were involved in specula-tion in pockets of unused land around the capital, Tirana. Among those named were Seit Mema (secretary of the 4th Primary Party Organization of the 10th District of Tirana) and Qemel Qafmolla (member of the People's Council of the village of Shish-Tufine – details from *SWB* EE/0312/B/2, 18 November 1988).

19 Smuggling

The DPRK

In October 1976, the Danish, Norwegian, Finnish and Swedish governments expelled a number of North Korean diplomats for smuggling alcohol, cigarettes and – most seriously – drugs into the Scandinavian countries. The Danish foreign minister claimed they were probably doing it under orders from Pyongyang, in order to earn much-needed hard currency (on this see *FEER*, 5 November 1976, p. 11, and *KCA*, Vol. 23, 1977, p. 28136). Although there were some doubts about the persuasiveness of this allegation, it is an interesting suggestion. If they were smuggling under orders from above, this would hardly be treated as corruption in their own country – even though it was by the Scandinavian authorities. This is thus an unusual case of 'grey' corruption.

Yugoslavia

In July 1985, it was announced by Tanjug that two inspectors of the Banja Luka Inter-Municipal Internal Affairs Secretariat were to be placed on trial for their role in a smuggling operating involving a total of 14 people. Between July and September 1984, this gang smuggled 18 tonnes of coffee into Yugoslavia from Austria; the two officials played a major role in this. The two – M. Vujinovic and V. Vuckovic – eventually received sentences of ten and six years' imprisonment respectively (details from *SWB* EE/7850/B/17, 16 January 1985, and *SWB* EE/7868/B/8, 6 February 1985).

20 Treason

Poland

In December 1982, the court of the Warsaw Military Region tried the former Polish ambassador to Japan, Zdzislaw Rurarz, *in absentia*; he was charged with high treason and sentenced to death. According to *Trybuna Ludu*, Rurarz had first supported Gierek, then Solidarity; once it became clear that Jaruzelski had taken control in Poland, the diplomat allegedly felt threatened and decided to sell Polish state secrets to a foreign intelligence service (in *SWB* EE/7215/B/10, 22 December 1982).

Cuba

What *Time* magazine (10 July 1989, p. 18) described as 'the most sensational corruption scandal to hit Cuba since Fidel Castro seized power three decades ago' was reported in the Cuban media in June and July 1989 (for all this see *Granma Weekly Review*, Vol. 24, No. 28, 9 July 1989, pp. 1–3; see too *NT*, No. 35, 1989, pp. 17–18). Early that month, Arnaldo Ochoa Sánchez – one of Cuba's most respected and decorated generals, and a member of both the Central Committee of the CPC and the National Assembly of People's Power – was arrested and charged along with six other military and law-enforcement officials with being involved in a large-scale smuggling operation. Although various items were involved, including diamonds and ivory, the most significant part of the operation related to drugs. In particular, Ochoa and his accomplices were accused of having made US $3.4 million by helping Colombian drug-baron Pablo Escobar Gaviria smuggle cocaine into the USA. For this, Ochoa was accused of treason. Ochoa pleaded guilty, described himself as a traitor, and was executed in July.

The Ochoa case was but the latest of a series of corruption trials of senior officials. One of the casualties of the affair was the Cuban minister of the interior, General José Abrantes Fernández; he was dismissed early in July 1989 for his failure to uncover Ochoa's activities. At the end of the 1980s, there were a number of other trials of very senior Cuban officials; indeed, at about the same time as Ochoa and his accomplices were being tried, another corruption trial – of former Vice-Premier Diocles Torralbas Gonzáles and five subordinates – was being held in Havana. Torralbas received a 20-year prison sentence.

Conclusion

There is little to be said here, by way of a conclusion, that has not already been said. Suffice it to make the point that many more examples of corruption – involving, for instance, Deng Xiaoping's son and Brezhnev's son-in-law – will be mentioned at appropriate junctures elsewhere in this book; this chapter serves only to provide the reader with a starting point and some of the more interesting cases encountered in the research. Moreover, we can expect to see far more examples of official corruption investigated and reported on in the 1990s, as post-communist governments seek to expose all the improprieties of their predecessors. The next chapter looks at cases from a very different – more aggregated – perspective; it is simultaneously a more systematic and less colourful chapter.

NOTES

1   It is interesting to note, however, that in one standard North Korean overview of the country and its system, the section on ideology and politics refers only to Juche, not Marxism or Leninism or Marxism-Leninism – see (unspecified authors), *Korean Review*, Pyongyang, 1982, esp. pp. 151–76. Other more recent sources *do* still refer to Marxism-Leninism, however.

2   In this particular case, it might be objected that I am being sexist in assuming it is Margot whose office-holding might be seen as improper. However, since Erich occupied a *higher* office than she, the main focus would normally be on him. As implied in the text, however, I myself do not see either Margot or Erich as corrupt (nepotistic) in terms of familial occupancy of high office. Indeed, although Honecker was charged in late 1989 with various forms of corruption, it was announced in March 1990 that the commission responsible for investigating the charges had been unable to find sufficient evidence against the former leader to bring him to trial. While some of the charges laid against senior East German communist officials in late 1989 were justified, those against Honecker were in my view laid primarily for political reasons, designed both to undermine him and his regime, and to enhance the legitimacy of the successor regime. In this sense, this is a classic example of the close relationship between official anti-corruption campaigns and legitimation that is at the core of this study.

3   Although this is not a case of alleged acceptance or demanding of bribes by indigenous officials – and is therefore not included in the main body of the text – it is interesting to note that the Beijing periodical *Youth News* claimed in March 1990 that an Australian embassy official had been accepting and/or demanding (this was still unclear at the time of writing) sex from young Chinese women in return for visa approvals to Australia. The Australian embassy in Beijing denied the allegations (details from *The Age*, 23 March 1990).

4   One of the most colourful cases of 'corruption' in Hungary is reported by Volgyes (1975, p. 30). In the early 1970s, a number of relatively high-ranking persons were put on trial for having 'gambled away on cards an entire collective farm, the Uj Elet (New Life) collective farm of Mezotur'. Unfortunately, Volgyes does not cite his source for this, and it is not clear that this constituted a case of official corruption as defined in this study. This interesting example is therefore mentioned here in a note, rather than in the main text.

4

Patterns of Corruption and its Reporting in the USSR and the PRC

It is very important to note at the outset of the present chapter that the findings reported in it must be treated with extreme caution. As will become obvious, a large number of methodological problems arose in the attempt to study corruption and its reporting in the USSR and the PRC. Some problems ultimately proved to be insurmountable. Although methods were devised for handling some of the others, such 'solutions' were frequently sub-optimal and subjective. A number of decisions had to be taken on somewhat arbitrary grounds. At one point, I even wondered whether the problems were so formidable that any attempt at quantifying corruption and its reporting would be scientifically worthless. After long deliberation and consultation, it was eventually decided that it would be even more irresponsible to abandon the project than it would be to process and present the data – on condition that the problematic nature of the data was emphasized. There were two main reasons why it was decided to classify the data anyway, warts and all. The first is that, after two to three years' solid work by both my research assistants and myself, there was a very considerable body of original data, and it seemed wasteful not to attempt to squeeze out of this whatever seemed academically respectable. Second, there was the all-important factor that I was interested in *perceptions* of corruption. The 'average reader' in a communist state does not quantify or classify articles s/he reads about corruption over the years, but rather forms an *impression* that the situation is deteriorating or improving. However, such an impression is based on the media reports – so that if we are to maximize our understanding of the kind of impression media reports might create among the citizenry, then those reports must be analysed as thoroughly as possible.

Much of the chapter concerns methodology, and it could be objected that this should be included in an appendix rather than in the main body of the text. This view is rejected on two grounds. First, the very inclusion of the methodology helps to endorse the point that the findings of the chapter must be treated cautiously. Second, many of the problems encountered in this project face researchers on other systems, particularly non-communist Third World ones. The inclusion of the methodology here might thus both help other researchers and/or warn readers to be wary of *all* 'empirical' analyses of corruption – not just this one – by highlighting the problems involved in research.

Having made these important caveats, we can now turn to consider how data sources were chosen, and the sorts of question it was hoped to be able to answer by analysing these sources systematically. Only following this can the results of the analysis be provided.

Selecting the Sources

It is surely obvious that it is not practicable for one person or even a small team of researchers to analyse all the media from one country – let alone 23 – for a period long enough to produce an indication of possible patterns and changes. Not only is this very expensive, both pecuniarily and temporally, but it is also not possible to gain access to all the local press, to monitor all radio and television broadcasts, etc. Hence, one must be highly selective.

For this study, it was decided to concentrate on just two countries, the USSR and the PRC. Given their significance within both the communist world and the world as a whole, such a choice does not appear to require much justification. But there are several other reasons why such a choice seemed appropriate. Although these two countries may, in the mid- to late 1980s, in many ways have been less distant from each other than they were in the 1960s and 1970s, they were still at very different levels of economic development, per capita income, etc. – so that hypotheses linking types and levels of corruption with particular stages of economic development could *a priori* be tested against these two. A second factor is that the PRC is even less of a 'clone' of the Soviet model than have been many countries of what was, until the end of the 1980s, often referred to as the Soviet bloc. Although China was highly emulative of the Soviet model until the mid- to late 1950s, it has largely pursued its own path since then. Thus – again *a priori* – if similar patterns of corruption could be identified for both countries, there would be less danger of being charged with having chosen two communist states that were *likely* to exhibit similar features. Third, there is the practical reason that there has been greater access both to indigenous printed sources and to translations of these from the USSR and the PRC than there has been for almost anywhere else in the communist world.

It was recognized that there is also at least one possible disadvantage in focusing on these two countries. This is that there are *some* ways in which they are not typical of communist states of the pre-1989 era. The communists took power in both countries largely on their own, which some would see as indicative of fewer problems of subsequent citizen alienation than in countries in which communism was 'imposed' from outside. While there is certainly some weight to this argument, it is not totally convincing. For instance, it does not explicitly recognize that the USSR was a multinational, federal state, in which – as again became very obvious by the late 1980s – many citizens felt at least as dominated by 'outsiders' (Russians, or even Azerbaijanis) as did Czechs/Slovaks or East Germans or Romanians. This factor applies much less to China, although some Tibetans, for instance, are as hostile to the Beijing government as some Lithuanians have been to Moscow. It should also be borne in mind that there were many more communist countries in which indigenous communists took power more or less on their own than is generally realized. In Cuba, Yugoslavia, Albania, South Yemen, Ethiopia and several other countries, communism can hardly be seen as a form of foreign domination. Finally, the findings of some analysts of political culture suggest that some states in which communism was 'imposed' (such as Hungary) have at times enjoyed a higher level of legitimacy than some in which communism was introduced by 'natives' (such as Yugoslavia since Tito's death). Thus the USSR and the PRC are not as atypical from this perspective as is sometimes assumed.

A more convincing charge of atypicality is that both countries are/ were extremely large, and that no other communist state even began to approach them in terms of either area or population. While this cannot be gainsaid, the assumptions behind such a charge need to be questioned. Is it *necessarily* the case, for instance, that large countries are likely to be more (or, for that matter, less) corrupt than small countries? It is surely obvious that *size* in itself is not the critical factor. More important is, for instance, the level of coercion and control. Political culture, including attitudes towards venality, is also very important – and does not necessarily correlate with size. Moreover, if corruption is linked with ethnicity – either in terms of cultural attitudes or in terms of it increasing as ethnic conflict increases – then the choice of the USSR (a large, ethnically diverse

country) and China (a large, ethnically *relatively* homogeneous country) is not clearly any less appropriate than, say, comparing communist Yugoslavia (a small, ethnically diverse country) with Hungary (a small, ethnically *relatively* homogeneous country).

The final possible charge of atypicality relates to the fact that both
the USSR and the PRC are/were widely *known* to have had major
campaigns against corruption, and in this sense might be seen to have
been selected to 'prove' what then becomes in reality a self-fulfilling
argument. My response to this is two-fold. First, it is quite clear
from the research carried out for this book that several other communist countries had anti-corruption campaigns in recent years (see
chapter 7 for details). Second, the argument here is that the USSR
and the PRC were amongst the trailblazers – that what was happening in them was likely to spread to those few parts of the communist
world that by the mid-1980s had still had no major campaigns.[1] It is
also argued here that the anti-corruption campaigns were to a
substantial degree part of a much more significant phenomenon – the
move *towards* the legal-rational state – which was discernible in
several communist states; this is elaborated in chapter 8. In short,
although it is acknowledged that the USSR and the PRC are not a
perfect choice in terms of typicality, it is argued that they are no less
suitable than any other pair of countries, since no two countries are
'typical' across a wide range of variables. If we add to this the much
better accessibility to Chinese and Soviet sources, their selection is
justified.

Having selected the countries, the next decision to be made related
to the choice of sources. To those who have not worked in the field
of communist studies, it might appear that one choice at least – that
between the printed and the electronic media – would be an obvious,
self-selecting one. This may once have been true. However, the
advent of high-powered short-wave radios and, more recently,
satellite television means that Western scholars have in recent years
had a far wider range of primary sources to choose from than was
formerly the case. Although most individual researchers would, for a
variety of reasons, find it relatively difficult to organize a long-term,
systematic monitoring of electronic media broadcasting, this can be
and has been done by various Western agencies – some of which
publish selections of what is considered to be the most interesting
and significant material. The BBC's *Summary of World Broadcasts*
(*SWB*) and the Foreign Broadcast Information Services (FBIS) *Daily
Report* are the best known of these in the English-speaking world,
and are an invaluable source of information. Thus, although access to
television broadcasts is still too recent to serve as the basis of an

analysis over time, it is possible to use monitoring service reports, in addition to the indigenous printed media, in order to obtain information on corruption. In fact, these reports were used extensively in this study, not only for information on the USSR and the PRC but for most communist countries (that is, to obtain the information for other chapters of this book).

Turning to the printed media, there are a number of Western translation services available; these are particularly useful for the comparative analyst. In the case of the USSR, for example, there is the invaluable *Current Digest of the Soviet Press* (*CDSP*) which provides either verbatim translations of complete articles, or extracts from articles, or abstracts of articles from a wide range of Soviet newspapers and journals, including some local ones. In the late 1980s, an English-language edition of *Pravda* became available. The Chinese have been less well served in terms of non-communist translations from original sources. Until 1977, there was a periodical somewhat akin to the *CDSP* known as the *Survey of the People's Republic of China Press*. Since this covered only half of the period analysed in this study, it was decided not to use it for this chapter, since to have done so could have seriously distorted our perception of scales of reporting.

All the sources mentioned so far, with the exception of *Pravda*, are what are in this study described as 'intermediate' sources. These are not secondary, in that they do not really constitute reporting and/or interpretation of other sources. On the other hand, neither are they primary sources *in stricto sensu*. One reason is that some of the translations – which are themselves to some extent open to question – have been edited or abstracted by someone else. Another is that the actual choice of what to translate has also been made by someone else. In these senses, there is interference between the researcher and the primary material. The first problem does not appear to be a serious one, however. For instance, random testing I have carried out of abstracts versus originals has not revealed a single instance of something I would judge important having been omitted. The same applies to the quality of translation; I have yet to discover a serious error or omission or what I perceive to be a misleading rendition in random testing. The other 'interference' factor is considered below. Thus, although for the sake of intellectual honesty I have highlighted the fact that Western translation services such as the *CDSP* are not primary sources in the strictest sense, such 'intermediate' sources unquestionably approximate far more closely to primary than to secondary sources.

Not all English-language sources used for this book are translations by Westerners. Both the USSR and the PRC have produced a number of English-language printed news media themselves. Of these, the weeklies *Moscow News*, *New Times* and *Beijing Review* are the most interesting and informative; of the dailies, *China Daily* is invaluable.

In comparing the 'intermediate' sources with these 'primary' sources, it soon becomes evident just how hazy the line between 'primary' and 'intermediate' can be, especially in using sources from the communist world. Just as there can be 'interference' (as defined above) between the researcher using intermediate sources and the primary data, so it must be borne in mind that the media have generally played a somewhat different role in most communist states from that played by the media in the liberal democracies. The level of censorship is one obvious difference (for a comparative analysis of East European communist censorship see Schöpflin, 1983). Another is that there has not traditionally been the same level of competition – trying to provide information and views that one's competitor has not – in the communist media as in the media of the liberal democracies. Instead of being in competition, communist media have – at least until very recently – been more overtly concerned with state-directed purposive socialization. Information is usually to be revealed selectively and often for explicit political objectives. This can lead to less information being available in communist newspapers than in capitalist newspapers looking for the exclusive 'scoop'. Cases can intentionally be reported by editors and journalists in such a way as to create a specific (false) impression, for example.[2] The intention here is not to make simplistic distinctions between media in the West and the East; rather, it is merely to argue that there can be 'interference' between the researcher and original data even when using 'primary' sources. Moving beyond the media to the publication of laws, we know that – at least until recently – not all laws were published in the USSR; an example relating to corruption is cited in chapter 7. Thus the 'interference' problems that arise in using 'intermediate' sources can and do arise in using 'primary' sources, too. Of course, they are in at least one sense exacerbated in the case of the former, since the interference that exists between the researcher and the primary source also exists between the translator or abstracter and the primary source, so that the researcher is subject to a double dose of interference. But it becomes clear that we are mostly talking about differences of degree rather than quality in comparing the usefulness of primary and intermediate sources.

In light of the above discussion, it becomes evident that the selection of 'appropriate' sources is more complex than might initially appear to be the case. Before identifying the sources used for systematic research, one final but very important point is that research is often limited by practical constraints – of availability of sources, of time and of funding. All three of these directly and significantly affected the selection for the present study. In particular, limited time and less generous funding than was requested meant that a thorough reading of *Pravda* for a 20-year period was not feasible.

The data on the Soviet Union were gathered from a systematic reading of the *CDSP* from 1966 to 1987.[3] It had been hoped to maximize the chances of discovering all cases of corruption cited in *Pravda* by using the *Index to Pravda* (plus a reading of potentially relevant articles) as a back-up to *CDSP*. Unfortunately, *Index to Pravda* was published only irregularly for three years in the mid-1970s and then ceased publication altogether. Only to have used those issues that did appear would have distorted the overall database, so that this method for discovering reports was rejected. Thus, any case actually cited in this book from *Pravda* has been traced from *CDSP* but then read in *Pravda* itself. For the purposes of comparing the reporting of corruption in what was for the period in question the main newspaper in the PRC and that in the USSR (that is, *Renmin Ribao* and *Pravda*), a sub-set of the *CDSP* articles was created consisting exclusively of *Pravda* items.[4] Although various cases and aspects of corruption in the USSR have been cited in this study from elsewhere in the Soviet press (for example, *Moscow News*), the data used for analysis in this chapter – with the exception of those on the scale of corruption – have been taken exclusively from these sources (that is, *CDSP*, *Pravda*).

The data on the PRC were gathered from a systematic reading of *Renmin Ribao* from 1966 to 1983 and of *SWB* from 1966 to 1986; although various cases of corruption in China have been cited in this study from elsewhere in the Chinese press (notably *Beijing Review* and *China Daily*), the data used for analysis in this chapter – again with the exception of those on the scale of corruption – have been taken exclusively from those sources. It should be noted that a shortage of funds meant that it was – most unfortunately – not possible to have *RMRB* thoroughly read and analysed for the years 1984–6; many readers will appreciate from their own experience that it takes considerably longer, and is therefore far more expensive, to analyse one year's run of *RMRB* than one year's run of the Chinese sections of *SWB*. Hence, the Chinese data for the period 1984–6 must be treated with even more caution than the rest of the data; while some *RMRB* reports are included (that is, those that have been referred to in *SWB*), not all are. It follows from this that the number of reports given for the years 1984–6 must be understood as a *minimum* number, since there is little doubt that several *RMRB* reports have been omitted.

It should be clear from the above that practical constraints have meant that the data used for the two countries are not strictly comparable. This is, of course, unfortunate, and is one of the reasons the findings of the present chapter cannot be treated as more than impressionistic. On the other hand, the two sets of data are *internally* consistent (with the partial exception of the Chinese data 1984–6), and do at least give an indication, based on the communist press itself, of patterns of reporting of corruption.

Problems of Identification

Having selected the sources for analysis, the next problem that arose was that of identifying reports, articles, speeches, etc., to be classified; there are several dimensions to this problem. The first is that some articles are entirely about corruption, others are mainly about it, while a third group contains references to it but is principally concerned with some other issue(s). The first type clearly should be included in the analysis. After deliberation, it was decided to include the second type but to exclude the third. The classification of an article as being of the second or the third types had, ultimately, to be somewhat intuitive; early attempts at quantifying articles in terms of the percentage of the article devoted to corruption proved to be too problematic to apply generally. This said, the number of questionable cases was very small; although resources did not permit a full second coding of all material, random checks revealed that coders rarely disagreed on the issue of inclusion or not. Where coders were in doubt, they were instructed to consult with me; a problem case would thus be identified, and a decision reached.

The next problem relates to the definitional problem analysed in chapter 2. Relatively few articles relate specifically to corruption as defined in this study. The distinction drawn here – for purposes of cross-system comparison – between 'officials' and 'non-officials' has rarely been made in the communist world itself, for example; yet only sources containing details of corruption by 'officials' have been included for the analysis over time. Unfortunately, even the identification of 'officials' is not as straightforward as it might appear, despite the fact that these had been disaggregated into six groups.

The problems of identifying 'officials' in group 6 – senior people, not covered in groups 1–5, who are in most societies expected to 'set an example' – have already been noted and are self-evident. But there are many individuals whose position does not *clearly* fall either within or beyond categories 1–5. In the USSR, for instance, did 'citizen inspectors' or lay members of comrades' courts count as 'officers of the law', even 'broadly understood'? Did gamekeepers – who, according to the Soviet press, frequently engaged in poaching rackets – constitute 'officers of the law'? Did an external auditor of factory accounts count as a state bureaucrat? There are no universally acceptable answers to these questions; decisions have to be made on subjective grounds. In this study, the notion of 'cross-system comparability' has been the dominant criterion in reaching decisions. In other words, if a position would not *clearly* count as 'official' in non-communist systems, then unless it is quite clear that it would be perceived by citizens of communist states as 'official', it is excluded from the analysis in line with our narrow definition of corruption.[5] Another criterion used is 'professional full-time' versus 'amateur part-time'. With the exception of committee members in groups 1 and 2, the latter are generally *not* accepted as 'officials' for the purposes of this study. Moreover, since the theoretical framework of this study emphasizes the notion of chiefs attacking their staffs, this general principle of 'when in doubt, leave it out' seems justified; there is in my view little doubt that the publication of an article on a corrupt minister, Central Committee member or senior police officer is more overtly 'political' and would cause more public concern and indignation than the publication of a case of a fishing inspector in a small village who has been permitting local people to fish illegally in return for bribes.

Even the identification of a crime or misdemeanour as 'corruption' can be problematic. Assuming the coder has determined whether an individual is an official or not, problems often arise because of vague references to 'abuse of office' or 'laxity'. Once again, the overall purpose of this study has determined whether or not such cases are to be treated as corruption. If there are general references to 'abuse of office', but it is clear from the context that this could be no more than turning a blind eye because of work-overload or uncertainty about how to deal with an ambiguous issue (as distinct from being clearly in the *interests* of the individual official), such cases have been classified as 'not clearly corruption'. The interest here is in overt attacks – campaigns, if these are visible – on *corrupt* officials, not general complaints about officials' occasional failings and inadequacies.

Classifying the Data

Having decided on sources, and on how to identify articles/officials/ crimes for inclusion, the next step was to decide on the kinds of information to be looked for. Having searched for definitions and explanations of corruption – the results of which appear elsewhere in this study – coders were asked first to look at who is involved; this question sub-divides into three – name, age, position. Including the name has two main functions. The first is that knowing the actual identity of an individual helps to minimize the problem of multiple-counting. By this is meant that if we are, for example, to form an impression of how frequently and under what circumstances officials are executed for corruption, then we must seek to avoid saying there were three such cases in Republic A in 1983 when in fact we have read three different reports of one and the same case. This example is a hypothetical one, cited to make a point forcefully; in fact, I am unaware of any actual instance of this particular kind. However, some cases certainly are reported more than once – the first time announcing that a crime has been committed and that one or more persons have been charged, the last time concerning the outcome, and sometimes with ongoing commentaries in between. Clearly one has to be wary of counting a given case more than once. In a sense, it would be perfectly reasonable to decide to treat these three reports providing different information on the same case as one 'case' for *all* purposes in the research project. However, it needs to be borne in mind that we are concerned with the phenomenon of *reporting* corruption as well as corruption itself, so that the total number of *reports* in the sources being used is of interest, as well as the number of *cases*. Perception by citizens is probably affected at least as much by frequency of reporting as by the actual number of cases, assuming the latter is different from the former. Thus, in the data analysis that follows, a distinction is drawn between the number of reports and the number of cases. The second reason for noting the name is that this can *sometimes* indicate a person's nationality and/or gender; unfortunately, this proved to be the case too infrequently to be of much value.

Following this, coders were asked to include the *age* of officials. The intention was to see if there was any generational pattern to corruption. Again, far too few reports included any information on this to be able to detect any patterns.

Next, coders were asked to classify officials according to the listing given in chapter 2. Very occasionally, articles merely refer to 'officials' or use alternative but similarly vague terms; if nothing more is said about the officials, they have been classified as 'unspecified' for statistical purposes. However, subsequent references in the report typically suggest strongly that such officials are state functionaries, party *apparatchiki*, etc.; if the evidence on this was considered convincing, they have been classified as such. Where a person's rank within a given hierarchy is made clear, this has been included on the data-sheet produced for each case reported. A difficulty arises when, for instance, the researcher encounters a case in which someone who may well be an official is not identified as such. For example, the director of an enterprise may be identified only in that role in a report on the director's misdemeanours; since we know (empirically) that the overwhelming majority of directors in both the USSR and the PRC are – or have until very recently been – not only party members but also members of the party committees in their places of work, a case could be made for inferring that such people are to be included as 'officials'. It was decided *not* to do this, on two grounds. First, it must constantly be borne in mind that a major aspect of this study is to examine the relationship between corruption (and its reporting) and legitimation; if it is not mentioned in a report that Director X is *also* a member of a party committee, many readers of the report within the USSR or the PRC will not necessarily be aware that s/he *is* an official. Thus the potential delegitimating aspects of an official being corrupt do not really pertain in these circumstances, even if Western observers are almost certain that this is a case of a corrupt official. Second, although we might be almost certain that a given director is a member of a party committee, there will be many other people whose economic crimes are reported on but about whose membership or not of party committees we have no way of knowing. Thus because both of the perception (through reporting) dimension and the fact that we should strive for maximum consistency, it was decided not to make inferences about a given individual's possible classification as an official, but only to categorize a person in terms of his/her confirmed position in reports.

One important aspect of noting not only whether cases of corruption involve officials or not, but also precisely what kinds of official are involved, is that subsequent analysis of the aggregate data will provide a pointer to the question of which functional groups seem to be most prone to corruption – and, at least as interestingly, which groups seem for the most part *not* to engage in corrupt activities. Of course, bearing constantly in mind that our perception of actual levels of corruption is primarily conditioned by the reporting of corruption, all we are doing is to show which groups are rarely reported on. But this in itself is interesting in terms of the question of legitimacy, a point to which we shall return later in the book when the results of the data analysis are presented.

In addition to considering individuals as members of functional groups, we also examined them in terms of their position within a given group's hierarchy. The primary concern here was to see how frequently higher-level officials were reported on relative to lower-level officials. Once again, the findings can provide only an impression. This is partially because Western scholars often disagree on the relative size of many functional groups in both the USSR and the PRC, so that one must be very cautious in making statements about the relatively higher or lower incidence of corruption among senior officials as compared with lower officials. This said, if reporting of corruption among senior officials is *very* rare, then clearly we need to speculate on the reasons for this. Moreover, any patterns that emerge over time will also require interpretation; one of the sub-hypotheses I wanted to test was that there is a tendency over time for anti-corruption campaigns to be directed further up the hierarchy (that is, to affect a growing number of higher-ranking officials).

At this juncture, it is necessary to specify what is meant by senior leadership on the one hand, and high-, middle-, low-ranking and workplace officials on the other. Such a distinction is frequently glossed over in the literature on elites, but must be drawn reasonably clearly for the purposes of empirical research. It is particularly important for the present study because of the distinction drawn by so many writers between 'chiefs' and 'staffs' (see chapter 1). In this book, therefore, the necessarily somewhat arbitrary borders are drawn as follows:

1 *Chiefs* (senior leadership). Members (full and candidate) of the Politburo; functional equivalents of the head of state and deputy head of state; members of the 'inner core' of the chief executive organ of the state (Council of Ministers in the USSR;[6] State Council in the PRC).

2 *Staffs* (n.b. all the positions listed *exclude* individuals already covered under 'Chiefs').
   (a) *High-ranking officials.* Members of the Central Committee; members of the central party apparatus; members of the Party Congress; members of the legislature; members of the chief executive organ of the state; officials of central ministries; central-level judges; military officers equivalent to general and above; other

'responsible officials' at the central level, whose position normally suggests that they might be expected to be on party and/or state central-level bodies at some point.

(b) *Middle-ranking officials.* Members of the republican (USSR) or provincial (PRC)★ party and/or state and/or legal elective and appointive bodies; all military officials not covered in (a); other 'responsible officials' at the republic/province level, who might normally be expected to be on party and/or state bodies at the republic/province level.

(c) *Low-ranking (that is, local) officials.* Officials not covered by any of the above and working at the local level, but above the workplace level.

(d) *Workplace Officials.* Officials working in factories, on farms or at other work-units.

The above listing will not satisfy all readers; no listing could. An acceptable argument can be made, for instance, that a local town mayor is a 'higher-ranking' (for example, in terms of social prestige) official than is a relatively junior administrator in a republic-level ministry. While such an argument is not explicitly rejected here, it is nevertheless maintained that a workable division has to be drawn for the purposes of this study, and that to distinguish officials primarily on the basis of the level at which they are working meets the requirements of this analysis as well as any other.

In addition to the *identity of officials* found or alleged to be guilty of corrupt acts, the *nature of the crime* committed was recorded, in line with the taxonomy provided in chapter 2. Sometimes, individuals are accused of and tried for more than one form of corruption; in such cases, all the forms listed in the reports have been entered on to the data-sheet unless it is clear that one type has dominated. This helps to explain why the sum total of the examples of different types of corruption is somewhat greater than the total number of cases identified.

Not only the nature of the crime but also the *time and place of the crime* were recorded, if such data are provided in the report (the latter, at least, are in the majority of cases). The location data have been used, *inter alia*, to test the view – common in the existing literature – that there have been discernible concentrations of corruption in particular parts of the USSR and the PRC (always bearing in

★Or equivalent – for example, the municipalities of Beijing, Shanghai and Tianjin in the PRC.

mind that we can only make inferences on the basis of corruption reported). Information on the temporal dimension of cases is also valuable, in particular for testing hypotheses that relate both corruption and its reporting to changes of leadership, major changes in economic policy, etc. For instance, it was hoped to be able to obtain – both by this method and by using published statistics – enough hard data on (detected) corruption in China to test the Chinese leadership's own assumption that corruption increased dramatically following the introduction of radical changes in economic policy in the late 1970s/early 1980s (causal inferences about the nature of such a relationship, if it appears to exist, are a different issue; this is considered briefly later in the book).

The next section of the data-sheet for each report contains information on the *sum of money* (or *value of goods*) involved and the *punishment* given. The thorny problem of disaggregation arises. Occasionally, a case will be reported in which a number of individuals and their respective punishments will be listed, but in which the loss to the state as a result of their crimes is given in aggregate. The decision taken here was to assume that, in the absence of any alternative indication, judges (broadly understood to include members of investigative committees as well as professional judges) have acted as if all defendants should be held equally responsible for the total loss rather than for a proportion of it. The justification for this decision is the mode of reporting by communists themselves. This is to say that if individuals are named but the loss is aggregated – perhaps because it is impossible or perceived as unjust for the authorities to apportion blame – then it seems reasonable to assume that the perception of the judges has been of the aggregate crime and that they have acted accordingly.

Each data-sheet also has a section at the end for 'other observations'. The sorts of information inserted here include whether or not there are other reports of this case, and whether there is other information in the report of relevance to the present study (such as details of new anti-corruption legislation, a definition of corruption, crime statistics, etc.). The latter information is mostly not included in the findings of this chapter, but is incorporated elsewhere in the book.

The reader may feel by this stage that the doubts expressed at the beginning of this chapter should indeed have led to the abandonment of any attempt at aggregate statistical analysis. But, as already argued, such a conclusion is overly pessimistic. The vast majority of cases classified do not require the 'guesstimates' and somewhat arbitrary decisions discussed above. There is a great deal of hard data available from both the USSR and the PRC on corruption, and if we are at least to *begin* to detect patterns, it is imperative that these data be maximally exploited. I have highlighted problems both for the sake of honesty and in order that the reader treat the following statistics with caution and not fetishize apparently 'scientific' research. Conversely, the reader must not gain the impression that *most* of the reports are highly problematic; had they been, I would not have proceeded with this part of the research. Moreover, it must be acknowledged that although the findings cannot be conclusive, nor are they necessarily incorrect. They can serve as a rough guideline until such time – should this ever come – as full details of all cases of corruption investigated become available. After all, many – perhaps even most – collections of data in social science research are problematic, deficient and to some extent subjective; if we were to be deterred each time we found a data gap, for instance, our understanding of social problems, which is a first step to overcoming these problems, would improve far more slowly.

Having decided that it was worth subjecting the data to statistical analysis, each variable had to be classified at the nominal, ordinal, interval or ratio level. At the outset, it had been hoped to be able to run complex correlation or regression analyses, which normally require at least interval-level variables. Unfortunately, such analysis proved not to be feasible. In the case of those variables that could be classified at the interval level (such as sum of money/value of goods involved), there were insufficient cases with adequate data to render analysis viable. Conversely, the variables for which we have complete or near-complete data (such as on locational distribution) cannot justifiably be classified at a level appropriate for correlation or regression analysis.[7] Thus, unfortunately, correlation and regression analysis of this data set proved to be inappropriate. But cross-tabulation was appropriate, as were various modes of sub-setting. The results of such computations, plus interpretations of these, form the basis of the next section.

The Findings

Number of Reports and Cases

Some readers may initially be surprised at the *relatively* small number of reports of corruption that were discovered; the principal reason for this is almost certainly because much narrower definitions of 'corruption' and 'official' have been used in this study than in most Western analyses of corruption, economic crime, abuse of office, graft, etc. In the case of the PRC, a total of 387 media reports were discovered; these involved 351 clearly identified individuals plus 48 groups of individuals (for the sake of clarity, aggregated numbers of individuals and groups are termed 'instances', to distinguish them from 'reports' and 'cases'). The groups have only been included in computations where this seems warranted; given the lack of information in the vast majority of cases on the size of the group, they have – regrettably – had to be coded simply as instances of 'more than one person'. In the years 1966–77, there were no years in which the number of reports reached double figures; in fact, there were no instances of the number exceeding 2. During this period, there were many general criticisms of corruption (see, for example, the article by Yang Gaochao and Qi Cheng in *RMRB*, 27 December 1969; one of the oft-repeated clichés in the press was the reference to the 'sugar-coated bullets' of bourgeois ways of thinking – see, for example, *RMRB*, 23 April 1975), but almost no actual cases cited. Indeed, many of the charges of 'corruption' were essentially figurative, and – during the era of the GPCR – officials could be accused of 'being corrupt' merely for espousing a political view that differed from Mao's. The first real 'jump' occurred in 1978 – not long after Mao's death – when there were 36 reports (13 in *RMRB*); the findings are summarized in table 4.1 below.

In only five years – 1980, 1982, 1983, 1985 and 1986 – did the number of reports clearly exceed 40; however, it seems highly probable that this was also the case for 1984. There has thus unquestionably been a substantial increase in the reporting of official corruption in the Chinese media, with 1982 (82 reports – with 40 in *RMRB* alone) being the peak year, reflective of the leadership's anti-corruption campaign. This said, the sudden leap in reporting came in 1978 – not following 1980, as some Chinese leaders have suggested. Although it would be unwise to draw too firm a conclusion on the basis of only one case of major leadership change (Mao died in September 1976, while Deng had clearly started his consolidation of power by 1978), it is interesting to note an *apparent* correlation between change of leadership and a marked change in the reporting of official corruption in the PRC.

A somewhat similar, though less extreme, pattern can be found in the Soviet reporting (see table 4.2). A total of 272 unambiguous reports was discovered; these involved 462 clearly identified individuals plus 66 groups of individuals; the latter have been treated in the same way as the Chinese groups. There was no example in the

Table 4.1   Number of reports of corruption per year in the Chinese media

Year	Number of reports	0–9	10–19	20–9	30–9	40–9	50+
1966		X					
1967		X					
1968		X					
1969		X					
1970		X					
1971		X					
1972		X					
1973		X					
1974		X					
1975		X					
1976		X					
1977		X					
1978					X		
1979				X			
1980						X	
1981				X			
1982							X
1983						X	
1984					X[a]		
1985						X[a]	
1986						X[a]	

[a] This figure is a *minimum* one, since not all reports in *RMRB* have been recorded, see text (pp. 126–7) for further explanation.

late 1960s of the number of reports reaching double figures, the lowest years being 1966 and 1968 (2 and 1 report(s) respectively).

The situation changed marginally in the 1970s, with the total number of reports being just into double figures in four years of that decade (1974, 1975, 1977, 1979). The highest number of reports in any one year of the 1970s was in 1975 (13 reports); this relates to the anti-corruption campaign mounted in several of the Central Asian and Caucasian republics in the early to mid-1970s (see chapter 7). The big increase in reporting comes in the early 1980s. Whereas 1980 and 1981 were very much in line with the 1970s (at 8 and 12 reports respectively), the figure rises to 14 in 1982 – the year in which Andropov replaced Brezhnev – and then increases substantially, to 35, in 1983. Interestingly, the number of reports in 1984 was exactly the same as in 1983. This could mean that the Chernenko team encouraged reporting of corruption just as much as Andropov did.

Table 4.2 Number of reports of corruption per year in the Soviet media

Year	Number of reports	0–5	6–10	11–15	16–20	21–5	26–30	>30
1966		X						
1967			X					
1968		X						
1969			X					
1970			X					
1971		X						
1972			X					
1973		X						
1974			X					
1975				X				
1976		X						
1977				X				
1978			X					
1979				X				
1980			X					
1981				X				
1982				X				
1983								X
1984								X
1985					X			
1986								X
1987					X			

On the other hand, it could be that this phenomenon is best explained by 'lag' – that is, that it took time for many of the investigations of corruption encouraged by Andropov to be completed and reported on. Even if this is the case, however, it is clear that there was no major clampdown on reporting during the Chernenko era. This finding is thus out of line with the view that the Chernenko era reversed the Andropov initiatives and represented a return to Brezhnevism.

In the year in which Gorbachev took power, there was a substantial *drop* (to 20) in the number of newspaper reports on official corruption (although this figure is still far higher than any in the period up to 1982). This might be explained by the 'lag' argument cited above; while Chernenko did not clamp down immediately, he may have encouraged a winding down of investigative reporting. This interpretation would be compatible with the big rise again in 1986, when there were another 35 reports; such an increase would tend to endorse the argument of those who maintain that Gorbachev emulated many of the policies of Andropov. It is thus particularly interesting that there was another substantial *reduction* in reporting – again to 20 – in 1987. On the basis of our data, and given the post-1987 change noted in note 3, it is not possible to say whether or not this represented an intended long-term trend under Gorbachev. Moreover, if we consider only *Pravda* reports, the pattern – while still clear – is less marked (7 reports in 1985, 20 reports in 1986, 13 reports in 1987). Nevertheless, if all this *was* symptomatic of a changed attitude at the top towards the reporting of corruption, then it could be argued that Gorbachev began to feel that too much reporting of official corruption might be dysfunctional in a period of *general* destabilization (represented by *perestroika* and *glasnost*); in a period of crisis, it is probably better to limit attacks on the 'staffs'. An alternative explanation is that there were so many other problems that he placed less emphasis on official corruption. A third possibility relates to the point about greater *glasnost* in the late 1980s, and shifts the focus away from the leadership's own intentions. The suggestion here is that Soviet journalists were so keen to investigate problem-areas which for years had been taboo that there was less interest on their part in official corruption. This argument would be compatible with the hypothesis – already intimated – that the Soviet leadership was in any case playing a less direct and directive role in the media in the late 1980s. Since all such speculation is based on only one year, however, it seems inappropriate either to prioritize explanations of the apparent change, or to make too much of it.

Let us now turn to consider the number of *cases* reported each year, as distinct from the number of reports.

In the PRC, there were again very few cases indeed reported in the later Mao era. The pattern of number of cases thereafter closely parallels the number of media reports. Thus the big jump comes in 1978; whereas, using our narrow definition of corruption, we could find a report on only one case of official corruption in 1977, 27 were publicized in 1978. The boom year was again 1982, when no fewer than 50 cases found their way into the media. Bearing in mind that the data on *RMRB* for 1984–6 are incomplete, it is interesting that the numbers remained relatively high for the rest of the period under investigation – at 27, 21 and 36 for the years 1984–6 respectively. Clearly, the Chinese campaign maintained steam.

Turning to the USSR, we find that the number of cases reported on there is also close to the number of media reports. Thus 1975 was the 'boom' year of the 1970s, with 22 cases reported; the next closest year was 1977, with a total of 13 cases. In the 1980s, there was a big increase in the number of cases. Whereas there were only 11 cases cited in 1981, this figure had shot up to 36 by 1983 and 44 by 1984. Interestingly, although the number of *reports* declined substantially in 1985, the number of cases cited dropped far less – to 32. In both 1986 and 1987 there were in fact *fewer* cases than reports (the number of cases was 30 and 13 respectively); this is explained by the fact that there were more follow-up reports than there had tended to be in the past.

Types of Official Cited

The salient features to emerge from the Chinese data are the following:

1   The group most frequently cited in reports of official corruption since reporting really 'took off' (that is, since 1978) is party officials. Of approximately 400 instances identified since then, the majority – 57.6 per cent – have included at least one corrupt party official.
2   State bureaucrats were the second largest group, accounting for 41.6 per cent of all instances.
3   There have been very few elected representatives (group 2 – only 2 per cent of all instances) or military officials (again 2 per cent) reported on, while only 6.8 per cent of all instances have been 'officers of the law'; as will shortly be demonstrated, this last feature is very different from the situation in the USSR.[8]

The four most interesting points to emerge from the Soviet data are the following:

1   If we consider *all* instances of corruption over the period 1966–87 the group that heads the list is state bureaucrats; these are followed by – in order – party officials, officers of the law, elected representatives, group 6 officials and military officers.
2   The group most frequently cited in reports of official corruption in the 1970s was 'officers of the law'. In the period 1966–79, for example, 59 of the total 156 instances identified (almost 38 per cent) were 'officers of the law'. These were followed by 'state bureaucrats' (almost 31 per cent of instances) and party officials (over 20 per cent). In the 1980s, the picture changes dramatically, with state bureaucrats being far and away the largest group. Thus, of 372 instances clearly

identified in the period 1980–7, 154 (over 41 per cent) were state bureaucrats. These were followed by party officials (just over 30 per cent), while 'officers of the law' accounted for under 15 per cent of instances.

3   Although state bureaucrats were the group most frequently reported on in the 1980s, a closer analysis of the data reveals that an interesting change occurred in the early Gorbachev era. Thus, there was not a single year in the period 1980–5 in which there was anywhere near as much reporting on corrupt party officials as on state bureaucrats. But in 1986, 41 instances of party officials were reported on, compared with only 17 of state bureaucrats; the respective figures for 1985 had been 14 and 25. Although the overall *numbers* declined in 1987, the relationship stayed the same as in 1986, with 13 instances of party officials being reported on and only 8 of state bureaucrats. If the imperfect methodology used for this chapter is reflective of the actuality of media reporting of official corruption, it certainly appears that party officials were singled out for particular attack (or, in less loaded language, investigation and report) in the early Gorbachev era.

4   Only one group was not cited at all until 1985 – the military. This might be simply because the Soviet military – probably like most military establishments – was far less prone to corruption than are civilians. But there could be other explanations; the notion that there was *no* corruption at all in the Soviet military until the 1980s, given the scales both of the military establishment and of economic crime generally in the USSR, seems highly implausible.[9] The most likely explanations are that the civilian authorities were wary of mounting major public attacks on the military, and that the military looked after its own house and did not encourage – perhaps even allow – the media to investigate its activities. These two explanations are not mutually exclusive, of course. It should be noted that only three instances of military corruption in the period 1985–7 were found; thus, although this represented a new development, we must be careful to keep its significance in perspective. One final point to note here is that a number of Soviet citizens with whom I raised this issue in discussions held in 1989 stated that 'corruption' was rapidly spreading in the Soviet military in the late 1980s. The most disturbing point is that some of my interviewees claimed it had become very easy to buy military weapons (especially rifles) on the black market. It is not clear whether or not many officers (that is, the military personnel included here as 'officials') were involved in this, and hence whether this was or was not corruption in the particular terms of this study. But the phenomenon is potentially very serious, since

two Soviet interviewees – quite independently of each other – claimed that this was a relatively new development that would make civil war that much more feasible in their country (or its successors).

Level of Officials Cited

Unfortunately, the period in which one would expect there to have been the most marked change of focus in Chinese reporting – proportionately, away from lower-ranking and towards higher officials – falls outside the scope of the systematic research engaged in for this chapter. It was only about 1986 that the call clearly and strongly went out from the senior leadership for citizens to pass on information concerning corrupt high-ranking cadres. Thus, while it can be said that there *should* have been a marked increase in the reporting of corruption among such officials in the latter half of the 1980s (at least until June 1989, following which the authorities may have decided that excessive emphasis on the corruption of senior officers would be dysfunctional), it is not at present possible to state on the basis of systematic empirical research whether or not this actually happened.

Apart from this absence of data for the late 1980s, one problem that arose in attempting to classify Chinese officials by 'level' is that it was in many cases not possible clearly to distinguish between 'workplace' and 'local' (low-ranking) officials. In the analysis that follows, therefore, these two lowest categories have been collapsed into one. Although this is unfortunate, it is still possible to distinguish this aggregated category from middle- and high-ranking officials – which, for the purposes of the argument in this book, is a more important division. Let us now examine the findings.

Until the 1980s, it seems, no detailed cases of corruption among high-ranking officials were reported in the Chinese press. This changed in 1980, when 3 instances were reported. This figure remained fairly stable – averaging 2–3 per annum – until 1986, when it suddenly increased to 6; this is in line with the 1986 changes in leadership approach. In percentage terms, this increase looks more dramatic – climbing from 4.4 per cent of identified instances in 1985 to 10.7 per cent in 1986 (for the record, the level of officials in 6.3 per cent of all instances 1966–86 could not be identified). Of course, the actual numbers are small, so that one should be wary of making too much of these data. On the other hand, if the data on high- and middle-ranking officials are collapsed and this aggregate figure is compared with that for local and workplace officials in the individual years, the pattern is not only at least as striking, but also – in that the actual number of instances is greater – that much more convincing as evidence for the argument put forward in this book. Thus, in 1978 – the year Chinese reporting 'took off' – there were only 3 instances of high- and middle-ranking corrupt officials reported in the media, compared with 36 local and workplace instances. Expressed another way, there were 12 times as many cases of the latter as of the former. In 1980, the proportions were rather similar, with 4 instances of high- and middle-ranking officials, compared with 46 instances of local and workplace officials. By 1982, the ratio had declined markedly to a little over 5 : 1 (53 local/workplace instances, 10 high- and middle-ranking instances), while in 1986 it was down to below 2 : 1 (34 local/workplace instances to 19 high- and middle-level instances). In percentage terms, corrupt high- and middle-ranking officials accounted for 7.3 per cent of reported instances in 1978, 8 per cent in 1980, 15.1 per cent in 1982 and 33.9 per cent in 1986. For all the rubberiness of our data, there can be little doubt that a major change in media targetting had occurred.

The Soviet data are somewhat less problematic than the Chinese, and can be presented in less aggregated form. Just as there was a change of focus in the USSR in the 1980s – away from officers of the law through state bureaucrats in the early 1980s to party officials under Gorbachev – so there was a clear and interesting development in terms of the level of officials being reported on. Thus we were able to find instances of only 4 high-ranking staff officials in the whole of the period 1966–79. In contrast, there were reports on 37 such officials in the period 1980–7 – a substantial increase by any criteria, even more so bearing in mind that the latter period is only just over one half as long as the former period. Similarly, whereas there were only 30 republican- (middle-) level instances 1966–79, 95 such individuals or groups were publicly disgraced 1980–7. If we take leadership 'reigns' instead of decades as our break-points, the picture is at least as interesting. Thus, only 11 instances of high-ranking staff officials were reported on in the 17-year period 1966–82, compared with 30 in the five years 1983–7; at the republican level, for the respective periods, the figures are 52 and 73. This said, the number of instances of republican-level officials reported on grew substantially in 1986 and 1987 (at 26 and 19 respectively) in comparison with the period 1983–5 (at 9, 9 and 10), while central-level figures stood at only 4 and 1 in 1986 and 1987, compared with 8, 10 and 7 in the years 1983–5. Clearly, then, there was some shift in the early Gorbachev era away from very high-ranking officials towards the middle-ranking level. The findings strongly endorse the hypothesis (see, for example, Shelley, 1988, p. 203) that campaigns against official corruption in the USSR were targetting higher-ranking officials in the 1980s, although, as just indicated, there was somewhat less emphasis on the highest levels in the early years of the Gorbachev era and considerably more stress on the republican level.

Finally, aggregating of the data to produce figures directly comparable to the Chinese ones yields some interesting results. Thus, if we aggregate the number of instances of high- and middle-ranking corrupt officials being reported in various years, we obtain the following pictures: 1966 – 100 per cent of all identified cases (*but* N = 2, so that this statistic is of very little significance); 1970 – 41.2 per cent (N = 17); 1975 – 15.6 per cent (N = 32); 1980 – 11.1 per cent (N = 18); 1982 – 42 per cent (N = 31); 1984 – 26 per cent (N = 73); 1986 – 38.4 per cent (N = 78); 1987 – 57.2 per cent (N = 35).

Types of Corruption

Too many reports of corruption provided insufficiently precise details on the type of corruption to justify supplying figures in this section. Rather, I shall provide an impressionistic overview, based on an analysis of the reports that did supply adequate information on the type of corruption.

In China, easily the largest number of cases were of embezzlement, although 'improper use of socialized property' was also a very large category. These were followed by forging of documents and accepting bribes; speculation and smuggling were also popular. Interestingly, false reporting was not a major form of corruption; there were considerably more cases of understatement than of overstatement. Although there were many cases of nepotism, there were relatively few cases of patronage based on shared experience or interests. We found no clear-cut cases of deception of supplicants by officials, and very few cases of blackmail, not earning one's salary, or treason.

There are several striking similarities between the Soviet and the Chinese data. Thus bribe-taking and embezzlement were easily the most frequently committed acts of corruption in the USSR – although there were more cases involving the former than the latter. Nepotism in the USSR, as in China, was more frequent than cronyism, and there were very few cases of blackmail, not earning one's salary or treason. On the other hand, there were proportionately more cases of extortion in the USSR, and far more cases of report padding (false reporting – overstatement). There appears to have been much less 'improper use of socialized property' by Soviet officials, and far less smuggling or speculation. It seems reasonable to infer that the last two kinds of corruption do indeed relate to economic policy; the 'open door' policy since the late 1970s is almost certainly the major reason why smuggling and speculation have been so common in the PRC in recent years, in comparison with the USSR.

Temporal and Locational Distribution

The data on when acts of corruption were committed in China are very incomplete, and should be treated with particular caution; of 271 cases of corruption identified, we were able to determine either the year (in the case of a one-off act) or the starting year (in the case of individuals or groups being corrupt over a period of time) in only just over half the cases (148). This said, if our incomplete data are an indication of the actual state of affairs, they produce a very interesting picture.

Of the 148 cases, 74 – exactly 50 per cent – started in 1979 or earlier. Given that reporting really only 'took off' in 1978 – so that most reports date from that year or later – one might have expected a higher percentage of cases in the later years. Considering the data from another perspective, of the 27 cases reported in the Chinese media in 1978 (that is, *before* the economic reforms), the (starting) date was given in 14; of these, 7 had commenced in the three-year period 1976–8. An examination of the 1986 data reveals that the (starting) date was given for 20 out of 36 cases; of these, 11 had commenced in the three-year period 1984–6. In 1983 – the last year for which a full analysis of *Renmin Ribao* is available – the total number of cases reported was 31; temporal information is available on 13 cases, of which 7 had commenced in the three-year period 1981–3. In sum, the picture looks remarkably similar in all three years considered.

As might be expected, the figures can be calculated in a different way, to create a rather different picture. This happens if we consider the percentage of cases reported on in the 1980s that started at or after the end of the 1970s. Thus, of the 20 cases in 1986 for which details are available, 16 (80 per cent) had started since the beginning of 1980. But I would argue that this is roughly what would be expected in any period of investigation and reporting, and that it does not undermine the interesting impressions generated by the first two methods. On the basis of our incomplete data, therefore, and not forgetting that we are concerned only with officials, the validity of the charges that leaders such as Chen Yun have made – that the economic reforms introduced at the end of the 1970s led to a substantial increase in corruption (in its broad sense, not *only* among officials) – can at least be questioned.

In the case of the USSR, we were able to determine the starting date for corrupt acts in only 24 of the 291 cases identified; this is far too small a proportion from which to make even tentative inferences.

Other commentators (see, for example, Liu, 1983, pp. 606–15; Feldbrugge, 1984, *passim*, esp. pp. 541–2; Critchlow, 1988, esp. p. 143) have already noted that some parts of China and the USSR have apparently – based on reports – been more corrupt than others. However, given the narrower definition of corruption adopted in this study, and the longer period analysed, it is interesting to compare the results obtained from our research with those of analysts using different definitions.

Considering China first, there have been considerably more cases of corruption in Guangdong Province reported than from any other part of China. A total of 38 cases of corruption in Guangdong were discovered, compared with 19 in Henan, 15 in Jilin, 13 in Heilongjiang and Beijing, and 11 in Fujian. Since corruption was hardly reported on in China until the late 1970s, it is not possible to answer with any confidence the question of whether corruption has increased more in border areas and areas of special economic development than elsewhere; this said, the greatest concentrations of corruption do *seem* to be in the areas adjacent to Hong Kong, in Henan, and in the North-East. At the other end of the spectrum are the parts of China from which very few cases have been reported. Autonomous Regions (ARs) figure strongly in this group. Thus only 1 case was found of official corruption in Tibet (Xizang), while there were 4 cases in Xinjiang, and 5 cases each in Inner Mongolia and Guangxi; no cases of corruption in Ningxia were discovered. Other areas with very few cases reported include Shandong, Qinghai, Jiangsu and Guizhou. It should be noted in concluding this Chinese section that the findings of this study are broadly similar to Liu's (1983), despite differences of definition and methodology; Liu provides very detailed analyses – which are beyond the scope of this study – of the possible reasons for high or low rates of corruption in individual provinces and regions.

In the case of the USSR, too, the results of this research are broadly in line with the findings of those who have studied corruption using different definitions and methodologies. On the basis of the republics in which reported crimes were committed, the RSFSR comes top, accounting for over 25 per cent of cases of corruption. This is hardly surprising, given both the size of the population of Russia itself and the fact that so many ministries were located in Moscow; to the extent that the figure causes any surprise, it should be because it is not higher. Second – at 15.5 per cent – is Azerbaijan; the dubious 'honours' of third, fourth and fifth places go to Uzbekistan (12 per cent), Georgia (8.2 per cent) and the Ukraine (5.8 per cent). Sixth equal, at 5.5 per cent of reported cases each, are Kazakhstan and Kirghizia. With the exception of the RSFSR, then, the reporting of corruption would suggest that corruption has been most highly concentrated in some of the Central Asian and Transcaucasian republics, particularly in Islamic areas (this is in line with Feldbrugge's findings – 1984, esp. p. 541). The republics *apparently* least prone to corruption were the three Baltic states (Estonia, Latvia and Lithuania) and Byelorussia (all at 0.7 per cent of cases), and – surprisingly perhaps – Tadzhikistan (0.3 per cent). If we create a subset and consider the period 1983–7 (that is, post-Brezhnev), the position changes, though not dramatically. Thus the RSFSR still has the highest number of cases cited in the press (at 29 per cent), followed by Uzbekistan (21.3 per cent), Kirghizia (9.7 per cent), Kazakhstan (6.5 per cent) and Georgia (5.8 per cent); these findings are broadly similar to Critchlow's (1988, *passim*). Only 5 cases were reported from Azerbaijan in the period, so that it dropped to seventh place (just below the Ukraine). Once again, Tadzhikistan and the Baltic States – this time together with Armenia – were at the bottom of the list, just below Byelorussia and Turkmenia.

It is tempting to make correlations between levels of corruption and, for instance, standards of living. Thus the Baltic states had among the highest standards of living and seem to have had the lowest incidence of corruption. However, such a correlation does not work well across the full range of republics; living standards in Tadzhikistan were among the lowest in the USSR, while those in Armenia were well below average. Moreover, cultural attitudes could well explain differences at least as well as any readily quantifiable variable, such as level of income. Finally, we must never forget that all that is being analysed here is *reported* corruption; this may or may not correlate closely with *actual* corruption. If it does not – and there is no way of knowing this – then it is even more questionable to make correlations.

It is worth noting in parenthesis that the Soviets themselves had by the 1980s become very interested in regional differences in crime rates (*all* crimes – not just corruption). One of the findings to emerge from such research that is of particular interest for the present study is that 'crimes of office' in Georgia occur mainly in the urban areas (see *CDSP*, Vol. 36, No. 20, p. 17). While this is hardly surprising, it is interesting that Soviet criminologists were themselves recently attempting to explain differences in crime rates across and within republics.

Value of Goods/Money and Punishments

The very incomplete data available suggest *some* correlation between the value of goods/money involved in a particular case and the punishment meted out. However, a number of complications make it impossible to draw even tentative causal inferences on the basis of these weak correlations. Since this dimension of the analysis ultimately relates to official reactions, the elaboration of these complications is more appropriately dealt with in chapter 7.

On the Scale of Corruption

It should be self-evident that it is quite impossible to measure the scale of official corruption in *any* state, not just communist ones. Even assuming there could be agreement on the meaning of the term 'official' and 'corruption', those engaging in the latter normally do so in a clandestine manner and do not want others to be aware of their activity. The very most one could hope to measure would be the scale of investigation and reporting of corruption. But even this has been extremely difficult in the case of communist states, for a number of reasons.

The major reason is that it was only very recently that some countries started publishing reasonably comprehensive crime statistics – a prerequisite for an analysis of *detected* corruption, at least. Notably, the USSR only began to publish such statistics in 1988 (see, for example, *NT*, No. 9, 1989, pp. 30–1), despite various pleas before this (see, for example, A. Vaksberg's criticisms in *Literaturnaya Gazeta*, 17 December 1986, p. 13). Thus, while analysts such as Lampert (1984, p. 376) are to be congratulated on their innovative approach in forming an impression of, for instance, the number of Soviet convictions per annum for 'corruption', such methodologies must be treated cautiously.

A second reason has been highlighted by Shelley (1988, p. 202, citing van den Berg, 1985, p. 61), who writes: 'prosecutions in this area [official and economic crime in the USSR] are very much affected by political circumstances'. The point is that the investigative and prosecution process, following whistle-blowing and other reasons why the authorities should examine possible cases of corruption, varies considerably according to whether the higher authorities *want* to know about and publicize the misdemeanours of their own officers or not. While this factor can apply to some extent in liberal democracies, too, the much greater freedom of the media in the latter means this is less pronounced than in communist states.

Third, it would in some ways be useful to study court reports – as Lampert, *inter alia*, has done. But there are three drawbacks to this method for the present study. The first is the purely practical one of time and access; however, this could have been overcome had the effort seemed worthwhile. But access to records of court proceedings has been partial for most (all?) communist states, so that we would ultimately still be dealing with impressions. Finally, in that the approach adopted in this study focuses on the *perceptions* of ordinary citizens, mass media reports are far more likely to steer us in the right direction than are relatively inaccessible law reports.

In view of all these problems, all we can hope to do is to form a very impressionistic image – which could well be misleading – both of the scale of corruption itself, and of the level of its detection. For what they are worth, it is of interest to note some of the pieces of the jigsaw that have been revealed in the Soviet and Chinese media; at the very least, such isolated reports can help us to form some impression of whether *perceptions* in these two communist states have been/were that corruption and related phenomena (such as economic crime) are/were increasing or decreasing.

Starting with the USSR, the author of an article that was published in *Sotsialisticheskaya Zakonnost'* (No. 1, 1978, pp. 54–6 – in *CDSP*, Vol. 30, No. 11, p. 13) claimed that the number of 'crimes of office' had declined by 85 per cent in the period 1967–77; whether this was true, or whether it merely reflected the 'stagnation' (that is, self-satisfaction and relative inactivity of the authorities) of the later Brezhnev era, cannot be determined. Certainly, as *glasnost* spread under Gorbachev, so more and more details on the extent of economic crime and corruption in the USSR became available. For instance, Soviet Procurator-General A. Rekunkov revealed in June 1986 that approximately 250,000 cases were discovered in the Soviet Union each year of state-owned vehicles being used for purposes other than those for which they were intended – mostly for reasons of personal gain (*Izvestiya*, 2 June 1986, p. 3). In the following March, Rekunkov revealed that some 200,000 individuals had been investigated in recent times for corruption (*The Australian*, 31 March

1987). In July 1987, the Ministry of Internal Affairs held a briefing session for the Soviet press. At this, three senior officials – including the first deputy director of the Chief Administration for Combatting the Embezzlement of Socialist Property and Speculation, K.V. Kosterin – answered questions on Soviet crime put to them by media representatives. So many details were revealed at this (see *Izvestiya*, 27 July 1987, p. 4) that only a selection can be included here. Thus it was revealed that speculation was growing (though no statistics on significant cases of this were provided), while embezzlement of socialist property, abuses and mismanagement, mostly by accounting personnel at the executive level, accounted for over one half of total losses in the economy. At that time, black marketeering accounted for 17 per cent of all reported crimes that had been investigated.

In the (northern) spring of 1989, the State Bank and the Ministry of Internal Affairs organized what was described as the first ever public discussion of the Soviet 'shadow economy'. It was emphasized at this meeting just how difficult it is to quantify the shadow economy. In order to give some idea of the range of figures generated by the use of different definitions and methodologies, three estimates of the amount of money circulating in the shadow economy – 5, 40 and 150 billion rubles – were cited (*MN*, No. 15, 1989, p. 12 – see too *MN*, No. 13, 1989, p. 12). Another estimate of the size of the Soviet 'shadow economy' appeared in an October 1989 issue of *New Times* (No. 42, pp. 32–4). In that, N. Andreyev revealed that 'experts' had calculated that the capital circulating in the shadow economy amounted to between 17 and 25 per cent of the national income, according to whether one accepts figures of 100 or 150 billion rubles (these figures are the same as those cited by A. Bunich, in *MN*, No. 13, 1989, p. 12, although the latter appear to be based on *Western* estimates; T. Koryagina – cited by Bunich – has provided a more conservative estimate of 80 billion rubles). Andreyev further argued that the shadow economy had higher growth rates than any branch of the (official) national economy had ever achieved – and that organized crime (a phenomenon that is beyond the scope of this study unless officials are explicitly involved) had been increasing since the early 1980s. One final statistic on the USSR is that the number of reported cases of bribery (involving both officials and ordinary citizens – disaggregated data do not appear to be available) increased by 9 per cent in 1990 in comparison with the 1989 figure; while this represented a fairly substantial increase, it was actually lower than the overall increase in reported crimes – which were up 13.2 per cent (data from *Pravda*, 15 February 1991, p. 6).

Even more data are available for forming some impression of the scale of corruption, and economic crime more generally, in the PRC than in the USSR. In 1979, the number of cases of smuggling detected – at 13,400 – represented an increase of 41 per cent over the 1978 figure; but in the first 18 months of the 1980s, the number of cases increased even more dramatically, with the annual average for 1980 and the first six months of 1981 running at 30,000. The value of goods involved in the 1979 smuggling cases was 7.3 million yuan, approximately three times the 1978 figure. But then the figure shot up to over 100 million yuan for the 18-month period January 1980–June 1981, giving an annual average of over 66 million yuan. Expressed another way, the value of goods smuggled had increased by a factor of approximately 27 in only two years (all figures from *SWB*/FE/6413/BII/13–14 and *BR*, No. 39, 1981, p. 8 – cited in Forster, 1985, p. 7).

In February 1983, the Central Discipline Inspection Commission (CDIC) met to assess the results of the 1982 campaign against economic crime, and revealed that 164,000 cases had been uncovered, of which 86,000 had been resolved. Some 30,000 offenders were in prison as a result of the campaign, while five and a half thousand CCP members had been expelled from the party; cash and goods to the value of 320 million yuan had been recovered (*RMRB*, 5 February 1983 – cited in Forster, 1985, p. 15). According to a Taiwanese source, the CDIC revealed two years later that a total of one million criminal cases of all sorts had come to light since the beginning of 1984. Most of these cases involved 'ideological degeneration' and corruption; a staggering 67 per cent of cases involved CCP members, although it is unclear what proportion of these would be officials in our terms, or how many crimes would constitute corruption (all data cited in Yeh, 1987, p. 13). A somewhat more precise picture, focusing on *economic* crime, was provided by the president of Beijing's Supreme People's Court in January 1986 (*Guangming Ribao*, 15 January 1986, p. 4 – cited in Yeh, 1987, p. 13). In 1982, courts at all levels in the PRC handled 35,176 cases of economic crime; this figure rose to 51,486 in 1983, declined to 36,625 in 1984, then increased again to 48,400 in 1985. These figures exclude all cases not dealt with by the courts, notably those handled exclusively by the CCP.

One of several indications of the rubberiness of many PRC statistics is that, according to Yeh (1987, pp. 18–19), two members of the Politburo provided – in the same year, 1986 – widely divergent estimates of the number of CCP members punished both by the courts and by the CCP itself for all kinds of crime. Thus Yu Qiuli put the figure at approximately half a million, whereas Hu Qili provided a far more conservative estimate of '80–120,000'. Whether this discrepancy reflected differences of interpretation, different time-frames, the different political stances of the two politicians (that is, wanting to create different images), or merely how essentially arbitrary such figures are, is unclear. However, it serves to endorse the argument that many statistics from the communist world should be treated with caution rather than as authoritative; as is being done here, they should in many instances be used only for creating general impressions.

The 'peak period' of economic crime in China apparently occurred from the second half of 1984 to the first half of 1985 (*CD*, 3 February 1988, p. 1). During this period, the local head of the CDIC in Beijing, Meng Zhiyuan, reported (in May 1985) that 563 CCP members and government officials had been disciplined recently for illegal involvement in private businesses. There were many cases of party members moonlighting; 460 cases of this had been proven. Among those penalized were 64 'senior officials', who had been 'earning' up to 500 yuan per month through illegal businesses (all from *CD*, 18 May 1985; as a yardstick, the average monthly earnings in Beijing at that time were 60 yuan). The problem of officials being involved in illegal businesses had become quite a serious one by the mid-1980s. Thus, early in 1986, *Newsweek* (3 February, p. 14) referred to a recent PRC government report that stated that more than 67,000 party and government officials were involved in nearly 28,000 illegal businesses.

In mid-1987, the Chinese newspaper *Economic Daily* reported that the people's procuratorates at all levels had been dealing with 22,740 cases involving economic offences in the 'first months' – these are not specified – of 1987. Of these, prosecutions had begun in 10,758 cases, and 1,552 cases involved bribes. A total of 185 CCP members had been arrested in this period for accepting bribes and had been expelled from the party (all from *CD*, 14 July 1987). During the whole of 1987, Beijing local courts handled more than 5,500 criminal cases. While this number represented a decrease in comparison with the previous year of over 9 per cent, the number of cases of civil and economic crimes – especially cases of bribery and embezzlement – increased markedly (*CD*, 27 January 1988, p. 3). At the national level, 59,000 cases of economic crime were filed with the people's procuratorates in 1987 (*CD*, 3 February 1988, p. 1); the number of cases of economic crime coming before the PRC's courts 'increased greatly' on 1986 (to 322,000) at a time when – as in Beijing – the number of criminal cases of all sorts decreased slightly (*CD*, 15

February 1988, p. 1). The minister of supervision, Wei Jianxing, revealed in a 1990 article explicitly on corruption (*BR*, Vol. 33, No. 4, p. 22) that supervisory organs at all levels in the PRC had received 168,700 reports of suspected violations during the first 10 months of 1989; almost 40,000 of those investigated resulted in prosecutions, including 1,200 cadres at the county head level, and 4 provincial governors.

In concluding this section on the scale of corruption – detected, at least – it needs to be emphasized that, even allowing for the considerable rubberiness, incompatibilities and even contradictions in many of the statistics cited, there can be little doubt that the examples of corruption published in the media are but the tip of the iceberg. Moreover, even if we could – somehow – ascertain the number of cases of corruption in a given country in a given year, this still would not tell us how many people feel *affected* by corruption; all we would know is that the number would be far higher than the number of people actually charged with corruption. It is important to bear this point in mind in view of the theoretical framework of this study.

Conclusions

The relative softness of the data generated and analysed in this chapter has been emphasized throughout. Bearing this in mind, and without repeating the detailed findings of each sub-section, what appear to be the salient aspects of the research, and how do the results relate to legitimacy and legitimation?

The first point to make is that, on the basis merely of these data, it might initially appear that I am making a great deal out of relatively little – at least in the case of the USSR (the increases in Chinese reporting are substantial by any criteria); although the Soviet percentage increases are marked, the absolute number (*N*) of reports and cases could be perceived as still relatively small. I would reject the notion that the changes are insignificant, on two grounds. First, it has been shown not only that there has been an increase in numbers, but also that the average *level* of officials being reported on has risen in recent years, and that the main groups targetted have changed markedly (more on the latter point below). Second, although the number of *unambiguous* reports of official corruption in the Soviet press did not increase as dramatically as might have been expected – given leadership statements, for instance – the number of reports that have had to be classified as 'not clearly corruption' is not insubstantial, and increased in the 1980s. There were 121 such Soviet reports in the 1980s, with a mean annual average of 15.1 (compared with an annual average in the 1970s of 12.1); if one considers only the period from the beginning of 1983 – the first complete 'post-Brezhnev' year – then the annual average rises markedly, to 20.6. It is almost certain from the contexts that many Soviet reports of official 'abuse of office' should be classified as corruption by our criteria; in the absence of sufficiently unambiguous information, however, such reports have been excluded from the analyses in this chapter.

Thus the reporting of official corruption did increase significantly in both the PRC and the USSR in the 1980s – though the process had already begun in the late 1970s in the case of China. Although the patterns of reporting vary somewhat in the two countries, there is too much similarity of basics for us not to be drawn towards the conclusion that similar processes were under way in countries with essentially similar systems but at very different levels of economic development. This does not disprove the notion that there is a correlation between official corruption and levels of economic development, since we are only measuring – imperfectly – the reporting of corruption, as distinct from corruption itself. On the other hand, the detailed discussion of methodological problems in this chapter should, at the very least, highlight the dangers of making unverified and unverifiable assumptions about the relationship between corruption and levels of development.

On the basis of an admittedly very limited number of cases, it does appear that there has been some correlation between increases (and decreases) of reporting and changes of top leaders. On the other hand, the tenuous evidence from the USSR in the 1980s suggests that it might have become easier to initiate a campaign than to limit it; but several more analyses of different kinds of campaign are required before any reasonably firm conclusions on this can be drawn.

The focus of media campaigns, and changes in this focus, in both the PRC and the USSR are interesting. In both countries, for instance, the military has rarely been reported on.[10] Without reiterating the possible reasons for this in detail, it would not be unreasonable to infer that this reflected a conscious policy on the part of the (civilian) leadership, who may have feared the potential backlash of too open or widespread a campaign against military officers. Both the Soviet and Chinese leaderships had reason to be wary of the power of the military, and both had concrete evidence in recent years of dissent within the military. In the PRC, for instance, not only has the official ideology long acknowledged that 'power grows out of the barrel of a gun', but the Beijing massacre of June 1989 appeared to reveal deep divisions within the army that could have threatened the position of either particular groups of civilian leaders or the leadership as a whole.[11] In the USSR, events in Vilnius following the newly elected parliament's declaration of Lithuanian independence in March 1990 suggested that the senior Soviet leadership might not have full control of the military.[12] Thus, a very low level of reporting of military corruption could suggest a sensitivity on the part of the civilian leaders, a fear that their rule might not enjoy a high level of legitimacy among the potentially most dangerous of all staffs.

Conversely, media campaigns in both Deng's China and Gorbachev's Soviet Union (have) targetted party officials more than any other group of officials. This may well reflect a growing perception by the top leadership that the masses become more alienated by corruption among what is supposed to be the most trustworthy, exemplary group – the 'vanguard' – than among any other group. Moreover, if the party is to supervise (*kontrolirovat'*, to use the Russian term) all other groups of officials – for instance, to ensure that the economy performs well for the purposes of eudaemonic legitimation – it must put its own house in order even more than any other group. If this interpretation is correct, it would endorse the argument that the leaders were indeed concerned about popular legitimation. As argued earlier in this book, this is not to say that the acquisition of popular (mass) legitimacy is *more* important to the chiefs than the gaining or maintaining of legitimacy in the eyes of the staffs; to repeat, the argument is that leaderships in recent years became more aware of the possibly dialectical relationship between popular and staff legitimation.[13]

Finally, and leading on from the last two paragraphs, the differential targetting of staffs in both the PRC and the USSR would lend weight to the argument that, in terms of chiefs legitimating themselves and the system to their staffs, some staffs are more important than others. Their varying degrees of importance can be viewed from at least two perspectives – their direct significance (even threat) to the chiefs, and the effects of their interaction with the masses on system and regime legitimacy.

NOTES

1   As noted earlier, the GDR was one such example for nearly the whole period covered by this study. This all changed in November 1989, at a time when the GDR was still communist. Moreover, the campaigns in Cuba at the end of the 1980s were far more significant than those earlier in the decade.

2   The Chinese have recently explicitly stated that 'reportage' – reporting that highlights and criticises specific social problems – has really only developed since 1980 (see *CD*, 28 September 1988, p. 4).

3   Originally, the research for this chapter covered an 18-year period (1966–83) for both the PRC and the USSR. However, a small additional research grant meant that I could choose to have a few more years' worth of primary or intermediate sources 'combed'. I eventually decided that the most interesting analysis would be of the *CDSP* for 1984–7 and of the Chinese section of the *SWB* for 1984–6. This would take the Soviet material well into the Gorbachev era and would make it possible to ascertain whether or not there was a decline in the reporting of corruption in the Gorbachev period in comparison not only with the Andropov but also the Chernenko era. On the other hand, there is at least one major reason why the methodology used for this chapter could probably *not* be applied to the USSR *beyond* 1987; it relates to the emergence and development of *glasnost*. Thus, it could no longer be assumed that the leadership had much direct influence over the direction of investigative journalism and the content of newspaper articles; the greatly expanded variety of views and news coverage in the Soviet press from about 1988, plus statements by journalists and others on the decline of censorship, support this assumption of significant change. In the case of the PRC, the most significant recent leadership changes occurred in 1988 and 1989, so that one would expect any changes to occur *following* these. In the circumstances, I believe the optimal choice has been made – even if it means that one country has been analysed for one year longer than the other and even though 21- and 22-year periods will not appeal to those who prefer their research periods to be in, for example, tidy blocks of quinquennia or decades.

4   As power and authority became more diffused and confused in the USSR by the late 1980s, so the role and status of *Pravda* could be seen to have changed. Expressed crudely, as the 'leading role' of the CPSU came under attack, so the authority of its Central Committee's newspaper declined. By the beginning of the 1990s, it was unclear that *any* Soviet newspaper could be treated as the most authoritative. *Pravda* almost ceased publication altogether early in 1992.

5   It is useful to remind ourselves that the issue of who is and is not a state 'official' is sometimes a difficult one in Western states too. A prime example derives from the West German *Berufsverbot* of the 1970s. Since all state employees were to be treated as state functionaries – and therefore liable to have their political views investigated – the somewhat absurd situation arose whereby train-drivers or postmen/postwomen were treated as potential security risks if they were members of, for instance, a communist party (on this see Cobler, 1978, pp. 33–6). It is to be hoped that one of the more useful aspects of the present study is to highlight the practical difficulties of applying abstract references to 'chiefs', 'staffs' and 'the public' to the realities of complex societies.

6   The Soviet Council of Ministers was replaced by a much smaller Cabinet of Ministers in December 1990 (which itself was dissolved and replaced by the Inter-republic Economic Committee in August 1991 – which in turn was disbanded by the end of 1991); these changes have no significant implications for the present study, however.

7   In an earlier draft of this chapter, I provided a detailed breakdown of the reasons for classifying each variable at a given level. Not only was this highly methodical approach somewhat tedious, but – more importantly – it would in my view have increased the very possibility of overfetishization of rather soft data that I

was so anxious to minimize. It is largely because of the potentially distorting effects on the perception of the data that I have opted not to incorporate a detailed exposition here. Instead, I have included some analysis of the categories within a given variable at what seem to me to be appropriate junctures in this book.

8   The observant will notice that the percentages here add up to more than 100; this is because I am presenting aggregate data that include cases where individuals or groups occupy more than one type of official post. To give the reader some idea of the scale of this 'double-dipping', a total of 64 instances out of 399 referred to an individual or group that was identified as being in two or more of our six official categories. Of these 64, 43 were simultaneously group 1 (party) and group 3 (state bureaucrat) officials. The point about double-counting applies to the Soviet data, too, since these are also presented in terms of 'instances'.

9   See next note.

10   This is true of the major national newspapers. However, it should be noted that the Soviet military did report corruption among its membership in its own main newspaper, *Krasnaya Zvezda* – for details see Jones, 1988, p. 245. The very fact that Jones cites a military newspaper rather than the mainstream press in providing evidence of corruption would tend to support my argument that the military was rarely targetted in the major newspapers. Jones herself states that 'there are no indications that this problem [corruption] is particularly acute in the Armed Forces', and provides explanations, largely in terms of the extensive 'oversight mechanisms' in the military, of why corruption there was on a much smaller scale than in other Soviet agencies and regions.

11   The allusion here is to the alleged conflicts between the 27th and 38th divisions of the People's Liberation Army.

12   Various Western media reports claimed that some of the Soviet military activities in Lithuania following the Lithuanians' declaration of independence had not been sanctioned by the political leadership in Moscow, who may not even have known about some of them in advance. Similar claims were made following the military clampdown in all three Baltic states in early 1991. If these claims are true, they would suggest not merely a breakdown of communication between sections of the military and the civilian leadership, but possible antagonism between them. Certainly, at the time of his surprise resignation in December 1990, Soviet Foreign Minister Eduard Shevardnadze warned of a coming dictatorship in the USSR, and implicitly linked this to elements in the military such as Colonel Alksnis (see *Izvestiya*, 21 December 1990, p. 5). Although Alksnis does not appear to have been involved in the August 1991 coup attempt, the Soviet defence minister, Marshal D. Yazov, certainly *was* one of the ring-leaders. Despite the failure of that attempt, it should not be too readily assumed that the threat from the Soviet (or CIS) military has now been completely removed; the post-coup USSR/CIS is still in a revolutionary situation, and with the collapse of the CPSU, middle-ranking military officers could increasingly feel that they are the only ones who can bring order to the country.

13   Of course, more extensive reporting of corruption among party officials in recent years could also reflect the increasing incidence of such corruption – an explanation that can coexist with that provided in the text. The negative implications for legitimacy of such an increasing deterioration of moral values within 'the vanguard' should be obvious.

5

Reasons for Corruption

The major focus of chapter 6 is the advantages and disadvantages of corruption (and its reporting) to the political order; in this chapter, we concentrate more on the costs and benefits of corruption to the individual or group that engages in it. This said, it is acknowledged that *some* factors included in this chapter could equally well be covered in the next chapter and vice versa. There is a vast range of factors to be covered; purely for the sake of analytical clarity, explanations have been divided here – sometimes rather arbitrarily and artificially – into three categories, viz cultural, general psychological, and more specifically system-related. In the real world, the boundaries between these three are frequently unclear, and others might prefer to locate individual factors under different categories; the most important point is the identification of variables, however, rather than their classification.

Two final opening caveats need to be made. The first is that many of the points raised below have to be speculative, since they are difficult to research empirically – either by their very nature, or because individual communist societies either still are or have until very recently been far less open than they might be. Second, many factors apply to economic crime and 'unofficial' corruption generally as much as to official corruption specifically. Comparatively few factors relate exclusively to officials, since they are part of a larger system within which they operate. In this sense, few of the factors are unique to official corruption; however, to avoid undue repetition, this point is made only once – here.

Cultural Factors

In many countries, both communist and non-communist, certain types of corruption are more or less acceptable – often depending on the scale – in the traditional political culture. As pointed out in chapter 2, ordinary citizens may well expect some corruption, and do not take major exception to it, within limits. For instance, the practice of promoting members of one's family or protégés and friends is, apparently, accepted by many citizens in several East Asian cultures and elsewhere (on African communist states see Jackson and Rosberg, 1984). Indeed, senior leaders may seek to capitalize on a tradition of dynasty and caring family leadership in a given country's culture, seeking both to enhance their own legitimacy and to indulge their personal preferences by promoting close relatives; Kim Il Sung in the DPRK would be the best example of this. Officials may take a similar view; alternatively, they may object to it – yet explain it largely in terms of the cultural legacy. Thus according to Sampson (1983, p. 54), some Romanian officials and social scientists saw the second economy – itself closely linked to corruption – as 'a manifestation of a "Balkan mentality"' (for a definition of this see P. Moore, 1984, p. 189) and 'a "legacy of Ottoman domination" which would gradually disappear'. Along somewhat similar lines, the Chinese leadership has often seen corruption as a hangover from China's feudalism. Thus Deng, in a speech made to the National Conference of the CCP in September 1985 (Deng, 1987, p. 130), spoke of the influence of both feudalism and capitalism, arguing that this influence had increased again in recent years. Similarly, the Vietnamese leadership has seen corruption as partially a vestige of undesirable Confucian traditions (Beresford, 1988, pp. 184–5; she notes that not *all* Confucian traditions are officially rejected, however. For the Soviets seeing bribery as a 'relic of the past' see *Pravda* 16 January 1975, p. 1, while Tomasevich, 1955, pp. 244–7 and 379, argues that Yugoslavia was riddled with corruption during the inter-war years).

One point to be made in assessing the validity of such cultural arguments is that different sections of society may look to different traditions in the past. Moreover, there is sometimes disagreement over what constitutes traditional practice. Thus a number of Westerners have argued that it is traditional to Chinese culture for trade officials to offer gifts to potential trading partners in order to be in an advantageous position. However, two Taiwanese officials interviewed by me in Taipei in July 1987 specifically denied that this was a tradition in Chinese culture. Of course, Taiwan seeks to discredit the PRC whenever it can, so that an official denial of common heritage in this particular area must be treated with caution. Nevertheless, the general point about different reference points in tradition still pertains.

Another cultural aspect is a weak tradition of the rule of law in most of these countries and, as a corollary, a low level of respect for the law. Several of the Asian and African communist states were formerly colonies (mostly of France or Portugal), and 'the law' has been seen by some citizens as 'theirs' (that is, of the imperialist power) and therefore not respected in the same way that it might be in a long-established independent country, such as many Western states. Conversely, three West German specialists interviewed in 1986 about the apparently very low levels of corruption in the GDR related this to the German tradition of respect for law and order.

The reference to imperialism in the last paragraph leads to another 'cultural' explanation for corruption. This is that colonialism can lead to the development of a bureaucracy in the colonized country that is largely dependent on the metropolitan country for various perquisites and privileges. Following the withdrawal of the colonizing country, remnants of the old bureaucracy, and of its way of thinking, can be carried over into a new communist system. In order to ensure the maintenance of the privileged position to which they have become accustomed and to which they even feel they have a right, some members of the bureaucracy will engage in corruption.

In multi-ethnic states, some ethnic groups have more of a reputation for corruption than others, partially because of traditional attitudes towards a number of factors such as the state, the family, the law, etc. Thus Lampert (1984, pp. 371–2) writes of the USSR:

> In the Transcaucasian republics especially (of these, Georgia has acquired the most notoriety), a number of influences have led to a systematic disregard of the law at certain periods. The strength of family ties, the role of the gift, the importance of 'macho' displays of material wealth, and perhaps the strength of entrepreneurial traditions, have helped to create enclaves in which some types of abuse have flourished to an extent that seemed astonishing to the outside world.[1]

Indeed, this whole issue of traditional loyalties is very relevant to the study of corruption, since there have been a number of communist countries (such as Afghanistan, Angola, Mongolia, Mozambique) in which a tradition of loyalty to the state (and hence obedience to general societal rule) was not well established at the time the communists took power, with loyalties to clan, etc., clearly dominating this more general commitment. Intimately related to this is the issue of commitment to the *nation*, as the basis of the nation-state. By the 1980s, several communist states were not only relatively new as *communist* units but as political units altogether – Yugoslavia and Czechoslovakia were established in 1918, for instance, South Yemen in 1904, the DPRK in 1948, the GDR in 1949, while several African states have yet to create a proper *national* (as distinct from tribal) identity in many of the citizens. A lack of commitment to the nation can also help to explain the lack of internal constraints on the would-be corrupt official.

Related to the last point is the fact that the *way* in which the communists took power has been seen by many commentators as an indicator of the subsequent popularity – popular legitimacy – of the new system. In some countries (such as the USSR, the PRC, Cuba, Yugoslavia), the communists came to power with considerable – though invariably far from universal – public support, while in others (such as Romania, Poland, South Vietnam), communism was virtually imposed upon a reluctant citizenry, in many cases by a foreign (Soviet) army. Although the communists appear in some cases to have had some success in making themselves more popular, in other cases – Poland being the most obvious one – they were never fully accepted by large sections of the population. In this sort of situation, some individuals will feel that performing corrupt acts is on one level a way of taking revenge on what they see as an illegitimate system with no tradition of popular endorsement.

Linking the last two points is a factor inferred from something Rasma Karklins noted in her fascinating study of ethnic relations in the USSR. She cites the case of a Kirghiz respondent who stated that if Kirghiz are promoted to high position, then they will attempt to surround themselves with other Kirghiz, especially kin – 'and the Russians get on with much more difficulties then' (1986, p. 83). In other words, nepotism can be a way of excluding 'them' (the dominant nationality) by promoting one's own. Moreover, whistle-blowing on members of another ethnic group can be a way of seeking revenge on a group with which one is in overt or covert conflict.

In an interview with me, the vice-president of the Soviet Academy of Sciences' Sociological Association, Professor Mikk Titma, explained differences in ethnic groups' attitudes towards corruption less in terms of the specificities of traditional culture or group tensions than in terms of what he called 'the level of development' of different cultures. For Titma – an Estonian – one of the reasons for less tolerance of corruption in the Baltic States than in, for instance, Georgia was because urbanization and economic development had gone further in the former, resulting in different attitudes towards personalized power, nepotism, etc.

One aspect of communist political behaviour that can and does have a profoundly destabilizing effect on culture and values is the practice sometimes adopted by new leaderships of severely criticizing their predecessors. Khrushchev's denunciation of Stalin; Deng's less extensive but nevertheless powerful critique of Mao, and in particular of the Cultural Revolution; Gorbachev's criticisms of the Brezhnev era; the limited criticisms Alia made of Hoxha (mainly of economic policy and policy towards youth – see *YICA*, 1987, pp. 261–2); Ali Salem al-Bidh's denunciation of Ali Nasser Mohammed (see *YICA*, 1988, pp. 437–9) – these and many other examples show just how confusing and destabilizing communist leaders' statements can be for ordinary citizens, who do not invariably appreciate all the nuances of ideological attacks on a predecessor. What they do know is that the vanguard that is allegedly guided by 'scientific socialism' is very much more subjective and confused than it is prepared to admit – which is hardly conducive to legitimacy; white becomes black when black becomes white.

It is clear from the above that political culture is affected by experiences under communism, as well as by pre-communist traditions. Certainly, what might be called the 'culture of expectation' can develop irrespective of the pre-communist traditions. By this I mean *inter alia* that officials can come to believe that certain perquisites – not all of them officially and explicitly sanctioned, but seen as tacitly accepted by the regime – are the norm when they reach a given level in the hierarchy. Citizens, too, can over time come to see *some* corruption as normal and/or beneficial. Thus Sharon Zukin, who interviewed many Yugoslav citizens on a range of issues for her book *Beyond Marx and Tito*, writes of Yugoslavia (1975, p. 31): 'In the citizens' eyes, whatever corruption exists serves to lubricate the wheels, rather than to bog down the works, of the political machinery.' Some communist commentators have clearly been disturbed by the fact that *some* corruption has become more or less accepted by the population. One *Izvestiya* correspondent noted in June 1983 how this is even reflected in changes over time in the use of the Russian language:

our language has very subtly captured this compromise, which expresses itself in the reluctance to call phenomena by their proper names. Nowadays, the vulgar little word 'pull' (*blat*) is no longer as popular as it was, say, twenty years ago. Now the fashionable terms among cer:ain people are the perfectly respectable verbs 'to obtain', 'to arrange' or even 'to make'. The euphemisms are now so commonly used that their original point has disappeared; it seems that the foul meaning inherent in them is not getting across. (*Izvestiya*, 26 June 1983, p. 6)

The fact that there has tended to be a much weaker tradition of initiative and risk-taking in most communist systems than in more market-oriented systems means that there may be less respect for one's superiors than in a situation in which one is subordinate to dynamic achievers; the *perception* that one's superiors have been promoted more because of time-serving and/or sycophancy than because of their own real merit may serve to weaken commitment to a hierarchy and, more generally, a normative commitment to the system.

According to my own interviews, another view that was common in several communist states is also more the product of experience under communism than of traditional values. This is that citizens were for so long and so frequently informed by the authorities that they owned the wealth in society that they came to believe it – or, perhaps more accurately, 'believed' it if it suited their purposes. A number of Poles and Russians interviewed, for instance, maintained that most of their fellow citizens had far greater respect than most Westerners do for their neighbours' property, yet far less for state property. A similar point was made explicitly by the then Soviet minister of justice, V.I. Terebilov, who in 1971 argued that:

> We must resolutely put an end to the attitude that regards state property as 'someone else's, as 'the public's'. Probably many of us know people with whom we can freely leave the keys to our apartments (they wouldn't take so much as a pencil!), but who may permit themselves 'to benefit a little from production'. Sometimes they do this without the slightest embarrassment, reasoning that the state will be none the poorer. (from *Trud*, 2 March 1971, p. 2 – in *CDSP*, Vol. 23, No. 12, p. 23: for further endorsement of this point see Grossman, 1977, p. 29 on the USSR; Liu, 1983, pp. 616–17 on China; S. Young, 1971, p. 683 on Vietnam)

Although the limited data available suggest that such an assumption may in *some* cases be a false one (see Kwasniewski, 1984, p. 105, for Polish data), it is widely believed that there is far more theft of socialized than of personal property in many communist states, in contrast to the situation in Western countries (for Czechoslovak evidence to suggest that this belief is correct see *SWB*/EE/7981/B/3, 19 June 1985). If this perception *is* correct – as I believe it is – then the attitudes described would have to be incorporated into any attempt at explanation, *in addition to* the far more obvious fact that considerably more property is socialized in communist states (and, by late 1991, still in most post-communist states) than in liberal democracies.

As a final point – and, in that it is simultanously a cultural and a psychological problem, a bridge to the next section – it can be noted that various Soviet studies of the reasons for criminality cite alcoholism as a major factor. According to an article published in 1977 by the then director of the Academy of the USSR Ministry of Internal Affairs, Professor Lieutenant-General S.M. Krylov, almost 63 per cent of all crimes in the Soviet Union at that time were committed by people under the influence of alcohol (*Sotsiologicheskie Issledovaniya*, No. 3, July–September 1977 – in *CDSP*, Vol. 30, No. 3, p. 6). A 1983 article by the USSR minister of internal affairs, V. Fedorchuk, gave a slightly lower figure – he stated that nearly one half of all crimes were committed by people under the influence of alcohol – but it was still a very significant percentage (*Pravda*, 10 August 1983, p. 3). There is no way of knowing how significant a factor alcohol is in corruption – assuming it is a factor at all. But given the whole culture of alcohol abuse in both the USSR and some other East European states (notably Poland – see, for example, *SWB*/EE/7987/B/5, 26 June 1985, and *SWB*/EE/8081/B/5, 14 October 1985), and given that this is known to affect many officials as well as ordinary citizens,[2] it does not seem inappropriate to infer that alcohol plays some role in the complex phenomenon of corruption – probably, in many cases, in breaking down resistance to the initial step on the path to corruption. Moreover, the severe limiting of access to alcohol in the early part of the Gorbachev era almost certainly encouraged criminal elements who were prepared to make alcohol available illegally and for a price, doubtless with some degree of official connivance. Similarly, the increased drug abuse in many communist countries was almost bound to lead to more corruption, both in terms of official involvement in drug trafficking and in order to fund individual officials' habits (for Soviet support of these arguments see *CDSP*, Vol. 33, No. 9, p. 20; Vol. 34, No. 12, pp. 14–15; Vol. 34, No. 16, p. 18: see too Powell, 1973, Kramer, 1988, and Kramer, 1990).

Psychological Factors

A number of psychological factors help to explain corruption in the communist world; most of them apply in any type of system. One sub-set of such factors can be labelled generally 'psychological problems'. For instance, some people simply 'get a buzz' from engaging in criminal activities – including corrupt ones – undetected; if individuals feel highly alienated from and hostile to 'the system', anomic behaviour can serve as a way of venting their frustrations. But not all deviants want to go undetected. In the West, the shop-lifter who steals sometimes hopes to be caught; according to psychoanalysts, such people are actually seeking attention and/or excitement (rather than wanting to acquire more goods), either because they are bored with their lives and/or because they feel they are receiving insufficient love and attention from others. If this applies to shop-lifting, there is no logical reason why it should not also apply to, for instance, embezzlement.

If some people definitely do not want to be caught whereas others do, there is a third category for whom the risk itself is the attraction. Many people take known risks simply because they find the risky act itself pleasurable or thrilling – smoking, drinking alcohol, taking drugs, sky-diving, illicit sexual liaisons and gambling are common examples of this. The last of these is particularly close to engaging in corruption, in that there is in both the possibility of real pecuniary gain in addition to the pleasure of the act itself.

Nowadays, there is increasing awareness among analysts of deviance that chemical and/or biological factors can explain some individuals' criminality. While intuition suggests that few acts of corruption are the result of chemical imbalances in the brain, any attempt at a comprehensive analysis of the causes of corruption must allow for this. Biological explanations for crime generally have certainly been used by psychologists and other specialists in the communist world (for a discussion of this factor by Soviet criminologists citing, *inter alia*, East German criminologists, see the discussion in *Literaturnaya Gazeta*, No. 48, 1967, p. 12, translated in *CDSP*, Vol. 19, No. 49, pp. 3–5). Moreover, although this reason seems to me to be particularly bizarre and unconvincing, it should be noted that at least one writer has in the past suggested that corruption among Russian officials working in Central Asia is partially a function of the 'state of mental imbalance' caused by people used to a colder climate living in a hot one (on this see Critchlow, 1988, p. 147).

Adopting a less physiological, more philosophical position, several people interviewed by me in various countries made the point that some individuals are 'naturally evil' and will commit criminal acts, including corrupt ones, in any type of system. While it might be surprising to hear such views from, for instance, a Marxist sociologist or political scientist, the fact is that such an explanation was given to me more than once by social scientists. Indeed, Fidel Castro has argued that vice grows more quickly – 'spontaneously, like weeds, and grows by itself' – than virtue, and that virtue is a matter of correct socialization rather than humanity's natural state (Castro, 1983, p. 342). A less extreme interpretation is that some people are just 'naturally selfish' (as distinct from 'not virtuous'); this too can explain corruption (for a fascinating Soviet analysis of crime that focuses *inter alia* on the personality of the perpetrator see Kuznetsova, 1975).

The focus so far has been on factors essentially internal to the individual. But the individual's relationship to the group is also important. The power of both peer-pressure and peer-comparison can be great, for instance. In the words of one lavatorial graffiti artist: 'When the best of people take bribes, isn't it the fool who doesn't?'. In other words, if individuals see others around them benefiting from corruption, they may well choose to indulge too.

It is obvious why fear of the consequences of being detected might act as a deterrent to would-be corrupt individuals. What is less obvious is that fear can also *encourage* people to act corruptly. Harking back to the 'fool who doesn't take bribes' – but this time in a hierarchical rather than peer-group situation – a subordinate may fear the consequences of not acting in a similar manner to his/her corrupt superiors. To cite a concrete example of this, the deputy director of the Soviet Union's All-Union Research Centre for Mental Health, Marat Vartanyan, told a Western visitor in the mid-1980s that any signing of questionable documents he had engaged in in the past (in the context, this presumably relates to the classification of criminals as mentally insane) he had done only 'under pressure from my superiors' (cited in Reddaway, 1988, p. 29). It is interesting to note in this context that the authors of a report on corruption presented to Gorbachev in 1986 argued strongly that legal proceedings initiated against corrupt officials should be directed only at the highest levels of the various hierarchies, precisely because superiors often force subordinates into corrupt activities (*MN*, No. 34, 1989, p. 10).

A different kind of fear is the concern many officials have of the consequences of underfulfilling the plan; this is simultaneously a system-related factor. This fear may lead individuals to engage in corrupt practices, either in order actually to fulfil the plan or else to *appear* to have done so (the 'false reporting' syndrome); this was common in Vietnam in the 1970s, for example (Beresford, 1988, pp. 115–6). Other individuals may act corruptly partially in order *actually* to fulfil the plan – not out of fear, but because they take a pride in meeting their targets; this, too, is primarily a psychological factor.

Yet another kind of fear can be particularly germane in explaining why some officials turn a blind eye. If a corrupt official reports on the misdoings of others, there is a real chance that the latter will then seek either revenge and/or to alleviate their own situation by informing on the official. This point can be inferred from the following quotation from a Soviet correspondent:

> Why do people whose official duties make it incumbent on them to uphold devotion to principle and the norms of party life suddenly turn out to be so inclined to give indulgences? The answer is not difficult. At times, some of them are themselves far from irreproachable; therefore, fearing that fingers will be pointed at them, they are prepared to shut their eyes to the 'sins of their neighbours'. (*Pravda*, 21 December 1985, p. 2)

A factor that may sometimes be linked with fear – but which is conceptually distinct and may in fact relate more to general personality traits – is human weakness. Thus, in an article published in *Pravda* (28 August 1982, p. 3), A. Chernyak argued that some people find it difficult to reject offers from a person of a 'generous' (that is, pushy) nature; if such a person also happens to be one's superior, then the fear factor may pertain here too. It can be noted parenthetically that the same source points out that genuine gratitude can lead people who should know better to offer 'bribes' (that is, gifts presented after the official has performed the act that has generated the feeling of gratitude). Developing this argument, it is quite possible that some officials will accept gifts because they know they have been particularly helpful to someone (*not* necessarily for premeditated self-interested reasons), and either feel they 'deserve' a reward (that is, they feel that a reward is not inappropriate), or else genuinely do not wish to offend or embarrass a grateful supplicant.

Although many Western theorists – especially Marxists or quasi-Marxists (see, for example, Marcuse, 1964) – see individual possessiveness largely in terms of the effects of dominant capitalist ideology, this is neither the sole nor necessarily the most convincing explanation. V. Rutgaizer, for instance, argued at the beginning of the 1980s (*Pravda*, 16 November 1981, p. 3) that material possessiveness generally, and the desire to accumulate consumer goods more particularly, is for some individuals 'a perverted form of self-assertion'. Corruption is often a way of helping to satisfy this 'perversion', which a psychoanalyst might relate to insecurity, feelings of sexual inadequacy, etc.

It has been argued that nepotism should be included as a form of corruption. This phenomenon can also be explained in psychological terms – the 'blood is thicker than water' syndrome, wanting to help one's own family. Considering this from another perspective, nepotism can also be explained in terms of individuals seeking to maximize their own power – and the lust for power is a psychological variable. Nepotism should not only be seen from the perspective of the official promoting relatives, however; sometimes the initiative will come from the family members, using what can border on emotional blackmail to encourage an official to 'look after' his/her relatives.[3] The family is, of course, a major source of latent socialization even in societies in which purposive socialization by the state is more visible and intensive than is the case in Western liberal democracies. Certainly, a number of Soviet criminologists have argued that the family can play a very influential role in the development of the criminal personality (see, for example, A. Sakharov's article in *Literaturnaya Gazeta*, 19 September 1979, p. 11).

The argument about 'lust for power' leads to the final point in this sub-section, which is that one has to consider what sort of individual joins the communist party. Innumerable reports and studies, including many from the communist states themselves, reveal that opportunists and careerists frequently become party members; many of these wish to – and do – become officials. The principal motive of such people in joining the party is ambition rather than revolutionary zeal; they may have been more widespread in the more established regimes than in the newer ones, although they were certainly to be found in the latter too.[4] Ambitious people not infrequently want 'the good life', and in many instances will not permit moral scruples to prevent them from achieving this; corruption can thus often be linked to an ambitious personality.

System-related Factors

The range of factors relating to the system and regime is vast, complex and interrelated. Moreoever, some of the factors are primarily related to communist ideology and practice, whereas others relate more generally to developing countries, large units, etc. In the first draft of this chapter, 'communist-specific' factors were separated from the more general ones. This division was eventually abandoned, for two reasons. The first is that it led to repetitiveness and an unnecessarily artificial separation of closely related factors. Second, such an approach can give the impression that there are factors that are *uniquely* communism-related; while a few factors could be argued to be so, most are not. Rather, the relative salience of individual factors does vary – sometimes considerably – from one kind of system to another, according to, for example, the balance between plan and market. The argument here is that since, for instance, no liberal democracy has a pure market economy and no communist state has a pure planned economy, so types of corruption relating to the planned economy or the market economy will never assume a 'pure' form and will never be unique. Similarly, communist states are not the only ones in which one political organization – such as a political party, the military – dominates, so that here, too, arguments about uniqueness are unconvincing. As already suggested, the balance of the factors may be unique to communist states; but this is best argued, not implied by artificial divisions of factors into 'communist-specific' and 'general'.

Two final introductory comments to this section are necessary. First, it must be emphasized that in many – probably most – cases of corruption several variables will be operating simultaneously; as elsewhere in this study, factors are treated discretely here solely for the sake of clarity of analysis. Second, although I have rejected the notion of classifying factors as 'communist-specific' and 'not specific to communism', I have somewhat artificially grouped factors into five major categories that will be examined in turn. The categories are:

1   The impact of modernization;
2   Inequality and inequity;
3   Factors relating directly to the economic system;
4   Factors relating directly to the political and legal systems;
5   Factors relating to the dynamism of the communist world and its growing integration into the world market.

Each of these groups involves a number of specific reasons for corruption that are elaborated below.

The Impact of Modernization

The rapid modernization of many communist countries, plus the relatively large scale of several of them, can exert a generally alienat-

ing influence.[5] Citizens may feel lost not only because of the changing values, but also because of the turmoil more generally – revolutions from above, for instance – that the new system has brought
into their lives, with families being divided, etc. In addition to this,
the greater social mobility not only frequently makes people more
susceptible to corruption for reasons outlined below, but also often
gives them much better opportunities to engage in it. As Sampson
(1983, pp. 61–2) has pointed out – and explained in some detail –
'second economy' resources and access to these typically become
more extensive during modernization ('industrialization and urbanization') phases. Let us now examine these factors more closely.

Many commentators on corruption, especially if they are focusing
on the so-called developing or modernizing countries, have pointed
either to a conflict between traditional and new ethical codes or else
to a breakdown of traditional codes without the concomitant emergence of a new set of values (see, for example, Nye – who derives it
from others – 1967, p. 418). The traditional values in communist
states often include an ethical code based on religion (such as Christ-
ianity, Islam, Buddhism, etc.), and the avowed anti-religious stance
of all communist states – even if some have been far less hostile than
others (see, for example, Miller and Rigby, 1986) – can serve to
undermine the respect for property and law that most religions
encourage.

The breakdown of traditional values is by no means confined to or
solely dependent on the basic atheism of communists. Partially
because of their Marxist orientation, and partially because of their
competition with capitalism, communists also seek to turn the
societies in which they take power into modern industrial ones – at
least in those cases (the vast majority) in which they take power in
predominantly agrarian societies. They attempt to implement this
transformation as rapidly as possible. Thus there is typically a
relatively sudden major change in traditional rural life (such as
colletivization) and a large-scale movement to the towns (urbanization). Because of the need for new skills in industry, plus a real
commitment to education as a right in socialist society (and, to some
extent, in order to enhance the opportunities for purposive socialization of the population), communist systems also typically mount
first literacy and later more general educational campaigns for the
population. These wide-ranging social changes – such as the urbanization – can also have profound effects on traditional values, and may
well break down old values without replacing them with sufficiently
strongly internalized new ones. This 'ethical deficit' – or, more
simply, decline of morality – factor helps to explain corruption.

Another, closely related aspect of the impact of rapid modernization is that the new status and wealth associated with rapid upward
social mobility can have a negative effect on morality at the same
time as it can encourage aspirations to run ahead of possibilities.
Zukin (1975, pp. 111–12 and 206) cites Yugoslav respondents who
made this point explicitly, particularly with reference to ex-Partisan
peasants who were promoted to positions of executive responsibility
after the Second World War.

It is not only the breakdown of traditional value-systems associated with rapid modernization that can lead to increasing crime rates,
including instances of corruption. Thus a Soviet analyst has argued
against what he claims is the Western, bourgeois notion that urbanization *per se* leads to an increase in crime (presumably, including
corruption). According to Antonyan (1975), in a socialist system it is
not the urbanization itself that leads to increasing crime but rather
factors relating to the process. For instance, rising material expectations are argued to lead to an increase in cases of embezzlement, if
aspirations outstrip possibilities. Moreover, the greater anonymity
of the city in comparison with the village means that there is less
peer-control in the former than in the latter. Few 'bourgeois criminologists' would accept that Westerners seriously argue that urbanization itself – as distinct from the ramifications of urbanization – lead
to increased crime rates, and in this sense Antonyan is knocking
down a straw-person; nevertheless, it is interesting to note that a
communist social scientist has correlated these aspects of modernization with crime.

Communists themselves frequently acknowledge the imperfections of their socialization processes, and sometimes explicitly relate
poor socialization of the young to later adult behaviour. Indeed,
children may well learn from the agencies of purposive socialization
the opposite of what they should be learning. Thus Eduard Shevardnadze, addressing the Central Committee of the Georgian Communist Party in November 1974, made the following observation:

> it is no secret that, starting in the schoolroom, we are giving young
> people practical instruction in the idea that work plans and resolutions
> can go unfulfilled. Unfulfilled measures are listed as fulfilled even in
> Young Pioneer organizations. This is how children begin to deceive
> themselves and others. That is how hoodwinking, lies and deception
> begin . . . Thus, we instill in many people while they are still children
> bad habits that may play a fateful role later on. (*Zarya Vostoka*, 15
> November 1974, translated in *CDSP*, Vol. 26, No. 46, p. 5)

One final aspect of modernization that can encourage corruption is the greater opportunities offered by more sophisticated and complicated technology. Thus commentators in both the Soviet and the Chinese press have in recent years referred to instances of accounting frauds made possible by the growing use of computers (see, for example, *Izvestiya*, 27 July 1987, p. 4, and *CD*, 11 February 1988, p. 3).

Inequality and Inequity

According to Dobel (1978, *passim*, esp. pp. 961–2), the single most important source of corruption is inequality. There is no question that inequalities have been widespread and multifarious in communist states (just as they are in other states), and that they can have an alienating effect on citizens. This is especially so if such inequalities are also widely perceived as inequitable. The usual argument in the West about such inequalities is that they are 'normal' or even 'inevitable' in developing economies, in which an emphasis on developing heavy goods industries (and finding the investment for this) is almost bound to lead to a shortage of consumer goods. Several communist states certainly have had highly skewed, imbalanced economies at some stages of development. As a consequence, access to consumer goods is usually very uneven. Communists themselves often argue along these lines. In April 1982, Fidel Castro argued that: 'Capitalists solve everything on a price basis, but socialists don't. So when there isn't enough of something, there is speculation' (Castro, 1983, p. 345).[6] In the following month, Castro provided an example of this. He stated that Cuba had only 10,000 cars to distribute to the population for the whole of 1982, and argued that the fairest way to distribute them was to sell them at near cost-price to vanguard workers and others (such as doctors) who most deserved them. However, he also pointed out that those eligible to purchase cars were sometimes tempted to sell them at profits of up to 400 or even 500 per cent to people whom Castro (1983, pp. 354–5) disparagingly referred to as 'Lumpen' elements; in that some of those selling cars would be 'officials' by our definition, this is an example of corruption.

There are a number of problems with this 'communist' approach to distribution, many of which relate to and help to explain those highlighted by Castro himself. One is that it does not necessarily relate at all to 'need' – the very fact that those eligible for cars are prepared to sell them for gain suggests that the cars are not vital to them. Although the socialist maxim for distribution is supposed to be 'from each according to his/her ability, to each according to his/her work', there will be many citizens who feel that the implementation of this should not directly clash with the longer-term communist goal of 'from each according to his/her ability, to each according to his/her need'. In the early days after the Cuban Revolution, at a time when Castro was claiming communism was still a long way off, consumer durables that were in short supply were typically distributed more or less along the lines of need. Thus refrigerators often went to parents with young children, whose milk had to be kept fresh in a hot country. The moves away from this method of distribution could lead to resentment and a decline in morals, both of which can relate to corruption. If there is a severe shortage of cars, it might be socially preferable to use them all as cheap taxis rather than to sell some as private vehicles. In addition, it could be argued that Castro is fuelling (sic) a 'need' for cars among ordinary citizens by emphasizing how only a few people are entitled to them, thus making them more desirable to others than might otherwise be the case. Few human 'needs' are really basic – certainly private cars are not. Rather, need itself is a largely subjective, socially determined phenomenon – and communists can and do themselves create, or at the very least exacerbate, 'needs'. Moves towards commodity fetishism are by no means exclusive to regular capitalism.

One point about shortages is that in some countries in which people have long been used to them, but do expect slow and marginal improvement in the supply situation, the shortages have actually become more serious. Cuba, Yugoslavia, Romania, Vietnam and the USSR are all good examples of a deteriorating supply situation for the consumer in recent years. Some officials who may be prepared to work hard and honestly, and to endure hardships as long as there is some prospect for improvement, may find that the disappearance of such a prospect is the straw that breaks their back. Formerly uncorrupt officials may in these circumstances become corrupt not to *improve* but merely to *maintain* their already low standards of living. One major reason for such shortages has been the introduction of trade embargoes by the West or the removal of MFN status; Vietnam, Cuba, Poland and Romania have all been affected in this way. Thus it is not only internal, domestic factors that can lead to shortages and other economic problems – although it should be noted that in most cases the embargoes, etc., are mounted as a reaction to domestic policies and politics.

Perceptions among the masses that distribution is inequitable are commonly intensified by the behaviour of members of the political elites themselves. The latters' own lifestyles and access to the 'third economy' (such as the special shops and hospitals available to many officials) can appear to many citizens to be incompatible with – even antithetical to – the professed *telos* of communists. Although communism as a political system requires *political* elitism – certainly at some stages of its existence (the vanguard concept epitomizes this) – the ideology has never fully succeeded in legitimating social and economic elitism, and the conspicuous consumption of some relatively senior communist officials can lead others to feel 'justified' in engaging in corrupt practices. For some citizens and lower-level officials, the conspicuous consumption is less irritating than the attempt by some more senior cadres to hide the fact of their privileged access to goods in short supply; the clandestine nature of many elite shops in the communist world can exacerbate the problems of perception, since the high walls around some elite shopping compounds (particularly in the USSR, such as the one in Granovskii Street in Moscow) give the impression that the elite is aware that what it is doing is indefensible and is trying to hide it (for further details on the 'special stores' see Connor, 1979, pp. 251–3). If senior cadres are attempting to obtain a bigger slice of the cake surreptitiously, then why should not their subordinates?

The point about perceptions of inequality does not cut only one way between officials and masses. Sometimes, non-officials may appear to have – and actually *do* have – greater 'privileges' than low-ranking officials. A Hungarian survey reported on in *Népszabadság* (27 May 1985 – in *SWB*/EE/7965/B/5, 31 May 1985) revealed that the proportion of income gained from sources other than what is officially designated as one's principal occupation was rising in Hungary. The report pointed out that the question of who has access to extra income becomes critical in such circumstances. Between 30 and 40 per cent of Hungarian workers – a figure which will almost certainly have included many low-level officials – had no such opportunities, according to the survey. In this situation, some officials may fear they are missing out relative not only to their superiors, but also to 'privileged' workers. Such a situation is conducive to corruption.

Yet another dimension of perceived inequity in distribution may be particularly relevant to corruption in federal communist states with ethnic tensions. Partly in an endeavour to counter criticisms of a privileged elite at the centre, the federal Yugoslav authorities permitted the development of a situation in which federal officials sometimes received less than officials and non-officials in the republics. For instance, according to official Yugoslav sources, the Yugoslav prime minister was in 1985 earning 110,000 dinars per month – the same as a good engineer in a successful factory in Croatia (*SWB*/EE/ 7966/B/9, 1 June 1985). It is highly probable that some federal officials will consider this sort of situation inequitable, and thus justify their own corruption to themselves on the grounds of 'correcting' inequities in the reward system.

Although this section on inequalities has – justifiably – concentrated on the negative implications of perceptions of an excessively *wide* range of differentials (of income, access to goods and services, etc.), it can be inferred from the previous paragraph that too *narrow* a band of income differentials can result in some of those shouldering a greater burden of responsibility 'helping themselves' to what they believe is appropriate and deserved extra income. Thus, according to the then deputy head of the Department of Sociology in the Hungarian Political Academy, T. Roszgonyi (see *SWB* EE/8135/B/3, 16 December 1985), managers and supervisors often earned either little more, or else even less, than their subordinates, despite their added responsibilities and irrespective of their performance. In such a situation, which could certainly apply to some officials, corruption is likely to become an attractive and 'justifiable' proposition to some.

The Economic System

Inequality and inequity in distribution is on one level a function of the economic system, on which we must continue to focus for several pages. One of the salient features of communist systems is that they have had, or have sought to have, both highly planned and highly socialized economies; the implications of this for corruption are several. First, such a system allows little scope for entrepreneurial skills as we normally understand these in the West; corruption can partially compensate for the frustration some enterprising individuals experience in an essentially non-privatized and planned economy. Another point is that the complexity of modern planned economies – both in terms of the sectoral/branch divisions and territorial scale and divisions – is such that there are almost bound to be problems, deficiencies and loopholes; both the need to overcome the problems, and the opportunities that loopholes provide, can encourage corruption. Related to this is the fact that the complexity and scale often result in serious delays in updating norms. A former Soviet minister for internal affairs, for instance, has argued that the existence of outdated (and, by implication, overly 'generous') norms for wastage and spillage in trade and supply makes it easy to cover up thefts (*Pravda*, 10 August 1983, p. 3). Moreover, the supremacy of the plan – the enormous significance communist authorities have attached to its fulfilment – is a major explicator of the false-reporting syndrome. According to a report on a 1984 plenary session of the Uzbek Central Committee: 'The ability to fulfil the plan at any cost was valued over all else. As a result, such alien and immoral phenomena as report-padding, hoodwinking and bribery have penetrated our lives' (from *Pravda Vostoka*, 26 June 1984, in *CDSP*, Vol. 36, No. 26, p. 13). The more centralized and planned an economy – for instance, the more sets of statistics are required of production units by ministries – the more scope and probably incentive there is to engage in false reporting when, as communists themselves have frequently acknowledged happens, problems (of supply, etc.) arise. Finally, aspects of the fact that so much is socialized are sometimes correlated – whether implicitly or explicitly – with corruption by communist analysts themselves. Earlier in this chapter, reference was made to the cavalier attitude many citizens in communist states display towards socialized property. In an interesting article that helps to explain some of the *reasons* for such attitudes, Soviet Procurator-General A. Rekunkov referred to the widespread practice of writing off damage caused by poor organization, negligence, carelessness and even abuse, arguing that this 'causes an indifferent and sometimes even scornful attitude towards public property', which in turn can lead to corruption (*Pravda*, 27 April 1982, p. 3). Readers familiar with classical Greek political theory will appreciate that Aristotle would not have been at all surprised to learn that citizens do not treat public property with the respect authorities expect and require.

Although communist states have had predominantly planned economies, many of them have in recent years explicitly encouraged the legal component of the 'second economy'. Not only the private plot in agriculture, but also various small scale businesses and service enterprises (such as shops, taxis, domestic repair services, private tuition, etc.) were developing in the 1980s, in some countries at an impressive rate. However, as argued earlier, the second economy can often encourage – almost necessitate – corruption if it is to function reasonably efficiently. This is largely because of ambiguities in official attitudes towards private, small-scale economic activity; although the authorities have in most cases acknowledged the economic benefits of private enterprise, their adherence to Marxism-Leninism has limited their enthusiasm for it. This in turn means that frequently they have not permitted, or at least have not encouraged, the necessary support systems/infrastructures to private enterprise, which is where corruption may well arise. Thus peasants find they are permitted to grow vegetables or rear pigs, but may not be told how they are to transport their produce to the private markets; to do this, they will sometimes bribe officials to 'lend' them state-owned trucks (on this problem, see *Sel'skaya Zhizn'*, No. 2, 1972, p. 3, in *CDSP*, Vol. 25, No. 10, p. 23). Hence the legal and illegal parts of the second economy are often intimately linked.

Some communist leaderships have shown themselves to be very aware of the potentially corrupting aspects of the legal part of the 'second economy', either in the narrow sense just described, or else in the broader sense that the moves towards more private enterprise in the economy have a negative impact on the development of a socialist consciousness. Under Hoxha, Albania rejected the introduction of any private trading for this reason; although small private plots were permitted for the farmers in both state and collective farms (Albania's socialization of agriculture was completed in 1970), these were only for personal consumption and not for the cultivation of produce to sell.[7] It should be noted, however, that under the new leader from 1985 (Alia),[8] even Albania changed this policy; peasants were by the late 1980s urged to grow more vegetables and rear more livestock on their private plots and to sell excess produce to the market (on this see Biberaj, 1987, esp. p. 181). Cuba has gone against the general trend in the communist world, although this looked set to change again at the time of writing. In order to increase agricultural production and supplies, Castro encouraged private farmers' markets in the late 1970s/early 1980s; by June 1986, however, he had decided that the negative implications for socialist consciousness of this policy were outweighing the economic improvements it brought, so that the policy was reversed (see *YICA*, 1987, p. 82). This policy change exacerbated economic problems and would have continued to do so. Given this, the Soviet announcements in 1991 that the USSR could no longer afford to subsidize Cuba, and the fact that Castro has himself argued that shortages in a socialist system often lead to speculation, he may well have to reverse this policy once again (there were a few signs at the 4th CPC Congress in October 1991 that this might happen, in that small-scale private enterprise in the service sector and private foreign investment in Cuba were both encouraged – this said, it must be acknowledged that Castro continued to reject private farmers' markets for the time being); if corruption (and poor socialist consciousness) is connected *both* with shortages *and* with a situation in which such shortages are being overcome, then surely the latter arrangement – which is less likely to lead to riots, or at least alienation and possible declines in motivation and legitimacy – is the lesser of the two evils.

Another aspect of the tolerance or even encouragement of the private sector in many communist systems is that the private sector can attract workers to such an extent that managers – almost necessarily in collusion with officials (for example, in the form of turning a blind eye) – have to engage in illegal or semi-legal practices simply in order to attract good workers and to secure a good day's work out of them. According to Kemény (1982, pp. 353–4), this was a common occurrence in communist Hungary.

The USSR was trying – with limited success – from the 1950s to overcome the imbalance in the economy caused by Stalin's prioritized approach to economic development. Nevertheless it still had definite priorities in industry, at least until recently.[9] One was that some enterprises were accorded special status. This was the group of so-called 'closed' enterprises that were involved either directly or indirectly with defence products.[10] According to Victor Zaslavsky's (unpublished) research on them, these enterprises rarely experienced the supply problems ordinary enterprises suffered. Given this, the need for managers to break rules – and for officials to collaborate with them – was less. While this does not mean that there was no corruption connected with this sort of enterprise, it is probable that the extent of corruption in them was less than elsewhere in industry. Given that several communist countries have had one part of the economy working primarily on defence, and since defence has traditionally been treated by communist countries as at least as important as it has by Western states, it is highly likely that this point has pertained in them too.

The poor quality – as distinct from availability – of (domestically produced) goods is another problem frequently identified by communist leaderships; many Western economists link this with the nature of communist economic systems. In many countries, the emphasis has often been more on gross output – on quantity – than on quality; this problem is common to many developing nations, whether communist or not. The Soviets made a great deal of this problem when the then prime minister, Kosygin, announced a major reform of the Soviet economy in September 1965. In order to alleviate this problem of quantity at the expense of quality, the Soviets attempted to introduce a system in which enterprises would be judged on sales rather than gross output. If a factory produced shoddy goods that no one wanted (reflected in its inability to sell them), it would be financially disadvantaged – even if its overall production increased. Unfortunately, this policy was poorly implemented, and there were still, in the late 1980s, frequent complaints in the Soviet press and by Soviet leaders that goods were of poor quality and did not meet consumer requirements. The relevance of this to a study of corruption is that producers will sometimes bribe trade officials to buy goods they would not be able to dispose of in a more market-responsive system – and other officials not to interfere in these transactions. In November 1987, for example, the Chinese press reported the case of 10 officials in Harbin who were found guilty of precisely this practice (*The Independent*, 17 November 1987). The problem can also be seen as a factor explaining why officials smuggle or in other ways illegally acquire goods of foreign manufacture.

One long-term effect of both skewing and the policy of subsidizing many basics (such as housing, some foods and public transport) that was very visible in the Soviet Union and some of the East European countries (such as Poland) is that citizens managed to accumulate relatively large sums of money which they were not – because of the shortages and poor quality of goods – using to purchase, for instance, better homes or consumer durables on anything like the scale they would in the West (on the problem of an excess of money and a shortage of goods see Rumer, 1984, pp. 25–6). The Soviet writer V.D. Belkin alluded to this problem when he wrote: 'The disproportion (excess of money in circulation) . . . has an unfavourable effect on the moral norms of people's behaviour' (cited in Feldbrugge, 1984, p. 532). Expressed another way, one of the prerequisites for many forms of large-scale corruption – large sums of uncommitted money – has been a feature of many older, more developed communist states that have been unable to 'absorb' the citizens' savings by providing consumer goods in sufficient numbers and of adequate quality. This situation may well change in the next few years, as transitional or post-communist states both improve the quality of goods and reduce their levels of subsidization.

The economy in many communist states has been in such poor shape – with even worse shortages than elsewhere, stagflation, major trade imbalances, etc. – that the governments have until recently attempted to ameliorate their position by keeping exchange rates at a very artificial level. One reason for this is to encourage visitors with hard currency to exchange as much of it as possible. Unfortunately, this can backfire and encourage corruption, as black marketeers offer visitors exchange rates that are more realistic. If the difference between black market and official exchange rates is not great – perhaps two to five times, a figure not uncommon in Eastern Europe during the 1980s – then many visitors will feel that the risks of being caught outweigh the financial advantages, so that the overall scale of illegal currency trading will be limited. But when I visited Vietnam in 1984, the official rate of exchange was 10 dongs to one US dollar, while black marketeers would offer up to 300 dongs. Not all of my fellow travellers were able to resist the temptation. It seems highly probable that some officials were paid to turn a blind eye to such currency speculation, while it is conceivable that some were themselves actively engaged in it.

Another ramification of hard-currency shortages is that the policy adopted by so many communist leaderships of allowing enterprises and/or sub-central level authorities to retain either very little or else none of the hard currency they generate through foreign sales can lead to perceptions at the workplace and/or sub-central level of exploitation by the centre. This was a major factor leading to the crisis in relations between Croatia and the federal Yugoslav authorities at the beginning of the 1970s. It is also a situation conducive to corruption, by both individuals and groups of individuals. On the one hand, some people will feel 'justified' in not declaring all hard currency income to the centre. On the other hand, where a very limited number of people *legally* receive some of their income in hard currency as an incentive, the possibilities for corruption are again enhanced. Thus one Polish émigré interviewed informed me that he had worked in a foreign trade corporation in which some employees received part of their bonuses in hard currency. He further explained that several of these people used to exchange at least some of their hard currency earnings for złoty on the black market. Add to this the fact that the government's policy of privileging some will lead to resentment in others and it becomes clear that, in a situation of both widespread shortages and a non-convertible domestic currency, preferential access to limited hard currency is likely to encourage corruption.

Many of the same basic arguments apply to the limited access to foreign goods in so many communist countries. According to a number of deputies to the Chinese National People's Congress (see *BR*, Vol. 32, No. 19, p. 9), an increase in the availability of foreign goods leads to an increase in official corruption. In one sense, and to a limited extent, this may well be true; the more goods available, the more officials may not only be tempted to but actually can engage in corrupt activity relating to such goods. However, it must be emphasized that this argument still relates principally to an overall situation of severe shortage in a country; in this sense, the notion of 'too many' foreign goods is potentially misleading.

It is clear that it is not merely the *structure* and *nature* (for example, the priorities) of a communist economy that need to be examined if we are to understand the relationship between communist economies and corruption better. In addition, the *state* of the economy – which is often correlated with the structure and nature – needs to be considered. In this context, it is worth noting that Gorbachev himself argued that it was originally a poorly functioning official economy that led to the growth of a shadow economy in the USSR (see *Pravda*, 24 October 1988, p. 2). But whereas Gorbachev seemed to believe that an optimal blend between the centrally planned and the market economy was the best way to solve the USSR's economic problems, others in the Soviet Union took a more radical position. They argued that the abolition of the centrally planned economy and its replacement with a full-blooded market economy (as distinct from the very partial marketization typical of so many communist systems in the 1980s and briefly referred to above) would of itself result in the disappearance of many types of economic crime. This line was adopted by some of the participants in the fascinating 'round-table' discussion on corruption that was published in *Moscow News* late in 1988 (No. 34, p. 10). There could surely be no clearer indication of the fact that many analysts in the communist world itself have seen a clear connection between the communist economic system and corruption.

The Political and Legal System

In communist states, the connection between the economy and the polity is even closer than it is in liberal democracies, and some factors explaining corruption are really located at the interface of the two systems. One very obvious factor here is that the scale of socialization of the economy, the communist commitment to planning of production and distribution, and the emphasis on purposive socialization all mean that the proportion of officials in the communist countries is higher than it would be in a similar-sized liberal democracy. *Ceteris paribus*, the scope for corruption is that much greater where there is administrative overkill.

Another factor at the interface of the political and economic systems is that, as Nye and others (Leys, Braibanti – cited in Nye, 1967, p. 418) have pointed out, the acquisition of political office is for many the primary means for gaining access to wealth in communist systems. In other words, if a given individual's principal aim, for whatever reason, is secure, long-term, legally earned income well above the national average (that is, to be relatively rich), then – in the absence of legal gambling opportunities (whether in the casino or on the stockmarket), opportunities for large-scale private enterprise, exceptional artistic or sporting ability, etc. – the best strategy is to make his/her way up one or other political hierarchy. Given the essentially 'mono-organizational' (to use T.H. Rigby's term) nature of communist systems, the scope for corruption in the form of patronage or even actual purchase of office is great.[11] This point requires elaboration.

Weber argued in the early twentieth century that there is only one group in society that can successfully act as a counter-weight to state bureaucracies, viz the business class. This arrangement refers, of course, to a capitalist system; in a communist system, there has until now been no autonomous business class to speak of. This is not only because managers, for instance, depend to a great extent on state bureaucrats for investment and other forms of finance, but also because of the pervasiveness of the *nomenklatura* system. There are several implications of this more unified system. One is that career opportunities are more dependent on a smaller number of organizations; in theory at least (though see below), if one blots one's copy-book in a communist system, there are not the alternative channels that exist in a politically and economically more pluralistic society. One way to redeem oneself in a communist-type society is to bribe superiors to give one another chance. A second implication is that if there is a state policy of granting greater security to officials – as a reaction to an earlier terror period and/or major restructuring, either of which can lead to a sense of insecurity in officials that is not necessarily conducive to them giving of their best – then this is good news for those in the upper strata of the hierarchy, but unwelcome to those lower down who see their promotion opportunities severely reduced. A further reason why such upward mobility paths can become blocked is because of the slowdown in economic growth and/or transformation that occurs in many economies, whether capitalist or communist, as they become more developed and complex. Again, individuals can hope to circumvent all of this in a less monopolistic society by transferring, for instance, from one firm to another – or even, given the greater freedom to travel and seek employment in the West, to another country; the liberalization of employment regulations within the EC exemplifies this. In a society in which there is in theory essentially one employer, the adoption by that employer of a policy of security of tenure is going to make it far more difficult for ambitious people to achieve the promotions they seek and feel they deserve. As was argued above, this can lead to frustration; in the absence of alternative channels for this frustration (such as the possibility of establishing one's own business, thus making oneself independent of an employer – or, indeed, the possibility of 'dropping out'),[12] engaging in corrupt activity may act as a release valve for some.

Ironically, perhaps, just as excessive stability can lead to corruption, so can high levels of insecurity. Where a political system is still being established and/or where offices are not regularized (for example, where there are no specified tenure arrangements), individuals may engage in corrupt activities in order either to gain or to maintain official posts. This applies – especially in the form of patron–client relations (on this see Rigby and Harasymiw, 1983, and Tarkowski, 1988) – at the very top, as well as at the lower levels; the absence until relatively recently of regularized leadership arrangements in every communist state other than Yugoslavia created a situation ripe for corruption (on recent moves towards regularization see chapter 8).

Most of this section on 'mono-organizationality' has focused principally on officials and career possibilities. But another very important aspect of the essentially mono-organizational nature of most communist systems is that, as Brzezinski (1967, p. 92) has argued, in systems in which there are no real opposition parties to act as a 'loyal opposition' and watch for misdemeanours among the officers of the ruling party, there is one important check less than in other types of system (this point is elaborated later in the chapter). One can extend this to argue that the absence of a free press, as this is understood in the West, can also work to the advantage of the corrupt; this is a point made by Šimečka (1984, pp. 130–1). Given that so many examples of corruption cited in this study have been taken from the communist press itself, one must of course be very careful not to overstate this argument; as so often in comparisons between capitalist and communist systems, the differences are of degree (albeit often considerable degree) rather than kind. There was an increasing amount of investigative journalism in the communist world during the 1980s, and this study would not have been feasible without it. The Soviet Union was – until its collapse – still in a phase of *glasnost*, for instance. And the Chinese leadership has in recent years often seemed remarkably open in highlighting flaws in its system – through rather less so since June 1989 – as part of its policy of *toumingdu* (transparency). But these policies and practices should not blind us to two very important facts. The first is that the patterns of reporting of corruption identified in chapter 4, assuming they are valid, do suggest political interference in reporting; until fairly recently, some groups and some levels in the hierarchy were rarely if ever reported on, even in 'liberal' periods. Second, many countries have reported little, if any, corruption; we should not fall into the trap of assuming that the smaller communist states were all essentially mirror-images writ small of the USSR or China.

An essentially political factor that has frequently been mentioned by communists in power is the ineffectualness of the bodies responsible for vigilance – the police, the party, youth leagues, etc. One general reason for this 'ineffectualness' might be that communism's expectations of its officials – in terms of loyalty, devotion and sheer capacity – are unrealistically high; in such a situation, some officials will collude with each other to hide their various imperfections. But before considering the charges made against the control agencies, and the reasons for the problems identified by communist analysts themselves, the point needs to be made that the highly voluntaristic approach to politics adopted by communists leads them to try to be directly involved in more areas of social activity than do most other kinds of political activist. Moreover, during the 1980s, when an increasing number of communist states were putatively attempting to move closer to the rule of law (and away from subjective political control), the extent of formal regulation increased significantly. One reason why there might appear to have been more corruption in modern communist states than elsewhere, therefore, is quite simply that it is easier to transgress the law than it is in less-regulated states. Conversely, the task of the legal and control agencies is that much more difficult where more actions are proscribed, especially in the economic sphere.

In the April 1982 speech on corruption by Castro already cited, the Cuban leader argued that corruption does not develop only in the context of 'neo-capitalist activities': 'No! It also develops in the context of purely socialist activities as a result of a lack of control, of weakness, a lack of strict vigilance' (Castro, 1983, p. 348). In the same month, Deng argued that the reason why various law enforcement agencies and bodies responsible for maintaining vigilance were not performing as well as they should was because many 'comrades' were unaware of the seriousness of the problem of economic crime (Deng, 1984, p. 381). But this is in fact only one of a number of reasons for inadequate 'control'. Some communists, for instance, have explained the problem less in terms of problems of awareness (that is, consciousness) than of structural problems. One of these is deciding who is responsible for investigating and trying those engaged in economic crime. In February 1986, for example, an article in *Guangming Ribao* referred to various defects of this nature in the Chinese judicial system (cited in Yeh, 1987, pp. 16–17), while the results of a Soviet attempt to delineate more closely responsibilities for investigating and prosecuting in cases of corruption, published late in 1979 (see *Pravda*, 1 December 1979, pp. 1 and 3), only highlighted the confusion that still existed in this area.

Yet another reason for poor vigilance is that inspectors of various kinds are often less well educated and less well paid than the people they are charged with investigating. They may thus be outwitted by the latter, at the same time as there is insufficient incentive for them to pursue their aims as vigorously as they might (on this see *Izvestiya*, 18 September 1968, p. 2). Indeed, their relatively low incomes could actually be an incentive to collude with their investigatees. Furthermore, control agencies, notably the police, may actually be praised and rewarded for reporting low crime rates in their area – so that there is an incentive *not* to investigate too many misdemeanours.[13]

Then there is the fact, noted by several commentators, that even when officials – especially higher-ranking ones – are discovered and tried for their economic crimes, the punishments are often relatively very light (for more details on this see chapter 7). But even when courts *do* impose appropriate sanctions, they are not always able to have them implemented. In Henan Province (PRC), for instance, of 18,106 economic cases handled by the courts in 1986, sentences were not enforced in almost a quarter of them. According to *China Daily* (16 July 1987, p. 4) among the various factors contributing to this phenomenon are:

- Interference from administrative leadership ('Some leading cadres tend to protect the losing parties in their own areas by hampering the courts that handle the cases');
- Some cadres having a weak sense of law and not taking court decisions seriously;
- Courts not always paying sufficient attention to the implementation of their own decisions;
- A shortage of personnel to implement decisions (in China in 1987 there were approximately 3,400 law courts, but they had between them only 1,301 people to enforce decisions on economic cases).

It is clear, then, that 'overload' and inadequate resourcing can also help to explain inadequate performance by legal agencies. But not all commentaries on this problem are negative; some propose at least partial solutions. For example, in an article published in *Literaturnaya Gazeta* (1 July 1981 – translated in *CDSP*, Vol. 33, No. 40, p. 17), A. Rubinov urged the public to engage in more whistle-blowing since, in his view, it was unrealistic to expect officers of the Department for Combatting the Embezzlement of Socialist Property and Speculation (see chapter 7) to combat economic crime and corruption on their own. One problem with Rubinov's proposal is that both the Soviet and the Chinese media have published cases in which whistle-blowers have come off worse than the superiors they have reported. Often, the superior will be able to quash an investigation, while the whistle-blower suffers in one way or another for being a 'trouble-maker' (see pp. 204–5 for details). This discourages whistle-blowing, at the same time as it can encourage corruption.

An even more extreme variation on this general theme of the law acting insufficiently as a deterrent is that some laws intended to reduce corruption are not applied at all in practice. Thus a report in *Izvestiya* (6 April 1969, p. 3) pointed out that, according to a 1929 law still technically in force, managers and officials may in some circumstances be obliged to cover the costs of acts of embezzlement committed by their subordinates; this particularly applies when it is demonstrated that the superiors' negligence was a factor contributing to the subordinates' corruption. But this law had not, it was claimed, been applied at all for many years.

In the light of the above points, if those engaged in corruption feel that they may well 'get away with it' even if discovered, and if their superiors are unlikely to be held materially responsible, then the disincentive to start engaging in or continue with criminal activities is correspondingly less, as is the incentive to investigate suspicious activities. Moreover, just as inequities in the distribution of *wealth* can lead to resentment, so the fact that many more senior people go unpunished or receive light sentences for corruption can alienate those lower down, and can encourage them to break the rules too. In short, inequality and perceived inequity in the application of *justice* can promote corruption.

Another reason why the legal agencies have sometimes been perceived to be acting in an unsatisfactory way is because the entire legal system in communist states has in practice so frequently been dominated by the party. Although judges are formally elected in many countries, this has in the vast majority of – if not all – cases been only after they have been approved by the communist party. The fact that many citizens and party members themselves believe that party members are to a greater or lesser extent 'above the law' does not help communist leaders to persuade their subjects that their country is run according to the rule of law. If the law does not really rule, respect for it will be less than where it does.

A second relevant aspect of communist parties is that they have typically been large organizations, in some cases having more members than many countries have citizens. Thus the CPSU had in the late 1980s a membership of some 20 million, while the Chinese Communist Party has almost 50 million members. It would be idealistic and naive to the point of absurdity to assume that *no* or very few party members or officials in organizations as large as these are going to succumb to the temptation of illicit pecuniary gain. In short, the law of averages tells us that the size and spread of these organizations is going to mean there will be some corruption.

A third problem relating to the party is that the growing size of the *nomenklatura* in some communist states in recent years was not matched by a commensurate growth in the scale of the agencies charged with monitoring those on the list. At a plenary meeting of the Uzbek Central Committee – held in mid-1984 and concerned very much with corruption – one of the speakers made this point explicitly: 'The inflation of these lists [the *nomenklatura* lists] makes it difficult to study thoroughly the political, work-related and moral qualities of people and to monitor their activity' (adapted from *CDSP*, Vol. 36, No. 26, p. 13).

Many of the problems elaborated in the preceding paragraphs are aspects of the general problems – only sometimes mutually exclusive – in communist systems of *overload* (including inadequate resourcing), *overlap* (confusion of responsibilities) and *overkill* (for example, inflated apparatuses relative to the tasks). Much of this is succinctly summarized in the following statement by Eduard Shevardnadze, made at a meeting of Georgian communist party activists in January 1982: 'The style and work practices of our supervisory organizations continue to be a very serious problem. We have an enormous supervisory apparatus, but so far no one has made a serious study of the style and systems of its work. No one coordinates the supervisory agencies' activity' (from *Zarya Vostoka*, 19 January 1982 – translated in *CDSP*, Vol. 34, No. 5, p. 14).

But another reason why the law has often been poorly applied is that both policy statements and actual legislation on economic policy (and, often as a corollary, what constitutes economic crime) have been ambiguous. And ambiguous legislation can be conducive to corruption. In considering the dynamics of communist politics, some analysts have argued – sensibly – that the desire to move away from terror and coercion towards a more normative-based form of government, coupled with the deepening division of labour and rising standards of education and awareness, has led to a situation in which communist leaderships have been more willing than they were to seek the advice of specialists before making decisions. Precisely because of the less controlled political climate, these specialists become less likely simply to make the recommendations they believe their senior decision-makers want to hear. Moreover, they are more willing to reveal differences of opinion among themselves.

If the leadership itself is more collective, and more prepared to reveal differences among its membership than in more terroristic phases (a prime example of this prior to the 1989–91 revolution occurred at the time Messner resigned as premier and dissolved the Polish government in September 1988), this too can encourage a more pluralistic input to decision-making. Some commentators (such as Hough, 1972, esp. pp. 28–9) have taken this line of argument even further, and suggested that communist leaderships may increasingly have to act as brokers between competing interests (as distinct from merely choosing between different sets of advice). In all events, it was clear in many countries by the 1980s that an increasing amount of legislation was ambiguous, to some extent because it represented a compromise between conflicting views (for a case-study of this see Holmes, 1981a). Ambiguity means loopholes and possibilities for interpretation to one's own advantage.

Not everyone who, from the perspective of leaders or judges, 'misinterprets' or 'misunderstands' ambiguous legislation does so deliberately and in their own interest. Some may commit corrupt acts not because they are consciously interpreting 'grey areas' to their own advantage, but because they do not appreciate that their actions (or non-actions) may subsequently be interpreted and condemned as corrupt. Indeed, some individuals may genuinely be ignorant of the law for reasons that some commentators believe are more the fault of the authorities than of the citizen (or, it may be inferred, some lower-ranking officials). One Soviet citizen (cited by A. Bezuglov and V. Usanov in *Pravda*, 18 April 1983, p. 3) pointed out that it is often difficult to ascertain what the law is for the simple reason that it is almost impossible to obtain copies of particular sets of laws (such as the criminal code); the solution proposed in the *Pravda* article was to make such laws readily available in bookshops and elsewhere.

In addition to policy ambiguities and poor dissemination, sudden changes in policy can mean that what is generally perceived as legal one day becomes illegal the next. Sometimes, it is not easy to change one's situation as quickly as the new policy requires. For instance, in the early summer of 1983, the Central Committee of the VCP issued a much clearer statement than previously to the effect that party cadres were no longer permitted to own land. This pertained overwhelmingly to cadres in what had, until 1975, been South Vietnam – 22 per cent of whom at the district level or higher still formally owned land. The notion that cadres could suddenly dispose of assets in the way decreed by the central authorities revealed an insensitivity and naivety on the part of the latter (details from *YICA*, 1984, p. 284).

Another effect of policy changes is that they can actually create a new situation in which the pre-conditions for corruption are enhanced. One example is the policy adopted by the Yugoslav government in August 1965 that was designed to make rents more nearly approximate the actual running costs of domestic properties. Such properties were revalued, rents increased accordingly, and 'housing enterprises' were established through which rents were collected and funds pooled for major repair work and investments in new housing projects. According to Rusinow's research (1977, p. 178), the establishment of these housing enterprises led to very little improvement in the maintenance of existing property, but to a big increase in various forms of corruption. And various Russian economists, including Tatyana Koryagina, have argued that the introduction in May 1988 of the Soviet law on cooperatives – which encouraged the development of cooperative enterprises – led to an increase in economic crime (*MN*, No. 34, 1989, p. 10). But unquestionably the best example from the communist world – in the sense that several communist leaders themselves have made so much of it – is the effect of economic reform policies in China since the late 1970s. Both the opening up to the West and the effects of more private initiative in agriculture and of some decentralization of decision-making in industry have apparently been major contributors to the rise in corruption, at least according to some Chinese. Certainly, the increases in rural incomes in recent years could lead to resentment in the towns. In 1983, for example, the average net income of peasants increased by 14.7 per cent, as compared with only 4.3 per cent in the case of workers and managers in the urban areas (Cheng Jin, 1986, p. 95).[14] Moreover, the emphasis on boosting foreign trade, and on using material incentives to increase production, creates a climate more conducive to corruption than that which existed earlier. Such, at least, has been the argument of those often described by Westerners in the 1980s as the 'conservatives' among the Chinese leadership (such as Chen Yun, Peng Zhen). However, some Chinese have disagreed with this argument; thus an article that was published in the CCP theoretical journal *Hongqi* in August 1982 'refuted the "mistaken idea" that economic policy had caused economic crime' (Forster, 1985, p. 10). According to this article, it was the shortage of commodities, plus weaknesses in management, that were the principal reasons for the big increase in economic crime.

Deng himself has used both types of argument. While he did link corruption to the economic reforms in his April 1982 speech, he also argued at a senior party meeting in October 1984 that:

By the year 2000, people's outlooks will be quite different. Material conditions are the foundation. With improved material conditions and a higher cultural level, the people's outlooks will improve greatly. Our effort to crack down on criminal offenders is necessary and we shall continue to pursue this. *But the ultimate solution lies not in such an effort, but in quadrupling the GNP.* (Deng, 1985, p. 59 – emphasis added)

Thus Deng placed rather less emphasis on purposive changing of the masses' consciousness than Mao would have done, and placed the main stress on increasing production. The notion that a mere increase in living standards will be sufficient to overcome or at least substantially reduce the problem of widescale corruption can certainly be questioned; factors such as the availability and quality of consumer goods (not just money or collective goods), the perceived equitableness in distribution, respect for the law, etc., will be part of the equation. Moreover, there is little doubt that the policy has made particular kinds of corruption more feasible and almost certainly more widespread; the opportunities for officials to engage in currency speculation, for instance, have expanded as trade with capitalist nations has increased. Nevertheless, it is interesting to note what the leader of the world's most populous communist state has seen as the major reason for economic crime and corruption.

A fourth dimension of policy is that legislation and policy statements may actually lag behind the implementation of, for instance, economic reforms, so that new possibilities for corruption arise before the exploitation of such possibilities has been explicitly identified and condemned by politicians and legislators. Once again, some of the Chinese leadership has overtly acknowledged this as a factor explaining corruption (Forster, 1985, p. 10).

Aspects of policy are not the only reasons for problems of vigilance, law enforcement, etc. As Rigby (1985, p. 9) has pointed out, some more senior officials may actually *favour* a certain amount of corruption among their subordinates 'because their corruption increases their dependence'. If it can thus sometimes be in the vested interests of higher-ranking officials to permit such corruption, it becomes clear why they may attempt to block investigations by judicial organs, party commissions, etc. Not only do they wish to maintain this dependence, but they themselves may be implicated by an investigation team that could accuse them of turning a blind eye (see the quotation cited above, p. 166). In trying to prevent such investigations, the chances are that they will themselves engage in other forms of corruption, most notably string-pulling, against the interests of society at large.

The nature of the legal system and ambiguities in policy-making can be a reflection of the overall political climate in a given country. Other things being equal, a society in which there is perceived to be widespread state terror (or even very high levels of coercion) is likely to have lower levels of corruption than it does in more liberal, less repressive periods. The reason is fairly obvious; despite the fact that the continued use of the death penalty in many communist countries for extreme cases of corruption has not deterred some individuals, most people will feel that the risks (including death) involved in engaging in economic crime in a terroristic period far outweigh the possible advantages. This all said, the general picture needs to be modified if it is to reflect reality more closely; caution must be exercised when drawing inferences about 'the' political climate. Thus apparently liberal (that is, more tolerant) phases may in fact be accompanied by selected campaigns against particular manifestations of social deviance, including corruption, in order to keep liberalizing tendencies among the population in check. Less arbitrary and more tolerant communist regimes are still communist, and must sometimes demonstrate in various ways that they are still committed to democratic centralism, discipline and the end-goal of a truly communist society.

A second very general point about the political system is that, if the old adage 'power corrupts' is true, then the highly concentrated nature of power in so many communist countries would be very corrupting. The Leninist emphasis on 'vanguardism', on the need for an elite party and on democratic centralism, did not begin to be widely and publicly questioned and rejected as time-specific (and thus no longer valid) by communists in power until the late 1980s[15] – even if, giving him the benefit of the doubt, Lenin himself *may* have considered the need for the Bolsheviks to be organized in this way to have been a temporary expedient in the specifically Russian conditions of the early twentieth century. Most officials and politicians in the communist world were not in any very meaningful sense exposed to public control prior to the end of the 1980s, even if there were signs in some countries before then that there would be greater control of and less security for officials in future (see chapter 8). Indeed, the concentration and centralization of power, together with the limited and controlled channels of political participation, can exacerbate the feelings of alienation and frustration in many citizens and lower-level officials, which in turn can create an atmosphere conducive to corruption (subject to the point made earlier about state terror). There is, in short, some truth in Adlai Stevenson's claim that 'Power corrupts, but lack of power corrupts absolutely.' In Western-type systems, there are various escape valves for alienated and frustrated citizens, such as the right to strike or demonstrate, and the right to join anti-system political organizations as long as their methods are legal. Such rights have been rare in the communist world. Thus, although strikes have sometimes occurred, they have not generally been accepted as a legitimate release valve.[16] To cite just one example of the level of alienation that can exist in communist states, Schöpflin (1984, pp. 390–1) refers to the Czechoslovak quip that 'he who does not rob the state robs his family'. It appears that some have felt that if one can neither beat nor join (here in the sense of reach the upper echelons of) 'the system', then at least one can cheat it. This is another factor *explaining* the phenomenon noted in the cultural section whereby many feel that state property is 'theirs', so that they respect it less than – or at least treat it differently from – their neighbours' property.

Reference was made above to the possible effects of ambiguous policies or laws on the incidence of corruption. In fact, it is the ambiguity not only of specific policies or legislation, but also of the general approach of senior leaders, that can be largely responsible for the confusion experienced by many officials. In addition to the argument already made about leaderships increasingly having to consult and make compromises, there is the point that some leaderships are simply inept; such an argument has been made forcibly about the Brezhnev era by well-known Soviet investigator Telman Gdlyan (*MN*, No. 34, 1989, p. 10). But there are also aspects of leadership approaches which relate to the 'dynamism of legitimation' argument that permeates this book. As communist leaders have reinterpreted the ideology and have themselves argued that pragmatism must sometimes dominate idealism – as part of the move away from teleological and towards eudaemonic legitimation – so it becomes understandable why some officials believe they are being urged to do everything possible to, for instance, increase economic growth or foreign trade. The references to 'realistic' or 'really existing' socialism in so many East European states in the 1970s are a classic example of the sort of leadership pragmatism being referred to here (further examples are cited in Holmes, 1986a, pp. 112–13). Once again, however, China exemplifies this problem particularly well. When Deng made his famous statement that 'it does not matter whether a cat is black or white as long as it catches mice' (that is, it is the end result that matters more than the method used to achieve it), he appeared to condone all sorts of practices as long as they achieved the desired results. If one adds to this the fact that the Chinese leadership was simultaneously stressing the need to boost trade with the outside world, then it becomes comprehensible why some officials have resented the fact that they have been chided for spending too much public money on *dachi dahe*, if such banquets have been arranged for foreign businesspeople in the hope that this will improve the climate for trade negotiations.

I shall return to the broader ramifications of the 'banqueting issue' below. Before doing so, however, one final aspect of the general political climate needs to be commented upon. In doing so, the focus shifts from the system and its policies both to those hostile to communism and towards the newer communist states. Thus there can sometimes be a conscious policy by a group opposed to the communist system to weaken it through widespread encouragement of corruption. This is more feasible in those countries in which the communists' hold on power has never been properly consolidated – notably some of the African communist states and Afghanistan. Thus, writing on one of these African states, Williams has argued that: 'In a civil war, economic sabotage can be more effective and less risky than a military offensive and, in Angola, concerted efforts have been made through smuggling and associated corruption to undermine the fragile economic position of the MPLA Government' (R. Williams, 1987, p. 94; for evidence of a somewhat similar phenomenon in South Yemen see *IB*, No. 19, 1987, p. 39).

Generalizing from the last point, the reader is reminded once again that not all communist states were, by the late 1980s, as old and consolidated as the two giants we have concentrated on. Not only were many of them – including Afghanistan, Angola, Ethiopia and Mozambique – relatively new, but the communists had never properly consolidated power; civil war was common in these. In several, the party, state and legal organs had been very underdeveloped both in comparison with other communist states and relative to the professed needs of the country. In Benin, for example, there were very few primary or base party organizations at all, a problem the Beninois leadership was trying to overcome during the 1980s (see, for example, Allen, 1988, esp. p. 53). The gross inadequacy in some younger communist states of the legal and ideological apparatuses, in terms of their capacity both to coerce and to educate the citizenry and members of the other apparatuses, is yet another of the vast number of reasons for corruption; *ceteris paribus*, this makes it easier for groups hostile to communism to operate in the manner just described.

Dynamism and Integration into the World Market

The earlier reference to Chinese confusion over banqueting relates to the fact that officials from the communist world often conduct business with people from the capitalist world and are having to use some common language – in this case, that of business etiquette. In the field of trade, capitalist etiquette has been seen by many even in the communist world as the norm, and this often does involve wining and dining potential trading partners. If a private company does this, there is rarely any suggestion of improper use of public funds.[17] Employees of a communist enterprise, on the other hand, are seen to be disposing of *public* funds, since the unit is socially owned. Here, then, there is a conflict of values not so much between communist and pre-communist traditions (although this may also be part of the equation in the particular case cited here) as between current communist and capitalist values. If communist leaders encourage their subordinates to interact with people of fundamentally different value-systems, then there are almost bound to be tensions and contradictions.

Thus, to no small extent, the ambiguity of leaderships' approaches can itself be a reflection of the tensions and even contradictions that often exist between a given communist system's multifarious general goals, and the dynamism of such systems (for an explicit statement by the Soviet Minister of Internal Affairs that one of the major reasons for crime in the USSR is the contradictions under socialism, see Fedorchuk, 1985). In addition to the problem of building communism in a capitalism-dominated world, there is the problem of skewing referred to earlier. This is partially a function of the tension between the short- to medium-term aim of economic modernization and the ongoing aim of better satisfaction of people's aspirations, for example. In the earlier stages of modernization, the shortage of material rewards that reflects the priority of investments in heavy industry is often less a problem than at later stages; typically, some citizens are coerced into the development programme, while others work largely out of the genuine enthusiasm for a better world that communists can and in some cases do generate in the short term. Later on, the situation begins to change. As has been pointed out, there are often large sums of money in circulation but very little to purchase with them, while the earlier enthusiasm has been replaced by both cynicism and much greater materialism and individualism. The latter 'development' is largely a result of the system's own emphasis now on economic performance (moves towards eudaemonic legitimation) rather than revolutionary idealism or charismatic leadership. By this stage, moreover, bureaucratic interests have become entrenched in a way they were not in the earliest days of revolution or during the terroristic phases, and these act as a major impediment to the structural rebalancing of the economy that is required. In these circumstances, trading with the West and/or seeking aid and investment from it may seem to many communist leaders to be a sensible policy at later stages – after the first 'revolution from above'.[18] It is partially for these sorts of reasons that, in the case of communist countries at least, the notion that corruption is more typical of the developing than of the more developed stages must be put seriously in question; this point is expanded upon in the concluding chapter.

Some communist leaders became very aware by the 1970s and 1980s of the tensions that can arise in the ideology and in social practice when trying to use the capitalist world to assist communist systems in overcoming their economic problems. It was in this context, for example, that the GDR's ideologists (such as Hager) developed the concept of *Abgrenzung* (demarcation) in the 1970s, whereby the SED leadership urged economic cooperation with the FRG but emphasized the need for ideological vigilance. Some of the Chinese leaders and senior cadres have also warned of this problem. Mao, for instance, used to warn of the dangers of 'sugar-coated bullets', by which he meant that communists have to be aware of bourgeois temptations that have negative repercussions (for a sophisticated Chinese argument – from the Mao era – to the effect that corruption increases as capitalist ideas and bourgeois property rights spread see Yao, 1975, esp. p. 6). More recently, Politburo members Peng Zhen and Chen Yun, and the Second Secretary of the CDIC Wang Hoshou, were in the 1980s warning CDIC members and others responsible for vigilance of the negative influence of capitalist ideology on cadres. They linked this influence to the 'opening to the West' policy and directly correlated it with the rising incidence of corruption in the PRC (Yeh, 1987, pp. 16 and 20). Somewhat similar arguments were made by hardliners in the South Yemeni Politburo (such as Abd al-Fattah Isma'il and Salih Muslih Qasim), who in late 1985 accused the president and others of being too liberal and, as a corollary, condoning corruption (*YICA*, 1987, p. 464). In sum, many communists have argued that an opening up of their system to foreign influences will lead to a decline in socialist values and an increase in the possessive individualism they see as a fundamental component of corruption.

But not all communist leaders seem to have accepted that the danger of value-pollution is as great as Hager, Chen et al. contend. Others have maintained that the economic improvements likely to occur by seeking trade and aid from the West outweigh the potential ideological disadvantages. In the 1970s, for instance, several East European leaders took advantage of détente to increase their economic interaction with the West. The best example of this, and of how it can backfire, is provided by Poland. Gierek borrowed heavily from the West in the early 1970s, and used much of this to bring real improvements to the standard of living of most ordinary Poles. Unfortunately, as the West moved into recession in the mid-1970s (this is often attributed to the 1973 oil crisis, although to explain it in terms of just one factor is simplistic), so Poland suffered the knock-on effects of this (for details see Pelczynski, 1980, pp. 414–21). The ensuing disappointment among many Poles was one of the major factors contributing to the mass unrest in Poland both in 1976 and again in 1980–1. Communist leaders have often been aware of the potential dangers of economic interaction with capitalist states, but their hold on power has in some cases been so precarious that they would rather run this risk than relinquish control – and their own long-term aspirations for their country – altogether. It is almost certainly in this light that one should see the signing of the Nkomati Accord between Mozambique and South Africa in 1984; Samora Machel and the rest of the communist leadership in the former Portuguese colony were not so much 'selling out' as accepting what appeared to be the lesser of two evils (see R. Williams, 1987, p. 91).

Summary and Conclusions

It is evident that there is an enormous range of factors that can encourage corruption. It would, of course, be highly desirable to be able to rank-order these variables, or even groups of variables. Unfortunately, this is not possible – situations change over time and across polities, and in most actual case-studies it is impossible to disentangle all the motives for a given individual's corruption. Even if we were able to interview many of those found guilty of corruption – an extremely unrealistic aspiration – most would not be aware of all of their own motives anyway. We must, in short, be satisfied merely with the identification of factors. Having said this, some speculation on the reasons for apparent changes in corruption patterns and likely future developments is both permissible and conducive to debate; I shall thus engage in this at appropriate points in this section.

As already indicated, some commentators – in communist states as well as in the West – have argued that the problem of corruption will dramatically decline or even disappear once the problems of shortages and the poor quality of goods are overcome. This seems to me to be a naive argument, given the point made earlier about 'need' being a socially determined construct. Nevertheless, some steps could be taken by communist regimes – in the unlikely event that those few still in existence survive for some years yet – to lessen the opportunities for corruption. If there is an excess of money chasing too few goods, then the removal or reduction of subsidies on so many basics (housing, public transport, basic foods, etc.) could help to overcome this. Alternatively, such states could follow the (communist) Hungarian example and either introduce or substantially increase income tax for the masses; many formerly communist states allowed for income tax, but it became payable in significant amounts at such a relatively high threshold that only a small proportion of people were affected by it to a perceptible degree. Either of these policy changes should generate more disposable income for the state, which in theory could be used to overcome skewing problems (by freeing more funds for investment in consumer goods industries) and satisfy consumer demands better. But there are, unfortunately, dangers in raising prices or introducing/increasing income tax. Not only Poland, but also the USSR (for example, in Novocherkassk in 1962), Romania, Yugoslavia and other countries have discovered that price rises sometimes lead to mass demonstrations and riots.

In an attempt to avoid this, at least two (at the time) communist states in recent years considered ways of introducing such rises without triggering mass unrest. In the USSR, advisers to Gorbachev such as Abel Aganbegyan argued that *proposals* for price changes should be announced in the press, and that citizens should then be free to comment on them for, perhaps, three to four months before they are introduced; this principle was accepted at the June 1987 plenum of the CPSU Central Committee (see Aganbegyan, 1988, pp. 181–2). This remained largely at the theoretical stage, and it remains to be seen whether or not it will be put into wide-scale practice, either in the post-communist CIS (which at present appears more intent on letting 'the market' determine prices) or in the few remaining communist states, and whether it will have the effect intended by the leadership. In one country where the former communist government did attempt something along these lines, the masses did not give sufficient support to the government's proposals;

on 29 November 1987, the Polish authorities held a referendum whereby they hoped a simple majority of the electorate would endorse proposals for price rises of up to 50 per cent on a number of basics, the increases to become effective in 1988. Unfortunately, only 44 per cent of the voters indicated their 'support' (perhaps 'reluctant acceptance' would be a more appropriate term); the reforms were subsequently adopted, but in a highly modified version (for Jaruzelski's interpretation of the referendum results at the December 1987 plenum of the Central Committee of the PUWP see *IB*, Vol. 26, No. 4, 1988, pp. 37–9). All this brings us back to the issues of mass attitudes, legitimacy and legitimation; but these are big, general issues and are therefore dealt with in the concluding chapter.

It has also been argued by some commentators that many of the problems relate to development; with the exception of the GDR and Czechoslovakia, all communist states were, or still are, developing countries.[19] The commitment to *rapid* and ostensibly *comprehensive* ('ostensibly' because of the skewing problems) development is generally stronger in communist states than in other developing countries. Moreover, the methods used are usually different. Communist states typically attempt development with as little recourse to aid from capitalist countries as possible – even if, in practice, many of them had limited success in this endeavour (on the problems of Angolan economic development see Somerville, 1986, pp. 131–51; on the Mozambican economy see Hanlon, 1984, pp. 72–120) and in recent years introduced radical changes of policy on this. Instead, in most cases they initially sought to modernize via internal accumulation and/or – in the cases of the newer ones – aid from older communist states, notably the USSR and China. In the case of internal capital accumulation, this often required high levels of coercion, especially of the peasantry. If the coercion is added to the need for a large-scale bureaucracy to administer the 'revolution from above', then it becomes clearer why the scale of officialdom is proportionately much higher on average than in other types of system. Other things being equal, the scope for corruption increases in this situation. Moreover, the coercion and the breakdown of value-systems are important factors leading to alienation from the system, which creates a fertile soil for corruption.

One point that has emerged at various junctures is that several of the reasons for corruption in communist states are, while rarely unique to such systems, far more a feature of them than of liberal democracies. The centrally planned and socially owned economy, and the centralized and in some senses mono-organizational nature of the political system, are the two most obvious features. This point is made forcefully in the *Moscow News* discussion referred to earlier (No. 34, 1989, p. 10). In that, two of the participants – Yuri Kozlov and Genri Reznik – argue that it is the *totalitarian* system itself that fosters corruption. Reznik argues explicitly that corruption in the USSR is closely related to the command economy and to the type of political system this engenders: 'We are doomed to our corruption by the economic and political system that we have. What we have today is not a sudden show of abnormality but a logical syndrome of the command economy.' More specifically, he relates corruption to a system in which there is a large number of low-paid bureaucrats who both wield enormous power and are subject to little if any meaningful control. Such an argument overlaps considerably with that of Weber cited above, and fairly explicitly reaches the same basic conclusion; unless there is an entrepreneurial structure to counter the bureaucracy, the latter will sooner or later abuse its power. But is it likely to be sooner or later?

Developing and integrating several of the points made in the previous paragraphs, I would argue that there is more likely to be endemic corruption in what Baylis (1974) has called 'mature' communist systems than during the mobilization phase (the first 'revolution from above'). Moreover, in line with the argument elaborated in chapter 1, it appears that one of the most significant reasons for corruption in many of the communist states is that these systems were very much in a contradictory transitional phase in recent years. All communist states are dynamic, and in a very real sense are in rapid and major transition once the communists take power. However, leaders in earlier phases had a clearer idea of the policies, structures and political style they would adopt as communists (for example, socialization of the means of production, industrialization, the leading role of the party, etc.), and of how these differed from those of their primary international class enemy, capitalism. Moreover, as Šimečka has explicitly argued was the case in Czechoslovakia (1984, p. 128), there are often many true believers in the early stages of communist rule, including many in the party–state apparatus. But leaders and others often lose both their radical vision and their ideals as the years pass; much corruption relates directly or indirectly to the identity crisis the communist world has recently been experiencing, as its leaders have felt increasingly compelled to move *towards* the policies, structures and even ideological tenets of capitalism. The identity crisis is heightened by the fact that the liberal democracies are themselves for the most part very imperfect examples of capitalism. In other words, the gap between the perceived reality of actual 'capitalist' states – with their social welfare provisions, in some cases minimum wage policies, etc. – and the reality of recent communist developments is *narrower* than that between the latter and the ideal-type of capitalism. It is this identity crisis – the results of which so dominated the world's media from 1989 to 1991 – which leads me to refer to a contradictory transitional phase, and to speculate that this has ultimately been the single most important reason for the apparent growth in official corruption in many of the countries considered in this study.

Finally, although the emergence of post-communism has meant that several of the structural/systemic reasons for corruption under communism either no longer pertain or else are far less significant than they were, it should be fairly obvious from the sheer range of causes identified and the arguments made in this chapter that official corruption, and campaigns against it, are both likely to be a salient feature of early post-communism. First, several of the factors analysed above can be found in *any* system. Second, a substantial proportion of the means of production in the post-communist world is still socially owned, with all the ramifications this point has for corruption. Third, the relatively serious economic problems all post-communist countries are currently experiencing suggest that regimes will feel a growing need for scapegoats to blame for these difficulties. Whereas many citizens may become increasingly racist – blaming other ethnic groups for the troubles – the authorities may consider it more functional to target corrupt officials. This said, the scope of campaigns may well be limited, since the new regimes need much of the expertise of the former communist staffs. Unfortunately, it is not possible to predict in advance – especially on a comparative basis – the likely balance between scapegoatism and dependency on the staffs.

NOTES

1 It is interesting to note that Khrushchev criticized what he saw as essentially the racism inherent in looking at the Georgians in this way – see Khrushchev, 1970, p. 305.
2 When Gorbachev came to power, he soon set about undermining his principal rival, Grigorii Romanov – particularly, it appears, by permitting rumours about Romanov's excessive drinking to circulate. Many Western observers believe that Boris Yeltsin is a heavy drinker – a rumour Yeltsin himself denies.
3 Cultural attitudes towards the family are of some relevance here; but these are more the domain of the anthropologist.
4 Several studies have suggested that many people joined the communist party in various East European states in the late 1940s because of a complex mix of

factors, including the desire for security, wanting to quash rumours that they were collaborationists with the fascists – and plain opportunism.

5   The term 'modernization' (and, it should be noted, 'development') is contentious and can be highly value-laden; this is particularly so if those using it argue or imply that the phenomena usually associated with it represent an improvement on the previous situation. No such implication should be inferred here. For our purposes, modernization refers to a range of social and economic changes that typify the transition from a predominantly village-based and agrarian society to a predominantly urban and industrial one. Among these are changes in the level and type of education; the kind of work people engage in; the nature and structure of the family; the individual's relationship with nature. Some of these and other factors will be elaborated in the textual discussion of the effects of modernization. The text should also make it clear both that and why I do not accept that such changes invariably or necessarily represent an improvement.

6   Rationing was introduced in Cuba in 1962. Although the situation generally improved over the years, as recently as 1980 consumers still spent an average of nearly one third of their total expenditure in markets on rationed products, and it was largely in the hope of overcoming this problem that 'free farmers' markets' were introduced in 1981.

7   There was some *illegal* private activity, though, in Hoxha's time – see Schnytzer, 1982, pp. 48–9 and 57–8.

8   Following parliamentary elections in Albania in March–April 1991, Alia was re-elected president by the Albanian parliament – despite having lost his parliamentary seat. In May 1991, and in line with the draft constitution that had recently been presented to parliament, Alia resigned as first secretary of the ALP, since no one individual could now head both the party and the state. In June 1991, at its 10th Congress, the ALP formally renamed itself the Socialist Party of Albania; F. Nano was elected chair of the 'new' party. And in April 1992, following parliamentary elections in March, Alia essentially left the Albanian political scene when he resigned as President.

9   By the end of the 1980s, it was far from clear what the priorities were – different leaders had different ideas on this. In theory, however, the notion of priorities, plan-targets, etc. still pertained until about 1990 – by which time, the country was in such chaos that it was difficult to determine not only what the policies on the economy were, but even whether or not there were any. The defence industry *may* well still have been a priority as of mid-1991, however – see next note. In all events, the point being made in the text helps to explain why corruption was probably more rife in some sectors of the economy than in others up to the late 1980s.

10 As part of the overall drive to improve economic performance and redress the structural imbalances in the economy, the Soviets introduced a policy in late 1988 of converting many defence-related closed enterprises to the production of consumer durables – see, for example, Yudin, 1989. However, there still existed a sizeable defence industry at the time of the collapse of the USSR, and I know of no concrete evidence to suggest that this was no longer privileged.

11 The term 'mono-organizationality' must be used with caution, not only because of increasing privatization in many parts of what little is left of the communist world, but also because of the realities of competition for skilled personnel; subject to these riders, the term is a useful one.

12 It should be noted that most communist states have had no unemployment benefits system as such, although Hungary introduced one in 1989. Although

several communist countries – even the USSR (see, for example, *MN*, No. 36, 1989, pp. 8–9) – were by the late 1980s acknowledging real unemployment, and although it appeared that a proper system of unemployment benefits would have been introduced in them in the 1990s (that is, had communism not been replaced by post-communism), communist constitutions typically specified that citizens had not only the right but also the *duty* to work.

13 This said, it should be noted that the Soviets, at least, became very aware of this problem in the 1980s, and introduced legislation that *required* the police to respond properly to all reports of suspected criminality – see *Literaturnaya Gazeta*, 29 August 1984, p. 10.

14 Urban workers were previously earning far more on average than their rural comrades, so that there was scope for catching up by rural workers anyway; but what matters is the *perception* by urban dwellers that they were now either less far ahead (an accurate perception) or even falling behind (in aggregate, an inaccurate perception).

15 There were, of course, occasional examples well before this; many Czechoslovak communist leaders certainly questioned various key aspects of Leninism during the Prague Spring of 1968.

16 On the role of trade unions and policies on strikes see Pravda and Ruble, 1986. There were signs of major change in official attitudes towards strikes in some countries, even before the momentous events of 1989. For instance, in Hungary's draft labour code that was published in the (Northern) autumn of 1988, there was provision for a formal right to strike (*Australian Financial Review*, 12 September 1988). The USSR formally recognized the right to strike – albeit subject to various provisos – in October 1989.

17 As is so often the case, however, the situation is not entirely straightforward. In several Western countries, there have been debates as to whether business lunch expenses, for example, should be taxed or not. One of the questions often raised in these debates is whether or not the state should use pecuniary means to dissuade private companies from entertaining more than is deemed necessary. However, this situation is not strictly comparable with the communist one, in which the actual costs of the wining and dining are funded by what are perceived to be publicly owned units. The latter phenomenon can exist in capitalist countries, of course – wherever enterprises are nationalized; but these constitute (increasingly) atypical enterprises in most capitalist states.

18 The reference here to the *first* 'revolution from above' is intended as an acknowledgement of the fact that Gorbachev introduced a second such revolution in the USSR, and that the Hungarian communist leadership did this in the late 1980s.

19 See note 5.

6

The Functions and Dysfunctions of Corruption and its Reporting

Although the term 'corruption' generally has a negative connotation, it can in some circumstances be a distinctly beneficial phenomenon, not only for those engaging in it – until they are caught – but also for the system in which they are operating. The advantages of corruption to the individuals involved in it having already been considered, both the positive and negative effects of corruption and the fight against it (leadership campaigns, media reporting, etc.), are the principal focus of this chapter; they are examined primarily in terms both of the system itself and of the regime. It is an interesting point in this connection that Western analysts of corruption in both the PRC and the USSR (see, for example, Feldbrugge, 1984, p. 541) have noted that the vast majority of items published in the communist mass media on crime were about *economic* crime – of which, as has been argued, corruption is often a major part. Indeed, if one were to adopt the broader definition of corruption favoured by many writers on communist politics, according to which economic crime and corruption are virtually synonymous, then corruption would emerge as far and away the most reported-on type of crime in several communist states. This may reflect the actual distribution of different types of crime; equally, it may not, and we need to ask *why* communist authorities often appear to want to wash their dirty linen in public. This issue is a major dimension of the present chapter.

The chapter is a short one. There are two main reasons for this. First, many of the factors overlap and are intertwined with the reasons for corruption that were analysed in the last chapter, and it would be inappropriate and tautologous to elaborate them again here. Second, the range of dysfunctions, etc., listed by communists themselves is a relatively narrow one.

The Advantages of Corruption and its Reporting

More than a dozen functions of corruption and its reporting can be identified, many of which directly or indirectly relate to system and/ or regime legitimacy.

One direct advantage of corruption is that a certain amount can help to make an economy operate more efficiently. Various problems, particularly relating to supplies, almost inevitably arise whenever attempts are made to direct a complex, large-scale economy from a central planning agency. The use of the *'tolkach'* (expediter or pusher) to overcome bureaucratic bottlenecks was common in the USSR and several other communist states (see, for example, Nove, 1977, pp. 100–1).

Closely linked to the last point is the fact that the ability of both production units and individual consumers to acquire via corrupt means goods and services they require or desire, but which are difficult or impossible to obtain through regular channels, helps to reduce levels of dissatisfaction. *Ceteris paribus*, the lowering of dissatisfaction levels should have positive ramifications for both regime and system legitimacy.

Similarly, the effect over time of corruption functioning in this way can be to expedite economic development, in that it can help to circumvent hold-ups in the economy that may arise from the cautiousness, errors and inefficiency of the bureaucracy. In that economic development is thus aided, and that communists may be able to claim that they are on target for their *telos*, corruption can again be seen as a potential legitimating agent (for an argument that corruption and modernization are usually closely correlated see Huntington, 1968, esp. pp. 59–71; see too chapters 1 and 8 of this study).

For reasons explained in the last chapter, communist states have relatively large bureaucracies. As with all bureaucracies, there is a constant, real danger that they will become estranged from ordinary citizens. A certain amount of relatively minor corruption can help to alleviate this problem, by humanizing relations both between citizens and officials, and between officials themselves. The fact that a citizen can break through a seemingly impenetrable wall of regulation by greasing the palm of an official, for instance, can render the whole image of officialdom less daunting (this point is made by McMullan, 1961, p. 196).

The legitimacy of the system or regime might also be enhanced through its encouragement of whistle-blowing. If citizens and officials feel both that they have the right to blow the whistle on corrupt officials (and others engaging in economic crime), and that allegations will be investigated and acted upon, then they may well identify more closely with the authorities, since the latter will be seen to be abiding more closely by their own professed ethical code than appears to be the case in some other circumstances (for example, in terms of their attitudes towards privilege). Moreover, if citizens feel that the authorities are prepared to respond to expressions of dissatisfaction, then it is reasonable to assume that fewer of them will be tempted to engage in disruptive political activism; this, too, is advantageous to regime legitimacy. And if uncorrupted officials feel that their interests are being protected by the leadership, then they are likely to perform better as administrators, etc. – which has positive knock-on effects for the system and society.

The points in the last two paragraphs notwithstanding, *some* toleration of corruption and economic crime by the authorities is useful, since there might be more political activism against the system or regime were it not for the release valve of corruption. If the claim of some writers on legitimation that political orders are particularly vulnerable when their own officers turn against them – or at least lose faith in them (see chapter 1) – are accepted, then *de facto* tolerance of some corruption among such officials can act as a release valve for these officials too. There is less incentive to turn to illicit political activity if one is in practice able to take pecuniary advantage of the existing system. Indeed, Šimečka (1984, pp. 134–5) argues that the Czechoslovak leaders actually *encouraged* (as distinct from merely tolerated) corruption in the post-1968 period known as 'normalization', precisely because they believed that they could in this way avert ('buy off') political unrest.

It is partially because of this ambivalence in official attitudes towards corruption and whistle-blowing that potential whistle-blowers in many communist states might – as mentioned briefly in chapter 5 – be well advised to think twice before reporting on officials. A couple of concrete examples will make the point. According to a recent Vietnamese report: 'Many people were subject to repression after they had submitted letters of denunciation [concerning, *inter alia*, corruption among cadres]; their material and spiritual lives were imperilled' (*SWB*/FE/0120/B/4, 8 April 1988). Members of the staff of the Georgian Republic Ministry of Trade who tried to expose the bribe-taking, nepotism and other forms of corruption of some of their colleagues were expelled from the CPSU for their troubles (*Zarya Vostoka*, 11 December 1985, p. 3 – in *CDSP*, Vol. 37, No. 51, p. 22; for another Soviet example of this problem see *Pravda*, 18 April 1983, p. 3), while a Beijing engineer was sacked twice for reporting corruption and economic crime at his workplace (*CD*, 21 October 1988, p. 3). It must be noted that it is by no means *only* ambivalence at the senior leadership level that leads to the unfortunate fate of so many whistle-blowers; bureaucratism, inadequate resources, and even – probably as a major factor – corruption itself among lower-level officials all help to explain this problem.

As argued in chapter 5, one of the reasons why some communist officials become frustrated is because their upward mobility channels are blocked. There is a certain irony in the fact that, in their endeavours to show in a concrete way their commitment to moving away from terror, some states have attempted to instil a new confidence and feeling of security among those groups once most subject to the whims of the leadership by seeking to minimize turnover among officials. The best-known example of this is Brezhnev's USSR, where the policy of 'stability of cadres' led to a situation in which people in the middle and higher echelons of officialdom could hope to keep their position for many years (on this see Rigby, 1970). Given that the leadership simultaneously wanted to keep the *size* of various bureaucracies within bounds, or even to reduce them, it is obvious why many junior officials became frustrated. Anti-corruption campaigns can thus be advantageous in that the removal of corrupt officials can create vacancies to which others can be promoted. This can help to reduce tensions between leaderships and their staffs. Moreover, if the removal of corrupt officials not only appears legitimate to the public (in contrast to the arbitrary way in which officials could be removed during terroristic, purge periods) but also helps to overcome the conservatism of bureaucracy that can and often does arise when a given group has been in the same position for a prolonged period, then leaderships can kill two or more birds with one stone. Thus both Andropov and Gorbachev hoped through anti-corruption campaigns to be able to change the complexion of the Soviet party apparatus, state bureaucracy, KGB, etc., without appearing to use Stalinist purge methods (whether they in fact succeeded in changing the complexion of various party–state hierarchies is a moot point, and is not our concern here).

A closely related point is that senior leaders may single out a particular part of their staff – such as the officials of an individual republic, a particular ministry, etc. – for an anti-corruption campaign. In this way, they can hope to overcome resistance (such as nationalism or 'departmentalism') that has built up in that unit. The replacement of corrupt officials can also give their superiors new opportunities for patronage. This can itself be a form of corruption, of course. But then the replacement of one form of corruption by another does not necessarily negate the effectiveness to the system or regime of overcoming the first.

Some Chinese leaders and other commentators have explained campaigns against corruption among high-ranking officials in somewhat different terms. Thus Hu Qili argued in 1986 that one of the main purposes of publicizing such cases is to *educate* other officials and the masses, in terms of both what constitutes corruption and why it is seen as detrimental to society, and to convey to everyone how the party–state deals with it; a somewhat similar argument has been made by the head of the China International Trust and Investment Corporation, Rong Yiren (cited in *Newsweek*, 3 February 1986, p. 15). Other Chinese officials and analysts have taken a more 'orthodox' Marxist approach to corruption, arguing that publicizing cases of it constitutes part of the class struggle against erosive bourgeois influences.

The legitimating effect of reporting has been noted by officials and commentators in other communist states. Thus the Minister of Internal Affairs for Georgia wrote in 1974:

> The Georgian Republic Ministry of Internal Affairs is aware of the enormous publicity it has received in the mass media in the past few years. Propaganda about the activity of the Soviet militia and criticism of shortcomings in the internal affairs agencies' work, if such accounts discuss the steps taken to combat these negative phenomena, enhance the militia's prestige and mobilize the public in the struggle to strengthen socialist law and order. (in *Zarya Vostoka*, 24 July 1974 – translated in *CDSP*, Vol. 26, No. 46, p. 27)

while the author of an article in the Vietnamese newspaper *Nhân Dân* in April 1988 argued that:

> It is a matter of concern that some key cadres contend that bringing this serious negative case [a cover-up by party, state and police officials] to court is tantamount to washing dirty linen in public, thus impairing the prestige of party committee echelons . . . They do not see that the effect is the opposite. In reality, the severe handling of cases of infringements of party discipline and state law consolidates, all the more strongly, the people's confidence. (*SWB*/FE/0120/B/4–5, 8 April 1988).

Involvement in anti-corruption campaigns can enhance the career prospects of rising politicians. Two former members of Gorbachev's

Politburo (itself now defunct), Aliev and Shevardnadze, have been seen by many Western observers as having been attractive to the general secretary largely because of their reputations for combatting corruption in Azerbaijan and Georgia respectively. It can be noted here that the creation of new bodies, or the enlargement of existing ones, to investigate corruption can also create new jobs and promotion opportunities; Chen Yun's promotion to head of the CDIC is an example of this, for instance.

If corruption itself can have a positive effect over time, so might the frequent long-term reporting of it. If a leadership feels compelled – because of the sheer scale of corruption and its demoralizing effects – to mount a visible campaign against corruption, it may also feel that a constant barrage of reporting will have one of three effects. First, it may actually lead to a significant reduction in corruption, which can have a legitimating effect. Second, and conversely, if it really finds it difficult to contain corruption, it may decide that the constant reporting of corruption will dull the senses of the masses to the problem of corrupt officials; people become accustomed to it. The latter is very much a 'second-best' approach, since virtual acceptance by the public of corruption as somehow an innate part of the system is hardly conducive to enhanced legitimacy. On the other hand, such a numbing of the senses is almost certainly better than widespread, strong indignation *in addition to* the feeling that the authorities are powerless and/or unwilling to control the problem. The third possible effect is a highly speculative one. A prolonged, high-profile campaign 'against' corruption might be seen on one level as a way of preparing the citizenry for a further uncoupling of the economy – in line with the general argument of this book concerning the relationship between eudaemonism and legal-rationality. Thus, one of the possible effects of such a campaign is that citizens will come to accept the idea that there is a great deal of entrepreneurial activity in the economy. If they also come to believe that this is a 'normal' – in some senses acceptable – situation, it should *ceteris paribus* be easier for a communist leadership to persuade the masses that it would be better to have a situation of *legal*, controlled entrepreneurship and market relations than one in which such activity is underground, with all the negative ramifications of this. The Polish communist leaders may have had such a strategy in the period up to 1988, when they suddenly legalized much of what had until then been classified as illegal economic activity. It can also be argued that the Soviet leadership was in recent years attempting to accustom the masses to a far higher proportion of (legal) entrepreneurial activity in the economy.

Another leadership-related dimension of the reporting of corruption is that leaders can use this to reveal human weaknesses in their citizens and officials. In doing so, they can hope to enhance their own reputations (and legitimacy) as superior beings who accept the responsibility of correcting defects in society and improving consciousness. In the absence of such flaws in society, and if a universal socialist (or even communist) consciousness has been achieved, the party's role – or at least its vanguard, directing function – comes into question, which in turn undermines the position of the party leaders.

There can be a dynamism to the reporting of corruption; it may assume different forms and play different roles at different stages of communist power. For instance, a relatively new communist regime may attempt to acquire greater support from the citizenry by reporting on the corruption of the former regime's elite (Castro frequently did this in the 1960s). At a later stage, previous *communist* leaders and/or current opponents – the latter especially during a power struggle – can be accused of corruption in a given leader's bid to increase support. To cite one case in which both groups were targetted, it has been demonstrated that the number of cases of corruption reported in the Chinese press increased dramatically from 1978 (see chapter 4); many people accused of corruption in the period to about 1980 were simultaneously charged with being supporters of the Gang of Four (that is, contemporary leading figures associated with the late Mao). It would be a mistake, however, to see the more recent (1980s) leadership encouragement of the reporting of corruption in China solely as an attempt to legitimate the present regime through an emphasis on the ways in which it is overcoming problems engendered by an earlier regime. In fact, it appears that some of the more 'conservative' leaders (such as Chen Yun, Peng Zhen) have been keen to have corruption exposed largely because they wanted to highlight some of the problems of Deng's economic reforms. This is not the same point as that made above concerning exposure of the *corruption* of a 'current opponent'; rather, corruption is being used as a way of raising certain critical questions about another leader's *policies*, primarily in the hope of seeing those policies modified or even abandoned. Expressed differently, individual members of a given leadership may have different reasons for wanting to publicize corruption, and a motive that is functional to one leader may be dysfunctional to others – not only past, but also present.

Developing the last point, some or all members of a leadership can attempt to use an anti-corruption campaign to engender support for a policy and/or legislative change they are intending to introduce. In the early 1960s, for example, Khrushchev's son-in-law Adzhubei – who was at the time editor of *Izvestiya* – encouraged the public to write in to his newspaper expressing their views on the most appropriate punishment for currency speculators. He claimed that he had received thousands of letters demanding the death sentence – which, in the colourful way the press had recently been reporting cases of currency speculation, may have been true (see Simis, 1982, pp. 28–31). Here, then, the media were being used by the authorities not only to report corruption but also in a bid to gain – or at least appear to gain – public support for the introduction of far more draconian laws that would be retroactively applied to those found guilty of currency speculation.

Leading on from this, the reporting of corruption can be seen by the leadership as a symbol both of its own commitment to a moral code (a campaign can be designed to demonstrate to the public that the leaders have not abandoned the ethical, normative dimensions of the *telos*), and of its commitment to the rule of law (legitimation in the legal-rational mode). Certainly, justice must be *seen* to be done if claims to be moving towards the rule of law are to be convincing; looked at from another angle, there must be no dual standards, no suggestion that some people are above the law. This issue – as well as the long-term importance of socializing the young to respect the law – is inherent in the following quotation from a Czechoslovak radio broadcast, in which the broadcasters discuss a recent article in *Rudé Právo* that had criticized the fact that many officials and managers were never prosecuted for their corruption and theft: 'This is particularly dangerous, because such practice distorts the young people's awareness of legality. If they encounter the so-called "double morality", and opportunist attitudes towards the law, they will then deduce that it is not necessary to respect the law' (*SWB*/EE/7981/B/3, 19 June 1985). In sum, the reporting of corruption and of the punishment of corrupt officials can improve the image of a regime by making it appear less hypocritical.

But there is another form of leadership commitment that a campaign might be seen to demonstrate. Thus, one possible function of the reporting of corruption – this must remain highly speculative at present – is that a smaller communist state may have emulated the USSR by introducing an anti-corruption campaign, primarily as a symbol of loyalty to the communist giant. In this case, the smaller regime may hope for various favours – for example, more advantageous trading arrangements – by sycophantically imitating an important policy of the larger power. The possibility that emulation of the USSR explains Bulgaria's anti-corruption campaign of 1985/6 has been raised by at least one observer (J.D. Bell, in *YICA 1986*, p. 268).[1]

As Alex Pravda (1986, p. 53) suggests, an anti-corruption drive is one way of diverting the public's attention away from the fact that living standards are not rising as quickly as consumer expectations. All this relates to the central argument of this book, concerning the problems of eudaemonic legitimation. Let us now focus even more explicitly on legitimacy-related aspects of reporting corruption.

One real advantage of publicizing cases involving corrupt officials is that such reporting can blame these people for problems that have arisen in the economy. In short, they become scapegoats. Although it is exceedingly difficult – perhaps impossible – to quantify this at all satisfactorily, it is highly improbable that corruption was the main, let alone the sole, reason for the relative failure of various economic reforms that were introduced in the communist world. Yet it is easy for the leaders to attribute problems to corrupt officials, and it is easier for most citizens to understand this reasoning than leadership explanations in terms of problems of accumulation, investment, distribution, sectoral or branch skewing, international market forces, etc. Certainly, it is from the leaders' own perspective far better to attack corrupt officials than to relate economic problems to deficiencies and ambiguities in their own policies. During the Stalin era of Soviet history, economic problems were frequently attributed to officials who were accused of deliberate sabotage and working in the pay of foreign agents. At the so-called 'Great Trial' of 1938, for instance, the chief Soviet prosecutor, Andrei Vyshinsky, referred to a number of senior Bolsheviks as: 'a band of felonious criminals . . . who have sold themselves to enemy intelligence services', and proceeded to argue that:

> In our country, rich in resources of all kinds, there could not have been and cannot be a situation in which a shortage of any product should exist . . .
> It is now clear why there are interruptions of supplies here and there, why, with our riches and abundance of products, there is a shortage first of one thing, then of another. It is these traitors who are responsible for it. (cited in Conquest, 1971, p. 563)

Thus a number of leading politicians – officials in our sense – were being accused of having sold themselves for personal gain, and of having caused, through various means, serious problems in the economy in the pursuit of their own pecuniary interests. That the Soviets later partially or fully rehabilitated many of those found guilty during the 'Great Terror' is of little relevance for our purposes; at the time, 'corrupt' officials were scapegoats for problems that arose in the implementation of Stalin's 'revolution from above'.

These sorts of extreme charge were not often made in the more industrially developed communist states in recent years. They were made from time to time in the less developed states, however. In November 1982, for example, the Albanian party leader Enver Hoxha accused his late prime minister, Mehmet Shehu, of having been a 'conspirator' who had worked simultaneously for the US, Soviet and Yugoslav intelligence services since the Second World War (a versatile and skilled man!); various problems, including economic ones, were linked to Shehu. In many countries, such charges would nowadays probably seem unconvincing; on the other hand, charges of more ordinary corruption by lower-ranking officials, and the linking of such criminality to economic problems, are perfectly realistic – and usually helpful to the regime and system. Examples can be found in both the more and the less developed countries of the communist world (on Mozambique, see Ottaway and Ottaway, 1981, p. 75).

Although leaderships in the more developed communist states do not appear to have engaged in Hoxha's style of scapegoatism, they certainly may have hoped to have benefitted from the publicity surrounding the trials of senior figures from an earlier administration. Perhaps the best example of this in the late 1980s was the well-publicized trial of Brezhnev's son-in-law, Yuri Churbanov (see, for example, *Pravda*, 30 August 1988, p. 6, and 6 September, 1988, p. 6). He was a candidate member of the Central Committee, and first deputy minister for internal affairs before Brezhnev's death in 1982; he went on trial in September 1988 charged with accepting bribes worth hundreds of thousands of rubles from officials in Uzbekistan – including the then head of the Uzbek Communist Party, Sh. Rashidov. His trial was symbolically very significant. Not only was Churbanov being charged with one form of corruption, but there was without doubt also the intimated charge against Brezhnev himself of nepotism. Indeed, 1988 witnessed extraordinary developments in official Soviet attitudes towards the former general secretary and head of state. The authorities began openly to tolerate and even encourage an image of Brezhnev as a thoroughly corrupt, mafia-style 'godfather' (on this see, for example, *Time*, 12 September 1988, p. 22). In doing so, the leadership almost certainly hoped to point out the contrast between its own implied moral superiority and an earlier regime, and thus enhance its own legitimacy.

Finally, a regime may hope (and may in fact succeed) to raise its legitimacy among the mass citizenry by mounting anti-corruption campaigns, in that, in doing so, it reveals both its awareness of the problem and its commitment and ability to do something about it. If a regime consistently turns a blind eye to corruption that is visible to most if not all, then any respect some citizens and officials do have for the authority of the regime, and perhaps even the system, would decline. Indeed, they may well start engaging in corrupt practices themselves – and if corruption becomes excessively blatant and widespread, the social fabric of society can be seriously weakened.

The Disadvantages of Corruption and its Reporting

There are probably as many disadvantages to both the existence of corruption and its reporting as there are advantages.

In terms of the economy, excessive tolerance of corruption can have serious negative implications for the official (first) economy. A major diversion of resources (finance, supplies, etc.) from the first economy into the black market – of which corruption is a part – can have a substantial knock-on effect for *both* parts of the economy in the medium to long term. The diversion of state funds to private pockets means there is less investment, at the same time that money expended in the black market, including that in corrupt transactions, is not taxed. In short, the state loses twice over, and there is inflationary pressure. If there is less state revenue, and not only worse shortages but possibly even declining real wages for the mass of citizens who cannot participate in either the black market or corrupt practices, then a regime seeking legitimacy largely on the basis of economic performance (eudaemonism) is clearly going to experience legitimation problems.

It is interesting to note an economic dysfunction of corruption that has been mentioned by Deng Xiaoping himself. In his key speech of April 1982, the Chinese leader referred to the heavy losses in foreign exchange that were being caused by the smuggling of gold and silver from the PRC into Hong Kong (Deng, 1984, p. 380). Losses of foreign reserves can be serious for *any* system; but when a system's own currency is soft and the country needs every cent of hard currency (including gold and silver bullion) it has for paying off debts and purchasing equipment abroad needed for its own modernization, the problem becomes that much more acute.

Another disadvantage of corruption in foreign trade is that it can tarnish a country's image abroad, and make foreign businesspeople wary of trading with a given communist state (for an explicit statement to this effect, see the editorial in *China Post*, 29 July 1987). The reporting of Li Huiquan's case in a Chinese newspaper that is available in foreign languages (see above, p. 108) can on one level be seen as an example of the Chinese authorities wanting to publicize, to foreigners as well as to their own citizens, the fact that corrupt foreign trade officials will be dealth with severely.

A major drawback of anti-corruption campaigns is that they can reduce initiative among the very people a regime is primarily looking to for economic growth and innovation. Forster (1985, p. 10) cites the example of certain cadres in Guangdong Province (PRC) who were confused by the leadership's anti-corruption drive in the early 1980s and became reticent about making contact with representatives of foreign companies unless there was a third party present. This was because they were unsure as to what might subsequently be construed as 'corrupt', and wished to safeguard their own positions. Thus empirical evidence shows that there can be a severe contradiction between anti-corruption campaigns and policies designed to foster economic growth. Given the argument in this book about eudaemonic legitimation, it becomes clear why this is a problem.

Some of the other economic disadvantages of corruption that have been identified – for instance by Joseph Nye (1967) in his classic 'cost-benefit analysis' of corruption and development – in non-communist Third World countries may also sometimes apply to the communist world, although there is limited evidence to support this. One is that there can be a serious problem with capital outflows – that is, wealth acquired through corruption may not find its way back into a domestic economy at all, but may instead wind up in, for instance, a Swiss bank account. Foreign aid may also be foregone if outsiders providing that aid feel that a regime is too corrupt and that the money is not reaching those for whom it was intended; a classic example of this in recent years has been aid to Ethiopia.

Already existing perceptions of *social* inequality that relate to the unequal (though not necessarily inequitable – it depends, of course, on the criteria selected) distribution of wealth by the system can be exacerbated if some citizens are perceived by others as having illegitimate access to goods, whether in the first, second or third economies. Such perceptions can have socially disruptive consequences – increased alienation, etc. – and in either subtle or explicit ways be dysfunctional to the system. Thus one serious danger of corruption identified by Yao Wenyuan (1975, p. 6) is that it can lead to polarization (between those who have access to goods through corrupt channels and those who do not) and exploitation in society that can ultimately lead to the re-emergence of antagonistic class relationships in allegedly socialist societies, and even to the restoration of capitalism. At its most extreme, then, too much corruption can so seriously undermine the social fabric of society and the legitimacy of the political order that both are seriously threatened and might even collapse. Corruption was one part of the crises that Czechoslovakia underwent in the late 1960s and Poland experienced at the beginning of the 1980s (see Hirszowicz, 1986, esp. pp. 129–35); moreover, it is interesting to note that some Soviet analyses of the December 1986 riots in Kazakhstan explained these largely in terms of a reaction to the corruption (and arrogance) of senior party officials (*CDSP*, Vol. 39, No. 11, pp. 11–12 – see below, p. 217, for a different perspective on these riots). Finally, the reader is reminded that it is a major thesis of this book that corruption, and public reaction to it, was a primary factor leading to the collapse of communist power in the USSR in 1991, Eastern Europe from 1989, and to the Tiananmen incident in the PRC in the latter year.

One very tangible danger of the effects of corruption, for a few individuals at least, is revealed in Soviet reports on corruption among leading psychiatrists. As a result of corrupt practices, a number of violent Soviets were classified not as criminals but as mentally insane; some were allowed out at weekends and/or released very early – and proceeded to murder people (Reddaway, 1988, p. 27).

In parenthesis, it can be noted that it is not only 'the system' or ordinary citizens that can be disadvantaged by too much corruption; the officials engaging in it can themselves suffer. If 'meat-eaters', for instance, become too rapacious and charge peasants what the latter perceive to be unacceptably high fees for permits to engage in legal or semi-legal private activity, then some peasants may prefer to blow the whistle on the officials rather than succumb to such pressure.

The disadvantages of the reporting of corruption are by no means restricted to economic and social issues; there are a number of overtly *political* ramifications too. For example, although it is generally assumed that criticism of the errors of earlier leaderships by a new leader or leadership team is beneficial to the latter, this is not invariably the case. Thus the post-Mao leadership in China may be perfectly justified in criticizing aspects of the Maoist era, but in doing so is rubbing salt into the wounds of many citizens and officials whose career prospects were seriously – in some cases irrevocably – damaged by the essentially anti-education atmosphere of the Cultural Revolution. Some of those people now suspect *all* communist leaders and the type of system that can allow the prolonged injustices of the GPCR. This is not conducive to regime or system legitimacy.

Similarly, any support for the system may actually *decline* as a result of anti-corruption campaigns. If local officials charged with investigating corruption are perceived by many ordinary citizens to be overstepping the mark, being unnecessarily officious and subjective, then attempts by communist leaderships to move towards a more legal-rational basis of legitimacy can backfire. This partially depends on the extent to which and how quickly senior leaders realize there is a serious problem of subjectivity among local officials and take measures to overcome this. If they react swiftly and decisively, the potentially delegitimating aspects of the officials' behaviour need not occur, and citizen support for the leaders may increase.

The relationship between officials and leaders (staffs and chiefs) can be negatively affected in various other ways by anti-corruption campaigns. For instance, such campaigns, if directed principally against officials, can lead to many of these people closing ranks and being at least uncooperative towards their superiors, and possibly even disruptive. If such officials are also very much at the interface between the public and 'the system', then their cynicism and hostility towards their superiors can contribute to a *general* undermining of authority. Moreover, it is clear from occasional articles in the press that not all lower-level officials agree with the policy of publicizing cases of corruption and other improprieties. Earlier, examples of officials publicly acknowledging the advantages of reporting were cited; now we can consider evidence of the opposite viewpoint. One of the most interesting articles – in fact a letter to the editors – from this perspective was published in *Pravda* in 1984 (15 October, p. 3); it is worth quoting from extensively. Party member Yu. Zhigulev wrote:

> There are a good many honest and conscientious people in party committees who sincerely believe that a discussion of an improper act by an official is not for everybody and not for the press, and that a discussion of his guilt can be permitted only behind closed doors, within a narrow circle . . . I have frequently encountered comrades who have been left bewildered and confused by critical articles in the central newspapers. 'Now why write about that?' they asked with alarm . . . Such people . . . sincerely believe that creating an atmosphere of uncommunicativeness and secrecy concerning improper behaviour by officials will maintain a local party committee's authority.

Even Zhigulev himself, while arguing that honesty and openness – *pre*-Gorbachev! – actually enhance the prestige of a party committee (in contrast to the comrades he is writing about), does see the need for secrecy in some cases. One of the interesting points made at the beginning of the quotation is that there are many *honest* (*chestnye*) comrades who oppose publicity – it is not just a matter of corrupt officials wanting to cover up their own dirty deeds. It does seem obvious that if many officials do not acknowledge the value of reporting official corruption, tensions may arise between them and their superiors. Thus can be sown the seeds of the legitimacy problems between 'chiefs' and 'staffs' that so many Western commentators see as crucial. In this sense, the reporting of corruption can be dysfunctional.

In the particular case of communist countries that are or have been perceived by many of their own citizens to be part of a larger whole (GDR, DPRK, PDRY), there is another legitimation problem. Such countries implicitly or explicitly wish (or have in the past tried) to demonstrate to their citizenry and their staffs the superiority of the communist system over the capitalist system in 'the other part' of the country.[2] For this reason, it does not usually appear to be advantageous to emphasize faults, such as corruption, in one's own system. Of course, if corruption is *so* widespread and visible that *not* to do anything would be potentially more dangerous than mounting a campaign against it, then a wise leadership will mount the campaign. In the cases of the GDR and North Korea, both of which had reported almost no cases of corruption until late 1989 (though see *SWB* EE/7146/B/4, 2 October 1982, for a rare example of explicit East German reporting of official corruption), it would appear that the phenomenon was/is not a serious problem. If this is the case, then factors to include in any attempt at understanding this would be culture, and perhaps levels of control and coercion (that is, people are less likely to engage in corrupt activities where there is widespread supervision and where the penalties for even mild forms of corruption are comparatively harsh). Although China is also divided (with capitalist Hong Kong, Macao and Taiwan as the 'other parts'), the sheer size of the communist part of the country is so great in comparison with the capitalist parts that the insecurity complex that (has) affected both East Germany and North Korea has not until now pertained there, to anything like a comparable degree. This might currently be changing, however, both because of closer relations with Taiwan and the planned integration of Hong Kong in 1997, and – intimately connected to the first point – because of the ongoing economic success of these 'Little Dragons/Tigers'.

Anti-corruption campaigns can have various other destabilizing effects. Investigating and reporting on corruption can trigger or exacerbate ethnic tensions. When a minority nationality believes that a putative anti-corruption campaign is in fact an attempt by the central authorities – associated with the ethnically dominant group – to discredit them, it is clear that hostility towards both those central authorities and the ethnically dominant group will increase. The investigation will often be at the level of the political unit of a minority (such as a republic in the USSR or Yugoslavia, an autonomous region in the PRC). But sometimes it will be of a group's formal leader (such as a first party secretary), who is involved in politics at the centre as much as – sometimes even more than – politics at the local level. If such a leader is found to be corrupt and loses his/her post, the ethnic minority may feel particularly aggrieved that they do not have a representative at the centre. In most communist countries, this problem is not usually a serious one, since the replacement leader will normally move into the central bodies that his/her predecessor occupied. However, if a corrupt first party secretary who is a member of the ethnic minority is replaced by an apparently uncorrupt person who is *not* a member of the ethnic minority, the minority may believe, justifiably or not, that they are worse off than before. The replacing of the corrupt Kazakh Kunaev as first party secretary of Kazakhstan by the Russian Kolbin in December 1986 is a good example of this problem. The riots that erupted at the time of Kolbin's appointment suggest that attempts by a central leadership to drive a wedge between a local elite and a local population can sometimes backfire (on the connection between corruption, anti-corruption campaigns and nationalism, with particular reference to Soviet Central Asia, see Critchlow, 1988).

The dysfunctions of reporting elaborated so far in this analysis have focused mostly on the general effects on the political order, the economy and society. Reports from the communist world itself reveal some interesting, more specific effects. One of these is what can be called the 'inspirational' effect. A Soviet chambermaid sentenced in 1982 for economic crime claimed at her trial that she had obtained the idea for her particular form of cheating from a newspaper article published in 1979; it seems perfectly feasible that some officials will also be influenced in this way by what they read, and thus engage in corruption.

Closely connected with this last point, one of the ramifications of Soviet *glasnost* – the unjamming of foreign radio broadcasts – *may* have had an inspirational effect on some potentially corrupt individuals. The first and more obvious way is through learning of corruption elsewhere and of some of the ingenious methods devised by others for making illicit gain. The second possible effect is potentially more dangerous. This is that broadcasts from the West may have made Soviet citizens (and citizens of other communist states) even more aware not only of the failings of their own system but also of the living standards of others. This might well have led to increased corruption, as well as to more general system/regime delegitimation.[3]

One final common dysfunction both of corruption and of its reporting, and which relates to the points just made, is that corruption by superiors can encourage it among subordinates – a point made clearly in an *Izvestiya* article (26 June 1983, p. 3): 'Any instance of abuse of office is striking and, moreover, corrupts the minds of the culprit's subordinates and encourages them to make compromises with their consciences and their duty.'

Conclusions

At first sight, it may appear that there are logical contradictions between some of the functional and dysfunctional aspects of corruption and its reporting identified in this chapter. How, for instance, can it simultaneously be advantageous *de facto* to condone corruption in order to improve the running of the economy *and* to condemn it and punish its practitioners? The answer is that there are many complex aspects of society in which apparently contradictory phenomena coexist; the all-important point is that there has to be an optimal *balance* of the various phenomena. Excessive condemnation combined with insufficient turning a blind eye can clearly be disadvantageous to a regime or system – as can the opposite proportionality. One can compare the existence and the reporting of corruption in a given society to what medical researchers are now telling us about the consumption of alcohol and exposure to sunlight – small amounts are better than none at all, whereas an excess is clearly damaging to the health. Unfortunately, unlike the situations regarding alcohol and sunlight, there can be no quantification of the optimal balance regarding corruption, either by social scientists or by communist leaderships. The balance in a given country and at a given time must be sought by leaders using a mixture of intuition and experience, both direct and vicarious.

Leading on from this, a serious misjudgement of the optimal balance can be one of the factors leading to revolution. While this might be seen as a desirable end by those opposed to communism, both within communist countries and beyond, it would not be seen as such by those at the apex of power in these systems.

Finally, it should not be assumed that, simply because we have considered corruption in terms of costs and benefits to a regime or system, this is how communist leaderships themselves have approached the phenomenon. While it is highly improbable that most leaders have not sometimes – I would argue mostly – approached corruption and its reporting from the functionality perspective, it would reveal a narrowness of vision and a high degree of cynicism on our part if we were not to allow for the possibility that some communists have at least occasionally concerned themselves with corruption because of higher ideals, a genuine commitment to a better society. Moreover, even when leaders have approached corruption from a functional perspective, they may at times have been only partially conscious of doing so; both capitalists and communists are in my view consciously manipulative – conspiratorial – rather less frequently than some of their critics maintain.

NOTES

1   It is interesting to note that the Bulgarian communists announced publicly in the late 1980s that they had until 1986 had a policy of *not* publishing details of corruption (presumably in both the broad and narrow senses); on this, the Bulgarian *glasnost* of the late 1980s more generally, and the limitations of Bulgarian *glasnost* as it related to corruption, see *YICA 1987*, p. 278, and Ashley, 1988. Whatever the official claim, some Bulgarian cases certainly were publicized before the mid-1980s, as is evident from chapter 3; this said, there does appear to have been a substantial increase from the time Gorbachev's influence reached Sofia. One traditionally loyal East European country that remained openly sceptical about both *perestroika* and *glasnost* until very shortly before the collapse of its own communist system was the GDR.
2   The term 'implicitly' is used because the GDR authorities used to claim that East and West Germany were two completely separate and independent states, and did not seek unification; this was the opposite position from that taken by the North Korean and South Yemeni authorities. The PRC is also part of a larger whole; its somewhat different situation from that of the other three countries is considered briefly later in the paragraph.
3   This could apply to Cuba, for instance, since the establishment of Television Martí by the USA in 1990. One must be careful not to *over*-emphasize this general point, however, at least as it relates to increases in corruption (as distinct from delegitimation). East Germans were long able to watch West German television – *apparently* with little or no impact on levels of corruption. Whether this relates to culture or not is ultimately unanswerable at present.

7

The Authorities' Reactions to Corruption

In the last chapter, the reasons why the political authorities some-times appear to 'turn a blind eye' to corruption were considered, as were the reasons why such authorities on other occasions seem to permit – even encourage – its reporting. In the present chapter, the focus is on their more overt reactions. The chapter sub-divides into two main sections. In the first, the history of anti-corruption cam-paigns, major policy statements and legislation – what in an earlier work (Holmes, 1981a) I have called 'macro-policy statements' and 'micro-policy formulation' – is outlined. The second part is con-cerned with the actual treatment meted out to corrupt officials. In both sections, the focus is once again on the USSR and China, although a 'brush-stroke' picture of several other communist coun-tries is also provided.

Official Policy, Campaigns and Legislation

The USSR

As the USSR was a federal state, a great deal of legislation and policy emanated from republican legislatures and executive bodies; it is way beyond the scope of the present study to analyse all this, and the more modest aim here is to concentrate on federal-level campaigns and legislation.

Corruption, and the fight against it, dates from the earliest days of the Soviet regime (Rigby, 1985, pp. 5–6). During the 1921–2 purge of the Russian Communist Party (Bolshevik) – the predecessor to the CPSU – some 9 per cent of the more than 136,000 members expelled lost their membership because of bribe-taking, extortion and other forms of corruption, for example (Schapiro, 1970, p. 236). And at the 19th Party Congress (1952), Malenkov complained about corruption – including false reporting, improper filling of office and speculation – among relatively senior officials, including several members of the Ulyanovsk Party Organization (see Malenkov, 1952, pp. 114, 119–21, 124–5).

Within the period focused on in this study, there were a number of identifiable campaigns – some national, others local – against corruption, and a series of legislative acts designed ultimately to reduce the incidence of corruption.

One major campaign occurred in the early 1960s, in the later years of the Khrushchev era (Khrushchev was ousted from power in October 1964); anti-corruption legislation was passed 24 May 1961 (on false reporting – see *Izvestiya*, 18 February 1973, p. 3) and 20 February 1962 (for bribery – see *Izvestiya*, 14 March 1970, p. 5), for instance. It was also at this time that the death penalty was reintroduced for serious cases of corruption; although this most draconian measure was applied mostly to 'entrepreneurs' in manufacturing, the campaign itself certainly affected a number of communist party officials and police officers, most of whom were charged with aiding and abetting (mainly in the form of turning a blind eye) the so-called entrepreneurs.

With the coming to power of Brezhnev, the anti-corruption campaign declined. As was shown in chapter 4, there were certainly individual cases of corruption reported in the late 1960s. There was also some new legislation, such as that of July 1966 establishing a Ministry for the Protection of Public Order (see *Pravda*, 27 July 1966, p. 2), that at least partially related explicitly to official corruption. And there were campaigns in particular parts of the country (for example, in Azerbaijan, with the coming to power there in 1969 of Geidar Aliev – see *CDSP*, Vol. 21, No. 32, pp. 9–12, and below). But there was no discernible *national* campaign; indeed, in an interview published in *Literaturnaya Gazeta* in February 1969 (12 February, p. 10), the deputy head of the Criminal Investigation Office of the Ministry of Internal Affairs explicitly argued that while it was desirable to publicize the struggle against crime (including economic crime), details of particular cases should not be published, since this might actually lead to an increase in crime. This statement was made less than two years after the then minister for the protection of public order (N. Shchelokov) made the somewhat absurd suggestion that the appropriate conditions now existed in the USSR for the complete eradication of all crime (*Pravda*, 31 July 1967, p. 2). This testifies to the generally sanguine attitude towards crime adopted by many officials in the late 1960s.

Although there was no national campaign in the early and mid-1970s, there was certainly some anti-corruption legislation (notably in July 1970, designed to combat embezzlement) and a great deal of reporting of corruption in Transcaucasia – especially Georgia, although Armenia and Azerbaijan were also involved. The Georgian campaign became publicly and nationally visible in March 1972, when the Central Committee of the CPSU issued a resolution on the Tbilisi City Party Committee, condemning *inter alia* the widespread 'misappropriation of state property, speculation, bribery and parasitism' in the Georgian capital (*Pravda*, 6 March 1972, pp. 1–2). At the December 1972 Plenum of the CPSU Central Committee, the problem of corruption was again raised, while in April 1973, the USSR Supreme Court called for harsher punishments against 'official and economic crime' (*Izvestiya*, 5 April 1973, p. 5). Within a very short time, the Georgian campaign had affected large numbers of party, state and law-enforcing officials – including the first party secretary of Georgia himself, V.P. Mzhavanadze. Mzhavanadze lost his first secretaryship in September 1972 and his candidate membership of the Politburo in December of that year. One of the main tasks of his successor in Georgia – a man who later became Gorbachev's Soviet foreign minister and in March 1992 *de facto* Georgian president, E.A. Shevardnadze – was explicitly to clean up corruption in the republic. The Georgian Communist Party Central Committee both condemned and provided details on aspects of corruption at its February and October 1973 plenary sessions. By 1974, four members of the Georgian Bureau (the Republic-level equivalent of the Politburo) had been dismissed, along with a number of senior state officials. One final, interesting point about the early 1970s Georgian corruption scandal is that even several members of the clergy – mainly senior clerics of the Georgian Orthodox Church – were accused of corruption (Reddaway, 1978, pp. 138–9; for further details on the Georgian corruption scandal see Law, 1974).

The scandals in Azerbaijan (see, for example, *Pravda*, 15 August 1973, p. 3), Armenia (see, for example, Demirchyan's comments on the April 1973 Plenum of the Armenian Central Committee at the January 1975 Plenum in *CDSP*, Vol. 27, No. 10, pp. 1–8, 15) and also the Ukraine (see, for example, Shcherbitskii's May 1975 criticisms in *CDSP*, Vol. 27, No. 21, pp. 4–5) were not as significant as that in Georgia, but it is interesting that some see Aliev's promotion to first secretary of the Azerbaijani party in July 1969 as symbolic of the central leadership's desire to crack down on corruption in that republic (Aliev had previously headed the KGB in Azerbaijan; for an example of Aliev condemning corruption in his republic see *CDSP*, Vol. 27, No. 31, pp. 1–7). Whether or not this is true, it is clear from the local press that there was still a great deal of corruption both in Azerbaijan (see, for example, *CDSP*, Vol. 29, No. 17, pp. 6–8 and 12) and in Armenia in the late 1970s.

Signs that the central authorities were once again becoming concerned about corruption as a general phenomenon emerged in the autumn of 1979. In September, *Pravda* (11 September 1979, pp. 1 and 3) revealed that the CPSU's Central Committee had passed a major new resolution on law and order; one section of this dealt specifically with 'attacks on socialist property' (an English-language version of the law is available in *CDSP*, Vol. 31, No. 36, pp. 1–4). Among the crimes that were particularly singled out were report-padding and hoodwinking. In the following year, the chairperson of the Criminal Chamber of the Supreme Court of the USSR accorded the necessity of dealing adequately with abuse of office top priority in a list of future tasks for the judiciary, arguing that it was: 'a very important task to increase the effectiveness of court practice in the struggle against embezzlement, waste, abuse of office, bribery, report-padding' (cited in Lampert, 1984, p. 374).

According to Zhores Medvedev (1983, p. 135), it was also in 1980 – in September – that the CPSU's Central Committee passed a secret resolution on measures to be taken to combat corruption among officials; although this was circulated to various party organizations, the fact that it was not published strongly suggests that the senior authorities did *not* wish to make a major, public issue of the problem of corruption. This would be in line with our own findings on Soviet reporting of corruption at the very beginning of the 1980s (see chapter 4). Similarly, although the subject of corruption was touched upon at the 26th CPSU Congress in 1981, it was not a major theme.

It is interesting that major political campaigns against corruption began in both the communist giants (the USSR and the PRC) in the same year, 1982. It is also important to note that the Soviet campaign was linked very much to the change of leadership in the USSR; Brezhnev died in November 1982, and his successor, Yurii Andropov, made the drive against corruption a top priority almost as soon as he became the new General Secretary.[1] The Politburo discussed the issue of corruption on 10 December 1982 – allegedly, at least partially in response to citizens' letters on this (*Pravda*, 11 December 1982, p. 1) – following which legislation was passed on 18 December 1982 that increased the penalties for various crimes, including corruption (the new decree became effective 1 January 1983 – see

Izvestiya, 19 December 1982, p. 4). One of the first major political casualties of the early Andropov era was Shchelokov who, as head of the Ministry of Internal Affairs, was accused of having tolerated widespread corruption for years. He lost his post on 17 December 1982. In Medvedev's terminology (1983, p. 60), Shchelokov had been a member of Brezhnev's 'Dnepropetrovsk mafia',[2] and Andropov was keen to make an example of someone who had, *inter alia*, a reputation for letting friends know (via his wife) in advance of any impending price increases, so that they could improperly stock up on items (for an accusation that Shchelokov's corrupt activities 'practically resulted in the militia beginning to turn into a sort of a symbol of lawlessness and corruption' see *MN*, No. 51, 1987, p. 3; it was acknowledged by the Soviet authorities in 1988 that Shchelokov had committed suicide in December 1984).

At a meeting of the Presidium of the Supreme Soviet held in January 1983, Andropov and other leading politicians called for an even more vigorous struggle against embezzlement, abuse of office, bribe-taking and other forms of corruption (*Pravda*, 13 January 1983, p. 2). This was followed by more calls to combat corruption at the June 1983 Plenum of the Central Committee. At this point, Andropov argued that there was a need 'completely to eliminate such phenomena as instances of the use of state and public property and official positions for purposes of personal enrichment' (*Pravda*, 16 June 1983, p. 2). In the same year (1983), there began a process of radical restructuring of the Ministry of Internal Affairs. In March, the minister (V. Fedorchuk) announced changes in the work-style of the police force designed to improve its responsiveness to citizen complaints; apparently, this change was the result of instructions issued to the Ministry by the CPSU's Central Committee, the Soviet government and Andropov himself (*Literaturnaya Gazeta*, 23 March 1983, p. 1). In addition, the number of management sub-divisions was reduced, while the operational units – including the Department for Combatting the Embezzlement of Socialist Property and Speculation – were strengthened. Not only was the Ministry restructured to render it more effective, but it also became subject to much closer scrutiny by the party, with the creation of new CPSU-based 'political agencies' within it. The main task of these bodies was to act as watchdogs over the ministry's personnel (all this from *Pravda*, 10 August 1983, p. 3).

In addition to these more general moves, 1983 also witnessed the targetting of certain groups. Campaigns were directed both at regions/ethnic groups (including Georgia, Kazakhstan and Uzbekistan) and functional groups; regarding the latter, it is particularly noteworthy that legislation was passed late in 1983 dramatically increasing the punishments for corruption and treason by members of the military (see *CDSP*, Vol. 36, No. 8, pp. 11–13; for further details on the Andropov era see Medvedev, 1983, pp. 135–44).

Although it is sometimes maintained that Chernenko, who succeeded Andropov as general secretary in February 1984, sought to reverse the policies of his predecessor, this is not clearly so in the case of corruption. For instance, at an election campaign meeting in Moscow in March 1984, Chernenko already pointed out that: 'The Party and the state have intensified the struggle against such disgraceful manifestations as the squandering of state funds, hoodwinking and the abuse of office, embezzlement and bribery. This is not a temporary campaign . . . In this, there is and there will be no special allowance made for anyone' (*Pravda*, 3 March 1984, p. 2). In a speech made six months later (see *Pravda*, 6 October 1984, p. 1) to one of the major groups charged with investigating corruption, the People's Controllers, Chernenko argued that an end had to be put to 'bribe taking and speculation, the squandering and theft of socialist property, the abuse of office'. He also argued that corruption was one of the factors hindering economic reform and productivity rises; this is interesting, in that this line of thinking by the top Soviet leader is almost the opposite of the way in which at least *some* senior Chinese leaders have perceived the causal relationship between corruption and economic reform.

Anti-corruption campaigns in particular parts of the USSR also continued under Chernenko. Among the republics whose first secretaries were particularly critical of corruption in them was Uzbekistan. At the June 1984 Plenum of the Uzbek Central Committee, for instance, Usmankhodzhaev called for a clamp-down on corruption and made reference to what was later to become the major cotton-growing scandal in this republic (see *CDSP*, Vol. 36, No. 26, pp. 1–6, 13–14 and 24).

The above points notwithstanding, Chernenko did not appear to commit himself to fighting corruption quite as wholeheartedly as Andropov had done. But within a year of Gorbachev succeeding Chernenko (this occurred in March 1985), he breathed new life into the anti-corruption campaign; the CPSU's last general secretary made it clear in a number of ways that Andropov was his role model among recent Soviet leaders, and this was reflected in the adoption of many of his predecessor's policies.

The full-blooded anti-corruption campaign did not emerge immediately after Gorbachev's accession to power, however. At first, the emphasis tended to be more generally on strengthening socialist legality; one early result of this was a formal resolution of the USSR Supreme Soviet to this effect in July 1985 (see *Kommunist*, No. 12, 1985, p. 67). Thus, while several others did (such as Boris Yeltsin; Uzbek First Secretary Usmankhodzhaev; Tadzhik First Secretary Makhkamov; Kirghiz First Secretary Masaliev; Turkmen First Secretary Niyazov; Kazakh Prime Minister Nazarbaev; and Chair of the CPSU Central Inspection Commission Sizov – for all these see *Pravda*, 26 February–5 March 1986), the new general secretary himself still did not treat corruption as a major issue at the 27th Party Congress in February 1986, for instance, although he certainly referred to it (see *Pravda*, 26 February 1986, pp. 5–10). Yet letters to the press at this time (see, for example, *Pravda*, 13 February 1986, p. 3) revealed a degree of public disquiet about corruption among officials, especially middle-ranking ones. Whether or not many such letters were published with the knowledge and the encouragement of the senior leadership is unclear; my own view is that they probably were. In all events, just a few weeks after the 27th Congress, in late March, the Politburo discussed the problems of economic crime, including corruption (*Pravda*, 28 March 1986, p. 1). Following this, in late May, major new legislation increasing the penalties for economic crimes was introduced. The CPSU Central Committee, the USSR Council of Ministers and the Presidium of the USSR Supreme Soviet all adopted resolutions of various kinds designed to clamp down on corruption, in particular unearned income by officials (see *Pravda*, 28 May 1986, pp. 1–2). The new legislation adopted at this time was intended in particular to clarify what constituted proper and improper types of unearned income, and to tighten up the February 1962 legislation on bribe-taking; it became effective from the beginning of July 1986 (for an analysis of this and related legislation, and of its significance, see the interview with USSR Procurator-General A. Rekunkov in *Izvestiya*, 2 June 1986, p. 3; *inter alia*, Rekunkov claimed that the struggle against bribe-taking was at its most intense ever, that it would be a prolonged campaign, and that bribe-taking officials were a particular target).

The leadership maintained its interest in corruption to the early 1990s – although there were clear signs that it was by the end of the 1980s beginning to feel that the whole campaign was getting out of hand and was becoming dysfunctional from a legitimation perspective. Following further calls for the general upgrading of law and order at the November 1986 Central Committee plenum (see *Pravda*, 30 November 1986, p. 1), Gorbachev was highly critical at the January 1987 plenum both of corruption specifically and of the moral malaise generally of the later Brezhnev era. He argued that the most important priciple of socialism is distribution according to work, and that there had been frequent violations of this principle. He also claimed that this resulted in 'spiritual emptiness and scepticism' among the masses: 'The facts of a scornful attitude towards laws, hoodwinking and bribetaking, and the encouragement of servility and glorification all exert a pernicious influence on the moral atmosphere in society' (*Pravda*, 28 January 1987, p. 1). Having referred to the indignation of the masses at the behaviour of both corrupt and self-centred state officials, he singled out regions and ministries where 'the degeneration of cadres' and 'violations of socialist legality' had been particularly acute; the regions/areas listed were Uzbekistan, Moldavia, Turkmenia, a number of Kazakh provinces, Krasnodar Territory, Rostov Province and the city of Moscow, while the two ministries named were those for Foreign Trade and Internal Affairs. Gorbachev then proceeded to criticize the rampant embezzlement, bribe-taking, report-padding (and alcoholism) within the CPSU, following which he explicitly argued that it was these sorts of negative phenomenon that had led to the adoption of the policies of 'acceleration' (of social and economic development – the Russian word is *uskorenie*) and *perestroika*. Thus two of the four domestic policies and buzz-words most directly associated with Gorbachev (the others being *glasnost* and *demokratisatsiya*) were here being justified as a reaction, *inter alia*, to corruption.

In June 1987, the Politburo again criticized the cronyism and nepotism in Kazakhstan (*Pravda*, 12 June 1987, p. 1). It also endorsed the notion that the Procurator's Office should be upgraded (*Pravda*, 5 June 1987, p. 1). In line with this, the Central Committee adopted a resolution designed to strengthen the hand of the Procurator's Office in investigating crime, including economic crime (see *Pravda*, 19 June 1987, p. 1). At the end of that month, the Supreme Soviet passed legislation designed to increase the rights of ordinary citizens *vis-à-vis* officials (see *Pravda*, 3 July 1987, p. 3). The latter legislation, in particular, was designed to encourage more whistle-blowing, as citizens have since then – in theory, at least – had a greater chance of having complaints against officials both investigated and acted upon.[3]

Corruption was a major theme at the 19th Party Conference of the CPSU, held in June–July 1988. Of particular note were the charges made by radical leader – and subsequently Russian president – Boris Yeltsin against the Party Control Committee. According to the then first deputy chairperson of the State Committee for Construction, the Control Committee was afraid to bring charges of bribe-taking against senior republican and provincial leaders; Yeltsin was particularly critical of Mikhail Solomentsev (head of the Party Control Committee) for being too slack and too tolerant in this regard (*Pravda*, 2 July 1988, p. 10).

But the charges of high-level corruption were not being made only *within* the confines of the 19th Party Conference. On the eve of the conference, two investigators who subsequently became household names in the USSR because of their unrelenting and very public struggle to expose corruption in the highest echelons of the Soviet elite, Tel'man Gdlyan and Nikolai Ivanov, published an article in the journal *Ogonyek* (No. 26, June 1988, pp. 27–9) in which they claimed there were four bribe-takers among the conference delegates; the editor of *Ogonyek*, Vitalii Korotich, endorsed these allegations at the 19th Conference. Three of the four were subsequently arrested for corruption – although one of them was later released and received a formal apology from the Procurator's Office (*Komsomol'skaya Pravda*, 23 May 1989, p. 1). Gdlyan and Ivanov had been in charge of the investigation into the so-called 'Uzbek corruption scandal'. This affair can be traced back to 1980, when the head of the Investigation Department of the USSR Procurator's Office (A. Buturlin) was sent to Uzbekistan to investigate alleged corruption. This investigation was stopped by the then first secretary of Uzbekistan, Sh. Rashidov. Following Rashidov's death (October 1983) the USSR Procurator's Office – under prompting from Andropov himself – eventually became involved again in investigating Uzbekistan. This time, the team was headed by Gdlyan, with Ivanov as his closest associate among a team of over 200 investigators. The team spent five years in Uzbekistan; eventually 70 people were charged with criminal offences, 19 criminal cases were tried in the courts and 40 defendants were found guilty and sentenced (details from the report of a Commission established by the Presidium of the Supreme Soviet in *Pravda*, 20 May 1989, p. 3; ironically – given his statements at the 27th Party Congress – among those found guilty was the former first secretary of Uzbekistan, I. Usmankhodzhaev).

To some extent in 1988, but much more so early in 1989, Gdlyan and Ivanov then started commenting openly in the media on corruption among officials – especially officers of the law, but also party and state officials. Among those singled out was Brezhnev's son-in-law, Yurii Churbanov, who had been arrested in January 1987 (certain aspects of this case were referred to on p. 211). Their revelations were apparently well received by a public eager to learn more about the improprieties of the elite (see *NT*, No. 25, 1989, p. 36). Indeed, such was their popularity that they were both elected – against powerful odds – to the Congress of People's Deputies in late March 1989 (Gdlyan) and May 1989 (Ivanov).

At first, their findings seemed to be well received by the senior leadership, too. But by April/May 1989, their attacks were becoming too sensitive – they were a little too close to home – for many of the top leaders. By this stage, not only were they accusing the courts of injustice and a lack of *glasnost* (details of the Churbanov trial, which ended in December 1988, were not given to the press, and Churbanov himself received a much lighter sentence than Gdlyan, Ivanov and many others felt would have been appropriate), but they were also attacking senior leaders of the Gorbachev era. In particular, Ivanov's claims on Leningrad television (12 May 1989 – see *Pravda*. 20 May 1989, p. 3) that not only (former) Politburo members Grigorii Romanov and Mikhail Solomentsev but also Yegor Ligachev – at that time, the most senior 'conservative' in Gorbachev's Politburo – were involved in corrupt practices were clearly causing embarrassment in some top circles. The Presidium of the Supreme Soviet immediately condemned such charges, in a statement published in all of the major Soviet newspapers on 13 May. Ligachev himself subsequently felt obliged to make a formal statement to the CPSU's Central Committee explicitly denying the charges of corruption (*Pravda*, 23 May 1989, p. 2).

It was in this general atmosphere of sensitivity that charges were laid against Gdlyan and Ivanov in the (Northern) spring of 1989. Most significantly, they were accused of having abused the law in holding people under investigation for more than the statutory maximum of nine months, and for using threats and actual violence to secure 'confessions' (see, for example, *Pravda*, 20 May 1989, p. 3). But as it appeared increasingly that certain people in high office might be attacking Gdlyan and Ivanov more because of what (and whom) they were exposing than because of the methods they used for obtaining this information, so – in what by now had become an atmosphere of real *glasnost* and emphasis on the rule of law – pressure built up for a full investigation into what was being called the 'Gdlyan–Ivanov Affair' (this is a very complex issue – for more detail on the early stages than can be included here see Wishnevsky, 1989). On 1 June 1989 the Congress of People's Deputies established its own 16-person special commission to examine the charges laid against the two investigators (*Izvestiya*, 2 June 1989, p. 10); the man elected to head this was the famous dissident historian, by now a deputy to the Congress, Roy Medvedev (*Izvestiya*, 11 June 1989, p. 2). At the time of the setting up of this commission, many deputies to the Congress made it clear that they believed it should investigate not only the charges against Gdlyan and Ivanov, but also the accusations the two investigators had made about senior CPSU officials (see *Izvestiya*, 29 May 1989, esp. p. 6, and 1 June 1989, esp.

pp. 7–10). Largely because of the latter charges, the CPSU had itself already established a special commission of the Central Committee (in addition to the Congress's Commission), a fact revealed by the then chair of the Party Control Committee – and a man later to play a key role in the failed coup attempt of August 1991 – Boris Pugo (see *Pravda*, 30 April 1989, p. 2). However, many ordinary citizens evidently felt that the authorities might be less than fair in their treatment of the two investigators, so that a Public Committee for the Defence of Gdlyan and Ivanov was also established (*NT*, No. 42, 1989, p. 4).

Unfortunately, the interim findings of the various commissions were ambiguous (see, for example, *NT*, No. 1, 1990, p. 9, on the Congress's special commission). Gdlyan and Ivanov *were* found to have detained suspects for more than the statutory maximum of nine months – but this was seen by many as reflective of the traditional lack of respect Soviet law had for those under investigation. On the other hand, Gdlyan and Ivanov were also found to have delivered vast sums of money to the state and to have been commended for their good work. By mid-1990 Gdlyan and Ivanov were still very popular with the masses (see, for example, *NT*, No. 19, 1990, p. 20, and No. 20, p. 22) and remained members of the Congress of People's Deputies; but they had lost their jobs with the Procurator's Office (on the basis of a decision of the Supreme Soviet, 18 April 1990). By this stage, both they and some of their supporters were making allegations about the very highest levels in the land. For instance, People's Deputy Polozkov publicly accused Prime Minister Ryzhkov of corruption – in connection with yet another scandal, the so-called 'Antgate' affair (for details of this see, for example, *NT*, No. 13, 1990, pp. 8–11; No. 15, pp. 30–1; and No. 17, pp. 30–2) – in March 1990, while Gorbachev himself was accused by Gdlyan and Ivanov of being involved both in corruption and in what many have seen as an attempted cover-up (see, for example, *Argumenty I Fakty*, No. 19, 1990, p. 4). By May 1990, according to Yurii Feofanov, 'the whole nation has been discussing the "Gdlyan versus Procurator's Office" problem for weeks, unmindful of everything else' (*NT*, No. 20, 1990, p. 22); while this is no doubt an exaggeration, it does help to convey the significance of the whole issue of official corruption in the USSR at the beginning of the 1990s – shortly before the collapse both of Soviet communism and of the USSR.

The most important ramifications of the Gdlyan–Ivanov affair relate very much to the main focus of this book. First, the methods the investigators used for extracting confessions were held to be typical of the way Soviet officers of the law exercised their power, while the level of political interference in court proceedings has also been described by Soviet commentators as typical of the Soviet system. Soviet (and now, probably, Russian) claims to be moving towards the rule of law have to be seriously questioned when this kind of activity is normal – although the fact that it was so openly discussed in the press did testify to change in the right direction. Second, it does appear that Gorbachev had by the beginning of the 1990s recognized a need for limits in the anti-corruption campaign, and – seemingly, even when a leading political rival such as Ligachev was the target[4] – preferred not to follow corruption trails to the very highest levels. At one stage, Gdlyan and Ivanov were arguing that the mafia (involving many officials) was to blame for economic shortages – an argument that could in more normal circumstances have been useful to the senior leadership if they were looking for scapegoats. But once the two investigators started to claim that even Gorbachev was involved with the Soviet mafia, the situation changed. If not only the staff but even present chiefs are implicated in corruption scandals, the dysfunctions of such campaigns in terms of legitimation may well be seen to outweigh the advantages.

This all said, the reader should not form the impression that the Soviet anti-corruption campaign suddenly stopped in mid-1990; indeed, new legislation was promulgated in October 1990 (see *Izvestiya*, 23 October and 1 November 1990), and was followed by an announcement in February 1991 that a new 'Chief Administration (within the Ministry of Internal Affairs) for the Combatting of Most Dangerous Crimes, Organised Crime, Corruption and the Drug Business' had been established (*Izvestiya*, 5 February 1991, p. 1). Rather, the leadership seems to have attempted to redirect attention, away from itself and more towards corrupt staffs *and* 'the mafia'; once it had recovered its composure, it seems, the leadership came to appreciate the value of using *some* of those *unofficial* groups identified by Gdlyan and Ivanov as scapegoats. Unfortunately, the Soviet leadership's realization came too late to save it.

While it would be reasonable to suggest that the anti-corruption campaign in the USSR had got out of hand by 1990 and had to be 'reined in', it would be ridiculous to suggest that the campaign itself brought about the collapse of Soviet communism. On the other hand, it certainly both contributed to and was symptomatic of the more general crisis in the Soviet Union, and unquestionably had serious (negative) effects on both regime and system legitimacy. For these reasons, one should not underestimate either the campaign itself or the seriousness of the Gdlyan–Ivanov Affair (for Gdlyan's own detailed story of his anti-corruption work, see Gdlyan and Dodolev, 1990).

The PRC

Although the USSR made much of corruption in the 1980s, even the Soviets could not match the Chinese in terms of public campaigning by the leadership against corruption. In fact, there has been so much legislation and so many official pronouncements that it would be impossible to refer to them all in a comparative book such as this, and I have had to be highly selective in what follows; the reader who is interested in obtaining more detail, but does not read Mandarin, is urged to start his/her search by looking at all issues of the journal *Issues and Studies* for the period in question – not forgetting to scan the section 'Chronicle of Major Events on the China Mainland' – and *Beijing Review*.

As in the Soviet Union, the recent campaign against corruption is not a total novelty in communist China. Within a couple of years of coming to power (1949), Mao initiated the so-called 'three-anti' and 'five-anti' policies of 1951–2; a nationwide campaign against 'three evils' (corruption, waste and bureaucracy) was launched in December 1951, and this was followed early in 1952 by a campaign against 'five evils' (bribery, tax evasion, theft of state property, cheating on government contracts and stealing economic information). Although the second of these campaigns, in particular, was targetted mainly at industrialists and businesspeople, they both had serious implications for officials too. According to others' research (Forster, 1985, p. 2; implicit in Liu, 1983, pp. 610–11, 615) this was the only full-scale central offensive against corruption during the Mao era (1949–76). There were certainly occasional complaints about corruption by senior leaders, but nothing that amounted to a major campaign.[5] Following Mao's death, there was a power struggle; by December 1978, the man who was eventually to win the struggle, Deng Xiaoping, had placed his foot firmly on the first rung of the ladder to the top. A major dimension of Deng's approach – at least until 1989 – has been to bring order and legality to China, following the chaos and near-anarchy of the so-called 'Ten Years of Cultural Revolution' (1966–76). Even before Deng had clearly emerged as a major force in the leadership struggle, the CCP – at its 11th Congress in 1977 – called for the establishment of a set of discipline inspection commissions. The first of these, a Central Discipline Inspection Commission (hereafter CDIC), was established in December 1978 (for further details on these bodies see Young, 1984). The principal task of the CDIC was 'specifically to deal with corrupt behaviour of members of the CCP' (Liu, 1983, p. 602). In the following year (1979), the Chinese established a number of Discipline Inspection

Commissions (DICs) at and above the county level. At the same time they adopted a number of new codes and laws designed to tighten up in the whole area of criminality. The new Criminal Law, for instance, dealt at length with the questions of economic crime and abuse of office (see esp. Articles 116–30, 150–6, and 185–92).

But the approach of Deng and other post-Mao leaders has not only emphasized order and a regularized legal system. They have also sought to develop China economically; the policy of 'The Four Modernizations', originally devised by Zhou Enlai, is aimed principally at raising productivity and living standards so that, by the year 2000, the PRC will have attained a per capita average income of US $800, in comparison with less than US $200 at the beginning of the 1980s. In order to achieve this, Deng has – sometimes against opposition from other members of the senior leadership – introduced what can only be described as radical economic reforms. Until the mid-1980s, probably the two most significant were the introduction of the household responsibility system in agriculture, and the establishment of special economic zones and 'open' status in fourteen coastal cities and the island of Hainan. The latter policy can be seen in part as one aspect of a policy designed to learn from the West and use the better features of capitalism to socialism's advantage.

Unfortunately for Deng, and as argued elsewhere in this book, many of these economic reforms seem to have encouraged criminality. Already by October 1980, the State Council noted a substantial increase in the number of cases of smuggling, and issued a document calling on local officials to clamp down hard on this. Two months later, the Central Committee held a work meeting at which Deng, on Christmas Day, criticized what he saw as an increase in various forms of corruption – not only smuggling, but also bribery, speculation and tax evasion. He explicitly stated that officials were involved in this. Within days, the State Council passed another directive aimed at combatting crime (*RMRB*, 1 January 1981), and an editorial in *Renmin Ribao* (16 January 1981) admitted that smuggling was rife.

In August 1981, the State Council discussed smuggling yet again, with Vice-Premier Gu Mu being highly critical of it. The State Council explicitly stated that the big rise in smuggling – and all the other economic crimes connected with it (including bribery of officials) – had started in 1980. The Council resolved to combat the phenomenon by adopting what amounted to a deterrence policy – by making a public example of those found guilty of the crime. This can be seen as one of the official 'triggers' for the wide-scale media reporting of corruption and other forms of economic crime in the early and mid-1980s.

Unquestionably, 1982 represents a high point of the present campaign against corruption in China. The New Year's Day editorial in *Renmin Ribao* specified two main tasks for the coming year – one of which was to fight economic crime. Shortly afterwards, the man who was subsequently to become president, Li Xiannian, emphasized the singular importance of the struggle (*RMRB*, 25 January 1982).

The leaders were not merely condemning corruption in speeches; they were also taking practical steps to reduce it. The body that had primary responsiblity for combatting economic crime in China, the CDIC, passed on details of a case in Guangzhou involving speculation by a high-ranking official to the Central Committee Secretariat in late 1981. The Secretariat discussed this, following which, on 11 January 1982, the Central Committee itself issued a major statement on corruption (for a translation of this document see *Issues and Studies*, Vol. 20, No. 7, pp. 116–18); as Forster (1985) observes, this represented the real beginning of the 1982 campaign. As part of this statement (section three), three members of the Central Committee Secretariat plus one senior member of the CDIC were sent to three coastal provinces in the south of China and to Yunnan to emphasize to officials there that decisive action had to be taken against all forms of economic crime. In addition, ordinary citizens were encouraged to blow the whistle on smugglers. Following the lead taken by Fujian Province, the central authorities decided to offer material rewards to citizens whose information led to the uncovering of cases of economic crime, particularly smuggling. However, Fujian Province was criticized (*RMRB*, 10 February 1982) by the central authorities for making the material rewards too large (up to 30 per cent of the value of smuggled goods); one problem here was that this could encourage connivance between whistle-blowers and smugglers. The central authorities opted instead to offer rewards of up to 10 per cent of the value of confiscated goods, with a maximum pay-out of 1,000 yuan to an individual and 10,000 yuan to a group. To demonstrate their commitment to tracking down smugglers, the central authorities even offered the reward to foreigners – whom, they announced, they were prepared to pay in hard currency.

In February 1982, *Renmin Ribao* published another editorial on corruption, and compared the contemporary situation with the crisis of 1951–2 that had necessitated the three-anti/five-anti campaigns. In March, the Standing Committee of the National People's Congress decided to increase the penalties for economic crime – especially if committed by officials. For the first time, bribery and smuggling became crimes punishable, in extreme cases, by death. Moreover, in another move aimed more at officials than at any other section of society, failure to prosecute criminals or connivance with them (such as turning a blind eye) could now lead to a prison sentence of up to five years.

Although the new measures were draconian, and although the central authorities were making it clear that they were treating corruption and others forms of economic crime as serious misdemeanours, they softened the blow by granting a one-month amnesty before the new, stiffer penalties became effective. Offenders were encouraged to turn themselves and their illegal gains over to the authorities within this period, in return for which they would be dealt with more leniently than they would from April. Some provinces in fact extended this amnesty into May and even later.

In April, the senior leadership again revealed its very real concern about economic crime. When the Politburo met on 10 April 1982, Deng spoke at length on the issue of economic crime. He made the point that although he considered the recent spate of corruption among cadres to be more serious than in earlier periods – notably in the three-anti/five-anti campaigns of 1951–2 (Deng, 1984, p. 380) – the leadership was not launching a *movement* against economic crime. This was almost certainly because the word 'movement' was too reminiscent of the horrors and chaos of the Maoist era, a point borne out by the fact that Deng now distinguished the present struggle from earlier ones, such as the 1959 campaign against 'Right Deviation'. The former was seen as being objective, concerned not with interpretations of political views but 'concrete' acts, such as theft of materials and money. Moreover, Deng wanted to avoid excessive involvement by the masses, since this had on a number of past occasions rapidly run out of control. However, the leadership's position was somewhat ambiguous. On the one hand, they claimed they did not want an anarchic mass movement. On the other hand, they stated that they did want citizens to whistle-blow – including on officials who in some cases, though charged with leading the campaign against corruption, were themselves corrupt. Instead of talking of a movement, Deng spoke of a 'constant and protracted struggle'. He also identified the combatting of economic crime as one of the four areas of struggle for socialist modernization, and even gave some idea of just how protracted the struggle against it would be: 'In my opinion, it [the struggle against economic crime] will last at least until the day the four modernisations are achieved. If that means the end of the century, the struggle will have to be waged daily for eighteen years' (Deng, 1984, p. 381). The supreme leader also argued that without this struggle, the modernization of the economy would fail; given the significance attached to eudaemonic legitimation, this is a clear indication of just how important the Chinese leadership has perceived the problem of corruption to be.

In his April 1982 criticisms of corruption, Deng directed particular attention to party members who engaged in economic crime. He argued that one way in which the party could be consolidated for socialist modernization would be to expel members found guilty of serious misdeeds and to discharge them from public employment. In short, Deng was implicitly arguing that party punishments were often inadequate. Moreover, he made it clear that confessing to a crime should not necessarily protect a person completely from punishment; embezzlers of large sums of money, in particular, should be both expelled from the party and dismissed from their posts, 'no matter how much leniency is shown them because they have confessed their crimes' (Deng, 1984, pp. 381–2) He went on to say that such people must not be promoted – implying that this did sometimes occur.

One final problem that clearly concerned Deng was the issue of just who might be corrupted. He emphasized the need to nip the corruption problem in the bud, since allowing it to continue could lead to far more people being led astray, including veteran cadres. One implication of this is that if even those whose ideological commitment is supposed to be strongest become corrupt, then the legitimacy of the system as a whole becomes undermined.

In order to give bite to his message, Deng called on every province to deal with some major cases of economic crime within two months – virtually a 'plan-target' approach. In dealing with such cases, judicial and party authorities were to be firm; in most cases, those found guilty were to be treated 'severely'.

Almost immediately following this Politburo meeting, a formal decision on 'Combatting Serious Criminal Activities in the Economic Sphere' was issued jointly by the Central Committee and the State Council (13 April 1982; for an English translation see *Issues and Studies*, Vol. 20, No. 2, February 1984, pp. 102–15). In that it represented a slight softening of the March legislation, it represented a concession to the many cadres who considered the earlier decree too harsh (see Forster, 1985, p. 8). On the other hand, since both party and state bodies were issuing the resolution, cadres would now find it more difficult to play one branch of the party–state complex off against another.

The 12th Congress of the CCP was convened in September 1982, and at that Deng once again made it clear that the achievement of the all-important socialist modernization and economic construction required a sustained attack on economic crime (Chinese Communist

Party, 1982, pp. 4–5). At the First Plenum of the newly elected Central Committee following the 12th Congress, convened 12–13 September, member of the Standing Committee of the Politburo Chen Yun was re-elected first secretary of the CDIC, a post he had held since the CDIC's establishment in 1978. Since Chen Yun was known as a hard-liner within the Chinese leadership, his re-election could be seen as yet another sign of the seriousness of the senior leaders' commitment to combatting economic crime.

In February 1983, the CDIC claimed that the 1982 campaign had scored a number of successes, including having basically put an end to smuggling (*RMRB*, 5 February 1983). However, this was wishful thinking; smuggling actually increased, certainly in some parts of China. In Guangdong Province (which borders on Hong Kong), for instance, smuggling was up in the first quarter of 1983 compared with the same quarter in 1982. The centre certainly recognized that economic crime as a whole was still a serious problem; in late August/early September, the Standing Committee of the National People's Congress discussed and passed the 'Decision on Imposing Severe Punishment on Offenders who Cause Grave Harm to the Social Order'; this was designed to increase the deterrent effect of the law on would-be criminals, including officials. It was followed by a renewed assault on corruption.

In terms of official statements, regulations, etc., the next 15 months were relatively quiet – certainly in comparison with the period from the beginning of 1982 through to mid-1983. Indeed, in October 1984, Deng revealed that he had now turned his attention away from economic crime towards other matters, such as the Hong Kong issue (Deng, 1985, pp. 55–6); this said, he did still see the need to crack down on criminals, partially to ensure that a new conscious-ness developed among the Chinese population by the year 2000 (ibid., p. 59). But generally during this period, the leadership seems to have been more concerned with catching criminals and ensuring they were being properly dealt with than with taking major initia-tives. Implementation was thus now more important than major new policy statements. In connection with this, it is interesting to note that when the CCP substantially reduced the overall number of posts on the Central Committee *nomenklatura* (August 1984), there was one group that went against the trend; for the first time, the heads of DICs in all central state agencies were *added* to the all-important list, 'giving these groups additional clout in their fight against corruption and bureaucratic abuses' (Burns, 1987, p. 38).

By December 1984, however, the central authorities were clearly feeling the need to issue further regulations to deal with corrupt officials. In that month, the Central Committee and the State Council issued new regulations – Central Document No. 27 – forbidding government employees from engaging in business (*BR*, Vol. 29, No. 8, p. 8; *SWB*/FE/8186/BII/2 – citing *RMRB*, 7 February 1986).

The year 1985 witnessed further developments in the Chinese leadership's fight against corruption. In two major speeches in September, for instance, CDIC Chairperson and member of the Standing Committee of the Politburo Chen Yun identified corruption as one of the most significant problem areas in Chinese society (Chen Yun, 1985a, esp. pp. 94–5; Chen Yun, 1985b, in which he stressed the need for developing ethics as well as the economy). This concern resulted in the adoption of yet more legislation and policy pronouncements in late 1985 and early 1986. In December 1985, the Central Committee and the State Council issued the 'Regulations Prohibiting Party and Government Organs and Cadres from Engaging in Business and Running Enterprises' (for a brief analysis see Yu, 1986). This was endorsed a few weeks later by the Central Committee's 'Document No. 6'. The regulations forbade officials in party and government organizations and affiliated institutions from participating in any enterprise unless this had been explicitly approved beforehand by both the Central Committee Secretariat and the State Council (see Yeh, 1987, p. 17). The party leadership was at this time making it quite clear – for instance at a major conference on corruption for 8,000 more senior officials organized by the Central Committee in Beijing, 6–9 January 1986 (see *BR*, Vol. 29, No. 3, pp. 4–6) – that they intended to deal resolutely with economic criminals, at whatever level the offenders worked. Deng himself said there had still been too much empty talk and insufficient action. As part of the new, intensified approach against senior cadres, Deng (apparently) decided that there was a need for new blood in the anti-corruption campaign. Put in charge of the new campaign was the then rising star Qiao Shi; his two deputies were Wang Zhaoguo and Qiang Xiaochu. They headed a new body – the 'Leading Group for the Rectification of Party Style in Central-Level Departments', which had as one major task the detection and countering of corruption among relatively high-ranking party officials – that was apparently established by Deng himself. All three were seen by Western observers as Deng supporters. Although the body may have been established to supplement the work of the CDIC, it could also be seen as being in competition with it. In this connection, it was revealing that the man who had headed the CDIC since its formation, Chen Yun, was conspicuous by his absence from the January 1986 meeting; as pointed out in chapter 5, Chen's views on economic reform and the reasons for corruption have been quite different from Deng's (for Western media interpretations of all this see *FEER*, 23 January 1986, pp. 28–9, and 30 January 1986, pp. 22–4, *Asiaweek*, 13 April 1986, p. 36, and *Newsweek*, 3 February 1986, p. 14).

One of the most significant aspects of the new regulations and approach was that it was specifically aimed at overcoming nepotism amongst officials. There were three specific measures taken to deal with this problem. First, in order to minimize the extent to which officials would have an illegitimate vested economic interest in the activites of enterprises and commercial organizations, not only were they themselves forbidden from taking up employment in state-run enterprises for at least two years from the time they ceased working for party or government bodies or affiliated organizations, but their children and spouses were *also* prohibited from taking up positions in commercial activites or operating the enterprises. Second, new regulations (of 28 January) in theory gave the right to lower-level government officials and party members to nominate candidates – by secret election – for promotion; according to the official Chinese newsagency *Xinhua*, this change was 'aimed at making the selection process more democratic, and preventing certain officials from promoting their own friends and relatives, regardless of competence' (*The Age*, 3 February 1986; *SWB*/FE/8174/BII/16–20; see too *BR*, Vol. 29, No. 8, pp. 5–7). To endorse the concept that senior officials should not interfere with the nomination process, the new regulations explicitly forbade them from suggesting who should be promoted; to endorse the point about nepotism, an official was in future to be obliged to withdraw from any party committee meeting at which the promotion of his/her children or other relatives was to be discussed. Finally, in a bid to prevent leap-frogging through the ranks by well-connected employees, the new regulations stipulated that officials would in future 'under normal circumstances' be promoted only one grade at a time. Unfortunately, this particular section of the legislation contained a loophole, in that it allowed for promotions by more than one grade for those with 'exceptional talent' or when there was an 'urgent need'.

In short, the traditional concept of *guanxi* (acquiring advantage through connections) was now under attack. But the senior leadership was to some extent divided on how the campaign should be organized. Some were still insisting that there was to be no mass movement against corruption; leading figures such as Hu Qili and Qiao Shi made it quite clear that the CCP would rely on education – including widespread publicity of cases involving high-ranking cadres – and the legal system to deal with the problem (*Asiaweek*, 13

April 1986, pp. 34–7). On the other hand, Li Xiannian urged the masses to exercise supervision over officials to ensure they observed both party discipline and state law. Evidently, some of the leaders were still concerned that the masses might perceive the anti-corruption campaign as a return to the subjectivity and unpredictability of the Maoist era, and therefore went to great lengths to make the whole process appear orderly and in compliance with all legal codes. Others felt that the urgency of the task did require mass involvement, and that the best way to deal with recalcitrant officials was to subject them to mass scrutiny. Although the differences of opinion here were more of degree and emphasis than of kind, such conflicting messages from the leaders sow confusion, doubt and nervousness *both* among the masses – wary of the local- and middle-level officials – and in these officials *vis à vis* the mass citizenry.

Probably in part because of this confusion and dilemma, the Central Committee ordered that a study be undertaken of the ways in which a number of aspects of the work of organizations could be improved (for example, in terms of decision-making, auditing, supervision, etc.) so as to help overcome corruption by party and state officials.

One further sign of the confusion that abounded in the legislation of late 1985/early 1986 was that in March 1986 the General Office of the Central Committee and the State Council issued a supplement to the December 1985 'regulations' to make clear what was intended by the ban on party and state officials engaging in commercial activities and being involved in business enterprises:

> Party and government organs and their cadres engaging in commercial activities and opening their own business enterprises refer to the instances where party and government organs and their cadres *use public funds* (including funds for the disbursement of administrative expenses, operating expenses, special fees, etc.), loans, and funds raised in one way or another to carry out commercial activites and open business enterprises *for the private benefit of their own units or of the individuals themselves.* (translation from Yeh, 1987, p. 13 – emphasis added)

Even now, there were a few minor exceptions to the above, aimed primarily at meeting the service requirements of both management and workers, but nevertheless representing a loophole susceptible to exploitation.

One final development of 1986 that must certainly be noted was the establishment of a Ministry of Supervision. This was set up largely as yet another body to investigate corruption and other forms of official malfeasance; it has in recent years played a major role in investigating official corruption (see, for example, *BR*, Vol. 32, No. 29, p. 8).

In mid-1987, another stage in the ongoing campaign became obvious when details of a new party directive – issued by the CDIC – were published. According to this, any party member found guilty of having committed extortion and/or taken bribes was to be expelled from the CCP, regardless of how small-scale the crime was. This measure was apparently taken because of 'rampant corruption' in some areas of the party (see *CD*, 14 July 1987, and *China Post*, 28 July 1987).

The issue of corruption was again a major one at the 13th Congress of the CCP (October–November 1987). General Secretary Zhao criticized widespread corruption in the CCP, and called for an intensification of the struggle against it: 'If we tolerate decadent elements in the Party, the whole Party will decline' (Chinese Communist Party, 1987, p. 66). He went on to advocate an approach to the problem that blended the carrot (education) and the stick (punishment). However, there was also a certain ambiguity in Zhao's position, in that he argued that the fight against corruption must not interfere with the economic reform: 'We certainly must not change our general principles and policies of reform and opening to the outside world just because of these few cases of corruption, or bring our work of economic development and reform to a halt in order to concentrate on sweeping the bad practices away' (ibid., p. 66). Although this attitude appears to have been similar to Deng's own at the time, it will be demonstrated below that Deng has since June 1989 used this aspect of Zhao's approach against the former general secretary. While space precludes a fuller analysis of the 13th Congress, one further important point to note is that Chen Yun was replaced by Qiao Shi as head of the CDIC at this time.

At the beginning of 1988, a number of supplementary provisions for the punishment of graft, bribery and smuggling were passed by the National People's Congress. Under the new laws, individuals found guilty of embezzling more than 50,000 yuan were to receive a minimum sentence of 10 years' imprisonment and a maximum one of the death penalty. According to this legislation, not only individuals but also state-owned enterprises and institutions that accepted bribes in return for favours could now be fined, while their managers and others diectly responsible were to receive up to 5 years' imprisonment (for further details see *RMRB*, 20 January 1988, p. 4; *RMRB*, 22 January 1988, p. 1; *RMRB*, 24 January 1988, p. 4;

CD, 22 January 1988, and 4 February 1988, p. 4). The adoption of these supplementary regulations seems to have been connected with the fact that, despite the campaign that had been underway since 1982, the appeals of corrupt activity were great for an increasing number of citizens (on increases in the number of cases of economic crime in Beijing during 1987, see *CD*, 27 January 1988, p. 3, and *RMRB*, 14 September 1988, p. 4). Indeed, not only were more and more ordinary citizens engaging in illegal economic activity, but the number of party members involved in bribery and other economic crimes was also increasing, according to *China Daily* (18 August 1988, p. 3).

In order to deal even more resolutely with official corruption, the Chinese party and state authorities adopted a number of further measures in 1988. For instance in the middle of the year, the CDIC released a set of provisional regulations on the kinds of punishment to be meted out to CCP members who behave improperly in matters relating to foreign affairs or foreign nationals, while the Ministry of Supervision announced its intention of promulgating several new regulations to deal with corruption and bribery among government officials (*BR*, Vol. 31, No. 34, pp. 5–6). The latter was followed in September by the passing by the State Council of the 'Provisional Regulations on Administrative Disciplinary Sanctions against State Administrative Personnel Involved in Corruption and Bribery' (*RMRB*, 10 September 1988, p. 1, and 18 September 1988, p. 3), plus various pieces of legislation concerned with leaking state secrets and taxing banquets (the latter presumably to help overcome the *dachi dahe* problem). Shortly after this rash of publicity and legislation, it was revealed in the press that a recent circular from the Supreme People's Court had encouraged local higher courts to be both more prompt in their handling of cases of serious economic crime, and more severe in the punishments handed down; this was because economic crime, especially 'official profiteering', had become particularly widespread recently (*CD*, 30 September 1988, p. 3). In October 1988, draft provisional regulations on civil servants were issued by the Ministry of Personnel; among the regulations were some designed to combat nepotism (*CD*, 31 October 1988, p. 1). In November, a report in *China Daily* (14 November 1988, p. 1) revealed that China's chief procurator had been instructed by CCP General Secretary Zhao Ziyang to mount a major new drive against embezzlement, bribery and speculation – especially among officials. Shortly thereafter, in December 1988, Zhao Ziyang informed the Central Committee that the 1988 campaign against bureaucratic corruption had largely failed, which was a major reason for intensifying the drive. At about the same time, and in line with Zhao's statement, the CCP urged the PRC's eight minor parties to establish corruption-reporting centres to monitor both government departments and the CCP itself (*BR*, Vol. 31, No. 48, p. 7).

An interesting development in Deng's anti-corruption drive during 1988 was that the supreme leader became so anxious to reduce corruption and to be seen to be doing so – no matter what or who was involved – that he now focused on a corruption case that related to his own eldest son, Deng Pufang. This was by no means the first occasion on which the crimes of children of leading officials had been publicly exposed and criticized; there was a major scandal early in 1986, for instance, when sons of three former senior officials in China's largest city, Shanghai, were executed for sex-related crimes (see *BR* Vol. 29, No. 9, pp. 5–6, and *FEER*, 6 March 1986, pp. 34–5). Deng Junior has a physical disability (he was paralysed in 1968, during the Cultural Revolution, as a result of a dispute with Red Guards) and had been in charge of the China Welfare Fund for the Handicapped since 1984. In late 1988, Deng concentrated much of his attention on 'corruption' (much of it unofficial in our definition) in eight large corporations – one of which, the Kanghua Development Corporation, was intimately linked with the China Welfare Fund. As will shortly be demonstrated, the Kanghua corporation was subsequently found to be highly corrupt – which would necessarily have had negative repercussions for Deng Junior's image.

As might be expected, the so-called 'turmoil' of April–June 1989 had various implications for the anti-corruption drive. Widespread corruption in high places had been one of the aspects of contemporary China most criticized by demonstrators, a fact that did not go unnoticed by the senior leadership. Towards the end of June, the Standing Committee of the National People's Congress met for a week–long session, during which it called on the State Council to intensify the struggle against corruption (*BR*, Vol. 32, No. 29, p. 4). The Politburo also met in late June; the problem of corruption was a major item on the agenda (*BR*, Vol. 32, No. 32, p. 5). There was an acknowledgement by the top leaders at this time that the anti-corruption campaigns of recent years had been less effective than they should have been; using familiar Chinese metaphors, they recognized that the masses' perception was that the authorities had been 'killing only mosquitoes and flies and not daring to fight tigers' (*BR*, Vol. 32, No. 33, p. 4). By July, the Central Committee and the State Council had resolved to accomplish seven tasks relating to the concerns of the masses. Many of the seven related to corruption (actual or potential), particularly among members – and their families – of the Politburo, the Central Committee Secretariat and the Executive of the State Council. It was resolved, for instance, that no child or spouse of a leader would be permitted to engage in commercial businesses or assume posts in trading companies from 1 September 1989. In August and September, several new regulations on various aspects of corruption were issued both by the State Administration for Industry and Commerce and by the Ministry of Supervision. One such was a clemency law (15 August), designed to encourage economic criminals of all sorts and at all levels to hand themselves over to the authorities by the end of October 1989; in return, they were guaranteed lighter sentences than they could normally have expected.

Another development during this period was the so-called 'clean-up and rectification' campaign against large-scale state-run corporations (see esp. *BR*, Vol. 32, No. 46, pp. 14–19). An attempt to stop official profiteering by such bodies had been started back in June 1985, but had enjoyed very limited success. A second attempt was made early in 1989, following an October 1988 decision of the Central Committee and the State Council. This resulted in an announcement at the end of July 1989 – following a Politburo meeting of 27–8 July – that two major corporations were to be dissolved. One of these was the one with which Deng's son had had such close connections, the Kanghua Development Corporation (see *BR*, Vol. 32, No. 33, p. 8). Following this, in August, the third stage of the campaign got underway; many more enterprises were to be scrutinized, the whole campaign being supervised by a 15-person team headed by Vice-Premier Tian Jiyun and responsible directly to the State Council.

The numerous new regulations were accompanied by various structural reforms intended to bring corruption more under control. For example, a new anti-corruption office (the Procuratorial Division on Graft and Bribery) was established under the Supreme People's Procuratorate, replacing the Procuratorial Office for Economic Affairs (*BR*, Vol. 32, No. 36, p. 8). The Ministry of Supervision's role also appeared to be increasing during 1989.

By the end of 1989, the intensified campaign of the second half of the year (see, for example, Premier Li Peng's comments to the National People's Congress on 20 March 1990 – in *BR*, Vol. 33, No. 16, p. iv) seemed to be having some effect. The clemency law, for instance, had resulted in more than 1,000 CCP and government officials turning themselves in for bribery and embezzlement, while it was claimed that by November all the spouses and children of senior leaders who had been working for private businesses had resigned from them (*BR*, Vol. 32, No. 46, p. 18). But some disturbing developments had also emerged by this stage. Thus, whereas the Chinese authorities had until June been encouraging their own limited form of *glasnost* (*toumingdu*), at least two senior leaders (CCP General Secretary Jiang Zemin and member of the Standing Committee of the Politburo Li Ruihuan) were by late November publicly arguing that the mass media should concentrate on publishing *positive* phenomena in the PRC, very much in line with orthodox communist views on the role of the media; although Jiang modified his argument somewhat by stating that investigative journalism was also necessary, the general message was by most criteria a depressing one (see *BR*, Vol. 32, No. 49, pp. 5–6, and No. 50, pp. 4–5). Moreover, at a time when the post-June leadership team was looking for scapegoats to blame for the mass unrest, Deng explicitly blamed disgraced former General Secretary Zhao Ziyang for having been too tolerant of corruption at the highest levels (*BR*, Vol. 32, No. 52, p. 21); as pointed out above, Deng's own views had earlier seemed very similar to Zhao's, while Zhao himself had in late 1988 explicitly identified and attempted to address the problem that anti-corruption drives had been less successful than they should have been.

An article that appeared in the very last issue of *Beijing Review* for the 1980s (Vol. 32, No. 52, pp. 19–23) repeated the claim that the anti-corruption campaigns of the 1980s – presumably referring mainly to the pre-June 1989 situation – had been more of words than of deeds, and far less effective than they should have been. But such a statement must be treated with caution and contextualized (that is, one must bear in mind that the authorities were still smarting from the ramifications of the June massacre). The Chinese leadership *had* been taking concrete measures against corruption in the 1980s, even if these were not as effective as had been hoped for. For example, as leadership concern about corruption among relatively high-ranking and middle-level officials increased, so the authorities urged ordinary citizens – at least by 1986 – to 'dare to touch the tiger's buttocks' (that is, dare to question and expose senior officials – on this see *Asiaweek*, 13 April 1986, pp. 36–7). In this context, a hot-line experiment was introduced in Beijing in September 1987, whereby citizens were encouraged to telephone the authorities if they had any information on corruption among officials. This was expanded in June 1988 (see *BR*, Vol. 33, No. 3, p. 25), and was available in most major cities by late 1988/early 1989 (see *BR*, Vol. 32, No. 30, p. 7); there should have been a countrywide system of 'corruption report centres' in operation by June 1989 (see *BR*, Vol. 31, No. 33, p. 8), although it is not clear that this had been fully implemented. Calls were directed – and, seemingly, currently go – either to local centres, the Ministry of Supervision (telephone number 202 5391!) or to the Supreme People's Procuratorate. According to *Beijing Review* (Vol. 31, No. 46, pp. 4–5), tip-offs from the public had led to the investigation of more than 40,000 cases of corruption (broadly understood – but including many cases of official corruption) by November 1988; the Shanghai Procuratorate Centre alone dealt with almost 2,000 cases in the first seven weeks of its existence (for a recent analysis of 'offence reporting' that includes many up-to-date data, see *BR*, Vol. 33, No. 3, pp. 25–8).[6] All this is certainly a form of 'deed', not just word.

It is also closely linked to the issue of legitimacy. *Hongqi*, the CCP's main theoretical journal until 1988, observed in February 1986, for instance, that: 'Corruption among leading officials harms the image of the party among the masses' (quoted in *Asiaweek*, 13 April 1986, p. 36). *Beijing Review* noted in November 1988 (Vol. 31, No. 46, p. 4) – possibly more as a symbol of wishful thinking than as a reflection of reality – that three facts (that the procuratorial bodies were now being urged to examine in particular cases of corruption based on public information; that a set of 1987 regulations was designed to ensure that no-one would suffer as a result of exposing or accusing corrupt party members or organizations;[7] and that major cases of corruption were now being both uncovered and prosecuted) had raised the public's confidence in the system. The legitimacy problem is not helped, however, by the fact that the Chinese leaders themselves had been divided on some aspects of corruption, including their assessment of the reasons for it, its overall significance, and of the best methods for dealing with it. Nevertheless, they are still treating it as a major problem, and have continued to do so even since the June 1989 events. While there appears to have been a slowing down in the promulgation of anti-corruption legislation in 1990 and 1991 – and a marked intensification of general ideological calls for 'cleaner' government and a much higher standard of ethics among officials – cases of quite senior officials being punished for corruption continue to be publicized. Two of the best examples are of the deputy minister of railways, Luo Yungang, in 1990, and of the ministers of communications and of construction (Qian Yongchang and Lin Hanxiong respectively).

In conclusion, it seems very clear that the anti-corruption campaigns in China will not be markedly less intense in the early 1990s than they were in the 1980s, although the emphasis at present seems to be more on ideological exhortation than on a more legalistic approach. What is also clear is that analysts of corruption will have an abundance of material for some time to come.

*Policies, Campaigns and Legislation Elsewhere in the Communist
World*

It is not possible to provide here anything like a comprehensive
picture of leadership views and legislation on corruption throughout
what was the communist world; the task is, quite simply, too big.
Instead, I shall cite just a few examples of leadership statements,
legislation, etc., so as to give the reader some impression of how
seriously corruption has been perceived by leaders in many communist states, and how various leaderships have approached the
problem. Before doing this, however, one important point to be
emphasized at the beginning of this section is that one would not
expect major campaigns in countries in which steps towards legal-
rationality had hardly been taken; this is another reason why information on some countries is very sparse.

Leadership concern about corruption and economic crime was
publicly articulated in most *East European* countries until the fall of
communism, and led to a number of clamp-downs, the strengthening of existing control bodies and/or the establishment of new ones,
and tougher sentencing. Corruption was seen by the *Polish* leadership as a major factor leading to the 1980–1 troubles, for example, so
that it is hardly surprising there was a major anti-corruption campaign in Poland in the early 1980s (see, for example, *QER, Poland/
East Germany*, No. 4, 1980, pp. 1–2, and No. 1, 1981, p. 7;
Tarkowski, 1989, esp. p. 56). Hirszowicz (1986, p. 130), citing a
Polish source, reports that among those officials denounced for
corruption following Gierek's fall (1980) were three Central Committee secretaries, 28 first secretaries of provincial party committees,
34 secretaries of provincial committees, 7 deputy premiers, 18 ministers, 56 deputy ministers and 51 heads and deputy heads of provinces. Political campaigns were endorsed by tougher anti-
corruption legislation. This process emerged in 1982, when the
courts began passing harsher sentences on corrupt individuals (*SWB/
EE/7896/B/13–14*, 11 March 1985). A number of anti-speculation
conferences were held during the 1980s at the Council of Ministers'
office in Warsaw (see, for example, *SWB/EE/7867/B/5*, 5 February
1985), and the Commission for Combatting Speculation was strengthened.

The communist leadership in *Hungary* long acknowledged corruption. For instance, a number of critical references to widespread
corruption in the HSWP were made at the 9th Congress, held in
November 1966 (*YICA*, 1968, p. 283). This was followed in 1967 by
publicity on various cases of corruption, such as that of the president

of the People's Control Committee (György Varga). But anti-corruption moves appear to have intensified in the 1980s. There was a major purge of corrupt party officials in Budapest in 1982 (*YICA*, 1985, p. 297). Following this, in April 1983, party leader Kádár acknowledged at a plenum of the Central Committee of the HSWP that corruption and parasitism were increasing, and called for action to combat it (*YICA*, 1984, p. 335). This resulted in a major campaign against corrupt officials, of whom Ádám Bonifert was perhaps the most prominent (*YICA*, 1985, pp. 296–7). In July 1985, in response to the perceived growth in fraud in Hungary, six new regional fraud squads (in Pécs, Miskolc, Szeged, Györ, Debrecen and Veszprém) were established; hitherto, fraud enquiries throughout the country had been conducted only by the Budapest fraud squad (*SWB*/EE/7966/B/5, 1 June 1985).

In *Czechoslovakia*, the politburo (Presidium) issued a statement in February 1983 concerning a campaign to fight against violations of socialist legality, morality and discipline (*SWB*/EE/8051/B/4, 9 September 1985); this was directed, *inter alia*, at corrupt officials. According to official sources, the Czechoslovak authorities then launched a major investigation campaign into bribery in the latter half of 1983 and throughout 1984 (*SWB*/EE/7965/B/3–4, 31 May 1985). In September 1986, a high-level Soviet delegation led by USSR Procurator-General A. Rekunkov visited Czechoslovakia, and had talks with senior Czechoslovak party and state officials; the main item on the agenda was the fight against economic crime and corruption (*Rudé Právo*, 5 September 1986, p. 2 – in FBIS-EEU-86-181, Vol. 11, No. 181, 18 September 1986). In January 1988 at a plenary session of the Slovak Communist Party's Central Committee, Miloš Jakeš made a strong plea for a more concerted effort against corruption of all sorts. He argued – perhaps with more prescience than he realized at the time – that openness (that is, the Czechoslovak equivalent of *glasnost*) is largely a matter of honesty, and that if the people are to trust the communist party, corruption must be eradicated (*Rudé Právo*, 15 January 1988 – in IB, No. 7, 1988, p. 45). And in December 1989, at the height of the crisis in Czechoslovakia, an extraordinary congress of the CPCS was convened at which the Central Committee was instructed to establish a commission to investigate cases of abuse of power and corruption among CPCS officials. Unfortunately for the communists, this was too little, too late.

According to Ghermani (1983, p. 317) there was a major clampdown on 'Several top functionaries from almost all branches of the economy and the administration' in *Romania* in 1982 (see too *QER*

Romania, Bulgaria, Albania, No. 3, 1982, p. 6 and No. 4, 1982, p. 7). This was followed in 1983 by a 'flood' of norms from the State Council, the Grand National Assembly and the President of the Republic, designed to strengthen the existing legislation on corruption and economic crime. Nevertheless, four years later, Ceauşescu was still calling for a more concerted struggle against corruption and misappropriation (*IB*, No. 23, 1987, p. 50).

Bulgaria, too, was adopting tougher legislation and more openly discussing the problem of corruption in the 1980s. In 1982, following various scandals including the Popov Affair (see p. 112), the National Assembly introduced a number of amendments to the penal code, increasing the penalties for economic crime (*QER Romania, Bulgaria, Albania*, No. 3, 1982, p. 14). But of greater significance were the more general criticisms of leading officials that appeared from 1985. Perhaps the most important 'trigger' article appeared in *Rabotnichesko Delo*, 23 September 1985. The party newspaper referred to the emergence of some 'very alarming symptoms' among the party and state officialdom. Most of the criticism was directed at improper office-filling (nepotism, cronyism, etc.). Although no senior leaders were identified by name, the implication was that this problem had reached the highest echelons. Certainly some lower-ranking officials were identified as guilty of corruption, including D. Gradev (director of the Centre for Propaganda, Information and the Press at the Committee on Culture), who was accused of having used state building labourers to work on his private villa during their normal working hours. The article in *Rabotnichesko Delo* was followed in early November by an expanded meeting of the State and People's Control Committee, which devoted much of its attention to corruption. Having considered economic crime among small-scale and low-ranking violators, the Committee vowed to target more clearly 'those who patronise and protect them' – a clear reference to higher-ranking officialdom (*SWB*/EE/8101/B/2, 6 November 1985). Legislation providing for much stricter penalties for corruption was passed in October 1986, at a time when more and more articles on corruption were being published in the mass media (see *KRWE*, 1987, p. 35518).

This said, the Bulgarian leadership in the 1980s also revealed some of the contradictoriness – a sensitivity to what it perceived to be excessively open and critical exposure of corruption among some leading dignitaries – that was a feature of the Soviet leadership by the late 1980s. Thus, the publication of details on the Mihailov family's corruption by the trade union newspaper *Trud* in June 1987 resulted in the expulsion of the investigative journalist responsible for the articles, Georgi Tambuev, from the BCP, on the orders of the party's Central Control and Revisory Committee (see Ramet, 1991, p. 259).

Moving away from what many saw until recently as 'the Soviet bloc', *Yugoslavia* also mounted campaigns and introduced legislation over the years in its fight against corruption. Thus, in the (Northern) autumn of 1950, the Central Committee adopted recommendations designed to abolish many hitherto legal privileges of the elite. In February 1958, the Executive Committee of the LCY circularized a letter to all party organizations urging them to be on the alert for party members engaging in corrupt practices. In the late 1960s, following the removal of the hated Ranković, there was a major press campaign against corruption in the security police (UDBa). Then in the early 1970s there was another identifiable media campaign against widespread graft and corruption (all the above information on Yugoslavia from Rusinow, 1977, pp. 57, 97, 187–8, 270 – see too Zukin, 1975, pp. 206–7, for more details and examples). In the 1980s, undoubtedly the most significant corruption scandal publicized in the Yugoslav media was the so-called 'Agrokomerc Affair' of 1987. This resulted, *inter alia*, in the forced resignation of the federal vice-president, H. Pozderac, in September 1987 amid allegations of his involvement in this major financial scandal.

Even the relatively closed system in *Albania* witnessed a marked increase in the reporting of corruption and economic crime in the 1980s (Zanga, 1988a, p. 2), a phenomenon that correlates temporally with Alia's replacement of Hoxha.

In April 1982, following a number of reports on corruption and profiteering in the press since early in the year, Fidel Castro launched a major drive against corruption in *Cuba*. He criticized the fact that a number of members of the Cuban Communist Party had recently been found to be corrupt, and, perhaps indirectly referring to legitimation problems, noted that 'bad things can foster . . . other bad things' (Castro, 1983, p. 342). He charged two bodies – the Ministry of Domestic Trade and the National Revolutionary Police – with the task of fighting corruption, although in May 1982 Castro stated that the Ministry of the Interior and the Cuban Mass Organizations were also to be involved. It is interesting to note that there was no reference on either occasion to party bodies dealing with the problem. This might reflect the fact that Castro at that time perceived the problem as being more one of ordinary criminals taking advantage of his tolerance of more private enterprise in the economy than of corrupt officials. Whether this was because the former were more visible and/or widespread than the latter, or whether it was because

Castro had reservations about clamping down too severely on his own officials, or whether there was some other explanation, is not clear. However, it is significant that Castro argued that investigating and prosecuting bodies should be 'much more severe' with people who commit theft than with 'those who commit administrative violations in order to profit from them' (Castro, 1983, p. 354). While the prime target in both kinds of situation was probably entrepreneurs, it is also clear that the latter notion could certainly be applied to some officials. On the other hand, as noted above, it is possible that Castro was being cautious about attacking his own staff too ferociously. Nevertheless, the campaign against both economic crime by non-officials and corruption itself has been waged in Cuba since then.

Castro seems eventually to have decided that it was the moves towards private enterprise and the greater stress on incentives that encouraged these undesirable phenomena. Thus he saw the only solution to this in reversing the privatization measures taken in 1981; this he did in 1986, so going against the trend in most of the rest of the communist world (Albania being a notable exception until recently). However, this has not totally eradicated corruption, and in July 1987, Castro referred in a major speech to the ongoing 'process of rectification' in Cuba; this has been directed, *inter alia*, at economic crime and corruption (*China Post*, 28 July 1987). Certainly, as was demonstrated in chapter 3 (see pp. 117–8), there were reports of some sensational cases of corruption among the highest echelons of the Cuban elite at the end of the 1980s; Castro was clearly both embarrassed and upset by these. Indeed, in September 1990, the Cuban authorities adopted a new programme – the 'Special Period in Peacetime' – that had as one of its principal aims the combatting of corruption (*KRWE*, 1991, p. 38229). Perhaps the final point to make about Castro's campaigns is that he has publicly acknowledged that crime – presumably including corruption – will endure even into early communism.[8] In a speech made in Havana 6 June 1986, Castro argued that: 'it would be illusory to believe that crime would disappear in the course of the transition from capitalism to socialism and from socialism to communism' (*YICA*, 1987, p. 81).

Despite J.C. Scott's (1972, pp. ix and 16) misinformed image of it as an almost 'squeaky clean' state, communist *Vietnam* too has both reported a number of cases of corruption over the years and mounted various campaigns to combat it. In August 1967, for instance, a major article was published in Vietnam's main theoretical political journal *Hoc Tap* in which To Huu was severely critical of a number of party functionaries in North Vietnam for their corrupt practices

(*YICA*, 1968, p. 643). In January 1969, in a major speech delivered in Vinh Phu Province, Truong Chinh referred to widespread corruption among cadres and party members. And in April 1970, Lê Duân signed a Politburo resolution condemning, *inter alia*, corruption among cadres (from *YICA*, 1970, pp. 697–8; *YICA*, 1971, p. 681). The situation did not improve following reunification. In June 1976 (that is, after *de facto* though shortly before *de jure* reunification), party leader Lê Duân once again castigated party cadres for bribery, misappropriation of private property and various other corrupt practices (*YICA*, 1977, p. 393). This was followed in 1977 and 1978 by an anti-corruption campaign and the expulsion of several cadres from the VCP. But there continued to be frequent official reports of corruption in Vietnam, and the problem was evidently perceived by the leadership as so serious that they established a new Party Central Organs Internal Affairs Department in September 1983. Although this body's brief was not fully clear, it appears that one of its tasks was to relieve the Central Committee's Internal Affairs Department, so that the latter would have more time for investigating the many charges made against party cadres and officials (YICA, 1984, pp. 282–3).

The fight against corruption in Vietnam increased its momentum in the mid-1980s. At the end of 1984, the VCP launched a major new campaign against five 'negative phenomena' at a party cadre conference chaired by the then head of the security services (and Politburo member) Pham Hung. The five phenomena to be overcome included four that could certainly be defined as corruption (for example, just 'one' of the five is 'smuggling, financial speculation, bribery, palmgreasing and loaning money at high interest rates' – see *YICA*, 1986, pp. 244–5). The campaign continued well into 1986, with party *apparatchiki* and legal officials being two groups singled out for particularly vehement attacks (*YICA*, 1987, pp. 251–2). Ordinary citizens were encouraged to criticize whatever they wanted to via letters to the press. In one weekend, about 1,300 letters arrived at a Ho Chi Minh City newspaper; in these, the second most criticized aspect of life in contemporary Vietnam (after the poor state of the economy) was of corrupt officialdom. At the 6th Congress of the VCP, held in December 1986, tackling corruption was identified as one of the party's major tasks (Beresford, 1988, p. 84).

The leadership condemnation and press campaigns continued into the late 1980s. For instance, in his Lunar New Year speech of February 1988 published in *Nhân Dân*, Nguyên Van Linh listed five main tasks for 1988, the last of which was to purify the party and state apparatus by weeding out degenerate and degraded elements, regardless of rank and position (*SWB*/FE/0080/B/4). On 9 June 1988, the party newspaper *Nhân Dân* reported that more than 500 members of the VCP in Cao Bang province had been expelled, while another 391 had been subject to 'disciplinary action', for 'embezzlement and other violations'; this is yet another result of the 'purification campaign' launched in Vietnam in the mid-1980s. According to an official report on the Cao Bang corruption, several of the party members were members of party committees (and thus officials by our definition) who had stolen large quantities of state property. It is interesting to note here that some Western commentators (see, for example, *The Age*, 22 June 1988) interpreted Do Muoi's 1988 promotion to the Vietnamese premiership as a symbol of the leadership's commitment to overcoming corruption; Do Muoi has been seen by many as the VCP's leading disciplinarian, and was elected general secretary of the VCP in June 1991.

However, even if Do Muoi's promotions in 1988 and 1991 did reflect a leadership decision at that time to intensify the struggle against corruption itself, there was also a clear change of policy on the *reporting* of this towards the end of the 1980s. From at least February 1989 – and hence before the East European revolution, though at a time when the dysfunctions of *glasnost* in the USSR and possibly Hungary were already becoming clear – even the relatively liberal general secretary of the VCP until June 1991, Nguyên Van Linh, was advocating a clamp-down on media reporting and criticism of negative phenomena, including corruption. The justification for this has been that such reporting has been undermining the prestige and credibility of the VCP. This policy was strongly endorsed by the VCP Central Committee at its seventh plenum in August 1989 (for details see M. Williams, 1990). As the Soviet leadership appeared to do in mid-1990, the Vietnamese seem to have reached the point where they have decided that the reporting of official corruption is more disadvantageous than advantageous; in the next chapter, I shall speculate on whether they have realized this in time to save communist power.

Give the different stage of communist power in them, it initially seems surprising that the *African* communist states were not markedly different from the general pattern outlined above; this said, the campaigns do not appear to have been as intense or prolonged as those in many of the more established communist states in recent years. If anything, the limited information available suggests that the African campaigns more closely resembled the situation in countries like Yugoslavia or the PRC in the early days of communist rule there. In *Ethiopia*, a major anti-corruption drive was launched in

1982, following the promulgation of an anti-corruption law in September 1981 that gave the government the legal wherewithal to investigate a number of former government and COPWE officials who were suspected of embezzlement, bribery and breach of trust (*YICA*, 1983, p. 16). As C.V. Scott has pointed out, evidence on corruption in *Angola* is difficult to obtain – although Scott himself maintains that corruption there appears to have been more widespread than in Mozambique (Scott, 1988, p. 35). There were certainly signs of leadership disquiet about corruption. Thus Neto launched a campaign against corruption in the provinces, especially Benguela, in 1978–9 (C.V. Scott, 1988, p. 3)). Following that, in June 1982, the Central Committee announced an anti-corruption drive (Somerville, 1986, p. 61). Later in that year, party leader dos Santos was attacked for corruption by a group of senior party officials; in this rather unusual case, he retaliated by purging his critics (*YICA*, 1984, p. 9).

Turning to *Mozambique*, President Machel launched a 'political and organizational offensive' in 1980 designed to rid the state sector of corruption and cronyism. He expicitly identified some forms of corruption as evidence of disloyalty to the masses and regime: 'If an administrator, or a dynamising group secretary, or a factory manager, or a member of an administrative commission steal, then they are not representatives of our people' (quoted in C.V. Scott, 1988, p. 31). Various new agencies were established in that year to deal with both corruption and incompetence, including new control and discipline offices within the ministries. However, it appears that some control agencies were themselves corrupt, and in 1981 Machel launched a campaign to combat both corruption and tribalism within the security forces (ibid., p. 36). The death penalty and flogging were reintroduced in 1983 as possible punishments for corruption and other forms of economic crime; this reflected the leadership's growing concern about this phenomenon (Hanlon, 1984, pp. 144 and 208).

Benin, too, witnessed a number of campaigns against corruption after the communists took power in 1972. In 1986, for instance, a Central Committee report identified corruption (including official corruption) as a major factor in the country's economic decline. At about the same time, a special new court was established explicitly to handle cases of corruption, economic crime and subversion; apparently, this dealt with its first case in October 1988 (all details from Allen, 1988, pp. 44, 74, 83, 88, 126).

Finally, a communiqué issued by the *Yemeni* Socialist Party Central Committee in late 1986 announced that, during the recent elections to the Supreme Council, a number of citizens had called for measures to combat abuses and corrupt practices by state officials, so as to strengthen respect for the law and the administrative services (from FBIS *Daily Report*/Middle East and Africa/No. 216/7 November 1986/pp. ii and C 1–2).

The examples cited above are but the tip of the iceberg. But the fact that corruption was perceived by communist leaderships as a significant phenomenon and that they visibly took a number of measures to deal with it in most parts of the communist world (the reader is reminded that the GDR and the DPRK were exceptions) should by now be established beyond doubt.

Official Range of Treatment

Party Punishments

Having given some indication of the responses of communist leaderships to corruption, we turn now to consider in some detail the range of penalties that were used in communist states; for reasons explained in the preface, the present tense is frequently used here, despite the fact that many of the practices appear to have become redundant in several – but not all – countries very recently.

The first point to make here is that, to a large extent, a distinction can be drawn between officials who are members of the communist party and everyone else, both officials and ordinary citizens. Theoretically, only members of the party can be subject to party discipline; as shall be demonstrated, the fact that one might be subject to party discipline may often be seen as a distinct advantage, since it is clear from our research that in many cases relatively minor party penalties are – or have in the past been – considered sufficient punishment for members. In other words, many party members found guilty of corruption have never had to face the regular law courts, and in that sense have not run the risk of severe punishments – such as imprisonment – faced by people who are not members of the party.

There is a core of punishments that has been common to most communist parties. For minor infringements, there are 'educational and influential' measures of various sorts, such as 'comradely criticism', 'advice', 'warnings before the members' assembly'. For more serious misdemeanours, there is a wide range of 'disciplinary' measures. In ascending order of severity, a typical set of punishments would be reprimand (or censure); severe reprimand (or severe censure); severe reprimand with the explicit threat of expulsion; expulsion. The question of whether these various punishments are to be entered in central party records and the member's membership book varies (for example, it depended on the situation in the USSR, whereas a record was always to be made in Czechoslovakia; in both cases, there was provision for subsequent erasure of the record). In some countries, there have been provisions for other forms of punishment. In Albania and Mongolia, for instance, full party members could be temporarily downgraded to candidate status; in other countries, such as China, this is expressed in terms of being put 'on probation'. In Cambodia, China, Cuba, Czechoslovakia, Hungary and some other states, members who serve on committees or occupy some other post can be either temporarily relieved or permanently dismissed from these posts. One final point about party punishments that is of relevance to the study of corruption is that a number of communist party statutes have explicitly provided for punishment of *groups* of party members, such as a base organization; Albania, China, Cuba, Romania, Vietnam and Yugoslavia all fit this category.

Many communist party statutes do not mention what can happen to party members once they have been punished by the party. But some – notably China, Cuba, the USSR and Vietnam – make the point explicitly that party members are subject to state laws and legal proceedings. Others have done so implicitly, by stating that party members found guilty of criminal behaviour will be expelled – for all sorts of crime in the cases of Bulgaria and the GDR, only if these are serious in the cases of China and Vietnam. The Mongolian communist party makes the point more openly than others that party members are to be tried by the party before they are tried by the administrative or judicial authorities. Thus, according to Article Thirteen of the Statute of the MPRP (1981 version): 'In those instances where a party member has committed offences punishable in a judicial proceeding, he shall be expelled from the Party, the administrative and judicial authorites being notified of the offence.' This is a significant point, to which I shall return later in the chapter.

At the beginning of this section on party punishments, the expressions 'to a large extent' and 'theoretically' were employed; the reasons for this can now be elaborated. In most (perhaps all) communist states, there has been a system of appointment to virtually all the most important posts in society – not only within the party, but in the state bureaucracy, management, education, the media, the trade unions, the military, etc. – which involves the party very directly. Most Western analysts use the Soviet term '*nomenklatura*' to refer to this system – after all, it was the Soviets who first devised it, back in the 1920s (see Rigby, 1988) – even when they are considering it in other communist countries. Under this system, the 'hiring and firing' of individuals to all positions on the list of posts (the *nomenklatura*) held by the party must involve the party, whether or not an individual moving in or out of one of these posts is a member of the party. Although empirical research reveals that most people who occupy *nomenklatura* posts are members of the party, not all are. Yet the communist party will – in the past, at least – have to have been involved in the case of the dismissal of a corrupt official from a *nomenklatura* post, even if that person was not a party member. This is one concrete way in which the party has been involved in the punishment of people who are not party members.[9]

In addition to the party measures just described, disciplinary measures against corrupt officials can be taken by either administrative or judicial bodies. Let us once again examine the USSR and the PRC to obtain a reasonably detailed picture of how the system has operated in two communist countries. In both cases, the focus will be on three issues – who is responsible for investigating crimes, who is responsible for administering punishments, and what is the nature of punishments.

Extra-party Punishments in the USSR

As pointed out earlier, most citizens' misdemeanours were dealt with administratively or judicially, according to the perceived seriousness of the crime. The classification of a given act as minor or more serious was not always obvious at the outset of an investigation, and what might have started as an investigation by administrative bodies could subsequently be transferred to the police, for instance.

Since Lampert (1984, pp. 372–3) has provided such a comprehensive and clear analysis of this dimension of criminal treatment, the following discussion is heavily dependent on his classification; it relates primarily to the situation pertaining in the 1970s and early to mid-1980s; in recent years, it became difficult to ascertain exactly how most Soviet institutions were actually functioning.

Within a given Soviet organization there were invariably a number of individuals who were authorized to exercise supervisory control and who would, as a corollary, have been at least partially responsible for investigating economic irregularities – certainly in the early stages of the investigation. The chief accountant and the legal consultant of an organization would normally have been included on the list of such supervisors. In addition, the trade union committee, the party committee and other bodies representing the workforce (such as production conferences, collective farm conferences) were supposed to exercise constant vigilance and to alert the appropriate supervisory and investigative bodies to any suspicious circumstances.

There were also a number of individuals and organizations beyond the particular unit that were responsible for monitoring behaviour. These included higher-level committees of both trade unions and the party, citizen-inspectors and Committees of People's Control, formal supervisors (such as ministerial officials *vis à vis* enterprises under their supervision) and financial and planning agencies such as the Ministry of Finance, the State Bank and the State Planning Committee.

Moreover, the media – especially the press – were to some extent expected to investigate cases. They were certainly to publicize cases of impropriety and to bring pressure to bear upon those agencies that would be responsible for detailed investigation and charging individuals.

But which organizations were ultimately responsible for investigation, trying cases and passing judgements? It has already been noted that the party itself was to deal with corrupt – or allegedly corrupt – party members and, often, other important officials. Beyond this, very minor cases of corruption could be dealt with by the so-called 'Comrades' Courts'; these very roughly approximated to magistrates' courts in the British legal system. But most cases of corruption were considered to be too serious for such courts, and formal investigation was carried out by the procuracy. The regular police – in particular, its Department for Combatting the Embezzlement of Socialist Property and Speculation – and even the security police (KGB) may also have been involved. This especially pertained to the most serious cases – notably embezzlement and bribery – although their overall role in investigation was a much smaller one than that played by the procuracy (this is borne out by the Gdlyan–Ivanov affair analysed earlier; Wishnevsky, 1989, p. 9, argues that there were by 1989 clear signs of a struggle between the KGB and the procuracy over who was responsible for investigating corruption).

Once an investigation had been completed, the procuracy was also responsible for mounting the prosecution case in court. Most cases were heard in the first instance at the district-level People's Courts. Defendants were *formally* entitled to defence lawyers, and all participants at a trial had the right to cross-examine witnesses. If an individual (or group of individuals) was found guilty, there were a number of channels available for lodging an appeal.

The Soviet Criminal Codes specified a number of sanctions that could be applied to those found guilty of corruption, according to the scale and nature of the crime. There was a wide range of penalties for relatively minor cases of corruption, such as fines (up to 20 per cent of one's salary for up to two years) or dismissal from one's post (that is, an administrative punishment meted out by a judicial body). More serious crimes could and did incur sentences in corrective labour colonies or prisons (for a detailed analysis of the different kinds of labour colony and prison see *Pravda*, 12 July 1969, pp. 2–3). Generally speaking, bribe-taking, bribe-giving, embezzlement and treason were considered the most serious forms of corruption; these could incur not only up to 15 years' imprisonment but, in cases involving very large sums of money and/or threats to others, even the death penalty. The Soviets on occasion stated that they intended to abolish the death penalty one day (see, for example, *Literaturnaya Gazeta*, 24 July 1969, p. 11 – in *CDSP*, Vol. 20, No. 31, pp. 13–15). But this change was not introduced, despite signs in December 1988 that the abolition might be imminent (for recent Soviet criticisms of the retention of the death penalty, see, for example, *NT*, No. 7, 1989, pp. 2–3, and No. 10, 1989, pp. 2–3; for an argument that the masses *want* to retain the death penalty in the USSR see *NT*, No. 43, 1989, p. 36; *NT*, No. 21, 1990, pp. 46–7, contains details of recent executions, while *Izvestiya*, 6 April 1991, p. 6, reveals that, in 1990, a total of 445 people were sentenced to death in the Soviet Union – mostly for aggravated murder).

Extra-party Punishments in the PRC

As in the Soviet Union, so in China there is a wide range of bodies that is expected to maintain vigilance against all forms of impropriety, including corruption. The kinds of individual and body *within* an organization are in essence similar to the Soviet arrangement. The picture is also similar beyond the individual unit, although the media tend to play more of a reporting than an investigative role in China (for an up-to-date analysis of the PRC's criminal justice system – albeit by scholars who are primarily specialists on particular aspects of crime rather than on China – see Troyer, Clark and Rojek, 1989).

One important difference between the USSR and the PRC, however, is that there have been the Discipline Inspection Commissions (DICs) at all levels in China, and these were in practice at least as responsible as the procuracy for investigating economic crime, at least until the late 1980s. However, there appears to have been confusion throughout much of the 1980s as to which organization(s) had primary responsibility for investigating cases. DICs were, theoretically, responsible for investigating only members of the CCP. But in practice – partially because many cases of corruption involve both CCP members and others – their nets have often spread much wider. This means that they have often overlapped with the state's legal agencies (notably the Procuracy, Public Security Bureaux and, more recently, the Ministry of Supervision) which are to investigate everyone – including party members. By the late 1980s, it *appears* that the Ministry of Supervision had taken over many of the functions the DICs had been performing. At least until then, however, this confusion of responsibilities constituted a classic example of the reason why the Chinese leadership has recently been so anxious to delineate and separate party and state more clearly (although differences among the top leaders often in practice result in the opposite effect).

As in the USSR, so in the PRC a distinction is drawn between administrative and legal sanctions, with the latter being applied in more serious cases. In Chinese terminology, 'unhealthy tendencies' (*wai feng* or *buzheng zi feng*) are to be dealt with administratively, whereas only clear-cut transgressions of the law (*weifa fanzui*) can incur legal sanctions. Administrative sanctions range from a public warning (such as 'recording a demerit') to suspension or even dismissal from public office. Only the courts may deal with what are classified as actual *crimes*, and special departments were established within the court and procuracy system in the late 1970s/early 1980s specifically to consider cases of corruption and other forms of economic crime. These sections also gather data on cases; figures on economic crime published in the Chinese press are based primarily on these data.

The range of sanctions against corrupt officials available to Chinese courts is similar to that in the USSR. Thus relatively minor offences can lead to a fine, whereas serious cases of embezzlement and bribery can result in permanent deprivation of political rights and/or a long prison sentence, or even the death penalty.

Appeals against a judgement can be made to higher courts. But these sometimes result in even stiffer penalties, so that convicts incur a risk in lodging an appeal against a sentence.

Extra-party Punishments Elsewhere in the Communist World

Once again, it is way beyond the scope of this study to examine in any detail the range of punishments for corruption in the 21 other communist (or formerly communist) states. Suffice it to say here that there appears to have been a similar range to those of the two countries examined above, with the notable exception that a very limited number of states (for example, Hungary, Poland, the GDR) abolished the death penalty altogether – either *de jure* or *de facto* – even before the communists lost power.

Actual Treatment of Corrupt Officials

Unfortunately, it is not possible on the basis of existing data to provide an acceptably reliable answer to the question of whether officials have tended to be more or less harshly treated than – or treated about the same as – ordinary citizens who have committed similar offences to those of the officials. There are three principal reasons for this. First, no two offences are ever identical, and a level of subjectivity is involved in comparing cases. For example, it might appear obvious that an official who has corruptly acquired 20,000 rubles has committed a graver crime than an ordinary citizen who has acquired a similar amount, let alone someone who has illegally acquired 2,000 rubles. However, it will be demonstrated below that communist judges and others responsible for assessing crimes often do not perceive the level of impropriety of action in such simple terms; motives, methods, past records, present attitudes – these and other factors are frequently brought into the equation when deciding on the appropriate punishment for a particular transgression. Second, there is some danger of being ethnocentric in assessing and comparing levels of punishment. It might seem obvious that a 10-year sentence in a labour camp is a harsher punishment than 10 years in a regular prison; Soviet law often perceived the situation otherwise, however (*Pravda*, 12 July 1969, pp. 2–3). Moreover, can we be certain that expulsion from the communist party was perceived in a given communist country as less severe a punishment than, say, a hefty fine? It is clear that in some communities the former would have brought greater social stigma than the latter. Third, there is the problem of disaggregation of data in some reports on corruption. Thus, in cases where a *group* has been engaging in corruption, it is sometimes impossible to determine quite who did what, and who benefitted by what proportion of the total sum involved. In such a case, it is of limited value knowing that official X received punishment Y, since we have only an impression of the precise nature of his/her crime, and of how much responsibility the judge feels should be attributed to that particular official. Moreover, the *impression* created by detailed analysis of cases in both the PRC and the USSR over a period of more than 20 years (see chapter 4) is that there is no clearly discernible pattern in comparing the treatment of officials and others performing similar acts.

The above problems notwithstanding, our primary concern is with *perceptions* of equity or inequity. Unfortunately, there is no systematic way of analysing this either at present. Instead, we consider random statements from the communist world about perceived inequities.

There is no doubt whatsoever that many citizens *and* officials have believed that, in the administration and application of 'justice', there is frequently one law for the masses and another – more lenient – for officialdom. An article on the inequity of the law that was published in *Literaturnaya Gazeta* in December 1986 provides some indication of this:

> In Orel Province, a 'thief' who secretly took two jars of homemade pickled cucumbers from his mother-in-law's cellar was sentenced to one and a half year's deprivation of freedom. In Ulyanovsk Province, another 'thief' managed to get himself a full two years for not having returned a friend's sunglasses on time . . . It would be interesting to know how many bribetakers and embezzlers, hooligans, speculators and slanderers did not get into the defendant's dock in these provinces over the same period. In pursuing imaginary criminals and bringing the punitive sword down on them, genuine, dangerous enemies are always allowed to get away; this pattern knows no exceptions. (*Literaturnaya Gazeta*, 17 December 1986, p. 13; the author of the article, A. Vaksberg, has long been concerned about dual standards in the Soviet application of the law – see, for example, his *Literaturnaya Gazeta* article of 19 October 1977 – in *CDSP*, Vol. 29, No. 14, p. 18)

Even where corrupt individuals *are* investigated and tried, the sentences are often perceived and even officially acknowledged as being too light relative to those meted out to others, and explanations for this can occasionally be found in the press. For instance, in May 1986, Vietnamese Politburo member Lê Duc Tho acknowledged that: 'for the same mistakes, only lower-echelon offenders are subjected to disciplinary measures, whereas no, or only mild, disciplinary measures are taken against higher-echelon offenders. This is also one of the reasons for the lack of confidence on the part of party members and the masses' (*SWB*/FE/8257/B/4, 13 May 1986). Looking at this from a somewhat different angle, Chief Inspector of the Polish State Trade Inspectorate P. Ostaszewski stated in a 1985 interview that: 'A situation where penalties for profiteering are so low that they cannot make these offences unprofitable cannot be tolerated' (*SWB*/EE/7956/B/10–11, 21 May 1985). Clearly, some people will see the inequity of all this and abandon their self-restraint. Moreover, this has an effect on higher-ranking people. Contrary to what might be *expected* in a so-called mono-organizational society, officials and executives have often been able to get back into senior positions. In November 1979, two *Pravda* correspondents investigated cases in which some cadres found guilty of improper conduct had been permitted to resign 'voluntarily', rather than be formally dismissed, and were then able to obtain other, similarly ranked posts and later even be promoted. As these correspondents noted: 'In the light of such facts, one can understand the psychology of people who, when they get into the orbit of executive positions, consider that they are in it for good. They may remove him, but he will find another portfolio' (cited in Lampert, 1984, p. 382). The authors of various letters published in *Pravda* (24 August 1987, p. 3) suggested that bribe-takers and other corrupt officials often received lenient sentences because of the pressure local authorities brought to bear on prosecutors. While such improprieties might often be because of bureaucrats' mutual interests and protection, this is not the only reason. One that can be inferred from a statement Eduard Shevardnadze made in July 1973 (*CDSP*, Vol. 25, No. 31, p. 7) is that there is a perceived *shortage* of officials. This would be in line with the point just made that officials found guilty of corruption and demoted often make their way back up the bureaucratic hierarchy within a relatively short period of time.

Other reasons why officials are often let off relatively lightly include the fact that they have voluntarily confessed, and/or that they have repented, and/or that they have on balance made a very useful contribution to society. In one recent case a Soviet party secretary received a punishment even below that stipulated in the Criminal Code as the minimum – because of his contribution in the 'Great Patriotic War' of 1941–5 and other factors (see *Pravda*, 30 May 1990, p. 8; it is interesting to note that this could on one level be seen to contradict the statement made by Soviet Minister of Justice V. Yakovlev in February 1990 that the law was now quite clear that higher officials involved in corruption would receive stiffer penalties than others guilty of the same crime – see *NT*, No. 6, 1990, p. 31). One final reason for light sentencing might simply be described as 'humane consideration'. Thus in another Soviet case, a woman convicted of economic crime was given a light sentence because she was pregnant; although she was not an official herself, it may well be that this line of judicial thinking has sometimes applied also to corrupt female officials.

Conclusions

It has been demonstrated in this chapter that many communist leaderships in recent years gave, both in their statements and their actions, a clear indication of their growing concern about corruption. Not only were there general policy statements, but there was tougher anti-corruption legislation, the establishment of new investigative bodies, and other concrete measures.

It has been argued that there was still often considerable confusion about the rights and responsibilities of various agencies charged with investigating and dealing with corruption during the 1980s. This was to no small extent a reflection of the broader confusion that has existed in most communist systems between the party and the state. It has been shown here, for example, how and why the party's disciplinary role can and does extend beyond its own membership. But the party has exerted influence in other ways too. Not only have judges and senior police officers been very much subject to the *nomenklatura* system, but the very concept of judicial autonomy has in practice frequently been disregarded by communist parties – much to the annoyance of some. The emphasis on the 'legal-rational mode' in several communist states in the late 1980s (see chapter 8 for further details) should in theory have led or be leading to a clearer delineation and separation of party and state. If such a distinction materializes in those few countries still communist, it should have ramifications for corruption and its treatment. First, lines of authority – to investigate, to charge, to punish – would become clearer, and this should have a positive effect in the fight against corruption. Not only will investigatory officials, for instance, have a better idea of who is responsible for what – and thus be less prone to leave the pursuit of corruption to others – but there should also be a clearer picture of what is or is not considered corruption. If there is, for instance, a clear demarcation between general political and ideological statements from the party on the one hand, and actual laws from what come to be widely recognized as the *actual* (as distinct from rubber-stamping) legislatures on the other, many of the current contradictory practices that can encourage corruption should be reduced or even eliminated. In one sense, then, senior politicans who are serious about wanting to reduce corruption should start by tidying up the mess of the communist party–state complex. Unfortunately, many communist leaderships did not realize this early enough. Others may have done for now, but are still pursuing contradictory policies in other key areas; merely changing the approach to the reporting and treatment of official corruption would not be sufficient in itself to rescue such communist regimes and systems. This is one of the major issues to be explored in the next – final – chapter.

NOTES

1 As seems evident from chapter 4, however, Soviet media coverage of official corruption had already intensified *before* Brezhnev's death. This may well reflect Andropov's growing influence (and/or the general secretary's declining role) in Brezhnev's last months – although this hypothesis must for the present remain speculation.

2 The term 'mafia' was by the late 1980s frequently being used in the Soviet media and even by Soviet politicians. At the 19th Party Conference (June–July 1988), for instance, the term was used by Boris Yeltsin (*Pravda*, 2 July 1988, p. 10).

3 It should be noted, however, that several Soviet commentators subsequently highlighted problems in the legislation – on this see *MN*, No. 50, 1987, p. 3; Savitsky, in *NT*, No. 18, 1988, pp. 19–20, and chapter 8 below.

4 Ligachev was widely perceived to be the leader of the main conservative grouping within the CPSU in the late 1980s, but was in essence removed from office and retired from politics in July 1990.

5 Liu has argued elsewhere that there was also a campaign in 1963, the so-called 'Four Clean-Ups Campaign' – see Liu, 1986, pp. 175–6. However, this was very minor in comparison with the early 1950s campaign, and most contemporary Chinese commentators make no reference to it (see, for example, Zhao Ziyang, in *RMRB*, 30 March 1982). It is interesting that Liu himself does not refer to it in his 1983 article focusing on corruption, whereas he does refer to the early 1950s campaign.

6 It is interesting to note that one of the ways in which the Soviets and the Chinese differed in recent years in their approach to corruption among officials is reflected in their most recent policies on whistle-blowing. As just indicated, the Chinese authorities still strongly encourage citizens to report 'corrupt' (that is, allegedly corrupt) officials; the accusers may remain incognito for fear of retaliation (see next note). The Soviet authorities adopted a similar policy in the mid-1980s. But in recent years, they became very sensitive to the fact that officials might be unjustly accused under such a policy. Thus, arguing that this was in line with the concept of the rule of law, the 'black boxes' – into which Soviet citizens had in the mid-1980s been encouraged to drop anonymous allegations about officials – were abolished, and the laws on slander tightened up (1987).

7 That such regulations were still inadequate by the beginning of this decade is revealed in the fact that a 1990 article in *Beijing Review* (Vol. 33, No. 3, p. 28) referred to temporary regulations, at that time being drafted by the Ministry of Supervision, that were explicitly intended to provide better protection to citizen 'crime-reporters'. According to this report, procuratorial organs in Beijing and 15 provinces and autonomous regions had recently dealt with 144 cases of retaliation against 'informers'. This problem of retaliation is a major reason why the Chinese authorities have continued to encourage citizens to make *anonymous* accusations against allegedly corrupt officials.

8 At the time of writing, however, it looked as if Castro might well be moving, albeit reluctantly, in the same direction as most of the rest of the communist world had done in the late 1980s – and thus away from communism as traditionally interpreted by communist parties in power.

9 It should be noted that the Soviets had by the end of the 1980s become reasonably open about the *nomenklatura* system, after having been very secretive about it for decades. Various references to it were made at the 28th CPSU Congress, and it was stated that the *nomenklatura* approach was being abandoned in personnel allocation (see, for example, *Pravda*, 30 August 1990, p. 2). Until the banning of the CPSU in August 1991, it was not clear how far this policy of 'abandonment' had actually been implemented; what was clear – from my own interviews – was that it was still operating in some key areas as of late 1990.

8

Conclusions

Since each of the preceding chapters has included a summary and conclusion, it would be tautologous to present the findings yet again. Rather, I shall now return to the hypotheses on corruption elaborated in chapter 1; following this, some observations on legal-rationality in late and transitional communism, on the emergence of post-communism, and on the relationships between communism, post-communism, modernity and post-modernity are presented.

Hypotheses Concerning Corruption

The Anti-corruption Drive under Andropov was a Temporary Phenomenon

It is clear that Feldbrugge's conclusion was premature. In fact, it appears that there was actually an *increase* in the reporting of corruption under Chernenko; although Chernenko himself did not concentrate on the problem to the same extent as his predecessor did, both corruption and its reporting were widespread in the mid-1980s. Gorbachev, too, made a major issue out of official corruption for much of his period in office.

Campaigns Against Corruption are Never Sustained and Decisive

The answer to this hypothesis depends very much on one's conceptions of 'sustained' and 'decisive'. On the basis of both the Chinese and the Soviet examples, it is clear that campaigns can last for several years. Indeed, the reader is reminded that Deng has argued that the Chinese campaign is likely to last until the year 2000; if it does, and given that it emerged clearly in 1982, it will have lasted for almost two decades – a sustained campaign by almost any criteria. This said, it should be borne in mind that campaigns are by their very nature *supposed* to be relatively short and sharp. If there is a hidden meaning in Law's statement – an implication that the brevity of campaigns itself represents an ambivalence in leadership attitudes or even a clear lack of commitment to the overcoming of corruption – then the evidence assembled here is itself mixed. The ambivalence is more obvious in some countries and at some periods than others, although it does seem that there is often a threshold – a critical point – beyond which leaderships have been unwilling to go in their pursuit of justice. This critical point varies according to time and place and circumstance.

If by 'decisive' Law means that the campaign is completely successful, then he is quite correct in arguing that campaigns are never decisive. If he means that they have led to a marked decline in corruption, then the evidence is inconclusive. And if he means that the leadership is not totally committed to the complete (or near-complete) eradication of corruption, then the hypothesis would in general, and as suggested above, be supported by the present study.

On the other hand, it could be argued that since the intense campaigns in the USSR, the PRC, some East European countries, Cuba and perhaps Vietnam were still *relatively* young by 1989, and that since the problem of corruption was so widespread and ingrained, then it would be unrealistic to have expected a 'decisive' victory against it by 1989 or 1990. From this perspective, then, and in those few countries that are not yet clearly post-communist, the answer must be more tentative – 'wait and see'.

Anti-corruption Drives are Often Associated with New Leaderships, But New Leaderships Do Not Always Mount Such Drives

New leaders in communist states have often been chosen or else have emerged largely because they represented a different approach and style from that of their predecessors. Expressed crudely, they have been a reaction to what preceded them.

It is quite clear even from the limited number of cases cited in this study that anti-corruption drives often *have* been associated with new leaderships. A major campaign was launched by Andropov within weeks of taking office, and Gorbachev seems to have reintensified this campaign fairly soon after taking office. It could be argued that Deng was hardly a 'new' leader by the time the anti-corruption campaign was launched in 1982. However, a number of Western specialists on Chinese politics (such as Nethercut, 1983, p. 30) have made the point that Deng only clearly got on to the senior leadership track at the end of 1978, and that it was not until the 12th Party Congress (September 1982) that he finally consolidated his position. In other words, in this interpretation of Deng's rise, the campaign is associated with the final stages of his consolidation. In this sense, it could certainly be argued that the major anti-corruption campaign was associated with a new leadership. The question of why new leaderships do not always mount such drives has been partially – if implicitly – answered above. New leaderships often wish to distinguish themselves from their predecessors; if a predecessor had been fighting a major battle against corruption – and generating considerable hostility in the process – the successor may seek to establish that his/her approach is different.

Of course, this is by no means the *only* reason why new leaderships do not mount such campaigns. One very obvious reason is that they do not perceive corruption as a serious problem. Another is that they do not feel they have sufficient power to attack corruption, particularly if it is rife among senior members of 'the staff'. Leading on from the last point, yet another reason they might desist from an attack on corruption is because they themselves are corrupt and do not wish to focus public attention on an issue that could backfire and weaken their own position.

The final point is that anti-corruption drives are not invariably associated with new leaderships. The major Bulgarian and Czechoslovak campaigns of the 1980s were launched when Zhivkov had been in power for some thirty years, Husák for somewhat less than half that time; this said, it must not be overlooked that their campaigns were remarkably similar to the Soviet ones, both in form and in timing – and the USSR *did* have several new leaders in the 1980s. In other words, there is *some* relationship between campaigns in these two East European states and new leaders. But Castro's campaign preceded the Soviet one by several months, and, unlike the two East European examples just cited, cannot be seen as a mere imitation of Soviet developments.

Corruption Increases or Decreases According to Levels of Development

The first point to make here is that any answer to this hypothesis must be speculative, on one level for the simple reason – emphasized throughout this study – that one can never be certain about levels of corruption in *any* society. With this caveat, a number of points can be made.

First, the case of China *could* be argued to endorse the notion that a country at the stage of 'economic take-off' is likely to become more corrupt. But it does not have to be interpreted – or certainly not exclusively – from this perspective. An equally plausible argument is that it is the *nature* of China's take-off that has caused the apparent surge in corruption, rather than the fact of the take-off itself. By this I mean that the breakdown in public morality caused by the GPCR and its aftermath, coupled with an ambiguous – even contradictory – economic development policy that has attempted to combine capital-ist motivation with some form of communist morality, can help to explain the apparently rampant corruption in the PRC as much as the fact of economic modernization itself. My own view is that, in China's case, it is both the modernization *per se* (the disruption caused by rapid urbanization, the breakdown of traditional values, etc.) and the particular circumstances of China's modernization that have caused the phenomenon.

There is, however, one other variable that must be included. This is the level of coercion. It *appears* that corruption was not a major feature of Stalin's USSR, despite the fact that it underwent a mod-ernization programme that could be argued to be at least as radical and rapid as the present Chinese one. If there really was less corrup-tion in Stalin's USSR, one part of the explanation could be that there was less contradiction in the modernization policy than in China's current approach. While Stalin's 'revolution from above' certainly contained contradictions (such as his policies on equality and strati-fication), it could hardly be argued that he toyed with capitalism in the way Deng has. Nor was there a substantial rejection of the previous *communist* – as distinct from pre-communist – economic approaches as there has been in China; in the case of the USSR, this rejection (Khrushchev's de-Stalinization) came decades *after* the major economic modernization drive had commenced. In short, China's problems can largely be attributed to the 'theory of contra-dictory transition' already elaborated. But in addition to this factor, Stalinism is synonymous with high levels of coercion and terror, whereas Dengism – at least until 1989 – has on the whole not been; this variable cannot be omitted from any analysis of the relationship between modernization and corruption.

Concluding this part of the argument, it may well be that corrup-tion does increase at the take-off stage, but for reasons that are more complex than is sometimes appreciated. In any comparative analysis, other variables that relate to the take-off must be incorporated if we are to understand apparent differences in rates of corruption between

communist countries. Apart from the obvious one of cultural tradition, these would include levels of coercion and the scale of the
divergence between the new values and the immediately preceding
ones (that is, *ceteris paribus*, the larger the gap, the greater the
likelihood of widespread corruption). In the case of the latter variable, the argument is not that the early values were necessarily
internalized by the population, but rather that the population perceives contradictions, even hypocrisy, between the values currently
being proclaimed by the leadership and those proclaimed by the
previous leadership. This could undermine the legitimacy of the
system.

It does *appear* to be the case that corruption is or has been rampant
in several relatively (economically) developed communist countries,
and that this corruption might be more widespread than in earlier
phases. Two reasons for this – declining levels of terror and even
coercion, and contradictions in policies – have already been identified. A third factor is closely related to the 'theory of contradictory
transition', but is discrete. This is that cynicism develops over time
about the *telos* – or, more precisely, about the regime's commitment
to the *telos* – and that the commitment at least some members of the
population *and* the staffs ('officials') previously had to the building of
a better, socialist society is replaced to some extent by a more
individualistic, self-regarding approach. The implication of this is
that corruption can *increase* at later stages of modernization – in
marked contrast to some of the views cited on pp. 46–7. If widespread
self-interest results first in radical societal change, then in systemic
change – towards a basically capitalist-motivated mixed economy –
then corruption *may* decline, as it is no longer as necessary (because
there are alternative, legitimate channels for pursuing self-interest).
On the other hand, corruption in the West does not appear to be
declining, and can be linked to the West's own consumerist ideology
and decline of ethical standards. As the communist world in the
1980s moved away from teleological legitimation towards legal-
rationality, with communist leaderships hoping subsequently to be
able to place primary emphasis on the eudaemonic mode, there arose
the real danger that the consumerist mentality and a further decline
of ethical standards there too would at least partially counter such
trends towards a decline in corruption. One implication of this is that
the consumerist ideology that may well become a salient feature of
post-communism will at least partially offset the decline in corruption brought about by the legitimation both of many forms of
private enterpreneurship and of the post-communist system more
generally.

Some Forms of Corruption are Peculiar to Communist Countries

If it were the case that there were clear-cut distinctions between the 'typical' communist system and the 'typical' capitalist system, then it might be possible to endorse the view of those who hold that some forms of corruption are peculiar to communist countries. However, just as the 'typical' capitalist state has in recent decades had a degree of state planning, nationalized industries, in many cases a growing state bureaucracy (even if this process has recently – and probably temporarily – been modified or even reversed in some English-speaking Western countries), and many of the other features one often associates with communist systems, so the 'typical' communist state in recent years permitted more private and cooperative enterprise, allowed the market a growing role in price-setting, etc. Although the shortages typical of so many communist countries are not typical of most Western countries, they certainly can be found in many non-communist developing countries, so that this feature is not unique to communist countries either. Nor is the one-party state or the centralized polity. In short, not one of the 20 types of corruption identified and exemplified in this study is exclusive tò communist countries.

However, just as the *balance* of private and public ownership, to take only one variable, differs considerably between the 'typical' communist state and the 'typical' capitalist state (it is more difficult to generalize about non-communist developing countries), so the balance between types of corruption varies across systems. *Ceteris paribus*, where there is a serious shortage of goods and housing, for instance, there is more scope for and likelihood of officials being involved in corruption than when there are no significant shortages. Where most enterprises are socially owned and subject to central plans, there is more scope for corruption of officials simply because more officials are more involved in the running of the economy than in a more privately owned and market-oriented economy. Conversely, buying votes and other forms of (private) vote-rigging are more likely to occur in genuinely competitive electoral systems (however, for a fairly early example of vote-rigging at the enterprise level in the USSR see *Izvestiya*, 30 November 1969, p. 6). Other things being equal, one would also expect there to be more opportunities for bribery relating to contracts for new roads or buildings in a competitive market system than where there is a state monopoly on such construction work. And 'insider trading' – to the extent that this involves officials – is still a form of corruption much more likely to occur in the West than it was in the communist world; although stock exchanges could by the late 1980s be found in Budapest and Shanghai – and even the USSR had introduced shares on a limited basis (see, for example, *MN*, No. 51, 1987, p. 9) – it will be some time yet before share-trading becomes a normal part of everyday life in those few countries considered in this study that are not yet post-communist. In sum, some *types* of corruption have both *a priori* and (apparently) in fact been more prevalent in communist societies than in other types of society, while other types have less frequently been encountered.

Corruption is More Destructive in Communist Countries Than Elsewhere

Analyses of various non-communist systems and/or regimes that have collapsed have sometimes linked these failures to corruption; the Marcos regime in the Philippines and Batista's government in Cuba are two prime examples. It has been argued in this study that corruption has also played or is currently playing a major role in weakening communist systems that either already have collapsed (Eastern Europe, the USSR) or else are likely to collapse in the foreseeable future (such as Vietnam, Cuba, the PRC).

In contrast, advanced and well-established liberal-democratic *systems* have rarely, if ever, collapsed; France in the 1950s is a debatable, rare exception to this generalization.[1] Certainly, *regimes* can collapse for reasons relating to corruption – Takeshita's in Japan, and arguably Nixon's in the USA, are prime examples. Moreover, senior officials and members of leadership teams often have to resign as individuals for corruption (for example, Speaker of the US House of Representatives Jim Wright), even if the regime as a whole persists. Despite the latter point, it does appear that advanced liberal-democratic systems are more resistant to the effects of official corruption than are communist systems – largely, it is argued here, because of the higher level of legitimacy the liberal democracies have enjoyed.

Having considered these six hypotheses specifically on corruption, we now return to the broader theme of this book, and draw such conclusions as are warranted.

Towards the Legal-rational Mode

The central theme of this book is that the reporting of official corruption in so many communist states has been (or, in the case of systems already at the stage of post-communism, was) symptomatic of a general tendency to place less emphasis not only on old traditional, charismatic and goal-rational modes of legitimation, but also on new traditional, official nationalist and eudaemonic – and to place an increasing emphasis on the legal-rational mode; this mode, it is argued, proved ultimately to be incompatible with Marxism-Leninism. Even in the early stages of the attempted transition to dominant legal-rationality, however, anti-corruption drives in themselves never had the potential to legitimate contemporary communist states in the legal-rational mode. Indeed, there was always the real possibility that they would backfire, further reducing whatever level of legitimacy a regime and/or system had hitherto enjoyed. Thus the argument is that anti-corruption campaigns usually formed part of a package of measures that *cumulatively* represented moves towards the legal-rational mode. It cannot be emphasized too strongly that the moves towards legal-rationality never *replaced* all other legitimation modes, simply that its significance *vis à vis* the others increased in the 1980s; in short, the balance between such modes changed. Let us now consider in what ways other than the reporting of corruption communist states tended in recent years towards the legal-rational mode of legitimation.

I have chosen to focus on nine variables to endorse the argument about legal-rationality, viz the codification of legal systems; greater control over the state's coercive agencies; greater control over leading officials; regularization of meetings of political bodies; increasing separation of party and state; changes in official attitudes towards mass participation; the moves from directive towards indicative planning and a system of contracts; boosting of the private sector; and increased overt interaction with the international market. Readers may disagree with the classification used here, but that matters little; the important point is to note the wide range of actual or proposed developments that can be seen to endorse the central argument of this book. Given both the space available and the nature of this study, it is not intended to examine each of these features at length; rather, a few basic points and examples – plus references to more detailed studies by others – will be given.

Legal and Political Developments – Towards the Socialist Legal State

Codification of legal systems According to S-C. Leng (1982, p. 5):

> The People's Republic of China made a genuine attempt in the mid-1950s to institute a formal and stable legal order. Whatever was accomplished, however, suffered a major setback in the Anti-Rightist Campaign of 1957–1958 and later an even greater blow during the Cultural Revolution of 1966–1969 . . . In the interest of restoring order and morals and attracting domestic support and external assistance for its modernisation programme, the current Chinese leadership has made vigorous efforts to revitalise and strengthen China's legal system.[2]

Leng proceeds to outline the several concrete steps taken to increase socialist legality in post-Mao China (for another analysis along these lines see Baum, 1986). Specialists on the USSR, Eastern Europe and several other communist countries have noted similar moves towards greater codification of legal systems taken by the respective governments. The Habeas Corpus Act, once seen as a bourgeois legal concept, was adopted in communist Poland, communist Czechoslovakia and Cuba, and there were calls for it in the USSR (see, for example, *NT*, No. 42, 1989, p. 39).

Of particular interest in the process of upgrading the law was the recently adopted Soviet concept of a 'socialist legal state'. Following more general leadership calls to enhance socialist legality made during both the Andropov era and, even more so, during the early Gorbachev era, Gorbachev himself was first publicly reported to have used the term 'socialist legal state' in April 1988 (see *Pravda*, 13 April 1988, p. 1) and explicitly used the term at a Central Committee meeting with ideologists and media officials on 7 May 1988 (see *Pravda*, 11 May 1988, p. 2); the concept was included in the Theses of the Central Committee of the CPSU for the 19th All-Union Party Conference (see *Pravda*, 27 May 1988, p. 2). An analysis of the concept by the head of the Socialist Legality Department of the USSR Academy of Sciences' Institute of State and Law, V. Savitsky, that appeared in *New Times* (No. 18, 1988, pp. 19–21) is very instructive:

> The concept of the legal socialist state has been universally accepted, at last, although I must say that its profound theoretical elaboration has just started. To put it briefly, the socialist legal state is that which

makes laws, bases itself on laws, and is governed by laws of its own making. That last point is of special importance in the light of the record of our historical development . . . Laws are not to be substituted for or replaced by individuals. In the socialist legal state all legislative activity should rest on democratic principles.

Thus the 'socialist legal state' is a state based on the *rule of law*.[3] In his frank and fascinating article, Savitsky went on to give examples of the way in which the rights of the individual had long been accorded second-rank status in the USSR, but argued that this was now all changing. To cite one of his examples verbatim:

In 1961, the national act – the Fundamentals of Civil Legislation – was promulgated. It provided for the adoption of a special law entitling anyone to material compensation for illegal imprisonment, conviction or deprivation. Do you know when such a law was adopted? In 1981. Its preparation took as long as twenty years . . . [This shows] that laws protecting citizens' rights were long considered of secondary importance and relegated to the bottom of the list. On the other hand, the laws that consolidated the powers of the state machinery came first.

Savitsky also referred to the fact that Poland had introduced the post of 'Citizens' Solicitor', at that time occupied by Professor Ewa Letowska. This post had been established so that citizens could obtain legal advice on their rights *vis à vis* various organizations and officials at all levels (for further Soviet analyses of the 'socialist legal state' see Institut Gosudarstva i Prava, 1987, esp. pp. 45–8; Kudryavtsev and Lukasheva, 1988; *Pravda*, 2 August 1988, pp. 1–2; Baglai, 1989; Manov, 1989 – and for a brief but interesting Soviet analysis in English, which also suggests that there needs to be much more ongoing publicity about the concept, see *NT*, No. 17, 1989, p. 23).

Another symbolically significant recent development in the Soviet legal system's attitudes towards the individual was the change in official attitudes towards defendants and defence lawyers. For many years, defendants in the USSR were typically treated by their judges as guilty – even before the trial had started – simply by dint of the fact that they had been accused by the state prosecutors. At the pretrial stage, defence lawyers nearly always played a minor role, and thus were typically in a weak position to question the prosecution's case in any fundamental way at the trial itself. But a spate of articles in the Soviet press in 1986–7 condemned this practice, and advocated an upgrading of the role of the defence lawyer. These arguments were accepted at the June 1987 plenum of the Central Committee, when it was agreed, *inter alia*, to enhance the role of the defence lawyer at the investigation stage of a case (on all this see, for example, *Pravda*, 22 March 1987, p. 3; *Literaturnaya Gazeta*, 15 April 1987, p. 11; *Pravda*, 19 June 1987, p. 1).

Although the emphasis here has been on developments in the PRC and the USSR, several communist states introduced elements of the rule of law in recent years, and a number of Western commentators noted the possible emergence of the communist *Rechtsstaat* (for one of the earliest articles – on Yugoslavia – see Fisk, 1969; on the GDR see Seiffert, 1980).[4]

Greater control over the state's coercive agencies In the 1950s, when many Western specialists on communist countries perceived them as totalitarian, some considered terror to be, in Fainsod's (1954, p. 354) words, the 'linchpin' of such systems. At the centre of the state's terror machine were the security police forces. In recent years, as shown in the collection edited by Jonathan Adelman (1984) and many other analyses, the status and power of most of these agencies were in marked decline. While they still played a greater role than many believe they should in allegedly 'socialist' systems – and while they were actually being strengthened in *some* communist states (such as South Yemen, as a result of the January 1986 plot – see *IB*, No. 19, 1987, p. 39) – there is no question that, on balance in the communist world, the trend during the 1980s was for their role to decline. Not only were their powers more limited, but their answerability to the state representative bodies and, in particular, to the communist parties increased.

A recent, symbolically important example of the decline in the powers of the state's coercive organs comes from the USSR. In January 1988, the Presidium of the Supreme Soviet published a new statute that transferred control of the notorious 'special' psychiatric hospitals from the Ministry of Internal Affairs (which supervised the police force) to the Ministry of Health. The law became effective 1 March 1988. It followed a crackdown on corrupt psychiatrists, and was accompanied by a general downgrading of the role of psychiatry in the treatment of 'dissidents'. Although this particular move towards a more legal and regularized mode of operation seems to be specific to the USSR (partially, it must be noted, because few other communist countries made such use of psychiatric hospitals for political purposes) and is therefore not generalizable, and despite the fact that many Soviets clearly felt as of 1990 that coercive agencies such as the KGB were not only still insufficiently under public control (see, for example, *MN*, No. 36, 1990, p. 14) but even becoming more powerful again (a justifiable perception, given the late 1991 revelations about the role of the KGB in the August 1991 attempted coup), it constitutes one example of the general dynamic identified in this study.

Greater control over leading officials   Two examples of the growing control of leading officials are the limitations that either were, or else were to be, introduced on terms of office, and the changes in the susceptibility to litigation of party and state officials.

At the beginning of the 1980s, only one communist system – Yugoslavia – had formal limits on the tenure of both party and state leaders. The situation changed dramatically during the 1980s. China introduced limits on the tenure of leading state offices, for instance. Under Gorbachev the question of limited tenure for both party and state officials was debated in the late 1980s, and several moves in this direction were taken; in advocating these, Gorbachev explicitly linked the notion of limited tenure to the concept of the 'socialist legal state' (see, for example, *Pravda*, 24 October 1988, p. 2). In January 1988, the Central Committee of the Bulgarian Communist Party approved proposals limiting leading party figures to a maximum of three 5-year terms in office; this rule was to have been ratified by the BCP Congress scheduled for 1991 – but this meeting did not take place, since the BCP was dissolved in April 1990 and replaced by the Bulgarian Socialist Party. At its April 1988 plenary session, the Central Committee of the Czechoslovak Communist Party resolved that in future a given general secretary was not to hold office for more than two terms, while the posts of first secretaries of regional and district party committees were not to be occupied by one individual for more than three terms (*NT*, No. 16, 1988, p. 31). Albania, Hungary, Mongolia, Poland, Vietnam, South Yemen and other communist states introduced or announced their intentions to introduce tenure limitations on a number of leading party and state offices in the late 1980s. Quite clearly, the trend in the communist world in recent years was to regularize and limit the occupancy of senior political posts.

As briefly alluded to in the last chapter, until the passing of legislation in June 1987 (see *Pravda*, 3 July 1987, p. 3) lower-ranking members of the *nomenklatura* and ordinary citizens in the USSR could not file civil suits against higher officials. The new legislation that changed this situation followed a number of articles published in the press during 1986 and 1987 on the abuse of the law by officials, and a discussion of this problem and the need to protect citizens' rights at the November 1986 Central Committee plenum (for further details and analysis of the change see Löwenhardt, 1987, esp. pp. 21–5). Although it is quite clear from letters and articles in the Soviet press following the June promulgation that many citizens, legal specialists and administrators felt that the system still needed improving – for instance, because citizens could only charge *individual* officials, whereas the collectives that usually made decisions on people's lives were still not subject to this law (see, for example, R. Livshits in *Izvestiya*, 29 September 1987, p. 3; Kudryavstev and Lukasheva, 1988, pp. 49–50) – there is no question that the passing of the 1987 legislation was symbolically, and *perhaps* practically, of great significance. It showed that the political elite was prepared, in theory at least, to subject everyone – including all officials – to the legal framework.[5]

In April 1989, following public discussion since November 1988, the National People's Congress in the PRC passed rather similar legislation which became effective 1 October 1990. Under this 'Administrative Procedures Law', Chinese citizens were for the first time unambiguously to have full legal rights to sue officials and official organizations. According to official Chinese sources, citizens had already been filing lawsuits against various levels of government in recent years – a fact that was described by some deputies to the Congress in March 1989 as 'part of a trend towards the rule of law in China' – but there had been no general administrative procedural law to guide and standardize the work of the courts in this area (*Xinhua News Agency News Bulletin*, No. 014679, 24 March 1989, pp. 45–6). Following the adoption of the new law, one commentator wrote: 'This is a major event in the construction of China's legal system as well as an important step towards the building up of China's political democracy' (*BR*, Vol. 32, No. 19, p. 4; for a similar argument and quite detailed analysis of the new law see *BR*, Vol. 34, No. 17, pp. 14–17; for further analyses of the connections between legality and democracy see, for example, Chan, Rosen and Unger, 1985). If one adds to this legislation the recent exhortations to citizens by Chinese leaders not only to 'kill off little flies' (that is, report the misdemeanours of low-ranking officials), but – since at least 1986 – also to 'dare to touch the tiger's buttocks' (see chapter 7), it becomes clear that in China, too, the leadership has been anxious to demonstrate to the public that no-one is above the law; how all this fits in with the traditionally personalized approach to politics (such as the role of *guanxi*), however, is far less clear.

Regularization and vitalization of meetings of political bodies   In theory, the congress is the supreme organ in any communist party. Despite this, it was only *relatively* recently in many communist states that congresses met regularly and according to the frequency specified in the party statutes. Examples of the long delays that could occur include the gap of 13 years between the 18th and 19th Congresses of the CPSU, the gap of 11 years between the 8th and 9th Congresses of the CCP, the 16 year gap between the 3rd and 4th Congresses of the Vietnamese Communist Party and the 7 years between the 11th and 12th Congresses of the Mongolian People's Revolutionary Party. Moreover, the Cuban Communist Party did not even convene a Congress until 1975, some 10 years after the party had been founded. By the 1980s, however, most of the established communist states were organizing regular (usually quinquennial) meetings of the party congress, in line with a general move to regularize meetings of political bodies. Moreover, party conferences had by then been reactivated. In June 1988, the CPSU convened its first party conference since 1941; but the communists in Bulgaria, China, Hungary, Korea, Laos, Mozambique, Poland, Romania and other countries all held conferences in recent years.

Not only did meetings of top political bodies become more regularized, but some larger, more publicly visible bodies were upgraded at the expense of smaller, less visible ones. At the same time, the *modus operandi* of many bodies also underwent significant change. An example of both these phenomena was the USSR's Supreme Soviet. Although this was drastically reduced in size (from 1,500 to 542 deputies as of 1989; its precise role and composition at the time of its disintegration, in late 1991, was not clear), its role was greatly enhanced from the end of the 1980s at the expense of smaller state bodies such as the Council (from December 1990 until August 1991 'Cabinet') of Ministers and even the most powerful party organs. One important symbol of its upgrading was the fact that it met for much of the year, rather than for just two or three weeks. The Hungarian Central Committee was substantially upgraded towards the end of the 1980s, seemingly at the expense of the Politburo (see *NT*, No. 17, 1989, p. 29).

Another example of the change in *modus operandi* is provided by the Chinese National People's Congress. Like many communist state legislatures, this long had a (deserved) reputation for being a dull, predictable body in which votes were always unanimous (at least as regards 'mainland' deputies). This recently changed quite dramatically. For instance, two members of the National People's Congress voted against Li Peng as acting premier in November 1987. Even more significantly, at the end of the March–April 1989 session of the Congress, 1,079 deputies (out of a total of 2,688 present) either voted against a bill to grant Shenzhen the right to pass its own legislation or else abstained. In fact, not one of the nine resolutions, bills, etc., put forward to the Congress at that session was passed unanimously; it was suggested in *Beijing Review* (Vol. 32, No. 16, p. 3) that: 'This situation of a "loyal opposition" is unique in the NPC's history and indicates further progress towards China's formation of political democracy.' While the actual rejection of a bill would be even more interesting, the symbolism of this recent development should not be underestimated. Majority opposition to a proposal might become even more likely if suggestions that the traditional method of voting in the Congress be replaced by a push–button voting system are acted upon (see *BR*, Vol. 32, No. 16, pp. 5–6; the push–button system was a feature of Soviet legislative voting by the early 1990s). Similar moves away from unanimous voting were repeated in party and state bodies in a number of other countries, and were symbolic of the significant change that was underway in the communist world in the late 1980s.

Increasing separation of party and state In a stimulating article that appeared in 1980, Rigby argued that there were serious difficulties in characterizing the Soviet system as a system of legal-rational authority. For him, the most significant difficulty was the vagueness in formal party and state documents about what he saw as 'this core aspect of the Soviet system', the party–state relationship. For Rigby, the law – rather than discretion – should regulate this relationship (Rigby, 1980, p. 12).

While one can agree with the basic thrust of Rigby's argument, it needs to be noted that various measures in the direction of legal regulation of the party–state relationship – in particular, clearer indications of their separate roles – were taken in several communist countries in the years following the publication of that article. Some empirical evidence to this effect can be found in a book edited by me and published in 1981 (Holmes, 1981b). In the period following the publication of that book, this trend intensified. For instance, a number of measures were taken to clarify the relationship between the premier and the head of the party. In China, Deng announced at the 13th CCP Congress (1987) that the party was to be removed from the decision-making process in a wide range of areas related to economic management. Moreover, there was in many communist countries increasing emphasis on the need to delineate more clearly the tasks of various organizations *within* both the party and state structures. A typical comment to this effect was made by the (at the time) new Hungarian leader, Károly Grósz, in an interview with a

Soviet journal that was published in May 1988; Grósz referred in that (*NT*, No. 21, 1988, p. 13) to 'changes which have taken place, within a short period, in the separation of the functions of parliament and government'. I would argue that such changes were symptomatic of the commitment of many communist leaders to more clearly defined roles for various political organizations and to a version of 'separation of powers'. Indeed, there were unmistakeable signs in some communist countries that the party was in decline relative to the state.

By 1990, this decline had become abundantly clear in the USSR; with the *de facto* collapse of the CPSU following the failed coup attempt of August 1991, the process appeared to be complete. But this was not the only example. In Yugoslavia, for instance, the 22nd plenum of the LCY's Central Committee (April 1989) approved for party-wide discussion the draft of a document – 'Basic Changes in the LCY' – that explicitly envisaged a decline in the role (and privileges) of the party. This formal downgrading of the LCY's role was at that time expected to occur at the next (extraordinary) Congress, originally scheduled for December 1989 (on all this see *YL*, Vol. 34, No. 4, pp. 1–2, and *NT*, No. 18, 1989, p. 36); in the event, the Congress took place in January 1990. Despite major conflicts at it, especially between the Serbian and Slovene delegations, the Congress did formally endorse the proposal that the LCY's constitutionally guaranteed leading role be abolished. It should be noted that shortly after this vote the Congress collapsed, before having debated all the ramifications of the downgrading of the LCY's role; immediately following the collapse, the Yugoslav premier, Ante Marković, announced in a nationwide broadcast that 'Yugoslavia continues to function with or without the LCY' (*KRWE*, Vol. 36, No. 1, 1990, p. 37172). Such a pronouncement from a federal *state* leader strongly endorses the basic argument here. Moreover, the emergence of genuinely contested elections at the republic level in 1990 (for example, in Slovenia and Croatia in April and May), and the Federal Assembly's formal recognition in July of the right to form pan-Yugoslav parties other than the LCY, made it clear that the communist party had been substantially downgraded. If one adds to this the references the Polish (see, for example, *IB*, Vol. 27, No. 3, 1989, p. 60), Hungarian (for example, at the November 1988 Central Committee plenum) and Afghan leaderships (see, for example, Najibullah's comments at the October 1987 PDPA Conference in *IB*, Vol. 26, No. 1, 1988, pp. 23–4 and 27) were making in the late 1980s to the need for the communist party to form some sort of coalition with other groups and even parties, then the intended dilution of the communist party's role becomes even more obvious.

It has to be acknowledged that *some* countries – such as Mozambique (see *IB*, Vol. 27, No. 2, 1989, p. 26) – were going against the general trend in the late 1980s, in terms of either separating party and state, or reducing the role of the communist party, or both; by 1990, however, Mozambique had fallen into line with the general trend. More significantly, the facts that so many general secretaries were simultaneously *also* heads of state, and that local party secretaries were in some countries also to be the head of the elected (state) councils, partially endorse Rigby's notion of confusion. Once again, however, it is necessary to consider the dynamism of the dominant developments. For instance, the electoral reforms that were introduced in so many communist states in the late 1980s were one early sign of the probable intended shift of power from the largely self-selecting party to a more popularly legitimated state, a point elaborated in the next section.[6]

Changes in official attitudes towards mass participation   In September 1987, the mayor of Beijing, Chen Xitong, introduced a 24-hour hot-line service for the citizens of China's capital city. Within a very short time, the hot-line was averaging 400 calls a month – and the number was increasing. This is just one of literally hundreds of examples one could cite of the growing concern communist authorities in many countries were showing for having closer ties with the masses. Although the word *glasnost* had by the late 1980s become a household word in the West, it should be acknowledged that the Gorbachev revolution in openness and communication was less a total innovation than an intensification and acceleration of processes that were already underway both in the USSR and elsewhere. The increasing use of public opinion surveys and referenda, the upgrading of local councils and works councils in enterprises, the election of enterprise directors, the changing nature as well as scale of the publication of letters in the press, the greater openness in reporting on a wide range of issues that were formerly taboo or close to it – in addition to the electoral changes referred to below – are all evidence of the growing concern to make the system more open and responsive to the masses.

One example of major change in political reporting concerns meetings of the Politburo. Until the beginning of the 1970s, no communist country regularly published details of Politburo meetings. Romania started publishing reports of meetings of its Political Executive Committee (the functional equivalent of an extended politburo in the Romanian communist system, which had no body actually called a Politburo) in 1970; this was followed by Politburo-meeting reporting in Poland (1971), the USSR (1982) and Afghanistan (1986); China now also sometimes reports Politburo meetings (see, for example, *BR*, Nos 7–8, 1988, p. 6).

A number of countries – including Bulgaria, Cuba, Hungary, Poland, the PRC and the USSR – altered their electoral procedures in the 1980s. Although the scope of the changes varied considerably – from essentially rather trivial modifications in the case of the PRC to far more serious and wide-ranging ones in the cases of Hungary and Poland – the general trend was towards more choice for electors and, to a limited extent, more secrecy (for details on some of the changes see Goodman, 1985; Bedeski, 1987; Hahn, 1987). This is not the place to examine in detail the moves towards contested elections and other changes in electoral practice. Rather, it is important for the purposes of this study to speculate on the reasons for and the significance of such political reforms.

Ordinary citizens in communist countries – as in other types of system – only voted in state elections; for reasons that are perhaps more obvious to West Europeans than to Americans, they do/did not vote in party elections. Yet it is widely agreed that the communist party still had more power than the state in most communist systems at the time the electoral reforms were introduced. The perceived significance of such reforms varied. Thus, the rapidly emerging shift of power from the party to the state in *some* communist systems towards the end of the 1980s (see previous section) meant that the electoral reforms there appeared to many to be of greater import than would otherwise have been the case. In those countries in which such a shift was not obvious, the changes in electoral practices would almost certainly have been perceived by many citizens as further evidence of the hypocrisy and cynicism of the communists. To a very limited extent, the mass cynicism generated by the communists might have been partially mitigated by the fact that some communist parties introduced, or were planning to introduce, changes in the intra-party electoral procedures – to render the internal processes of the party, at least, more democratic.[7] However, not only would this still not have had any direct effect on state elections, but the countries in which such reforms were being introduced (such as the USSR, Poland) were in most cases precisely those in which the more general shift to the state was occurring anyway. In this sense, the relevance of changes in intra-party electoral procedures should not be exaggerated.

In an interesting argument on legitimation Graeme Gill (1986, esp. p. 249) has seen the growing participation of the populace in 'the structures and channels provided by the system' as a discrete mode, which he calls 'participatory legitimation' (for a somewhat similar argument see Sasinska-Klas, 1988). Although there is something to be said for isolating this phenomenon and seeing it as a mode of legitimation in its own right, it seems to me that 'participatory legitimation' is more appropriately seen as a sub-division of legal-rational legitimation (Gorbachev himself came close to saying this – see *Pravda*, 24 October 1988, p. 2). This is because one of the most basic aspects of the latter is that legality is equated with decreasing subjectivity or arbitrariness and with decreasing amounts of personalized power – and one of the principal ways in which this occurs is through greater visibility of the power-holders to the masses. Thus I would argue that greater exposure of the 'chiefs and staffs' to the masses, plus greater mass participation, are as much a part of the essence of legal-rational legitimation as the sovereignty of universally applicable laws and norms. Unless the latter can be widely *seen* to be universally applicable, legal-rational legitimation is unlikely to take hold among the masses. Although, as has been indicated, several contemporary commentators feel that mass legitimation is not as important as self-legitimation by the chiefs and legitimation by them to their staffs, there can be no doubt that demonstrated and genuine mass support can greatly enhance total legitimacy, raising a given elite's position from one of low to high legitimacy at the same time as it has positive implications for that elite's own self-perception.

So far in this section, I have concentrated on the ways in which many communist states sought in recent years to improve the quality of mass participation and render the system more open. A related development that was gaining momentum at about the same time was the tendency for officialdom to accept that society is divided into various groups of interests, and that pluralism – albeit 'socialist' pluralism – is legitimate in a communist state. The two countries which officially and explicitly recognized this earliest were Yugoslavia and Hungary, and it is interesting to note in this context that when the Hungarian leadership team was changed in May 1988, one of those promoted to the new Politburo (Imre Poszgay) was a man who in the 1960s was already calling for recognition of different interests in society and who had more recently explicitly advocated a multi-party system. Both the Soviet Union and China had by the late 1980s *officially* recognized the legitimacy of conflicting interests in society, and the term 'pluralism' ceased to have the pejorative connotation it once had in almost all communist systems.[8]

Economic Developments

It is a major part of the thesis presented in this book that some uncoupling of the economy was an integral part of the communist world's move towards the legal-rational mode of legitimation. Indeed, given both the (former) Marxist orientation of all these countries and the intimate connections between the political and the economic systems, it is difficult to imagine how there could have been meaningful legal and political moves *without* concomitant economic changes. Three examples of the uncoupling phenomenon – some briefly touched upon in earlier chapters – are sufficient to make the point.

Moves away from central directive planning   Many writers on comparative communism (see, for example, S. White, Gardner, Schöpflin and Saich, 1990, p. 4) cite the centrally planned economy as one of the salient features of such systems. While it is true that such an economic system *is* a salient feature of communism in power, it must also be acknowledged that important changes were taking place in several communist countries in the 1980s. Yugoslavia started the trend back in the 1950s, following which it moved increasingly towards self-management. Far more recently, the USSR, the PRC, the GDR, Hungary and Bulgaria – among others – were moving away from central directive planning towards a mixture of central indicative planning and direct contractual ties between enterprises and regions. Another aspect of declining central control was the upgrading of profit-and-loss accounting, especially at the level of the production unit. Moves in this direction (such as the 1987 Soviet Law on the State Enterprise/Association) were not particularly new – a number of East European countries and the USSR introduced economic reforms involving this in the 1960s and 1970s; but they were intensified in several countries in the late 1980s. Moreover, they were formally extended in the 1980s to allow for the concept of bankruptcy in countries such as Hungary, the USSR and the PRC. On one level, all this can be seen to have reduced the power of the centre. On another, if this had increased economic efficiency, it could have enhanced the role of eudaemonic legitimation as the citizens-consumers' 'needs' were more satisfactorily met. At the same time – and to a certain limit – if economic problems arose, the centre could more readily have blamed officials in (sub-central) production units, regions, etc., than it previously could. In hindsight, however, it is clear that – in most countries – such moves came too late and were still too partial to have the desired economic (and legitimating) effects.

Boosting of the Private Sector With few exceptions (Cuba being one 1986–91), communist systems were through the 1980s advocating an increasing role in the economy for private enterprise (for an early, book-length study of private enterprise in the GDR and Poland see Aslund, 1985). This refers not only to the agricultural sector, but also the service sector and in some cases even small-scale industrial manufacturing. In November 1984, for instance, the Kampuchean government began explicitly to encourage the private sector (see *NT*, No. 20, 1989, p. 10). In January 1987, The Czechoslovak government adopted its '37 Principles' of economic reform; many of these related to privatization and marketization. In April 1988, the Vietnamese government legalized several aspects of free market trading and private property. In November 1988 the Yugoslav Federal Assembly adopted nearly 40 constitutional amendments, many of them intended to set the stage for the adoption of a series of laws designed to encourage the private sector and market forces. In the late 1980s, beginning with the major experiment in Estonia, the Soviet authorities started to encourage private entrepreneurship in the service sector. At about the same time, the maximum permissible staff size for private manufacturing enterprises in both the PRC and the USSR was increased to such an extent that, in theory, it was now possible for the owner of a small factory to live off the profits generated.

One other important development in the Soviet economy in recent years that relates to this whole issue was the development of the cooperative movement. Although cooperatives can be traced back, in their most recent guise, to 1978, their development really took off following the promulgation of the Law on Cooperatives in 1988. Thereafter, and despite opposition to them from various quarters, the cooperatives became a significant component of the Soviet economy, accounting for approximately 5 per cent of total output in 1989. Some five million Soviets were employed in them as of mid-1990, and they were to be found in most sectors of the economy (including construction, consumer goods, trade and engineering; for a detailed analysis of the cooperatives see Slider, 1991). In addition to the cooperatives, the Soviet Union encouraged 'small businesses' – small, private businesses attached to state enterprises.

Increased overt Interaction with the International Market The PRC's establishment of Special Economic Zones and 'open' coastal cities has already been referred to (see chapter 7) and is well documented. But this is just the best-known example of a widespread phenomenon in the communist world in recent years. Several communist leaderships (including the Vietnamese, Laotian, Hungarian, Yugoslav and Soviet) introduced legislation in the 1980s designed to encourage greater interaction with the world (capitalist) market. The various measures taken – such as the encouragement of joint ventures and the establishment of special zones somewhat akin to the Chinese ones – have had limited success, for a number of reasons. For instance, new legislation has often been ambiguous and/or has not covered all sorts of everyday problems that arise. In many cases, the communist officials involved in joint ventures have been unused to the risk-taking and displays of initiative of which their counterparts from the capitalist world have long experience. The non-convertibility of communist currencies has been another problem. For all these teething problems, many communist leaderships (have) committed themselves to further integration of their economies into the world market, largely with the aim of improving the domestic economy. For instance, the now-defunct Comecon formally recognized the EC (and vice versa) in June 1988, and several CMEA members – including the USSR – subsequently sought much closer cooperation with the West European body; Yugoslavia was also trying to move closer to the EC. Moreover, communist leaderships may have believed they had a scapegoat here too if their own economies faltered; 'the market' might have been seen as an even better cushion long term than the local officials referred to above, p. 286 (for the Hungarian leadership explicitly blaming the world economy for various problems at the May 1988 HSWP Conference see *IB*, Vol. 26, No. 15, 1988, p. 43).

These three examples of economic 'uncoupling' are all consistent with the argument that communist leaderships generally were in the 1980s attempting to 'depersonalize' (in a broad sense) and anonymify power – in this case, as it relates to the economy – as part of the shift towards the legal-rational mode. In that they were all largely intended to improve economic performance, they were also fully consistent with the longer-term aim of attempting to move back towards eudaemonism as the *dominant* mode of legitimation.

Moves Away From Goal-rational Legitimation

Although the primary aim of this part of the chapter has been to provide evidence of recent moves towards the legal-rational mode of legitimation in many communist states, it is appropriate, as a concluding point, to provide at least some evidence of the de-emphasizing of the goal-rational mode. Two examples should suffice. The first was the emergence in the 1970s in so many states of Eastern Europe and the USSR of the concept of 'realistic' or 'really existing' socialism. In some of the official advocacies of this, there were explicit criticisms of unrealistic aspirations for the achievement of communism, and a call for greater realism. A prime recent example of this can be found in a speech Gorbachev made in Moscow in September 1987 to a visiting French delegation, in which the Soviet leader stated that: 'We are not offering a utopia. We are offering a realistic philosophy, realistic initiatives' (*Pravda*, 30 September 1987, p. 2). Although this concept of 'realistic socialism' can and should *also* be seen as a way of limiting citizens' economic aspirations (thus potentially rendering eudaemonic legitimation more effective), the development of the concept of 'realistic' socialism represented a significant reduction in the emphasis on teleological legitimation.

The second example is related to the first, but is discrete. This is the deferment of deadlines for the achievement of communism. In 1961, the CPSU's Party Programme claimed that basic communism would be achieved in the USSR by 1980; in the new, more sober version of this programme adopted at the 27th Congress of the CPSU (1986), deadlines for the achievement of communism were replaced by deadlines for far more modest (and potentially realizable) goals. By the year 2000, for instance, labour productivity was to increase by 130–50 per cent, the production potential of the country was to double, and 'practically every Soviet family' was to have its own living quarters (*The Programme of the CPSU*, 1986, pp. 29–30 and 43). Indeed, the emphasis in the new version was on how *gradual* the transition to communism would be (for a fuller analysis see Gill, 1987, pp. 40–55). Similarly, the Chinese Communist Party announced at its 13th Congress (1987) that the present (primary) stage of socialism could last approximately 100 years from the 1950s – thus delaying beyond the lives of most currently living adults the promise of a much better society. While such moves do not mean that goal-rationality has disappeared *altogether* as a mode of legitimation in the few communist states left, it does mean that the goal is now so distant that it cannot realistically be expected to motivate the masses. Moreover, especially given the recent events in Eastern Europe and the USSR, it seems highly improbable that more than a tiny minority of chiefs and members of the staffs still believed in the *telos* in recent years.

It should by now be clear that there is a wealth of evidence to support the argument that the communist world – or at least many parts of it – was by the 1980s beginning to move into what I have chosen to call the legal-rational mode. The term 'chosen to call' is used to make the point explicitly that the conception of 'legal-rational' employed here is broader than that preferred by many analysts. But in that several of the policies adopted represented moves away from arbitrariness and towards regularization, depersonalization and 'norms', the term legal-rational seems to be the most appropriate. It might be objected by advocates of the 'goal-rational legitimation' image of communist systems that the types of participation, etc., identified here as symptomatic of the legal-rational mode were or are in fact fully consistent with the long-term *goals* of those systems (that is, that they could also endorse the goal-rational argument). Although there is some justification for this argument, it is insufficiently sensitive to two points. First, the ultimate *telos* is of a stateless (though not anarchic) society, so that moves designed to render the state more legitimate are not necessarily compatible with the *telos*. Second, many communist states became primarily concerned with the *means* to the end rather than with the end itself, more interested in present arrangements than future goals – an argument largely endorsed by the examples cited above of the Soviets, the Chinese and the East Europeans delaying 'the millennium' still further and advocating realistic approaches to socialism. It is largely this focus on means rather than ends that leads me to reject the notion that goal-rationality was the dominant mode of legitimation in the 1970s and 1980s.

There is no question that all of the countries studied here – even the growing number that are already post-communist – still have a long way to go before the legal-rational mode of operation is really the salient feature of their systems. Perhaps the best example of this is the continuing personalization of politics. Communist systems – and, apparently, early post-communist systems – are still far too oriented towards individual leaders for the depersonalization of politics that is a major aspect of the legal-rational mode to be seen as really dominant (post-communist Hungary might be argued to constitute a rare exception to this). If the ordinary Soviet citizen still believed in 1988 that the very nature of the political system depended on whether Gorbachev or Ligachev – and in 1990–1 Gorbachev or Yeltsin – won the struggle for power; if the average Chinese citizen had similar beliefs at the beginning of the 1980s about Deng and either Hua or Hu or Chen (and in April–June 1989 about Deng, Li Peng, Qiao Shi and Zhao Ziyang); and if the average Pole or Albanian still places greater faith in Wałęsa or Berisha respectively than in the new political institutions – then it is clear that individual leaders are still dominating systems rather than vice versa. Indeed, in the case of China, as Myers implies (1989, p. 210), the fact that Deng–who is neither head of the party nor head of state nor head of the government – has continued to rule from behind the scenes means that references to the institutionalization of politics and the legal system remain at present largely rhetoric. Looked at from a slightly different angle, if the right of the masses to be involved in a meaningful and self-motivated way in politics is still not fully established, at least in the communist or transitional states – if we continue to witness the 'more open' and 'more closed' phases symbolized by the rise and demise of Beijing's 'Democracy Wall' or the Tiananmen Square demonstration and massacre in China, or the (temporary) 'move to the authoritarian right' in Soviet politics in late 1990 following a more open phase – then this too suggests excessive arbitrariness, a level of personalized (leadership) politics that is incompatible with the legal-rational mode in its pure form.

The argument here is only that there was an observable *trend towards* the legal-rational mode, not that the goal was reached; indeed, the logic of the argument here has led to the unambiguous conclusion that it cannot be reached within the framework of a communist system. Nor is it being argued that the trend was observable in all countries. In Romania, for instance, such attempts at mass legitimation as there were under Ceauşescu were based primarily on official nationalism and charisma, and there were few signs indeed of moves towards the legal-rational mode. In several of the newer communist states of Asia and Africa (such as Afghanistan, Angola, Mozambique and Ethiopia), power had still not been properly consolidated by the end of the 1980s, and rulers continued to exercise power far more through coercion than through legitimation (to the masses, at least). In several communist countries, then, legitimation was still very much a secondary factor in the exercise of power, with coercion being the dominant form; in these countries, there were relatively few signs of legal-rationality.

From Communism to Post-Communism

By late 1991, it had become abundantly clear that the moves taken in the communist world away from goal-rationality and towards eudaemonism and legal-rationality had in most cases failed to save communist power. Earlier predictions that communism would fall into crisis, but then might be able to save itself, had proven at best only partly correct.[9] By then, of the 23 countries that had in the 1980s been classified as communist, only five (China, Cuba, North Korea, Laos and Vietnam) could still *relatively* accurately be described as such. However, there were clear signs in three of these countries that the transition to post-communism was starting.[10] A further 10 states (Afghanistan, Albania, Angola, Benin, Cambodia, Congo, Ethiopia, Mongolia, Mozambique and Romania) and parts of both the CIS and what used to be the SFRY were at various stages of the transition from communism to post-communism. Four countries (Bulgaria, Czecho-Slovakia, Hungary and Poland) were already post-communist but intact as sovereign states, while the remaining two – the GDR and the PDRY – were not only post-communist but had ceased to exist as separate entities. Parts of the former USSR and SFRY were by this time also clearly post-communist.[11]

The process, nature and direction of change has varied from state to state, depending on a wide range of factors; these include political culture, geography, the nature of the communists' original accession to power, level of dependence on the USSR, level of ethnic homogeneity, availability and accessibility of resources, level of economic development, etc. Nevertheless, there are two factors – both of which have already been briefly referred to – that are common to all communist states and which help to explain why, eventually, they all move to post-communism. The first is that Marxism-Leninism, both as a system and as an ideology, is ultimately incompatible with legal-rationality. The relatively high level of voluntarism typical of Marxist-Leninist systems, symbolized by the concept of the vanguard party, cannot be fully reconciled with the depersonalization that is crucial to legal-rationality proper. Legal-rationality as a concept and an ideology cannot *ultimately* privilege groups or individuals, even if the day-to-day practice of states based on legal-rational principles almost invariably does privilege some groups over others. Second, attempts at eudaemonic legitimation precede attempts at legal-rational legitimation in communist systems. This means that communist systems cannot revert to legal-rationality when economic performance is sub-optimal; this point is strongly endorsed by the argument that Marxism-Leninism is ultimately incompatible with legal-rationality anyway. In contrast, legal-rationality as a dominant mode typically precedes eudaemonism in liberal-democracies. This reverse sequentiality means that liberal-democracies have an established and reliable legitimation mode to resort to in times of economic crisis, which in turn renders them more resistant and durable than communist systems.

To argue that Marxism–Leninism is ultimately incompatible with legal-rationality might initially appear to run counter to the 1989–91 developments in some countries. The domino effect, for instance, seemed to be limited; while it eventually appears to have applied to all of Eastern Europe, it did not seem to pertain to developments in many Asian communist states. However, it is argued here that, while the domino effect has slowed down, the dynamism leading to total crisis does apply to all communist systems, and will become obvious sooner or later in every one of them. For various reasons analysed below, some states were by 1989 much closer to the point of ultimate contradiction and collapse than others. What were these factors?

One of the principal reasons why some communist states fell very rapidly, while others have thus far survived, was briefly alluded to earlier. Thus it does appear to be the case that systems in which communist power is widely perceived to have been imposed by an external agent, and/or in which contemporary leaderships are considered to be ultimately responsible to – even sycophantic towards – such an external agent are, *in a crisis situation*, more fragile than others. Such a broad generalization needs to be treated and applied with caution, however, and the peculiarites of the situation in a given country must always be borne in mind. Let us consider the individual countries of Eastern Europe in turn.

The hypothesis would certainly fit Albanian developments; together with Yugoslavia, it was the country in which Soviet influence – both in the 1940s and in recent years – was the most limited, and it is the European country that started its transition last of all.[12] The hypothesis would also *partially* fit the Yugoslav case, in which crisis was prolonged, and the collapse occurred in stages; the individual republics were moving to post-communism at different rates, with two – Serbia and Montenegro – opting in late 1990 to retain their nationalistic brand of communism and charismatic leader (in the case of Serbia) for a little longer. This said, the very obvious crisis of the second half of 1991 – which was initially particularly visible in terms of the fighting between Croatian nationalists and the Serbian-dominated federal military forces, subsequently so in terms of the collapse of the Yugoslav federation – can be seen as a variation on the double rejective revolution, in that component parts of an existing federal unit feel dominated by the federal authorities and/or the numerically dominant ethnic group. The argument is fully consistent with the very rapid transitions in Czechoslovakia, the GDR, Hungary and Poland.

The two East European states which could from some perspectives be argued to fit this hypothesis least well are Bulgaria and

Romania. In Bulgaria, it appeared by mid-1990 – largely because of the June elections – that it might have been only the Zhivkov regime, as distinct from the communist system, that had been rejected. However, following President Mladenov's resignation in July, and – even more significantly – the collapse of the communist-dominated government in December 1990 and its replacement by the coalition 'Government of National Unity' under Popov, it became clear to most that Bulgaria fitted this first hypothesis well. The election results of October 1991 revealed – to those who had any lingering doubts – that the process of transition to post-communism in Bulgaria was now complete. Its path may have been a little longer than in Czecho-Slovakia, for example, for reasons that include the Bulgarian tradition of greater proximity to the Russians and other Soviets, the fact that Bulgaria had had little tradition of dissidence (so that there was a much smaller pool of experienced people than in Czecho-Slovakia to wrest power from the communists and in whom others would have confidence), the fact that it did not have Soviet troops stationed on its soil (which was a very alienating factor in the GDR, Czechoslovakia, Hungary and Poland), etc. Nevertheless, on the grand scale of history, there is little difference between a few weeks and the year or more it took Bulgaria.

Romania shares some features with Bulgaria, but is in other ways different again. Since the early 1960s, communist Romania had had a reputation for being a maverick within the Soviet camp; in this sense, many would see it as having been the least deferential of all the Soviet bloc states. Its people certainly never felt as close to the Russians as the Bulgarians did. Yet it *was* a member of both the WTO and the CMEA (that is, of Soviet-dominated organizations), for all its nationalist declarations. Moreover, few would dispute that communism was imposed on the country with considerable external (Soviet) support. As was the case with Bulgaria until late 1990 (or, arguably, October 1991), it could be suggested that the Romanian masses – and the military – overthrew a particular communist regime rather than the communist system, an argument that could be endorsed by reference to the results of the May 1990 elections. However, the protests of late 1990 in Timişoara and other cities, plus the kinds of policy and public attitude adopted by the Iliescu–Roman regime, demonstrated that Romania, too, was clearly in transition to post-communism. The days of the Iliescu–Roman regime were clearly numbered – as was revealed by Roman's forced resignation in September 1991 (for two excellent, single-author analyses of the 1989–90 events in Eastern Europe, both individually and from a comparative perspective, see Glenny, 1990, and J. Brown, 1991 – for further analyses see Hawkes, 1990, and Sword, 1990).

Applying this first hypothesis – initial and/or recent dependency on the USSR or another communist state – to Asia, it again holds up rather well. Thus the Soviets played a significant role in the establishment of communist power in Mongolia, which was subsequently highly dependent on the USSR; it is one of only two Asian states to have belonged to the CMEA. As of 1990, Mongolia had by some criteria – particularly the political ones – proceeded furthest of all Asian communist states along the path to post-communism. In Vietnam, the communists took power with relatively little Soviet assistance and for long had a very independent – even charismatic – leadership. In recent years, however, the Vietnamese leadership was highly dependent on the USSR both for economic assistance (for example, via the CMEA) and in terms of policy guidance and/or emulation. If this first hypothesis is correct, a major crisis followed by far more overt moves towards post-communism could be expected in Vietnam in the first half of the 1990s; however – and although my own hunch is that this is unlikely – such a collapse *might* be delayed, for reasons relating to developments in China that are considered shortly.

Let us now turn to the other two Indochinese communist states. As indicated earlier in this chapter, Laos has in recent years certainly been engaging in the uncoupling of the economy that constitutes a major indicator that a country is moving into the transitional phase to post-communism. While the Laotian leadership has shown *some* deference towards Vietnam, the history of relations between these two countries before the communists came to power in both suggests that we should be wary of too readily assuming that such relatively warm relations between the Vientiane and Hanoi governments evokes widespread hostility in Laos. Laos does not have particularly close ties to Moscow, and was not a member of the CMEA. Cambodia, too, has recently been much closer to Vietnam than to the Soviet Union; Vietnam had not undertaken as much fundamental and public questioning of its own system as did the USSR, and at the time of writing was actually becoming less open. On the other hand, the Vietnamese military withdrawal in 1989 occurred at much the same time as a number of both symbolic and concrete changes in Cambodia revealed that it was starting what *could* be a rather more protracted transition to post-communism than occurred in many East European states. In fact, it certainly *looked* clear by October 1991 – as the terms of the latest peace agreement were revealed – that Cambodia was now taking the final steps to post-communism; this said, the history of failed accords in Cambodia suggests that one should be wary of too readily accepting that peace and stability really have come to the country this time.

Afghanistan is an interesting case, but can – as with all countries considered in this type of comparative overview – be considered only briefly. Suffice it to say here that the delay in the fall of communism in that country can *on one level* be related directly to the Soviet military withdrawal completed early in 1989. The somewhat longer transition would thus be compatible with our first hypothesis, since Najibullah's regime was now – until its collapse in 1992 – far less sympathetic towards and dependent on Moscow than it once was.

As of late 1991, North Korea was the Asian country that was, in terms of changes already made, furthest away from the transition to post-communism. It is a country that has in recent years consciously sought not to move too close to Moscow, Beijing or Hanoi (although it has moved closer to the latter two as communism in Europe and the USSR has collapsed). On the other hand, it is a country in which the communists came to power with considerable external assistance. Like the now-defunct GDR and PDRY, it has faced particular problems of legitimation because of the success and even existence of 'the other half' of a once-unified country. In my view, the dominant form of the exercise of power in the DPRK is coercion; the (subordinate) attempts at legitimation manifest them-selves primarily through the charismatic and official nationalist modes. Although one must be very careful not to over-emphasize these – because the DPRK has been far more independent in recent years than was Ceauşescu's Romania; because Kim Il Sung seems to be more genuinely revered than was Ceauşescu; because traditional Korean culture is very different from Romanian, etc. – there are *some* similarities between the North Korean regime and the fallen Ceauşescu dictatorship. Partly for this reason, it seems likely that North Korea will start moving quite rapidly towards post-communism in the next few years. Indeed, it would not be at all surprising if, fairly soon after Kim Il Sung's death, a reunification of the two Koreas were to take place; if this were to happen, it is considerably more probable that the new, united Korea would be based primarily on the ROK's system and values than on the DPRK's.[13]

This brings us to the most powerful and significant of all the communist states of Asia, the PRC. The Chinese communists took power in 1949 with very little assistance from the USSR; apart from the first few years of communist power, the Chinese have by no means been sycophantic towards or in any meaningful sense even emulative of the Soviets. According to the first hypothesis, there-fore, the moves towards post-communism would come later and probably not as rapidly in China as in many of the East European states; its revolution would be essentially single rather than double rejective.

The second hypothesis is that a domino effect works more powerfully among geographically proximate – even contiguous – countries than among countries geographically remote from each other; indeed, if the domino metaphor is to be reasonably accurate, this is necessarily the case. This argument seems to me to be a rather obvious one, and requires little elaboration. However, the point should briefly be made that the impact of media reporting from nearby countries can very rapidly raise political awareness within a country already in crisis. This factor helps to explain recent developments *within* what has sometimes been called the Soviet 'internal empire' (that is, the republics of the former USSR), as well as in Eastern Europe.

Third, one can generalize from one of the observations made above concerning the difference between Bulgaria and Czecho-Slovakia to argue that there appears to be *some* correlation between dissident traditions under communism and the speed at which systems collapsed in Eastern Europe. Thus, those states in which there had been a strong tradition of dissidence in recent decades – Czechoslovakia (Charter 77, Havel, etc), Poland (Kurón, Michnik, arguably Wałęsa), Hungary (Konrád, Haraszti, etc.) and the GDR (Harich, Havemann, Bahro, etc.)[14] – fell more rapidly than those that did not. One ramification of such dissidence is that dissatisfied citizens may well have believed that there was an alternative leadership to the communists in those countries in which there was a strong critical tradition. *Ceteris paribus*, this would suggest that another crisis in the PRC could lead to rapid collapse. This said, it needs constantly to be borne in mind that *several* factors explain the nature and pace of the transition to post-communism in any country, and that it is difficult to predict which features will be most salient in a given case.

Fourth, there is some correlation between the pace at which post-communism was reached in Eastern Europe and traditions of mass unrest under communism. Thus the GDR (1953), Poland (1956, 1970–1, 1976, 1980–1), Hungary (1956) and Czechoslovakia (1968–9) had all experienced widespread, anti-system mass unrest under communist rule, whereas none of the Southern states had (Yugoslavia is a special case – but I would argue that, even there, unrest over the years had tended to be concentrated in particular areas, such as Croatia in the early 1970s and Kosovo in the early 1980s). As with the third hypothesis, and subject to the same caveat, the final transition to post-communism in China – once the process is underway – should, according to this argument, be relatively rapid.

Fifth, the point about the sequentiality of legitimation modes may be useful in understanding the reasons for the different paths taken in and since 1989 – though in applying this argument, it becomes clear that it requires further elaboration and refinement. Thus, it has been argued that eudaemonism typically precedes legal-rationality in the communist world. It has also been suggested that if eudaemonism is seen to be reasonably effective, then there is less stimulus to communists to experiment with imperfect legal-rationality, with the ultimate contradiction in which this results. Let us now consider the PRC in the light of all this. The economic reforms initiated by the Chinese leadership from 1979 were generally far more successful than those introduced in Eastern Europe and the USSR in the 1960s and 1970s (on the latter see, for example, Ellman, 1969, Höhmann, Kaser and Thalheim, 1975; on China, see Joseph Cheng, 1989). Many of the economic problems in China of the mid to late 1980s can be seen as resulting from an overheating of the economy followed by inappropriate measures taken to cool it down (see, for example, Prybyla, 1989); in a sense, then, the problems could be interpreted as symptomatic of 'overly-successful' economic reforms. The reasons why the Chinese reforms were relatively so successful are complex, and can be considered only superficially and partially here. One factor was that the Chinese – whether or not they were prepared openly to acknowledge this – were able to learn certain lessons vicariously from the East European and Soviet experiences. A second is that, in the aftermath of the Cultural Revolution, the Chinese leadership had a much less entrenched and resistant bureaucracy ('staff') than the Soviet, and to a lesser extent the East European, leaderships had had to contend with. They were therefore better able to have radical new policies implemented than their comrades to the West had been. It would be easy to infer from this argument that, since economic reform – potentially a major component of eudaemonic legitimation – has been so much more successful in the PRC, China may be able to avoid the type of crisis other communist systems have faced. This would be an incorrect inference. The very fact of the June 1989 Beijing Massacre is suggestive of crisis.

The question now arises as to why the PRC is, according to the argument put forward here, heading towards a similar fate to that of Eastern Europe and the former USSR. Surely, it could be countered, this is unlikely if the economy is performing so relatively well. In answering this, we need to consider the *nature* of Chinese economic reform and its relationship to eudaemonism. The reforms of 1979 on were not only more radical than the Soviet and East European reforms of the 1960s and 1970s, but also moved more clearly away from a communist model; indeed, at least one commentator has argued that the reforms moved the PRC unambiguously in the direction of capitalism (see Chossudovsky, 1986). At about the same time, and as demonstrated earlier in this chapter, the PRC did take steps in the direction of legal-rationality in a number of fields, not just the economic. While it is quite true that the moves in the non-economic sphere were in most cases far more modest than those taken in the USSR – one need only compare Chinese and Soviet electoral reform in the 1980s, or the Chinese concept and application of *toumingdu* with *glasnost*, for example – the fact is that the Chinese also moved into an increasingly contradictory position, a growing identity crisis. In a sense, they sought eudaemonic legitimation through economic policies that were at least as close to those of capitalist, legal-rational systems as they were to those of any traditional conception of a communist system; to the extent that they attempted to retain elements of communism in the political sphere, there was a profound tension in this approach. Although, for reasons about to be elaborated, crisis and collapse *may* be avoided in both China and Vietnam in the short term, these fundamental contradictions between communist structures and values on the one hand, and economic policies on the other, are a feature of the PRC just as much as anywhere else. Let us now turn to a sixth hypothesis about the pace of transition to post-communism, which relates explicitly to the future of the two largest Asian communist states.

It was argued in chapter 1 that the 1989–91 revolution in Eastern Europe should be seen more as the rejection of a particular type of system (as well as of Soviet domination) than as the positive adoption of a reasonably well-defined alternative. Although in the early, euphoric days of the East European revolution many Western analysts – particularly in the mass media – gloated over the collapse of communism and rather unquestioningly assumed that 'post-communist' systems would soon look essentially like Western systems, it had by 1991 become increasingly clear that such an assumption may have been premature. Within 12 to 18 months of the 1989 events, there were signs of increasing problems and even crisis not only in those countries, such as Romania and Yugoslavia, in which the rejection of communism had not yet been fully completed (that is, in which, following the logic of the present study, one would *expect* continuing contradiction and crisis until post-communism had been reached), but even in the fully post-communist countries. In Czecho-Slovakia, one of President Havel's major and most difficult tasks in 1990 was to prevent the division of the country into two; by 1991, there were indications that *some* citizens in the renamed Czech and Slovak Federative Republic might even want the country to divide into three. In Poland Wałęsa had experienced difficulties in appointing a prime minister and cabinet in December 1990 – and, following the indecisive elections of October 1991, made many Poles apprehensive when he suggested he could be president and prime minister simultaneously. Strikes and disillusionment were spreading in Hungary. And many former citizens of the GDR were becoming increasingly disappointed with the rising prices, growing unemployment, and the resentment shown towards them by many West Germans prior to and following unification. The reasons for the growing crisis of post-communism were several, and in some cases peculiar to a particular country. However, the severe shortage of indigenous private capital in most countries, and the West's limited capacity and commitment to 'bail out' the transitional and post-communist states, were two major reasons for the economic problems in these countries, which in turn were leading to disillusionment and crisis.

In the light of all this, our sixth hypothesis is that the problems and tensions of both the transition to post-communism and post-communism itself *might* be sufficiently severe in the early 1990s to provide communists still in power with enhanced opportunities for delaying the inevitable collapse of their system. If, for instance, extreme authoritarian governments were to take power in various post-communist states (this could include various parts of the CIS – see below), and if such governments were to mix coercive rule with an economic situation that is at least as serious as that in the still-existing communist states, the worldwide collapse of communism might be slowed down still further. Unfortunately, writing at the beginning of the 1990s, the international debt situation, the Middle East crisis and signs of prolonged economic downturn in the West (here including Japan) give one little reason for being very optimistic about the short-term prospects of the post-communist states.

This all said, it should not too readily be assumed that either the leaders or the masses in the Asian communist states will be as influenced by developments in Eastern Europe as the above scenario might suggest. In some communist states, mass dissatisfaction with communism may well be a far more powerful factor than 'rational' comparisons between one's own lot and the fate of citizens on another continent. Moreover, to the extent that citizens *do* look to other countries for inspiration, the Chinese or Vietnamese masses might just as well look to their NIE (Newly Industrializing Economy) neighbours – the 'Four Little Dragons/Tigers' of Taiwan, Hong Kong, Singapore and South Korea, as well as Thailand and perhaps also Malaysia – as to Poland or Hungary or the former USSR. When one bears in mind that three of the four 'Little Dragons' are Chinese-speaking, then it becomes even more obvious why the East Asian masses – at least the PRC citizenry and the Hoa still in Vietnam – might relate more to them than to the European post-communist states. Whether or not such comparisons in the Chinese mass consciousness appear to an external analyst to be valid (the scale of the economy, for instance, is obviously very different in each of the NIEs from that in the PRC) is ultimately irrelevant; the indigenous *perception* that China might be able to emulate the NIEs is what matters. If we add to all this the fact that the post-communist states might somehow do better than the 'worst possible' scenario outlined above, it becomes clear why the sixth hypothesis empha-sizes only the *possibility*, not the *probability*, that communist power may be granted a stay of execution. There are, ultimately, too many unknown and unpredictable variables involved both within the communist world and in the international order to determine with any accuracy how long communism will be able to survive in those few countries in which it has clung on to power.

This said, the profound contradiction of contemporary commun-ism – which surely *is* recognized by Chinese, Vietnamese and other communist leaders still in power – is such that it would not be at all surprising if the same kind and level of identity and systemic crisis were to become evident in China in the 1990s as the USSR and Eastern Europe so recently experienced. Given the unrest that has sometimes followed the death of a leader in the PRC, it could well be that Deng's death will trigger a process that results in China moving into post-communism. Vietnam may already have entered that phase by then; if not, and if its leaders manage to hold on to power partially by orienting their country away from the Soviet Union and more towards their traditional enemy, China, the collapse of the latter, too, as a role-model would almost certainly trigger an irreversible move in Vietnam in the direction of post-communism.

Communism was already being rejected in all of the African communist states at the time of writing (Congo and Ethiopia were the latest to begin to do so); given its emphasis on class as the major cleavage in society, Marxism-Leninism was never a very appropriate ideology in Africa anyway.

This leaves Cuba and the original role-model itself, the former USSR, for consideration. Certainly, there is some evidence to sug-gest that Fidel Castro still enjoys a relatively high degree of popular support among the Cuban citizenry; by the end of the 1980s, he was one of only a very few leaders in the communist world who still enjoyed some prestige through having led the communist revolution in his own country. He was unquestionably one of the most trusted and charismatic communist leaders. This *might* be sufficient to delay the transition to post-communism in Cuba, perhaps until after Castro's death. On the other hand, there are also many signs of crisis in Cuba (such as the major extension of rationing announced in September 1990, Cuban reactions to the announcement of massive reductions in Soviet subsidies/aid in 1991, references to the need for political reform at the 4th CPC Congress in October 1991), and the collapse of communism in so many other parts of the world can only contribute to an undermining of the Castro regime. Cuba is increasingly isolated, and is not presently in a position to reverse the severe economic decline of recent years. For these reasons, and given that – having celebrated his 65th birthday in August 1991 – Castro is still *relatively* young for a communist leader (for instance, in comparison with Deng, Kim and many of the East European leaders ousted in the late 1980s), it would not be at all surprising if the Cuban transition to post-communism were to start while Fidel is still alive.

To some extent like the position in the post-communist states of Eastern Europe, the current crisis in what was the Soviet Union is such that an authoritarian backlash is a real possibility, at least in some of the new 'independent' states. By late August 1991, one pan-Soviet attempt by conservative communists had been made and had failed miserably. In late 1991, many commentators – particularly in the media – were arguing that the USSR had at long last experienced the attack from the 'right' (that is, old-fashioned communist *apparatchiki* plus leaders of the state's coercive organs) that had been threatening the transition to post-communism for at least two years, and had survived. But many went beyond this, to claim that the failure of the coup attempt represented the victory of 'democracy'. On one level, the failure represented indecisiveness, incompetence and misjudgement on the part of the plotters. On another, it did represent a major step (probably the final step, although it is too early to be certain) towards post-communism, especially with the subsequent banning of the CPSU.[15] But to go beyond this to argue that the former USSR is clearly on the path to Western-style democracy seems to me to be at least premature. The very fact that so many Russians looked to their president, Boris Yeltsin, to lead and save them during the August 1991 coup attempt reveals that many citizens are still tending to look too much to the strong, charismatic leader to improve their lot rather than to themselves. Thus, the potential for a new, post-communist authoritarianism must not be underestimated. Indeed, if the economy fails to pick up rather rapidly – and it is currently in such a sorry state that one must doubt its capacity in the short term to improve substantially – then the likelihood of a new form of authoritarianism, even if popular, will become that much greater. This is not to argue that such a system would necessarily be long-lived. But a culture in which initiative and entrepreneurship are not merely called for and accepted but actually encouraged and understood will take time to develop.

This said, there are no obvious reasons why many Russians, Ukrainians, Kazakhs, Lithuanians, etc., cannot develop full entrepreneurial skills in the longer term, and why reasonably well-functioning economies far less dependent on the state cannot emerge. To reject such an argument on 'cultural' grounds (for example, 'the Russians don't have the inherent business skills the Chinese have') smacks of racism; now that the communist structures and socialization processes have been destroyed, the structural impediments to initiative and risk-taking in the former USSR have been substantially reduced. Similarly, a pluralist system in which legal-rationality is firmly established will eventually come to the lands that until now constituted the USSR. Such developments will almost certainly occur sooner in some parts (such as the Baltic states) than others (such as Georgia, Moldova – which may merge with Romania). Moreover, the precise form will vary from state to state – just as legal-rationality and democracy assume different forms in every 'Western' state, despite important commonalities. In the next section, these arguments about the former USSR are explored in a more general, comparative way.

Before doing this, however, the present section can be concluded with a model of the final stages of the political transition to post-communism. This has been created on the basis of an analysis of actual developments in recent years in Eastern Europe and the Soviet Union. As with most models, it fits the perceived 'realities' of some countries better than others. In particular, it should be noted that the sequence of stages is an averaged-out one; not every country has clearly gone through every stage, and the sequence varies in some countries from that in the model. Partly because of these exceptions and limitations, I have provided only several examples of each point, not a comprehensive listing; ultimately, the concern here is with a general pattern, rather than the details of each country.

In the first stage, there is a crisis at the top of the leadership, and the person generally perceived to be 'the' leader – who may well have been in office for many years – typically resigns (often under pressure) or is removed. Examples of this include Kádár in Hungary, May 1988; Jaruzelski in Poland, July 1989; Honecker in the GDR,

October 1989; Zhivkov in Bulgaria, November 1989; and Ceauşescu in Romania, December 1989. In the second stage, the formal commitment to the communist party's 'leading role' is dropped (Hungary, February 1989; Czechoslovakia, November 1989; Bulgaria and Poland, December 1989; Yugoslavia, January 1990; USSR, March 1990; Albania, November–December 1990). The third stage is reached when governments formally accept the notion that opposition parties[16] have the rights both to exist and to compete against the communist party in elections (Hungary, January 1989; Poland – with some limitations – in April 1989; the GDR in November 1989; Romania, December 1989; Albania, November 1990). Fourth, the communist party changes its name and/or splits into two parties (Hungary, October 1989; the GDR, December 1989; Poland, January 1990; Albania, June 1991). Fifth, competitive general parliamentary elections are held (Poland – with limitations – in June 1989; Hungary, March–April 1990; Bulgaria and Czecho-Slovakia, June 1990; Albania, March–April 1991). The sixth stage is primarily of symbolic significance – the formal name of the country is changed, usually to reflect the fact that it is no longer necessarily a 'socialist' or 'people's' republic and sometimes to indicate a looser federal arrangement (Hungary, September 1989; Poland, December 1989; Czechoslovakia, April 1990; Albania, April 1991; while the Soviet Union ceased to be the USSR in August 1991 and, in truncated form, became the CIS in December 1991). The seventh – final – stage is reached when either a brand new constitution is adopted or else the existing one is so radically modified as to be virtually a new document (for example, Hungary, October 1989; Albania, April 1991; Bulgaria, July 1991; Romania, December 1991 – and a Polish one due in the early 1990s).

On Communism, Post-Communism, Modernity and Post-Modernity

It has been argued in this study that it is easier to specify what post-communism is *not* than what it is. Thus it presently rejects many of the basic tenets of communism in power, including the leading role of the party, democratic centralism, the ideology of Marxism-Leninism, the *telos* of communism, attempts to suppress religious belief, attempts to suppress divergent political views, faith in the centrally planned and predominantly state-owned economy, and devotion to Moscow or any other foreign 'centre'. In a sense, it is also the partial reassertion of civil society over the state, even if 'civil society' has only a limited self-understanding and knowledge of where it is going. Although there were slogans in 1989 (and since, in the case of those countries that have transited to post-communism only more recently) to the effect that citizens wanted 'democracy', a 'market economy', etc., the significance of these slogans needs to be contextualized.

First, many citizens had really very limited knowledge of what a Western-style democracy really meant. For some, it was little more than a deduction. For others, even if they did know what phrases such as 'a Westminster system', 'separation of powers', 'pluralism', etc., meant in theory, they had not experienced such phenomena first hand. The example of the FRG in the decades after 1949 demonstrates well that even where near-perfect conditions pertain – the almost total discrediting of an authoritarian system; stability; excellent economic growth and development; integration into and acceptance by the international community of established democracies; a counter-model that had to suppress its own people in June 1953 and physically hem them in from August 1961 – it takes time for a democratic culture to develop in *any* country. Second, *even if* we put all the above considerations to one side – an extremely unrealistic proposition – nobody in either the East or the West really knew how to create 'democracies' and 'market economies' overnight.

It is for these reasons that I argue that post-communism was, and *could only be*, committed to the 1989 slogans in a very limited and ultimately superficial way. What are the implications of such an argument for the future of post-communism? One is that post-communism, though emerging from the crisis of late communism, itself starts off in an identity crisis. In one very real sense, however, this identity crisis cannot be a full-blown legitimation crisis, since there is no established 'system' to legitimate; indeed, in all of the already existing post-communist states, even the regime is as yet insufficiently consolidated and stable for there to be meaningful talk of legitimating it. New elections and constitutions in the early 1990s *should* help the process of stabilization and consolidation, although the short-term economic problems will not help these processes. Ironically, the only major phenomenon that might be argued to enjoy a high degree of 'legitimacy' is leadership rejection of communism as a system of power; however, to use the term 'legitimacy' in such a context is to engage in such conceptual stretching as to render the term almost worthless.

It has been argued that the state of the world economy at the time of the emergence of the first post-communist states is such that they are likely to face severe economic problems – in the short term, at least. In the longer term, the facts that they represent huge new markets and sources of cheap and relatively skilled labour, and that they are slowly acquiring some of the world's latest technology in their factories, suggest that they may be able to start to catch up with 'the West'; if this happens, regimes can expect to be legitimated in the eudaemonic (and other) mode(s) and should eventually be able to form relatively stable, fundamentally legal-rational systems. Unlike communist systems, there is no *inherent* reason why post-communist systems should find themselves in identity crises as they move closer to full legal-rationality. But now let us briefly consider possible alternatives to the (longer-term) scenario just outlined.

As argued in the previous section, there is no question that a very real danger exists in the post-communist states – and in most of those in transition to post-communism – that the economic problems and ideological void of the post-euphoric era will result in new authoritarian regimes[17] arising before the weak, legal-rational basis presently existing has had time to establish itself. These authoritarian regimes would be predominantly nationalistic, and in some cases possibly even quasi-fascist. In the case of multi-ethnic states, it is already clear that boundaries are being and will be redrawn, and that many states are breaking up and will continue to break up into much smaller units (for an early overview of nationalism in the post-communist era see Brzezinski, 1990). Already – as of December 1991 – the former USSR had largely disintegrated, and may well disintegrate further. The same is true of Yugoslavia. Beyond this, the Czech and Slovak Federative Republic might be radically restructured and may yet break up; many nationalists in both Slovakia and Moravia were arguing strongly by 1991 that they were no longer willing to be 'dominated' by the Bohemians. Hungarians in Transylvania may soon demand to break away from Romania, and formally join with Hungary. Tibetans – and perhaps other minorities – may well make far more concerted efforts to break away from China in the next few years. And it seems to me to be not totally inconceivable that a new form of autonomism, possibly even separatism, might arise in the former GDR, as some East Germans increasingly yearn for certain aspects of their former existence; many currently feel that they are being dominated or even swallowed up by the West Germans, which might yet result in calls for either a confederal arrangement in Germany or, at its most extreme, the creation of a new sovereign successor to the GDR. It would be possible to continue listing other potential restructurings of existing 'national' state boundaries. But that it is not my primary objective here. Rather, I wish to explore other aspects of the future of post-communism in both the shorter and longer terms.

It has already been argued that nationalistic, new authoritarian regimes might well emerge in the 1990s in at least some of the post-communist countries. Growing unemployment, inflation and general economic and social insecurity mean that it is also feasible that such regimes may even bring back elements of 'communism', in particular high levels of state subsidization of the economy and social security; by 'communism', here, I mean some of the values and policies of former communist systems and regimes, as distinct from communism as a system of power. Certainly, there have already been tangible indications that many citizens – though still only a minority – want to retain or return to some 'communist' values; perhaps the best symbols of this were the results of the various East German elections in 1990,[18] and the Bulgarian and Polish election results of 1991. It might be assumed that a return to some of the 'cradle-to-grave' mentality in the post-communist world would represent the so-called 'third way' that many left-oriented intellectuals have advocated in recent decades. However, the use of the term 'third way' in this particular context would be inappropriate – unless one is prepared to call the National Socialism that Germany had in the 1930s and 1940s the 'third way'. The 'third way' surely implies *both* a high level of security for citizens provided by the state *and* extensive citizen control over the state. It implies a situation, then, in which the state really is the servant of society, not its master – and this is *not* a scenario that is likely in the short term in the post-communist countries. Even if citizens appear to *want* a form of benign dictatorship – as surveys conducted in Romania at the beginning of the 1990s suggested might be the case in that country (Shafir, 1991) – it would be absurd to label this the 'third way'. It is precisely because the post-communist countries currently have such fragile economies and polities that they will, for some time to come, essentially have to choose between satisfying their individual consumers and providing collective goods and services; there is simply insufficient wealth in these countries at present to permit both a Western-style consumer society *and* the very high levels of security/ welfarism some leaderships appear to want to offer. Citizens themselves may well divide sharply on this choice – which in turn could further intensify divisions in society and have adverse effects on the democratization process. In short, the fact that many citizens might favour a return of many 'old' communist values by no means suggests that these systems will succeed in finding that elusive, optimal balance between consumerism and security in the foreseeable future.

If anything, the West is currently closer to the 'third way' than any of the post-communist countries. It is true that there are signs that much of the West is moving away from state intervention at present; not only is this very visible in the privatization and deregulation that has been such a feature of the English-speaking West since the late 1970s, but the collapse of the social democratic regime in Sweden in September 1991 – which in some ways came closest of all to the 'third way' – symbolizes this trend particularly forcefully. This all said, Western governments have been far more involved in their economies in the twentieth century than was the case in the nineteenth century. Against the recent privatization and deregulation must be weighed the role of the state in health and education, affirmative action programmes, consumer protection, exchange and interest rates, superannuation schemes, etc. All of these can be seen as part of the move away from the *relatively* pure capitalism of the nineteenth century towards the mixed economy and voter-oriented state of the twentieth century that can on balance be seen to be heading *towards* something that is neither socialism nor capitalism (nor national socialism) but – in the absence of any better term – the 'third way'.

But the question of which kind of system is closest to the 'third way' is not my principal concern here either. I have argued that there are reasons for believing that new authoritarian regimes of one kind or another might well arise in the post-communist countries during the 1990s. Even if they do – and the best chance of avoiding them is for the economies of these countries clearly to turn the corner – they are unlikely to last very long. They will be required by the people to deliver the goods in a very real sense. On the other hand, the more authoritarian and anti-democratic they are, the less the West – especially the EC – will be prepared to help them, which will further exacerbate their economic problems. The masses and the intellectuals have already experienced their own power in bringing down authoritarian regimes that failed to deliver; the next time should be even easier, since the new authoritarian regimes will be less consolidated than the old communist regimes. Nor can the new regimes expect to motivate the masses with grandiose schemes and long-term promises; the era of teleologism and meta-narratives is over for the foreseeable future.

Even if – somehow or other – new authoritarian regimes succeed in dramatically improving economic performance, the demands for democratization will sooner or later become overwhelming. There are quite unmistakeable signs from the NIEs – especially the 'Little Dragons' – that demands for democratization will be made by the masses eventually in any country, whether or not there is a 'democratic' tradition and even if the economy performs well. In short, and while I am fully aware both of the present unpopularity of modernization theory and of the reasons for this unpopularity, the evidence seems currently to be clearly in its favour (for a fairly recent defence and update of modernization theory see Almond, 1987). This is *not* to argue that there is only one type of modern system *nor* to argue that all countries sooner or later adopt their own version of whatever the 'American' model may be. Rather, it is to argue that greater answerability of the state to an increasingly sophisticated and complex civil society is a feature that accompanies economic development. Quite when and how the demands arise and are made varies from country to country, depending on culture, the success rate of the economy, etc.

This is an appropriate point at which to consider the relationship between recent events in the communist and post-communist worlds and the heated debates of the last 20 years or so on both modernity and post-modernity. As with so many other dimensions of the argument in this chapter, the following analysis is intended to be primarily a provocative introduction rather than a fully developed line; if it serves to put what I consider to be certain very important questions more clearly on the agenda for future debate, then it will have served its main purpose.

In a stimulating article published in February 1990, Zygmunt Bauman argued that the 1989–90 crisis of socialism represented the final stage of the crisis of modernity. I have elsewhere dealt at some length with Bauman's argument (Holmes, 1992b), and do not wish to repeat all the details here. Rather, I shall – to some extent in response to Bauman's argument – consider the recent crisis and collapse of communism in terms of aspects of the debate on modernity and post-modernity. The basic argument is that, unlike Bauman, I do *not* see the recent revolutions as evidence of the final crisis of modernity. Indeed, I do not accept that these revolutions had very much relevance to the debate on this crisis; to the extent that they did, one of the main features of them is that sooner or later they are likely to result in a swelling of the ranks of the systems that can be called 'modern'. Such a position should not be interpreted to mean that I do not think there is a crisis of modernity; this is a quite separate question that I shall briefly address below. Rather, it is simply to argue that the 'double rejective' revolution was only marginally related to the alleged crisis of modernity. It is now time to consider modernity, post-modernity and the anti-communist revolutions.

For most analysts – including Anderson (1986b), Kolb (1986), Habermas (1987), and Giddens (1990) – modernity is a recent phenomenon, emerging at the time of the European Enlightenment, and thus dating from the seventeenth and eighteenth centuries. For analytical and heuristic purposes, it is useful to construct an ideal type of modernity; for me, such an ideal type should incorporate the following, closely related components:

- Humanism;
- An ideology of rationality and rational discourse;
- Teleologism;
- Dynamism;
- A belief in the possibility and desirability of constructing grand theories or meta-narratives;
- A division of functions or 'spheres of existence'

Each of the above requires some elaboration.

By *humanism*, I mean a faith or belief that humans are predominantly both responsible for their own destiny and capable of controlling this. This humanism essentially rejects supernaturalism or mysticism of any sort. It involves an essentially voluntaristic approach to the world.

The *ideology of rationality and rational discourse* is a logical extension of humanism. The distinguishing feature of humanity is taken to be that it can both think creatively and reason (the Enlightenment is often called 'The Age of Reason'). If humans are to assume most of the responsibility for their own condition, they must take decisions on the basis of some perceived order, a paradigm. For instance, they need 'information' and a belief that there are 'objective facts'. They need also to believe that there are relationships – causal and otherwise – between 'objective facts', and that such relationships are more or less discernible. The modern condition as described thus far necessarily implies a normative element, in that the very notion of making decisions implies choice. But such a choice is, ideally, limited by the 'objective facts'; the notion is that, to a considerable extent, better knowledge of the facts results in better decisions, while poor decisions are in many cases a function of inadequate information. In short, decision-making ideally becomes almost automatic – the better the information, the more obvious the solution to a problem becomes.

On the basis of constantly refined information – science – humanity can work towards a goal of total control of nature and happiness maximization. There is thus a goal – a *telos* – at the end of an *essentially* unilinear path.

It follows from the last point that the modern condition is a *dynamic* one, in which there is a belief in historical development from point A to point B – a concept of *progress*. This almost unquestioning belief that, despite hiccoughs, humanity is basically progressing towards something better is a key feature of modernity.

Again following on from the preceding points, modernity in its pure form implies a belief in discernible patterns of human behaviour and development and, with the refinement of appropriate techniques, in the capacity of humans to identify and label such patterns. For example, Darwinism is postulated on the assumption that we can work out and comprehend how humanity evolved from lower forms of life; it constitutes a good example of the belief in *grand theory* – or what is nowadays more frequently referred to as *meta-narratives* – that typifies pure modernity. Similarly, social scientists who embrace various forms of historicism – here meaning the belief that there are discernible patterns and 'laws' to historical development – are adopting what on one level can be seen as a particularly modern approach.

Finally, modernity implies rather clear-cut *divisions*, for what are perceived to be both practical and desirable reasons. The most obvious example, perhaps, is the division of labour; modernity's emphasis on rationality and efficiency suggests that individuals should become specialists, in contrast to the ideal of the rounded generalist of the Renaissance. But the notion of separate spheres of existence goes far beyond this. Within the fields of knowledge/science itself, boundaries become more sharply defined, and new disciplines (including political science) emerge; 'rational' analysis implies the dissection of complex wholes into more manageable parts, in theory the better ultimately to understand the whole. In the political sphere, there is both a horizontal divide between the newly emerging concept of 'the state' and 'civil society', and the vertical divide encapsulated in the American conception of 'separation of powers'.

In the discussion to this point, I have considered only what I take to be the basic epistemological and ontological tenets of modernity; as yet, there has been almost no consideration of how this abstract set of principles relates to the 'real world' of modernity. Before considering the latter, let us now – again, primarily for analytical and heuristic purposes – construct an ideal-type of post-modernity.[19] It must be strongly emphasized that such an ideal-type is highly subjective – there is an extensive and heated debate at present both on what post-modernity might be, and on whether it even exists.[20] The latter question will be briefly addressed at a later – more appropriate –point in the discussion. For now, a useful introductory suggestion is that post-modernity is above all a late-twentieth-century, Western reaction to the self-assuredness of modernity. Despite certain differences with Bauman, I can agree with his general definition of post-modernity, which he sees as: 'no more (but no less either) than modernity taking a long and attentive look at itself, not liking what it sees and sensing the urge to change . . . Post-modernity is modernity coming to terms with its own impossibility' (Bauman, 1990, p. 21). If we consider each of the six (closely related) component parts of modernity listed above from the point of view of post-modernity, the significant differences between the two approaches soon become obvious.

The faith of the modernists in the ability of humans to control the world around them is not shared by the post-modernists. Given what so many post-modernists see as the disastrous state of the world in the late twentieth century – with environmental pollution; mass starvation in the Third World; cold, hot and potentially nuclear wars; widespread alienation; etc. – there is a profound questioning of both the ability and the right of humans to believe they can and should and do control the universe. Such questioning means that mysticism becomes more acceptable (many 'new age' ideas, for instance) though not necessary; indeed, one of the salient features of post-modernity is that little, if anything, is prescribed.

Equally, the modernist faith in 'rationality' is cast in serious doubt by the post-modernist. The structured way of thinking typical of modernity is questioned, so that post-modernity often overlaps with post-structuralism. Post-modernity questions the very notion of trying to structure human thoughts and actions and creativity into set patterns – which is seen as an essentially limiting and even oppressive activity. The tendency towards technical, near automatic decision-making inherent within the modern project is seen as dehumanizing and, in a sense, too deterministic by the post-modernists. Conversely, the role of intuition in total understanding – knowledge – is treated with far greater respect. The post-modernist does not reject an 'explanation' simply because it does not fit into what are perceived to be essentially narrow and definable paradigms of rationality.

Teleologism is also anathema to the post-modern approach. Whether one is considering an explicit long-term goal (such as communism) or a more implicit one (such as the consumer-oriented pluralist democracy that seeks to maximize the satisfaction of the individual), the post-modernist rejects the notion of essentially gearing humanity towards any predetermined and structured goal.

Likewise, the post-modernist questions the very notion of progress and dynamism, being at least as aware of the negative aspects/ implications of what the modernist might call the 'march of history' as of its positive achievements.

In line with the above, post-modernity rejects the notion of what it calls meta-narratives, which – once again – can be seen to limit thought processes at least as much as they can be argued to bring order and rational interrelatedness to a multitude of phenomena. One major reason for this is that no theory can incorporate and explain *every* aspect of whatever phenomenon it is attempting to order and make sense of; in omitting those aspects that do not fit the theory, it is seen to be both inadequate and dishonest. At the same time, the devising and application of grand theories can on one level be seen as a form of domination, in that humans are attempting to impose order on complex phenomena that may or may not in fact have some internal logic.

Finally, the post-modern approach rejects the compartmentalization – the discipline and disciplinarity – of the modern approach to knowledge, perception and life generally.[21] It is argued that separating wholes into component parts – spheres of existence – is ultimately destructive, and that, for example, analysts in most cases do not in practice attempt better to understand the whole by reconstructing the (analysed) component parts. Instead, the 'modern' analyst tends to work within a given 'discipline', thus simultaneously having a very limited understanding of the whole at the same time as the discipline itself becomes in a sense fetishized, an activity in its own right that may have relatively little to do with a component part it was originally supposed to analyse. Such an approach is in essence exclusionary, and thus can obfuscate and mislead as much as explain. The post-modern approach, in contrast, is – to the extent that it can and/or should be labelled at all – best described as interdisciplinary and non-exclusionary.

The reader who is new to theories of modernity and post-modernity could well be forgiven for assuming that post-modernity is an essentially pessimistic, destructive way of approaching the world. In some senses, it is; it questions many of the most fundamental assumptions of the Western *Weltanschauung*, and this can be very unsettling for many people. In a sense, it is also highly introverted. It implies contemplation of everything we do, think, feel. But it can simultaneously be seen as a very liberating epistemology.

For instance, the self-reflexivity of the subject that is associated with the post-modern approach can on one level be seen as questioning the very notion of observer and observed in all forms of knowledge (science), which in a sense might be seen to lead to a worse understanding of the observed. On the other hand, it also means that we are less prone to treat the observed as 'other', at the same time as we become more aware of our own subjectivities. At one and the same time, therefore, the observer is dominating the observed far less, and possibly enhancing his/her understanding of both him/herself *and* the observed by being aware of his/her own subjectivities and acculturation. Partly as a consequence of this self-reflexivity and 'decentring the subject', the post-modern approach does not privilege or rank-order in the way modernity tends to. Post-modernity acknowledges the limitations of human endeavour, the negative implications of the clear and expansionist – and in many ways dominating – visions of modernity. It rejoices in diversity and tolerance; in post-modernity, no culture is to be privileged or to dominate any other. Genders and sexual preferences, races, religions, value-systems – all are to be treated on one level as being of equal worth. At the same time, they are not to be homogenized, standardized, reduced to universal sameness. Everything is 'other' – including oneself. By now, the more positive aspects of post-modernity should be emerging. Its emphasis on tolerance, non-domination and flexibility, plus its awareness of humanity's limitations, can be seen as attractive features. Moreover, its refusal to treat any theory or way of thinking as sacrosanct means it has a far greater potential to laugh at itself and the world than the more rigid ideal-type of modernity has. It is not obliged by its own logic to take itself seriously. This, together with the argument about the moves away from domination – including intellectual domination through structuring – is a major reason why post-modernity does not have to be seen as an exclusively pessimistic and destructive approach to life. To be sure, it has a number of disadvantages. Since it prefers not to privilege, it can be argued that it provides no guidance for the formation of any ethical bases to social formation. Its emphasis on tolerance can lead to a position in which the individual finds it difficult to make choices for fear of privileging one factor over another.[22]

But enough of such general observations on post-modernity. So far, both modernity and post-modernity have deliberately been treated as abstractions; the very use of the term 'ideal-types' implies this. Now we can turn to consider the so-called 'real world', to see how and to what extent the ideal-types can be related to our perception of that world.

In some aspects of the world around us, the distinction between a modern and a post-modern approach can be quite stark. In architecture, for instance, the differences between a 'typical' modern and a 'typical' post-modern building can be very obvious (for a particularly accessible introduction to this see Harvey, 1989, pp. 66–98). The post-modern building is less threatening and dominating, less overtly rational and functional, more decorative, etc. The differences between a modern and a post-modern building are thus often more visible and tangible than those between modern and post-modern social formations and/or modern and post-modern interpretations of such formations; the term 'social formations' is here used very broadly, to include economic and political formations.

Inasmuch as modernity is principally associated with Europe in the past two to three centuries, and the subsequent spread of the European 'model' to other parts of the world, it is also associated with the social, political and economic formations that have typified European development. In the early phases of modernity, this can be seen as a move away from a predominantly rural and towards an urbanized society; away from a predominantly agriculture-based and towards an industry-based society; away from feudalism and towards capitalism; away from autocracy and towards a legal-rational form of democracy; away from local/regional political formations and towards the large state (it is often overlooked that Italy, for instance, only came into existence in 1861, while Germany dates from 1871). Since so many analysts of modern politics argue that one of its principal features is the growing salience of the state – which by the nineteenth or twentieth century has in most developed countries become the key political actor – it is appropriate briefly to consider the major features of the modern state. According to Stuart Hall (1984, pp. 9–10), the distinguishing traits of the modern state are that:

1   Power is shared.
2   The rights to participate in government are legally or constitutionally defined.
3   Representation is wide.
4   Power is fully secular.
5   The boundaries of national sovereignty are clearly defined.

For Gianfranco Poggi (1978, esp. pp. 95–8) the four distinguishing features of the modern state are that it is:

1   consciously created or 'engineered';
2   teleological (it 'constantly operates with reference to some idea of an end or function to which it is instrumental');

3   functionally specific (it 'does not claim or attempt to encompass and control the totality of social existence');
4   'internally structured as a formal, complex organisation'.

As one begins to compare these actual developments and models of the component parts (in this case, the state) of modernity with the ideal-type, one can see many ways in which they interact with and reflect each other. For instance, the moves away from autocracy – often monarchy – towards parliamentarism and the rule of law are in line with the notions of humanism and rationality. Industrialism and urbanization brought with them a much clearer division of labour. Most of the major ideologies of the modern era – liberalism, socialism, communism, even fascism – incorporated in their different ways a commitment to dynamism and a better future. At the same time, and again in their various – often quite divergent – ways, they were ideologies based on meta-narratives. And much of both Hall's and Poggi's approaches to the modern state can readily be related to our ideal-type.

But we have also reached a point at which we need to reveal some of the most glaring contradictions of modernity. One of the most obvious of all is that the dominant economic formation of what many see as *actual* modernity is market-based capitalism. The stress on market economics is fundamentally at odds with the humanistic rationality and voluntarism of modernity, and – the pleas of Western economists notwithstanding – must be acknowledged as such.[23] Similarly, if perhaps not as immediately obviously, if pluralist democracy is supposed to be the least worst form of political arrangement, and if it is to be what its own name implies, then it must be seen to be in conflict with the essentially technocratic decision-making process that the logic of modernity would imply must be the optimal form. Thus, as one begins to compare the theory and practice of 'modernity', it becomes clear how vague and contradictory the term really is.

One can go further, and point to the substantial and fundamental differences between the practice of early and later modernity. Following 'The Great Crash' of October 1929, to take a good example, capitalism underwent a fundamental transformation. In response to economic problems, some countries went much further down a path that had already emerged in the 1920s, viz fascism. Other countries responded by introducing a 'new' form of economic management, associated nowadays above all with John Maynard Keynes, although one should not overlook the fact that Roosevelt's 'New Deal' was announced some three years before *The General Theory of Employ-*

ment, Interest and Money was published. Whether fascist or Keynesian, the notion of free-rein capitalism and genuine market economics was now clearly out of fashion, and was basically to remain so until the Friedmanite and Thatcherite counter-revolutions of the 1970s and 1980s; until this latest phase, the state was to become far more involved in the economy. During this phase, the very image of the state and its role changed dramatically. The emergence of the welfare state meant that earlier images of the state that had focused primarily on its coercive and dominating roles (*à la* Weber) had to be seriously modified. The coercive state had to become more caring; in a sense, it was to become more feminine. It could be argued that all this means is that later modernity has moved closer to the ideal-type than earlier modernity was. Perhaps this is indeed the case. But if it is, then the validity of talking about 'early' modernity must be questioned. Moreover, if the crisis of modernity in the West that Bauman and others refer to occurs precisely at a time when the practice of 'modern' systems more clearly approximates the ideal-type, then the fundamental contradictions of modernity become that much more pronounced.

This is even clearer if we examine Poggi's argument a little more closely. Thus – in contrast to the logic just followed – he argues that the nineteenth-century constitutional state (typically European) was closer to the ideal-type of the modern state than is the contemporary Western state; he describes the latter as 'the modern state in the post-liberal era' (p. 132). There are thus at least three discernible conceptions of the modern state in Poggi's book – the ideal-type, its nineteenth-century manifestation, and the twentieth-century version. This ambiguity – about just one aspect of modernity – is another example of the vagueness of the term 'modern'; if it can mean at least three different things to one analyst considering primarily just one dimension of it (the state), then it should be clear that it can have a very wide variety of meanings to the political science community as a whole (for further analyses of the modern state see, for example, McLennan, Held and Hall, 1984; Anderson, 1986a, Held, 1989).

What of the practice of post-modernity? There is probably even more debate over what, if anything, constitutes post-modern economics and politics than there is about the post-modern project as a theoretical exercise. What follows must necessarily be highly subjective and highly contentious. But I have no particular desire to avoid controversy – especially if, in being 'controversial', I am better able to make more sense of the communist and post-communist worlds.

To the extent that post-modernity is a conscious contemplation and often rejection of many of modernity's basic values, so many of these values are replaced. For instance, economic growth and constantly rising standards of living are no longer accepted, virtually uncritically, as a good thing; quality of life within a sustainable environment becomes more important than essentially crude conceptions of 'standard of living'. The efficient and rational approach to production typified by Fordism – such as the production line approach, in which the more like robots human workers become the better – is replaced by attempts to rehumanize the workplace. As basic values and structures change, so do sub-societal allegiances and formations; classes cease to be the single best predictor of political allegiance, and other cleavages become salient. Added to this is the fact that technological advances – themselves a reflection, to some extent, of the profit motive and wanting to out-perform one's competitors – lead to a change in the employment profile of societies. As the primary and secondary sectors of the economy decline (at least in relative terms) and/or become more automated, so the blue-collar workforce declines as a proportion of the total workforce. Conversely, service industries – and the workforces required to staff these – boom. Such developments and related ones have led writers such as Daniel Bell (1971, 1974), Ronald Inglehart (1977), Alain Touraine (1985) and others to refer to 'post-industrialism', 'post-materialism' and 'the new politics'. Although some see such developments as actually part of late (high) modernity, I have already argued that, in my view, the term modernity has now been used in such contradictory ways and to refer to such diverse social formations that it seems to me to be all but discredited; like the term totalitarianism, its main worth is as an ideal-type, for heuristic purposes.

Thus, again largely for analytical purposes, I shall here assume that post-industrialism, post-materialism and new politics are typical manifestations of the transition from modernity to post-modernity (for endorsement of the notion that new politics is often seen as a feature of post-modernity see Giddens, 1990, p. 46). While the meaning of the first two terms is virtually self-evident, the third requires unpacking.

'New' politics refers to both a style and a content of politics. Thus it places more emphasis than 'modern' politics on direct action, and it attempts to change what Touraine (1985, pp. 754–5) calls the 'main cultural patterns'. Unlike what many hold to be the dominant style of politics in modernity – parties based on class interests and ideologies, and groups trying to secure their interests by working through and/or with the formal institutions of the state – a prominent feature of the new politics of post-modernity is that groups or new social movements, which are not typically based on class or economy-related macro-ideologies, seek to transform basic values of society, as distinct from merely the policies of a government. It is believed that, in a competitive political system, the latter will change anyway if the former change occurs. These movements typically appeal to the public at least as much to the officers of the state. In a sense then, new politics is a means of asserting the dominance of (civil) society *over* the state, as distinct from elements of society appealing *to* the state. It is a form of enhanced citizen responsibility and the breaking down of traditional role differentiation; this is a major reason why such politics can be considered post-modern. Unlike typical West European parties, let alone the former East European communist parties, the new social movements 'have a loose and fluid structure; their membership is amorphous; they form spontaneously and can disappear quickly' (Jennett and Stewart, 1989, p. 1; for a more detailed definition see Pakulski, 1991, pp. 25–6). Moreover, most new social movements are less directly concerned with questions such as the ownership of the means of production and the distribution of wealth than with issues that do not fit neatly onto a left–right spectrum. These include the environment, war and peace, and the rights of various 'marginalized' groups. The emergence of green politics, peace activism, feminism, animal rights activism and the gay and lesbian movements are prime examples of the new type of social movement Touraine, Habermas (1981), Melucci (1981 and 1988), Offe (1985) and others focus on.

In the previous paragraph, reference was made to the changing attitudes of the citizenry towards the state. It has already been argued that the role of the state has undergone at least one major, perceptible change in the twentieth century (that is the emergence of the state's welfare functions). By the late twentieth century, it has become clear to many that the role of the state is changing in a fundamental way once again. Most notably, the notion of state sovereignty is in question, as countries either 'voluntarily'[24] yield some of their decision-making powers to supra-state organizations such as the UN or the EC and/or else *de facto* have to share some of their economic decision-making powers with transnational corporations. Even though, as the 'new institutionalists' (see, for example, Evans, Rueschemeyer and Skocpol, 1985) so forcefully argue, it would be premature to predict the imminent demise of one of the quintessential structures of modernity, the modern state, there can be little doubt that this state's role and even existence is being threatened and put in question by various developments in the contemporary world. Post-modernity cannot privilege the state in the way modernity did, and the term will have to be at least reconceptualized, if not abandoned, in the new political discourse.

Having produced ideal-types of both modernity and post-modernity, and having very briefly considered both some of the actual developments in Europe in recent centuries and analyses of some of the key political components of modernity and post-modernity, we are at last in a position to compare communist and post-communist systems with these more general abstractions and observations. Since I can see no good reason for structuring the argument in any but the most obvious way, I shall first consider communism in terms of modernity and then post-modernity, following which I shall analyse post-communism in the same way.

For Bauman, to the extent that he is consistent on this, socialism seems to represent an alternative model of a modern system from the capitalist liberal democracies of the West. Indeed, there can be little doubt that he is absolutely correct in suggesting that, in some cases, communist systems represented the epitome of modernity. Thus they went far beyond the average capitalist state in their belief that humanity could conquer nature and that reason can explain and dominate all; their policies on religion, moreover, were compatible with this humanism. They went far beyond the average capitalist state, too, in their belief in the advantages of economic and social planning, in their unquestioning faith in progress and production, in their overt teleologism, and in their historicist interpretation of social development. And there is no question that, in practice, they firmly adhered to and indeed advocated various divisions and specializations. In all these senses, then, they were the quintessential modern formation. But they were distinctly *un*modern in some of the key factors of political organization, and this incompatibility between modern goals and values on the one hand and modern formations on the other was one of the many factors leading to the collapse of communism. One of the drawbacks about not sufficiently involving the masses – about being so *relatively* undemocratic, in comparison with the liberal democracies – is precisely that the goals and values were not questioned enough in public until very late in the day. By suppressing open discussion, there was inadequate awareness among the officers of the state that they were pursuing *ideal* modern values which were too extreme and too pure for the real world. Only where there is a legitimate airing of a full range of political views are the excesses of the modern dream (or nightmare, according to one's perspective) contained. Rationality can only be limited; not everything can be explained by pure reason. 'Progress' is not without costs; it is precisely the arrogance of modernity – the notion that humanity can dominate the universe – that is leading to nature's backlash in the form of environmental degradation.

These were not the only ways in which the communist system was inadequate from the political perspective. If Weber, Poggi, et al. are correct in their assumption that the only form of legitimation appropriate to the modern state is legal-rationality, then – as this book has sought to prove – the communist states failed to meet the test. Of course, like the communist state, the modern liberal democracy *also* places considerable emphasis on eudaemonism, to the extent that it is sometimes seen as the dominant legitimation mode. The difference is that liberal democracies always have legal-rationality to revert to as their bedrock; communist states do not.

Yet another feature of the European communist states that was out of line with most interpretations of modernity was their class structure. To the extent that modernity is associated with late feudalism and, in particular, the capitalist epoch, it connotes private ownership of the means of production and a particular type of class structure derived from that. Without becoming embroiled in the old debate about whether or not there was a ruling class in communist systems, what is clear is that there was neither a regular bourgeoisie nor even a landed nobility to speak of in these countries. Indeed, one of the reasons there are so many problems for such countries in transition to a market economy is the near absence of a private property-owning class.

Let us now turn to consider the communist world – especially the USSR and Eastern Europe – up to 1989 specifically from the point of view of the state, using the criteria identified by Hall and Poggi. It soon becomes clear that several of these variables can indeed be applied to these countries. In all of them, state power was as secular as one ever finds; the boundaries were clearly defined, if not invariably uncontested; the states were consciously created; and they were clearly teleological – at least until towards the end. Controversially, perhaps, I would argue that they did not meet the condition of a 'formal, complex organization' as well as they might have done; while they were on one level complex, the nature of the relationship between the party and the state was still often unclear and operated in an informal manner. Nor were leadership arrangements properly formalized for the most part (Yugoslavia from 1980 was an exception). Hall's third point – about representation being wide – did not properly apply to communist states either. Although formal representation was extensive, this was generally of a superficial rather than a substantive nature. Representation patterns were basically decided by the state, which barely tolerated citizens' demands for more autonomous representation and involvement; while this varied from state to state – with Yugoslavia, Hungary and perhaps Poland at one end of the spectrum, Romania and Albania at the other – the fact is that citizens became increasingly irritated that they were not properly represented. Indeed, the very notion of a 'vanguard party' that leads the state and society is in some ways incompatible with this notion of wide and genuine representation. Of Poggi's features, the third is the one that East European states met least well; I shall return to this point below. Returning to Hall's criteria, the first was implemented only in a very inadequate and superficial way. There was no Weberian business elite to act as a counterweight to the politicians; the military and the various branches of the bureaucracy were to a large extent controlled by the communist party, via the *nomenklatura* system and other methods; the masses had little real say. The second criterion was again very imperfectly and superficially implemented in the communist world.

In sum, the argument here is that while socialism/communism represented an extreme form of *some aspects of* modernity (a point on which I am in full agreement with Bauman), in others – notably the political system, the actual economic system and some important aspects of social structure – it was either extra-modern or pre-modern, according to one's interpretation. Communism in Eastern Europe was never a complete, alternative version of modernity, but rather something *sui generis* that was *partially* modern in incorporating *some* values of modernity at the same time as it was out of line with others. For instance, inasmuch as the typical East European communist state *did*, until recently, 'claim or attempt to encompass and control the totality of social existence' (Poggi's third criterion), it was out of line with a key dimension of the politics of modernity. It follows from all this that the collapse of East European communist states could not *per se* represent a crisis of modernity, since they never adopted enough of the *actual* modern 'package' to be considered properly modern. The failure of their highly planned systems does not *necessarily* prove that planning, the commitment to technology and rationality, the belief in progress, etc., are redundant. Extreme forms of the modern idea were imposed on societies not yet ready for or wanting these forms, so that failure in such countries does not in itself tell us very much about the possibilities of such concepts and practices in other contexts. Even if the advocates of post-modernity are correct in their claim that the modern dream is fundamentally flawed, such conclusions do not have to relate to Eastern Europe at all; the arguments can be made purely on the basis of Western practice, or by subjecting the very *concept* of modernity to rigorous analysis (in terms of its own internal consistency, for instance). While one may well agree – and I do, to a limited extent – with the general point that modernity itself is in crisis (for instance, in that it has far less confidence in its own basic values than it once had), references to Eastern Europe as a major plank of such an argument seem to me to be unnecessary and misguided, even potentially misleading. The likelihood of eventual crisis in modernity was ever-present, since it has always contained potentially significant contradictions (the notion of pursuing liberty *and* equality simultaneously, for instance).

In what ways, if any, might communism be seen to have contained elements of post-modernity? At first sight, there is precious little that would seem even potentially and tentatively to qualify for the description 'post-modern' in the communist world. But one area in which some signs of post-modern politics could from *some* perspectives be argued to have become visible by the 1980s was in the emergence of a form of new social movements, as part of a nascent civil society. Possibly the clearest examples were to be found in the GDR, where opposition to the communist state was initially centred on an unofficial peace movement that was closely allied with the Evangelical Church (on this see Holmes, 1986b); this subsequently spawned and then interacted with both environmentalist and feminist groups. The effects of the Chernobyl disaster on consciousness-raising about the environment, plus the widespread concern about industrial pollution, acid rain, etc., led to the emergence by the late 1980s of small but often vocal green 'movements' in both the USSR (see Painter, 1991) and several of the East European states. For instance, the 'ecoglasnost' movement had by the late 1980s become the most significant unofficial political grouping in Bulgaria (see Crampton, 1990). Moreover, unofficial peace movements had become a feature of the Hungarian political landscape by the late 1980s. In a sense, it could be argued that such developments reflect the seeds of post-modern politics in the final stages of communist power. One could go further, and suggest that a new version of the 'law of uneven and combined development' might have been operating. By this I mean that some important changes in the communist world during the 1980s could have led to the inference that imperfectly modern societies might under certain circumstances be able to move rapidly towards post-modernity without having to traverse full modernity. Once the wheel – in this case, the post-modern condition – has been invented, there is no need for others to reinvent it; they can learn vicariously. But this line of argument is not very persuasive – and becomes less so if one examines a little more closely the nature of the 'new social movements' in late communism, and general political developments in the early years of post-communism.

Considering the former first, the activity of such movements needs to be contextualized. It must be seen, at least to some extent, as an example of what is sometimes referred to as 'Aesopian' political activity. For instance, the peace issue in the GDR was taken up by many citizens as much because it appeared to represent a method of demonstrating against the state with minimal risk (for a while, it could even result in an exit visa) as because of their commitment to the issue itself. 'New' politics was thus in many ways merely a form of anti-state politics, which is not particularly post-modern. Moreover, the significance of the examples cited should not be overstated. In Poland, for example, Solidarity was clearly the major unofficial political movement, and in my opinion should from most perspectives not be seen as post-modern, either in its aims, or in its methods, or in its structures (this point is elaborated in Holmes, 1992b; for a rather different – also very sophisticated and interesting – interpretation of Solidarity, see Pakulski, 1991, pp. 123–57; and for an argument that the percentage of post-materialists in Polish society by 1980 was higher than in most Western countries, see Inglehart and Siemienska, 1988, esp. p. 444).

As post-communism crystallizes, so it becomes clearer that many of the developments are more typical of what might be called actual modernity – in many ways, the *early* stages of modernity – than of post-modernity. Despite a professed commitment to the rule of law (legal-rationality), limited government, etc. the point has already been made that there are several indications that governments might become more authoritarian and autocratic – a feature typical of the early modern phase in Western Europe. Even in the country many have claimed has the strongest tradition of Western-style democracy and the best chances of re-establishing this, Czecho-Slovakia, there were by 1990 clear signs of a somewhat unhealthy personality cult developing around Václav Havel (see Glenny, 1990, pp. 44–7) – while popular faith in the strong leader was very overt in many parts of the former USSR by September 1991, not the least significant example of which was the cult developing around the increasingly autocratic Boris Yeltsin in Russia. The emphasis at present on creating a market system[25] is again a feature of early modernity rather than post-modernity. Moreover, as a (probably imperfect and distorted) version of capitalism develops, so might we see a class structure and societal cleavages that are closer to nineteenth-century Western Europe than to post-modernity.

Another very important reason why it would be premature to assume that post-communist systems might be in transition from modernity to post-modernity is that the basic economic problems of Eastern Europe and the former USSR will take many years to solve. While this is happening, most citizens are likely to be far more concerned with basic economic issues than with the post-materialist 'luxuries' of their Western counterparts. There will be some continuation, even development, of what might be called post-modern political formations, especially in the form of environmental movements. But the latter must currently be seen as being of marginal significance. Other 'new social movements' – feminist, gay/lesbian, peace oriented, animal rightist, etc. – are currently of even more limited relevance (on feminism, for instance, see Molyneux, 1990). While certain issues, such as abortion in Germany and perhaps Poland, could render such movements more significant, it seems – regretfully – that they are unlikely to become salient aspects of the political scene in most post-communist systems in the short to medium term. Thus the fact that what by some criteria looked like 'new social movements' with 'post-materialist' values played a role – sometimes significant – in the collapse of communism in some parts of Eastern Europe and the USSR should not *per se* be interpreted as a symbol of post-communism's ability to bypass full modernity and take a short cut to post-modernity.

One final point is that, to the extent that 'the West' (a misnomer, since it is generally taken to include Japan, Australasia, etc.) invests in the post-communist world, it is likely to be predominantly in more traditional industrial, as distinct from post-industrial, projects. In this sense, too, the post-communist states are further from the post-modern ideal-type than are the Western states.

All the above notwithstanding, there are just a few indications that post-communism incorporates elements of post-modernity. Two of the most obvious candidates for inclusion are the apparent rejection of meta-narratives and teleologism, and what could be argued to be the declining role of the state. Regarding the former, for instance, many commentators in the Western media have claimed that, with the rejection of communism, many citizens of the former communist states have lost faith in grand theories altogether.[26]

As for the role of the state, the ongoing disintegration of what were Yugoslavia and the USSR – plus the possibility of the break-up of Czecho-Slovakia and perhaps even other states – can on one level be seen as grounds for arguing that the concept of the state is currently being questioned in the post-communist world. Certainly, side by side with these disintegrative processes, there are indications that integrative processes not unlike those currently underway in Western Europe might also be occurring in at least parts of Eastern Europe. Most notably, the so-called Visegrad Summit of February 1991 provided evidence to suggest that Hungary, Poland and Czecho Slovakia (perhaps eventually just Bohemia or the Czech lands) might well form an economic bloc in the future, in which each country will more or less voluntarily yield some of its sovereignty in the economic sphere. There is also a possibility that something along these lines could emerge in the Balkans, and even between various East European economic blocs and parts of the former USSR (a sort of revamped and far more egalitarian CMEA). However, one must again be careful not to pursue this argument about the emergence of a new kind of state too far and prematurely. The break-up of existing multi-ethnic states and the formation of new, smaller units might in some ways be seen as a correction of another of the misnomers of political science. In much of comparative politics, the term 'nation-state' is used to refer to political units that were in many ways artificial creations, often the product of Great Power negotiations and/or domination, with relatively little regard for traditional ethnic sensitivities. Present developments might lead to the creation of what can more correctly be called 'nation-states'. In that they are more overtly part of the world economy – the so-called global village – and must therefore accept limitations on their sovereignty, as must Western states, there is a limit to the extent that they can legitimately be compared with West European states of the nineteenth century. But if the assumption here is correct that many, perhaps most, citizens in the post-communist systems will still look – indeed, increasingly look – to the state and/or politicians to solve their problems, the notion that they should be seen as being in transition to a post-modern political condition would appear to be quite inappropriate. At the very least, such a conclusion must presently be seen as premature.

Where does all this leave us? I have argued that both modernity and post-modernity are themselves problematical, contradictory and vague as concepts – and even more so when we try to apply them to the 'real world'. Nevertheless, I have also accepted that – *within limits* – they are useful as heuristic devices, for helping us to understand better the various 'realities' something inside many of us makes us want to analyse. I have argued that communist states had many modern values – often taken to an extreme level – but few modern forms. I have further suggested that the post-communist states display rather more features of what can, in the absence of any better term, be called early modernity than of late modernity or of post-modernity – even though elements of both of the latter can be found.

The future of post-communism is very uncertain, although I have argued that the short-term future is, on balance, less encouraging than the long-term future. Some have suggested that the example of Southern European transitions from dictatorship to democracy in the 1970s (Spain, Portugal and perhaps Greece) indicates that it is possible for countries successfully to make a relatively smooth and rapid transition to a liberal-democratic system in its broad sense – and that this gives us grounds for optimism about the future of the post-communist states. There is, however, one major flaw in this argument and analogy. This is that the economy in the Southern European states was already largely privatized and marketized at the time of the collapse of the dictatorships. Nor did any of those countries have economic problems on a scale that at least many of the post-communist states have. In short, one should be wary of making inferences on the basis of such a comparison. For different reasons, one should also be wary of too readily drawing comparisons with either the NIEs or Latin America. Cultural, structural, geopolitical and other differences between the post-communist states and either the NIEs or Latin America are in many cases substantial. For these reasons, the short-term future of post-communism is particularly difficult to predict. While my own view is that liberal democracy in its broad sense is an arrangement towards which all societies move sooner or later, the paths to it are highly divergent and often involve considerable pain. Not the logic of social science, but mere human optimism, leads me to hope that the future of post-communism will be brighter than many of my own arguments would lead me, rationally, to conclude.

A Final Observation

A fortuitous observation about anti-corruption campaigns in the early 1980s has led to an analysis of the fall of communism and the problematical emergence of post-communism. For all the uncertainties and confusions identified in the last few pages, one thing is clear; many of the factors that resulted in corruption in the communist world will pertain in the post-communist world, whichever direction(s) it takes.

NOTES

1   Interestingly, it was again France that came closest to systemic collapse during the 1968 'events' in the First World. Some analysts have argued that although Western systems survived 1968, the seeds were sown for the *possible* emergence of a new, socialist world-system – on this, but also on the possibilities of much bleaker alternative scenarios, see Arrighi, Hopkins and Wallerstein, 1989, esp. pp. 97–115.

2   It is interesting to note at this point that while Vietnam has shown signs of moving towards 'modernity' and legal-rationality in terms of several of the variables listed here, some of its legal norms were still different in North and South in the late 1980s – see *IB*, Vol. 25, No. 21, 1987, p. 57.

3   For a Soviet argument that Lenin favoured the 'socialist legal state', and that Stalin's prosecutor, Vyshinsky, was largely to blame for the decline of the rule of law in the USSR, see Y. Feofanov's article in *Izvestiya*, 11 August 1987, pp. 1 and 3. During a discussion I had with Savitsky in Moscow in June 1991, the latter acknowledged that he had now come to the conclusion that the notion of a *'socialist* legal state' was in many ways contradictory.

4   Note, however, that Seiffert concluded that the law-based state is incompatible with a system based on Marxism-Leninism.

5   It should be noted that the law contained provisions designed to protect officials against slanderous attacks by individuals – yet another symbol of the desire to develop the rule-of-law culture.

6   In connection with the point about general secretaries also being heads of states, it should be borne in mind that there were signs that this could be part of the transition process too, whereby one individual would seek to occupy both posts partially in order to oversee personally the decline of the role of the general secretary and the enhancement of the role of head of state. Gorbachev's actions in 1990 (that is, his filling of the new post of Soviet president in March while retaining the general secretaryship at the 28th Party Congress in July) conform well with this interpretation. Gorbachev renounced the general secretaryship in late August 1991, by which time the CPSU had lost virtually all credibility and respect; this constituted yet another stage – arguably the last major one – in the transition to a post-(communist) party political arrangement and hence to post-communism.

7   Indeed, Gorbachev let it be known at the time of the March 1989 Soviet elections that Politburo members (that is, senior *party* officials) who were rejected by the electorate – in *state* elections – might lose their party offices. It thus came as no surprise when Solov'ev, who was rejected by the Leningrad electorate, lost his candidate membership of the Politburo in September 1989.

8   In 1987, Zhao Ziyang officially acknowledged conflicting interests in Chinese society, and spoke of the need for the party to reconcile and coordinate different kinds of interest and contradiction. Michel Oksenberg (1987, p. 13) has described the implications of Zhao's remarks as 'profound', in that they (implicitly) represented the first official acknowledgement by the Chinese communists of the legitimacy of a form of pluralism (for a Chinese analysis of interest groups in the PRC see *BR*, Vol. 30, No. 48, 1987, pp. 14–15). For party leader Jakeš arguing that socialist pluralism was acceptable in communist Czechoslovakia, see *IB*, Vol. 26, No. 5, 1988, p. 31, and No. 14, 1988, p. 17.

9   According to Arato (1982, p. 196): 'the inherent crisis tendencies of state-socialist societies can be "managed" in the long-run only if, on the level of system integration, there is a transition from a high level of penetration of the socialist spheres by the political institutional core (positive subordination) to a lower level of penetration (negative subordination)'. He went on to argue (see esp. pp. 207–10) that the communist – or state-socialist, as he prefers to call them – states would seek to reform the economy in a major way, while at the same time preventing the constitution or reconstitution of civil society. In this way, the crises that would be caused by the emergence of civil society in a system that is organizationally incapable of recognizing civil society can be avoided:

> It is possible for the political-administrative system to execute a withdrawal from the economic sphere, and even to institutionalise this in terms of legal reform, without depoliticising the socio-cultural sphere and without generally pluralising the political sphere itself. The possibility exists of restructuring the 'dual state' within which the prerogative state must remain predominant over the normative state. Its restructuring would combine the features of a Rechtsstaat in relation to a reformed economy with the elements of the political prerogative state whose limits of intervention in culture, everyday life and the non-economic dimensions of administration will be defined only by itself. In other words, in order to establish a higher degree of depoliticisation of the economy without 'spillover', the party–state structure must execute the kind of 'uncoupling' (Habermas) or 'disjunctivity' (Offe) of administrative and political institutions, or rather of those institutions that would protect the link between the prerogative state and the socio-cultural sphere from the demands of legality, rationality and publicity. (Arato, 1982, p. 209).

Clearly, Arato accurately – and impressively – predicted many of the most important developments in the communist world of the mid to late 1980s, including the partial emergence of the *Rechtsstaat*. On the other hand, he underestimated the degree of contradiction that existed between economic reform and the emergence of civil society. This may have been because he believed economic reform could be more successful than it was in most communist states; the fact that so many of them – including the USSR – provided inadequate, misleading or even mendacious economic data would be a very understandable reason for this. This all said, it is possible to argue that the PRC accords well with his argument – though only if one believes that the 1989 'events' did not reflect a fundamental crisis.

For a recent analysis of the emergence of 'civil society' in the USSR see Kukathas, Lovell and Maley, 1991. A more comparative analysis of civil society in communist countries can be found in R. Miller, 1992.

10 It should not be overlooked, for instance, that China's, Vietnam's and Laos's economic policies revealed the abandonment of several key aspects of communist rule, while there were clearly chinks even in North Korean and Cuban communism.

11 Since this book went to press, Albania has clearly moved to post-communism proper (March–April 1992), and most would agree that Afghanistan also had by April 1992. Other countries – such as Congo and Mongolia – had also moved closer to post-communism.

The classification of a given country as 'in transition to post-communism' or clearly post-communist' must, ultimately, be a matter of judgement. For the purposes of classification in this book, I have opted to call a given political unit 'transitional' if there are clear indications that the communists have renounced their 'leading role' and are prepared to compete against other political parties (that is, I focus on *political* aspects of the rejection of the communist system, rather than economic ones). Typically *after* this stage has been reached, a government – here meaning the principal decision-making body in the system – might be formed in which the communists constitute a minority; this can be seen as the first stage of post-communism. A higher stage – what might be termed 'post-communism proper' – is reached when the population has, through elections, chosen a parliament in which non-communists outnumber 'communists' (the latter term includes former communists who have re-named themselves but whose statements and/or actions reveal that they retain many of their earlier values and attitudes).

12   The term 'double rejective revolution' was employed earlier in this study to encapsulate the essence of the 1989–91 events. Like most such forms of shorthand, the term has its limitations. Thus Albania's revolution was not in any meaningful sense a rejection of perceived external domination, and should therefore more correctly be described as single rejective. Another exception might – according to one's perspective – be the GDR; it can be argued that, unlike other East Europeans, the East Germans gave up their own separate identity/sovereignty, and in this sense engaged in a *triple* rejection.

13   Since the unification of Germany in October 1990, many South Koreans seem to have become less enthusiastic about reunification, largely because of the enormous costs that are likely to be involved. But patriotism and nationalism can be very powerful forces, and I remain of the view that the two Koreas will unite despite the costs – of various kinds – involved. This will be even more likely if the teething problems of German unification are successfully over-come.

14   The GDR is a very special case, however, and I have argued elsewhere (Holmes, 1992a) that dissidents played a much smaller role in the collapse of communism there than they may have done in several other communist states. Hence, although the correlation outlined in the third hypothesis does work with the GDR, one should be wary of over-hasty and inappropriate inferences about causal relationships.

15   It is interesting to note at this juncture that one of the many reasons for failure symbolized how far the USSR had moved towards legal-rationality; even the hard-line plotters of the 19 August coup – KGB Chief Kryuchkov, Interior Minister Pugo, Defence Minister Yazov, etc. – apparently felt the need to make the attempted takeover appear more or less constitutional. Had they been more Machiavellian (or Stalinist) – more ruthless and efficient – they might have been able to retain power for more than the approximately three days they did.

16   It should be noted that many of the new political organizations that have been identified by Western observers as 'parties' did not, in fact, include the word 'party' in their formal titles; examples include the Union of Democratic Forces in Bulgaria, Civic Forum and Public Against Violence in Czecho-Slovakia, and Democratic Forum in Hungary. The three most common reasons for this were that the word 'party' was associated in most citizens' minds with the *communist* party, from which the new organizations typically wished to distance them-selves as much as possible; many such organizations were essentially coalitions; and some were established *before* formal legalization of opposition parties, and

sought not to give the communists too obvious a reason for clamping down on them.

17 The term 'new authoritarianism' has frequently been used in recent analyses of Chinese (PRC) politics – for one of the most comprehensive collections on this see Liu and Li, 1989 (I am grateful to Dr Michael Dutton for having alerted me to this source and translating some key passages of it for me from the Mandarin).

18 Fehér (1990, p. 37) argues that what was for many analysts the unexpectedly high level of support for the former communist party in the GDR can best be explained in terms of 'a hypertrophically enlarged state bureaucracy, which has no special affinity with communism, but which does have a very strong sense of job security in the new situation and which finds a shield in the successor party'. His argument may well account for *some* of the success, although it seems unlikely that it was mostly bureaucrats who supported the PDS in the many cities in which, at the time of both the March general elections and the May local elections, the former communists secured some 25–30 per cent of the vote (for details and analysis of the electoral results see Winters, 1990a and 1990b). Fehér does not spell out why the bureaucracy would be very different in the GDR from that in other East European countries in which support for the communists was much lower; presumably, one of the biggest differences was that many bureaucrats in other East European states may have felt that their expertise would still be required by a post-communist state, whereas the East German bureaucrats could well have feared that West German counterparts would replace them.

19 Despite reservations about drawing too sharp a distinction between the arts and the social sciences, I broadly accept the distinction Giddens (1990, esp. pp. 45–6) draws between 'post-modernism' and 'post-modernity' – certainly for analytical and heuristic purposes. However, I know of no tidy way of distinguishing between an individual who advocates 'post-modernism' and one arguing for 'post-modernity'; thus, in the following discussion, the latter is called a post-modernist, despite my awareness of possible ambiguity here.

20 In a (typically) confusing approach, Lyotard (1984, p. 79) writes 'What, then, is the postmodern? . . . It is undoubtedly a part of the modern.' Not only does this render it difficult to distinguish post-modernity, but it also further muddies the concept of modernity.

21 As argued here, the blurring of differences and breaking down of set roles is usually held to be one of the salient features of post-modernity. This comes out nicely in Kellner's excellent introduction to post-modernity, in which, *inter alia*, he paraphrases Baudrillard:

> Whereas modernity was characterised by the explosion of commodification, mechanization, technology, exchange and the market, postmodern society is the site of an *implosion* of all boundaries, regions and distinctions between high and low culture, appearance and reality, and just about every other binary opposition maintained by traditional philosophy and social theory . . . Thus while modernity could be characterised as a process of increasing differentiation of spheres of life . . . postmodernity could be interpreted as a process of *dedifferentiation*. (Kellner, 1988, pp. 242–3 – original emphasis)

It is worth noting that towards the end of his article Kellner – possibly unwittingly – highlights an irony and contradiction in the post-modernists' own desire to eradicate classifications and binary oppositions in knowledge when he writes: 'Habermas and other Critical Theorists tend to reject the borderline between modernity and postmodernity that many new French theorists are eager to defend' (Kellner, 1988, p. 266). It is also worth pointing out that although most of the major theorists of post-modernity are anti-Marx (Fredric Jameson being an exception), some of their most basic arguments seem to be for the breakdown of divisions, *even within the individual*, that Marx advocated in *The German Ideology* – on one of several occasions when Marx appeared to be more post-modern than modern.

22 However, these criticisms have limited validity. Tolerance itself can be seen as an ethical code, while it is the *imposition* of value systems, rather than the right of the individual to choose and privilege freely, that is attacked by many post-modernists.

23 The 'rationality' of the market is really an inferred rationality, based on an assumption about the aggregate effects of 'rational' (self-interested) choices by individuals.

24 The word 'voluntarily' is in inverted commas in order to indicate that many – perhaps all – states yield sovereignty because they feel there is no viable alternative, rather than because they have a strong normative disposition to do so.

25 It should be noted that there were still, by 1990–1, major debates within several late-communist and post-communist states on how far and fast one should proceed with the creation of a market system. The differences between Havel and Klaus in Czecho-Slovakia constitute a fine example. During 1990, the debates between Yeltsin/Shatalin/Koryagina on the one hand and Ryzhkov/Abalkin on the other represent a good Soviet example.

26 As indicated earlier, my own view is that there was initially a *vague* belief in a new ideology and practice – 'the' Western-style system – but that disappointment in this is already setting in and being replaced by an ideological vacuum. It will be recalled that I argued that many citizens had ultimately a very limited understanding of both democracy and market economics; visits during 1990 and 1991 to a number of late communist and post-communist states (Poland, Czecho-Slovakia, Eastern Germany and Russia) only strengthened my conviction that such people had never really appreciated the costs, of various kinds, of these concepts and practices. This is part of the reason for the disappointment, which in turn strengthens the rejection of *any* teleological ideology or meta-narrative at present – at the same time as there are the rather contradictory and unrealistic aspirations *some* leaders and citizens have for the 'third way'.

Bibliography

Adelman, J. (ed.) (1984), *Terror and Communist Politics: The Role of the Secret Police in Communist States* (Boulder, Co: Westview).

Aganbegyan, A. (1988), 'The Economics of Perestroika', *International Affairs*, Vol. 64, No. 2 (Spring), pp. 177–85.

Allen, C. (1988), 'Benin', in C. Allen, M. Radu, K. Somerville and J. Baxter, *Benin: The Congo: Burkina Faso* (London: Pinter), pp. 1–144.

Almond, G. (1987), 'The Development of Political Development', in M. Weiner and S. Huntington (eds), *Understanding Political Development* (Boston: Little Brown), pp. 437–90.

Althusser, L. (1971), *Lenin and Philosophy and Other Essays* (New York: Monthly Review Press).

Anderson, J. (ed.) (1986a), *The Rise of the Modern State* (Brighton: Wheatsheaf).

Anderson, J. (1986b), 'The Modernity of Modern States', in Anderson (1986a), pp. 1–20.

Antonyan, Yu. (1975), 'Sotsial'no-psikhologicheskie posledstviya urbanizatsii i ikh vliyanie na prestupnost', *Sovetskoe Gosudarstvo i Pravo*, No. 8 (August), pp. 67–73.

Arato, A. (1982), 'Critical Sociology and Authoritarian State Socialism', in Thompson and Held (1982), pp. 196–218.

Arrighi, G., Hopkins, T. and Wallerstein, I. (1989), *Antisystemic Movements* (London: Verso).

Ashley, S. (1988), 'Corruption and Glasnost', *RFE Research*, Vol. 13, No. 14, Pt. 2 (8 April), pp. 3–7.

Aslund, A. (1985), *Private Enterprise in Eastern Europe: The Non-Agricultural Private Sector in Poland and the GDR* (New York: St Martin's).

Baglai, M. (1989), 'Pravovoe Gosudarstvo: Ot Idei K Praktike', *Kommunist*, No. 6 (April), pp. 38–47.

Banfield, E. C. (1961), *Political Influence* (New York: The Free Press of Glencoe).

Baum, R. (1986), 'Modernization and Legal Reform in Post-Mao China: The Rebirth of Socialist Legality', *Studies in Comparative Communism*, Vol. 19, No. 2, pp. 69–103.

Bauman, Z. (1990), 'From Pillar to Post', *Marxism Today*, February, pp. 20–5.

Baylis, T. (1972), 'In Quest of Legitimacy', *Problems of Communism*, Vol. 21, No. 2, pp. 46–55.

Baylis, T. (1974), *The Technical Intelligentsia and the East German Elite: Legitimacy and Social Change in Mature Communism* (Berkeley, CA, and Los Angeles: University of California Press).

Bedeski, R. (1987), 'Elections in China: A Comparative Overview', *Asian Perspective*, Vol. 11, No. 2, pp. 201–17.

Bell, D. (1971), 'The Post-Industrial Society: The Evolution of an Idea', *Survey*, Vol. 17, No. 2, pp. 102–68.

Bell, D. (1974), *The Coming of Post-Industrial Society* (London: Heinemann).

Beresford, M. (1988), *Vietnam: Politics, Economics and Society* (London: Frances Pinter).

Berg, G. van den (1985), *The Soviet System of Justice: Figures and Policy* (Dordrecht: Martinus Nijhoff).

Bialer, S. (1980), *Stalin's Successors* (Cambridge: Cambridge University Press).

Biberaj, E. (1987), 'Albania's Economic Reform Dilemma', *The World Today*, Vol. 43, No. 10 (October), pp. 180–2.

Binns, P. and Hallas, D. (1976), 'The Soviet Union – State Capitalist or Socialist?' *International Socialist*, No. 91 (September), pp. 16–27.

Brown, A. and Kaser, M. (eds) (1978), *The Soviet Union Since the Fall of Khrushchev* (London: Macmillan).

Brown, J.F. (1991), *The Surge to Freedom* (Durham, NC: Duke University Press).

Brugger, B. (1977), *Contemporary China* (London: Macmillan).

Brunner, G. (1982), 'Legitimacy Doctrines and Legitimation Procedures in East European Systems' in Rigby and Fehér (1982), pp. 27–44.

Brzezinski, Z. (1967), *The Soviet Bloc* (Cambridge, MA: Harvard University Press).

Brzezinski, Z. (1989), *The Grand Failure: The Birth and Death of Communism in the Twentieth Century* (New York: Scribners).

Brzezinski, Z. (1990), 'Post-Communist Nationalism', *Foreign Affairs*, Vol. 68, No. 5, pp. 1–25.

Burns, J.P. (1987), 'China's Nomenklatura System', *Problems of Communism*, Vol. 36, No. 5, pp. 35–51.

Castro, F. (1982), *Speeches at Three Congresses* (Havana: Editora Politica).

Castro, F. (1983), *Our Power is that of the Working People* (New York: Pathfinder).

Chalidze, V. (1977), *Criminal Russia: Essays on Crime in the Soviet Union*, (New York: Random House).

Chan, A., Rosen, S. and Unger, J. (eds), (1985), *On Socialist Democracy and the Chinese Legal System* (Armonk, NY: Sharpe).

Chen Yun (1985a), 'Speech at the National Conference of the Communist Party of China', in *Chinese Communist Party* (1985), pp. 89–96.

Chen Yun (1985b), 'Speech at the Sixth Plenary Session of the Central Commission for Discipline Inspectors', in *Chinese Communist Party* (1985), pp. 105–10.

Cheng Jin (1986), *A Chronology of the People's Republic of China 1949–1984* (Beijing: Foreign Languages Press).

Cheng, Joseph (ed.) (1989), *China: Modernization in the 1980s* (Hong Kong: The Chinese University Press).

Chinese Communist Party (1982), *The Twelfth National Congress of the CPC* (Beijing: Foreign Languages Press).

Chinese Communist Party (1985), *Uphold Reform and Strive for the Realization of Socialist Modernization* (Beijing: Foreign Languages Press).

Chinese Communist Party (1987), *Documents of the Thirteenth National Congress of the Communist Party of China* (Beijing: Foreign Languages Press).

Chossudovsky, M. (1986), *Towards Capitalist Restoration? Chinese Socialism After Mao* (London: Macmillan).

Clarke, M. (ed.) (1983a), *Corruption: Causes, Consequences and Control* (London: Frances Pinter).

Clarke, M. (1983b), 'Introduction', in Clarke (1983a), pp. ix–xix.

Cliff, T. (1974), *State Capitalism in Russia* (London: Pluto).
Cobler, S. (1978), *Law, Order and Politics in West Germany* (Harmondsworth: Penguin).
Comisso, E. and D'Andrea Tyson, L. (eds) (1986), *Power, Purpose, and Collective Choice* (Ithaca NY: Cornell University Press).
Connolly, W. (ed.) (1984a), *Legitimacy and the State* (Oxford: Blackwell).
Connolly, W. (1984b), 'Introduction: Legitimacy and Modernity', in Connolly (1984a), pp. 1–19.
Connor, W. (1979), *Socialism, Politics and Equality* (New York: Columbia University Press).
Conquest, R. (1971), *The Great Terror* (Harmondsworth: Penguin).
Crampton, R. (1990), 'The Intelligentsia, the Ecology and the Opposition in Bulgaria', *The World Today*, Vol. 46, No. 2, pp. 23–6.
Critchlow, J. (1988), 'Corruption, Nationalism, and the Native Elites in Soviet Central Asia', *The Journal of Communist Studies*, Vol. 4, No. 2, pp. 142–61.
Csapo, L. (1988), *The General Crisis of the Soviet Model of the Collectivist Society* (Bundoora: La Trobe University School of Economics).
Dallin, A. and Breslauer, G. (1970), *Political Terror in Communist Systems* (Stanford: Stanford University Press).
De Flers, R. (1984), 'Socialism in One Family', *Survey*, Vol. 28, No. 4, pp. 165–75.
Deng Xiaoping (1984), *Selected Works of Deng Xiaoping* (Beijing: Foreign Languages Press).
Deng Xiaoping (1985), *Build Socialism with Chinese Characteristics* (Beijing: Foreign Languages Press).
Deng Xiaoping (1987), *Fundamental Issues In Present-Day China* (Beijing: Foreign Languages Press).
Denitch, B. (1976), *The Legitimation of a Revolution: The Yugoslav Case* (New Haven: Yale University Press).
Denitch, B. (ed.) (1979), *Legitimation of Regimes, International Framework of Analysis* (Beverly Hills: Sage).
Dobel, J. (1978), 'The Corruption of a State', *American Political Science Review*, Vol. 72, No. 3, pp. 958–73.
Drewnowski, J. (ed.) (1982), *Crisis in the East European Economy* (London: Croom Helm).
Ellman, M. (1969), *Economic Reform in the Soviet Union* (London: PEP).
Evans, P., Rueschemeyer, D. and Skocpol, T. (1985), *Bringing the State Back In* (Cambridge: Cambridge University Press).
Fainsod, M. (1954), *How Russia is Ruled* (Cambridge, MA: Harvard University Press).
Fedorchuk, V. (1985), 'Neuklonno Ukreplyat' Pravoporyadok', *Kommunist*, No. 12, pp. 67–79.
Fehér, F. (1990), 'The Left After Communism', *Thesis Eleven*, No. 27, pp. 20–39.
Fehér, F., Heller, A. and Márkus, G. (1984), *Dictatorship over Needs* (Oxford: Blackwell).
Feldbrugge, F. (1984), 'Government and Shadow Economy in the Soviet Union', *Soviet Studies*, Vol. 36, No. 4, pp. 528–43.
Fisk, W.M., (1969), 'A Communist Rechtsstaat? The Case of Yugoslav Constitutionalism', *Government and Opposition*, Vol. 5, No. 1, pp. 41–53.
Fleron, F. (ed.) (1969), *Communist Studies and the Social Sciences* (Chicago: Rand McNally).
Forster, K. (1985), 'The 1982 Campaign against Economic Crime in China', *Australian Journal of Chinese Affairs*, No. 14, pp. 1–19.

Frankland, M. (1966), *Khrushchev* (Harmondsworth: Penguin).

Frentzel-Zagorska, J. (1989), 'Semi-Free Elections in Poland', unpublished paper presented at the Australasian Political Studies Association Conference, Sydney (September).

Friedrich, C.J. (1966), 'Political Pathology', *The Political Quarterly*, Vol. 37, No. 1, pp. 70–85.

Gdlyan, T. and Dodolev, E. (1990), *Piramida-1* (Moscow: APS).

Ghermani, D. (1983), 'Rumänien im Kampf gegen die Korruption', *Südosteuropa*, Vol. 32, No. 6, pp. 317–26.

Giddens, A. (1977), *Studies in Social and Political Theory* (London: Hutchinson).

Giddens, A. (1990), *The Consequences of Modernity* (Cambridge: Polity).

Gilison, J. (1972), *British and Soviet Politics: Legitimacy and Convergence* (Baltimore: The Johns Hopkins Press).

Gill, G. (1982), 'Personal Dominance and the Collective Principle: Individual Legitimacy in Marxist-Leninist Systems', in Rigby and Fehér (1982), pp. 94–110.

Gill, G. (1986), 'Changing Patterns of Systemic Legitimation in the USSR', *Coexistence*, No. 23, pp. 247–66.

Gill, G. (1987), 'The Programmatic Documents of the 27th Congress' in Miller, Miller and Rigby (1987), pp. 40–60.

Gitelman, Z. (1970), 'Power and Authority in Eastern Europe', in Johnson (1970), pp. 235–63.

Glenny, M. (1990), *The Rebirth of History* (London: Penguin).

Goldman, M. (1983), *USSR in Crisis: The Failure of an Economic System* (New York: Norton).

Gonzalez, E. (1974), *Cuba under Castro* (Boston: Houghton Mifflin).

Goodman, D. (1985), 'The Chinese Political Order After Mao: "Socialist Democracy" and the Exercise of State Power', *Political Studies*, Vol. 33, No. 4, pp. 218–35.

Gorbachev, M. (1986), *Political Report of the CPSU Central Committee to the 27th Congress of the Communist Party of the Soviet Union* (Moscow: Novosti).

Gorbachev, M. (1987), *Perestroika* (London: Collins).

Grossman, G. (1977), 'The "Second Economy" of the USSR', *Problems of Communism*, Vol. 26, No. 5, pp. 25–40.

Grossman, G. (1979), 'Notes on the Illegal Private Economy and Corruption', in US Congress Joint Economic Committee, *The Soviet Economy in a Time of Change*, Vol. 1, (Washington: US Government Printing Office), pp. 834–55.

Habermas, J. (1973), 'What Does a Legitimation Crisis Mean Today? Legitimation Problems in Late Capitalism', in Connolly (1984a), pp. 134–79.

Habermas, J. (1976), *Legitimation Crisis* (London: Heinemann).

Habermas, J. (1981), 'New Social Movements', *Telos*, No. 49, pp. 33–7.

Habermas, J. (1987), *The Philosophical Discourse of Modernity* (Cambridge, MA: MIT Press).

Habermas, J. (1990), 'What Does Socialism Mean Today? The Rectifying Revolution and the Need for New Thinking on the Left', *New Left Review*, No. 183, pp. 3–21.

Hahn, W. (1987), 'Electoral Choice in the Soviet Bloc', *Problems of Communism*, Vol. 36, No. 2, pp. 29–39.

Hall, S. (1984), 'The State in Question', in McLennan, Held and Hall (1984), pp. 1–28.

Hanlon, J. (1984), *Mozambique* (London: Zed Books).

Hannan, K. (1988), 'A Weberian "Understanding" of Chinese Economic Reform', unpublished paper presented at the Australasian Political Studies Association Conference, Armidale (August).

Harasymiw, B. (1969), 'Nomenklatura: The Soviet Communist Party's Leadership Recruitment System', *Canadian Journal of Political Science*, Vol. 2, No. 3, pp. 493–512.

Harris, P. (1986), 'Socialist Graft: The Soviet Union and the People's Republic of China – A Preliminary Survey', *Corruption and Reform*, Vol. 1, No. 1, pp. 13–32.

Hart, H. and Keeri-Santo, E. (1978), 'Approval and Rejection of the "Basic Idea of Comunism" (Czechoslovakia, Hungary, Poland)', *Communications*, No. 4, pp. 361–4.

Harvey, D. (1989), *The Condition of Post-Modernity* (Oxford: Blackwell).

Hawkes, N. (ed.) (1990), *Tearing Down the Curtain* (London: Hodder and Stoughton).

He Baogang (1989), 'Legitimacy in Chinese Politics – A Critical Re-Appraisal', unpublished paper presented at the conference 'China 40 Years after the Revolution', Sydney (September).

Heidenheimer, A. (ed.) (1970a), *Political Corruption* (New York: Holt, Rinehart and Winston).

Heidenheimer, A. (1970b), 'Introduction', in Heidenheimer (1970a), pp. 3–28.

Held, D. (1982), 'Crisis Tendencies, Legitimation and the State', in Thompson and Held (1982), pp. 181–95.

Held, D. (1989), *Political Theory and the Modern State* (Cambridge: Polity).

Heller, A. (1982), 'Phases of Legitimation in Soviet-type Societies', in Rigby and Fehér (1982), pp. 45–63.

Heller, A. (1990), 'The End of Communism', *Thesis Eleven*, No. 27, pp. 5–19.

Heller, A. and Fehér, F. (1988), *The Postmodern Political Condition* (Cambridge: Polity).

Hirszowicz, M. (1986), *Coercion and Control in Communist Society* (Brighton: Wheatsheaf).

Höhmann, H., Kaser, M. and Thalheim, K. (eds), (1975), *The New Economic Systems of Eastern Europe* (London: Hurst).

Holmes, L. (1981a), *The Policy Process in Communist States* (Beverly Hills: Sage).

Holmes, L., (ed.) (1981b), *The Withering Away of the State?* (London: Sage).

Holmes, L. (1986a), *Politics in the Communist World* (Oxford: Oxford University Press).

Holmes, L. (1986b), 'The State and the Churches in the GDR', in Miller and Rigby (1986), pp. 93–114.

Holmes, L. (1988), 'Legitimation and Legitimation Crisis in the Communist World', unpublished paper presented at the Australasian Political Studies Association Conference, Armidale (August).

Holmes, L. (1992a), 'The Significance of Marxist Dissent to the Emergence of Postcommunism in the GDR', in R. Taras (ed.), *The Road to Disillusion: From Critical Marxism to Postcommunism in Eastern Europe* (Armonk, NY: M.E. Sharpe), pp. 57–80.

Holmes, L. (1992b), 'An Alternative View on Communism, Post-Communism, Modernity and Post-Modernity', in J. Frentzel-Zagorska (ed.), *From a One-Party State to Democracy* (Amsterdam: Rodopi, forthcoming in 1992).

Hough, J. (1972), 'The Soviet System – Petrification or Pluralism?', *Problems of Communism*, Vol. 21, No. 2, pp. 25–45.

Huntington, S. (1968), *Political Order in Changing Societies* (New Haven: Yale University Press).

Inglehart, R. (1977), *The Silent Revolution* (Princeton, NJ: Princeton University Press).

Inglehart, R. and Siemienska, R. (1988), 'Changing Values and Political Dissatisfaction in Poland and the West: A Comparative Analysis', *Government and Opposition*, Vol. 23, No. 4, pp. 440–57.

Inoue, S. (1984), *Modern Korea and Kim Jong Il* (Tokyo: Yuzankaku).

Institut Gosudarstva I Prava (1987), 'Yuridicheskaya Nauka i Praktika v Usloviyakh Perestroiki', *Kommunist*, No. 14, pp. 42–50.

Jackson, R. and Rosberg, C. (1984), 'Personal Rule: Theory and Practice in Africa', *Comparative Politics*, Vol. 16, No. 4, pp. 421–42.

Jasinska-Kania, A. (1983), 'Rationalization and Legitimation Crisis: The Relevance of Marxian and Weberian Works for an Explanation of the Political Order's Legitimacy Crisis in Poland', *Sociology*, Vol. 17, No. 2, pp. 157–64.

Jennett, C. and Stewart, R. (1989), 'Introduction', in C. Jennett and R. Stewart (eds), *Politics of the Future* (Melbourne: Macmillan), pp. 1–28.

Johnson, C. (ed.) (1970), *Change in Communist Systems* (Stanford: Stanford University Press).

Jones, E. (1988), 'The Armed Forces and Soviet Society', in Sacks and Pankhurst (1988), pp. 239–58.

Jowitt, K. (1974), 'Political Innovation in Rumania', *Survey*, Vol. 20, No. 4, pp. 132–51.

Kaminski, A. (1989), 'Coercion, Corruption and Reform: State and Society in the Soviet-type Socialist Regime', *Journal of Theoretical Politics*, Vol. 1, No. 1, pp. 77–101.

Karklins, R. (1986), *Ethnic Relations in the USSR* (Boston: Allen & Unwin).

Katsenelinboigen, A. (1977), 'Coloured Markets in the Soviet Union', *Soviet Studies*, Vol. 29, No. 1, pp. 62–85.

Katsenelinboigen, A. (1983), 'Corruption in the USSR: Some Methodological Notes', in Clarke (1983a), pp. 220–38.

Kellner, D. (1988), 'Postmodernism as Social Theory: Some Challenges and Problems', *Theory, Culture and Society*, Vol. 5, pp. 239–69.

Kemény, I. (1982), 'The Unregistered Economy in Hungary', *Soviet Studies*, Vol. 34, No. 3, pp. 349–66.

Kenedi, J. (1981), *Do it Yourself* (London: Pluto).

Khrushchev, N. (1970), *Khrushchev Remembers* (Boston: Little, Brown).

Kolb, D. (1986), *The Critique of Pure Modernity* (Chicago: University of Chicago Press).

Kramer, J.M. (1977), 'Political Corruption in the USSR', *Western Political Quarterly*, Vol. 30, No. 2, pp. 213–24.

Kramer, J.M. (1988), 'Drug Abuse in the Soviet Union', *Problems of Communism*, Vol. 37, No. 2, pp. 28–40.

Kramer, J.M. (1990), 'Drug Abuse in Eastern Europe: An Emerging Issue of Public Policy', *Slavic Review*, Vol. 49, No. 1, pp. 19–31.

Krutogolov, M.A. (1973);, 'Korruptsiya', in *Bol'shaya Sovetskaya Entsiklopediya*, 3rd edn, Vol. 13, (Moscow: Izd. Sovetskaya Entsiklopediya), p. 216.

Kudryavtsev, V. and Lukasheva, E. (1988), 'Sotsialisticheskoe Pravovoe Gosudarstvo', *Kommunist*, No. 11 (July), pp. 44–55.

Kukathas, C., Lovell, D. and Maley, W. (eds) (1991), *The Transition from Socialism* (Melbourne: Longman Cheshire).

Kusin, V. (1988), 'Corruption Trial in Bratislava: The Party Metes Out Penalties', *RFE Research*, Vol. 13, No. 10, t. 1 (11 March), pp. 23–7.

Kuznetsova, N. (1975), 'Ukreplenie Sotsialisticheskoi Zakonnosti i Organizatsiya Bor'by Prestupnost'y v Svete Reshenii XXIV S'zeda KPSS', *Sovetskoe Gosudarstvo i Pravo*, No. 3 (March), pp. 122–30.

Kwasniewski, J. (1984), *Society and Deviance in Communist Poland: Attitudes towards Social Control* (Leamington Spa: Berg).

Lampert, N. (1983), 'The Whistleblower: Corruption and Citizens' Complaints in the USSR', in Clarke (1983a), pp. 268–87.

Lampert, N. (1984), 'Law and Order in the USSR: The Case of Economic and Official Crime', *Soviet Studies*, Vol. 36, No. 3, pp. 366–85.

Lampert, N. (1985), *Whistleblowing in the Soviet Union* (London: Macmillan).

Landy, P. (1961), 'What Price Corruption?', *Problems of Communism*, Vol. 10, No. 2, pp. 18–25.

Lane, D. (1979), 'Soviet Industrial Workers: The Lack of a Legitimation Crisis?', in Denitch (1979), pp. 177–94.

La Palombara, J. (ed.) (1963a), *Bureaucracy and Political Development* (Princeton, NJ: Princeton University Press).

La Palombara, J. (1963b), 'An Overview of Bureaucracy and Political Development', in La Palombara (1963a), pp. 3–61.

Law, D. (1974), 'Corruption in Georgia', *Critique*, No. 3, pp. 99–107.

Leng, S-C. (1982), 'Crime and Punishment in Post-Mao China', *China Law Reporter*, Vol. 2, No. 1, pp. 5–33.

Lenin, V. (1964), *Collected Works*, Vol. 23 (London: Lawrence and Wishart).

Levine, V. (1975), *Political Corruption – The Ghana Case* (Stanford: Stanford University Press).

Lewis, P.G. (1984a), 'Legitimation and Political Crisis: East European Developments in the Post-Stalin Period', in Lewis, 1984b, pp. 1–41.

Lewis, P.G. (ed.) (1984b), *Eastern Europe: Political Crisis and Legitimation* (London: Croom Helm).

Linden, C. (1966), *Khrushchev and the Soviet Leadership* (Baltimore: The Johns Hopkins Press).

Lipset, S.M. (1960), *Political Man* (New York: Doubleday).

Lipset, S.M. (1981), 'Social Conflict, Legitimacy and Democracy' in Connolly (1984a), pp. 88–103.

Liu, A. (1983), 'The Politics of Corruption in the People's Republic of China', *The American Political Science Review*, Vol. 77, No. 3, pp. 602–23.

Liu, A. (1986), *How China is Ruled* (Englewood Cliffs, NJ: Prentice Hall).

Liu, Jin and Li, Lin (eds) (1989), *Neo-Authoritarianism* (in Chinese) (Beijing: Beijing Economic Institute Publishing House).

Łos, M. (1982), 'Corruption in a Communist Country: A Case Study of Poland', unpublished paper presented at the International Sociological Association World Congress, Mexico City.

Łos, M. (ed.) (1990), *The Second Economy in Marxist States* (London: Macmillan).

Lovenduski, J. and Woodall, J. (1987), *Politics and Society in Eastern Europe* (London: Macmillan).

Löwenhardt, J. (1984), 'Nomenklatura and the Soviet Constitution', *Review of Socialist Law*, Vol. 10, No. 1, pp. 35–55.

Löwenhardt, J. (1987), 'Political Reform under Gorbachev', unpublished paper presented at the State University of Gröningen (December).

Ludz, P. (1979), 'Legitimacy in a Divided Nation: The Case of the German Democratic Republic', in Denitch (1979), pp. 161–75.

Lyotard, J-F. (1984), *The Post-Modern Condition* (Minneapolis: University of Minnesota Press).

Malenkov, G. (1952), *Report to the Nineteenth Party Congress of the Work of the Central Committee of the C.P.S.U. (B.)* (Moscow: Foreign Languages Publishing House).

Mann, M. (1970). 'The Social Cohesion of Liberal Democracy', *American Sociological Review*, Vol. 35, No. 3, pp. 423–39.

Manov, G. (1989), 'Sotsialisticheskoe Pravovoe Gosudarstvo: Problemy i Perspektivy', *Sovetskoe Gosudarstvo i Pravo*, No. 6, pp. 3–10.

Marcuse, H. (1964), *One Dimensional Man* (London: Routledge and Kegan Paul).

Marx, K. and Engels, F. (1980a), *Collected Works*, Vol. 14 (London: Lawrence and Wishart).

Marx, K. and Engels, F. (1980b), *Collected Works*, Vol. 16 (London: Lawrence and Wishart).

Mayntz, R. (1975), 'Legitimacy and the Directive Capacity of the Political System', in L. Lindberg (ed.), *Stress and Contradiction in Modern Capitalism* (Lexington: Heath), pp. 261–74.

McCarthy, T. (1981), *The Critical Theory of Jürgen Habermas* (Cambridge, MA: MIT Press).

McLellan, D. (1979), *Marxism after Marx* (London: Macmillan).

McLennan, G., Held, D. and Hall, S. (eds) (1984), The Idea of the Modern State (Milton Keynes: Open University Press).

McMullan, M. (1961), 'A Theory of Corruption', *Sociological Review*, Vol. 9, No. 2, pp. 181–201.

Medvedev, R. and Medvedev, Z. (1977), *Khrushchev* (Oxford: Oxford University Press).

Medvedev, Z. (1983), *Andropov* (Oxford: Blackwell).

Melucci, A. (1981) 'Ten Hypotheses for the Analysis of New Movements', in D. Pinto (ed.), *Contemporary Italian Sociology: A Reader* (Cambridge: Cambridge University Press), pp. 173–94.

Melucci, A. (1988), 'Social Movements and the Democratization of Everyday Life', in J. Keane (ed.), *Civil Society and the State* (London: Verso), pp. 245–60.

Meyer, A. (1970), 'Theories of Convergence', in Johnson (1970), pp. 313–41.

Meyer, A. (1972), 'Legitimacy of power in East Central Europe' in Sinanian, Deak and Ludz (1972), pp. 45–68.

Millar, J.R. (ed.) (1987), *Politics, Work and Daily Life in the USSR* (Cambridge: Cambridge University Press).

Miller, R.F. (1989), 'Communism in Crisis', unpublished paper presented to the Workshop on China's Democracy, Canberra (June).

Miller, R.F. (ed.) (1992), *The Developments of Civil Society in Communist Systems* (Sydney: Allen & Unwin).

Miller, R.F. and Rigby, T.H. (eds) (1986), *Religion and Politics in Communist States* (Canberra: Australian National University).

Miller, R.F., Miller, J.H. and Rigby, T.H. (eds) (1987), *Gorbachev at the Helm* (Beckenham: Croom Helm).

Molyneux, M. (1990), 'The "Woman Question" in the Age of Perestroika', *New Left Review*, No. 183, pp. 23–49.

Monteiro, J.B. (1966), *Corruption: Control of Maladministration* (Bombay: Manaktalas).

Moore, B. (1967), *Social Origins of Dictatorship and Democracy* (Harmondsworth: Penguin).

Moore, P. (1984), 'Bulgaria', in Rakowska-Harmstone (1984a), pp. 186–212.

Motyl, A. (1989), 'Reassessing the Soviet Crisis: Big Problems, Muddling Through, Business as Usual', *Political Science Quarterly*, Vol. 104, No. 2, pp. 269–80.

Myers, J.T. (1989), 'China: Modernization and "Unhealthy Tendencies"', *Comparative Politics*, Vol. 21, No. 2, pp. 193–213.

Nas, T., Price, A. and Weber, C. (1986), 'A Policy-Oriented Theory of Corruption', *American Political Science Review*, Vol. 80, No. 1, pp. 107–19.

Nethercut, R. (1983), 'Leadership in China: Rivalry, Reform and Renewal', *Problems of Communism*, Vol. 32, No. 2, pp. 30–46.

Nove, A. (1977), *The Soviet Economic System* (London: George Allen & Unwin).

Nye, J.S. (1967), 'Corruption and Political Development: A Cost-Benefit Analysis', *American Political Science Review*, Vol. 61, No. 2, pp. 417–27.

Offe, C. (1985), 'New Social Movements: Challenging the Boundaries of Institutional Politics', *Social Research*, Vol. 52, No. 4, pp. 817–68.

Oi, J. (1989), 'Market Reforms and Corruption in Rural China', *Studies in Comparative Communism*, Vol. 22, Nos. 2 and 3, pp. 221–33.

Oksenberg, M. (1987), 'China's 13th Party Congress', *Problems of Communism*, Vol. 36, No. 6, pp. 1–17.

Ottaway, D. and Ottaway, M. (1981), *Afrocommunism* (New York: Holmes and Meier).

Painter, J. (1991), 'The Green Revolution: Ecology, Politics and Social Change in the Soviet Union 1985–1990', unpublished Master of Arts Dissertation, University of Melbourne.

Pakulski, J. (1986), 'Legitimacy and Mass Compliance: Reflections on Max Weber and Soviet-Type Societies', *British Journal of Political Science*, Vol. 16, Pt. 1, pp. 35–56.

Pakulski, J. (1987), 'Ideology and Political Domination: A Critical Reappraisal', *International Journal of Comparative Sociology*, Vol. 28, Nos 3–4, pp. 129–57.

Pakulski, J. (1991), *Social Movements* (Melbourne: Longman Cheshire).

Palmier, L. (1983), 'Bureaucratic Corruption and its Remedies' in Clarke (1983a), pp. 207–19.

Pano, N. (1984), 'Albania' in Rakowska-Harmstone (1984a), pp. 213–37.

Pelczynski, Z. (1980), 'Poland under Gierek', in R.F. Leslie (ed.), *The History of Poland Since 1863* (Cambridge: Cambridge University Press), pp. 407–43.

Peters, J.C. and Welch, S. (1978), 'Political Corruption in America: A Search for Definitions and a Theory', *American Political Science Review*, Vol. 72, No. 3, pp. 974–84.

Poggi, G. (1978), *The Development of the Modern State* (London: Hutchinson).

Powell, D. (1973), 'Drug Abuse in Communist Europe', *Problems of Communism*, Vol. 22, No. 4, pp. 31–40.

Pravda, A. (1986), 'Elections in Communist Party States', in White and Nelson (1986), pp. 27–54.

Pravda, A. and Ruble, B. (eds) (1986), *Trade Unions in Communist States* (Boston: Allen & Unwin).

Prybyla, J. (1989), 'China's Economic Experiment: Back from the Market?', *Problems of Communism*, Vol. 38, No. 1, pp. 1–18.

Pye, L. (1968), *The Spirit of Chinese Politics* (Cambridge, MA: MIT Press).

Rakowska-Harmstone, T. (ed.) (1984a), *Communism in Eastern Europe* (Manchester: Manchester University Press).

Rakowska-Harmstone, T. (1984b), 'Introduction', in Rakowska-Harmstone (1984a), pp. 1–7.

Ramet, S. (1991), *Social Currents in Eastern Europe* (Durham, NC: Duke University Press).

Reddaway, P. (1978), 'The Development of Dissent and Opposition' in Brown and Kaser (1978), pp. 121–56.

Reddaway, P. (1988), 'Soviet Psychiatry: An End to Political Abuse?', *Survey*, Vol. 30, No. 3, pp. 25–38.

Remington, R. (ed.) (1969), *Winter in Prague* (Cambridge, MA: MIT Press).

Rigby, T.H. (1970), 'The Soviet Leadership: Towards a Self-stabilising Oligarchy', *Soviet Studies*, Vol. 22, No. 2, pp. 167–91.

Rigby, T.H. (1980), 'A Conceptual Approach to Authority, Power and Policy in the Soviet Union', in Rigby, Brown and Reddaway (1983), pp. 9–31.

Rigby, T.H. (1982), 'Introduction: Political Legitimacy, Weber and Communist Mono-organisational Systems', in Rigby and Fehér (1982), pp. 1–26.

Rigby, T.H. (1985), 'Political Corruption: The Soviet Case', unpublished paper presented at the Australian National University, Canberra (April).

Rigby, T.H. (1988), 'Staffing USSR Incorporated: The Origins of the Nomenklatura System', *Soviet Studies*, Vol. 40, No. 4, pp. 523–37.

Rigby, T.H. and Fehér, F. (eds) (1982), *Political Legitimation in Communist States* (London: Macmillan).

Rigby, T.H. and Harasymiw, B. (eds) (1983), *Leadership Selection and Patron–Client Relations in the USSR and Yugoslavia* (London: Allen & Unwin).

Rigby, T.H., Brown, A. and Reddaway, P. (eds) (1983), *Authority, Power and Policy in the USSR* (London: Macmillan).

Rootes, C. (1983), 'Intellectuals, the Intelligentsia and the Problem of Legitimacy', unpublished paper presented at the European Consortium for Political Research Conference, Freiburg (February–March).

Rose, R. (1969), 'Dynamic Tendencies in the Authority of Regimes', *World Politics*, Vol. 21, No. 4, pp. 620–28.

Rose-Ackerman, S. (1978), *Corruption: A Study in Political Economy* (New York: Academic Press).

Rothschild, J. (1979), 'Political Legitimacy in Contemporary Europe' in Denitch (1979), pp. 37–54.

Ruane, K. (1982), *The Polish Challenge* (London: BBC).

Rumer, B. (1984), 'Structural Imbalance in the Soviet Economy', *Problems in Communism*, Vol. 33, No. 4, pp. 24–32.

Rusinow, D. (1977), *The Yugoslav Experiment, 1948–74* (London: Hurst).

Sacks, M.P. and Pankhurst, J.G. (eds) (1988), *Understanding Soviet Society* (Boston: Unwin Hyman).

Sampson, S. (1983), 'Rich Families and Poor Collectives: An Anthropological Approach to Romania's "Second Economy"', *Bidrag till Öststatsforskningen*, Vol. 11, No. 1, pp. 44–77.

Sasinska-Klas, T. (1988), 'The Spiral of Delegitimization of Political Power in Poland', unpublished paper presented at the American Political Science Association Conference, Washington, DC (September).

Schapiro, L. (1970), *The Communist Party of the Soviet Union* (London: Methuen.)

Schnytzer, A. (1982), *Stalinist Economic Strategy in Practice: The Case of Albania* (Oxford: Oxford University Press).

Schöpflin, G. (ed.) (1983), *Censorship and Political Communication* (London: Frances Pinter).

Schöpflin, G. (1984), 'Corruption, Information, Irregularity in Eastern Europe: A Political Analysis', *Südosteuropa*, Vol. 33, Nos 7–8, pp. 389–401.

Schwartz, C.A. (1979), 'Corruption and Political Development in the USSR', *Comparative Politics*, Vol. 11, No. 4, pp. 425–43.

Scott, C.V. (1988), 'Socialism and the "Soft State" in Africa: An Analysis of Angola and Mozambique', *The Journal of Modern African Studies*, Vol. 26, No. 1 (March), pp. 23–36.

Scott, J.C. (1972), *Comparative Political Corruption* (Englewood Cliffs, NJ: Prentice-Hall)

Seiffert, W. (1980), 'Die DDR – ein Rechtsstaat?', *Deutschland Archiv*, Vol. 13, No. 7, pp. 765–6.

Senn, A. (1990), 'Toward Lithuanian Independence: Algirdas Brazauskas and the CPL', *Problems of Communism*, Vol. 39, No. 2, pp. 21–8.

Shafir, M. (1985), *Romania: Politics, Economics and Society* (London: Frances Pinter).

Shafir, M. (1987), *Political Legitimacy in Eastern Europe – A Comparative Study* (Munich: Radio Free Europe).

Shafir, M. (1991), 'Sharp Drop in Leadership's Popularity', *Radio Free Europe Background Report*, 3 April.

Sharlet, R. (1967). 'Concept Formation in Political Science and Communist Studies: Conceptualising Political Participation', in Fleron (1969), pp. 244–53.

Shelley, L. (1988), 'Crime and Criminals in the USSR', in Sacks and Pankhurst (1988), pp. 193–219.

Shmelev, N. (1987), 'Avansy i Dolgi', *Novyi Mir*, No. 6 (June), pp. 142–58.

Šimečka, M. (1984), *The Restoration of Order – The Normalisation of Czechoslovakia* (London: Verso).

Simis, K. (1982), *USSR: The Corrupt Society* (New York: Simon and Schuster).

Simons, W. and White, S. (eds) (1984), *The Party Statutes of the Communist World* (The Hague: Martinus Nijhoff).

Sinanian, S., Deak, I. and Ludz, P. (eds) (1972), *Eastern Europe in the 1970s* (New York: Praeger).

Skocpol, T. (1979), *States and Social Revolutions* (Cambridge: Cambridge University Press).

Slider, D. (1991), 'Embattled Entrepreneurs: Soviet Cooperatives in an Unreformed Economy'. *Soviet Studies*, Vol. 43, No. 5, pp. 797–821.

Smart, C. (1990), 'Gorbachev's Lenin: The Myth in Service to Perestroika', *Studies in Comparative Communism*, Vol. 23, No. 1, pp. 5–21.

Smith, H. (1976), *The Russians* (London: Sphere).

Somerville, K. (1986), *Angola: Politics, Economics and Society* (London, Frances Pinter).

Staats, S.J. (1972), 'Corruption in the Soviet System', *Problems of Communism*, Vol. 21, No. 1, pp. 40–7.

Stubb-Ostergaard, C. (1986), 'Explaining China's Recent Political Corruption', *Corruption and Reform*, Vol. 1, No. 3, pp. 209–33.

Sword, K. (ed.) (1990), *The Times Guide to Eastern Europe* (London: Times Books).

Szajkowski, B. (1981), 'Socialist People's Republic of Albania', in B. Szajkowski (ed.), *Marxist Governments – A World Survey*, Vol. 1 (London: Macmillan), pp. 34–61.

Tarkowski, J. (1988), 'Patronage in a Centralized Socialist System: The Case of Poland', *International Political Science Review*, Vol. 4, No. 4, pp. 495–518.

Tarkowski, J. (1989), 'Old and New Patterns of Corruption in Poland and the USSR', *Telos*, No. 80, pp. 51–62.

Teague, E. (1988), *Solidarity and the Soviet Worker* (London: Croom Helm).

Teiwes, F. (1984), *Leadership, Legitimacy, and Conflict in China* (London: Macmillan).

Thompson, J. and Held, D. (eds) (1982), *Habermas: Critical Debates* (London: Macmillan).
Tismaneanu, V. (1986), 'Byzantine Rites, Stalinist Follies: The Twilight of Dynastic Socialism in Romania', *Orbis*, Vol. 30, No. 1, pp. 65–90.
Tismaneanu, V. (1988), *The Crisis of Marxist Ideology in Eastern Europe* (London: Routledge).
Tökés, R. (1972), 'Analysis of A. Meyer's "Legitimacy of Power in East Central Europe"', in Sinanian, Deak and Ludz (1972), pp. 79–85.
Tolz, V. (1990), *The USSR's Emerging Multiparty System* (New York: Praeger).
Tomasevich, J. (1955), *Peasants, Politics and Economic Change in Yugoslavia* (Stanford: Stanford University Press).
Touraine, A. (1985), 'An Introduction to the Study of Social Movements', *Social Research*, Vol. 52, No. 4, pp. 749–87.
Troyer, R., Clark, J. and Rojek, D. (eds), (1989), *Social Control in the People's Republic of China* (New York: Praeger).
Vickery, M. (1984), *Cambodia: 1975–1982* (Sydney: George Allen & Unwin).
Volgyes, I. (ed.) (1975), *Political Socialization in Eastern Europe* (New York: Praeger).
Wallerstein, I. (1990), 'Marx, Marxism-Leninism and Socialist Experiences in the Modern World System', *Thesis Eleven*, No. 27, pp. 40–53.
Weber, M. (1918), 'Politics as a Vocation' in H.H. Gerth and C. Wright Mills, *From Max Weber* (London: Routledge and Kegan Paul), pp. 77–128.
Weber, M. (1947), *The Theory of Social and Economic Organisation* (Glencoe, ILL: The Free Press).
Weber, M. (1968), *Economy and Society*, Vol. 3 (New York: Bedminster Press).
Werner, S. (1983), 'New Directions in the Study of Adminstrative Corruption', *Public Administration Review*, Vol. 43, No. 2, pp. 146–54.
White, L. (1988), 'Changing Concepts of Corruption in Communist China: Early 1950s vs. Early 1980s', *Issues and Studies*, Vol. 24, No. 1, pp. 49–95.
White, S. (1986), 'Economic Performance and Communist Legitimacy', *World Politics*, Vol. 38, No. 3, pp. 462–82.
White, S. and Nelson, D. (eds) (1986), *Communist Politics – A Reader* (London: Macmillan).
White, S., Gardner, J., Schöpflin, G. and Saich, T. (1990), *Communist and Post-Communist Political Systems* (London: Macmillan).
Willets, H. (1962), 'The Wages of Economic Sin', *Problems of Communism*, Vol. 11, No. 5, pp. 26–32.
Williams, M. (1990), 'Vietnam's New Hard Line – The Seventh Central Committee Plenum', *Journal of Communist Studies*, Vol. 6, No. 1, pp. 112–13.
Williams, R. (1982), 'Corruption in Africa's Politics', unpublished paper presented at the 12th International Political Science Association World Conference, Rio de Janeiro (August).
Williams, R. (1987), *Political Corruption in Africa* (Aldershot: Gower).
Wilson, I. (1988), *Political Reform and the 13th Congress of the Communist Party of China* (Canberra: Australian National University Strategic and Defence Studies Centre).
Winters, P.J. (1990a), 'Zum ersten Mal frei', *Deutschland Archiv*, Vol. 23, No. 4, pp. 497–501.
Winters, P.J. (1990b), 'Die CDU liegt auch in den Rathäusern vorn', *Deutschland Archiv*, Vol. 23, No. 5, pp. 641–3.
Wishnevsky, J. (1989), 'USSR – the Gdlyan–Ivanov Commission Starts Work', *Radio Liberty Research*, 21 June 1989.
Wraith, R. and Simpkins, E. (1963), *Corruption in Developing Countries* (London: Allen & Unwin).

Yao Wenyuan (1975), 'On the Social Basis of the Lin Biao Anti-Party Clique', *Peking Review*, No. 10, pp. 5–10.

Yeh, M. (1987), 'Modernization and Corruption in Mainland China', *Issues and Studies*, Vol. 23, No. 11 (November), pp. 11–27.

Young, G. (1984), 'Control and Style: Discipline Inspection Commissions Since the 11th Congress', *China Quarterly*, No. 97, pp. 24–52.

Young, S. (1971), 'Vietnam: Democratic Republic of Vietnam', in R.F. Staar (ed.), *Yearbook on International Communist Affairs 1971* (Stanford: Hoover Institution Press), pp. 678–87.

Yu, Yulin (1986), 'Unhealthy Tendencies among Chinese Communist Cadres', *Issues and Studies*, Vol. 22, No. 1, pp. 5–8.

Yudin, I. (1989), 'Ekonomicheskie Aspekty Sokrashcheniya Vooruzhonnykh Sil i Konversii Voennogo Proizvodstva', *Voprosy Ekonomiki*, No. 6, pp. 48–53.

Zanga, L. (1988a), 'Open Criticism in Albania', RAD Background Report No. 58 (Albania), *RFE Research*, Vol. 13, No. 13 (31 March), Pt. 2, pp. 1–3.

Zanga, L. (1988b), 'Albania's Smuggling Operation?', RAD Background Report No. 3 (Albania), *RFE Research*, Vol. 13, No. 2 (14 January) Pt. 2, pp. 1–3.

Ziolkowski, M. (1988), 'Individuals and the Social System: Values, Perceptions and Behavioural Strategies', *Social Research*, Vol. 55, Nos 1–2, pp. 139–77.

Zukin, S. (1975), *Beyond Marx and Tito* (London: Cambridge University Press).

Index

Escobar, P. 118
Espín, V. 97
Estonia 4, 104–5, 146, 287
'ethical deficit' 169
Ethiopia 53, 122, 192, 213, 291
  anti-corruption campaigns 253–4
  collapse of communism 3
  transition to post-communism 292,
    301
Europe 315, 324
  Central 66
  Eastern ix, xi, 1–3, 9, 12, 20, 21–5,
    35, 55, 56, 57, 60, 178, 191, 214,
    273, 293–4, 297
  Southern 327
  Western 324, 326
European Community 181, 288, 319
extortion 78, 143
  definition 85
  examples 103, 108–10

Fainsod, M. 277
false reporting 82–3, 143, 165, 175
  examples 101–4
  see also pripiski
fascism, as a modern ideology 316
Federal Republic of Germany – *see*
  Germany, West
Fedorchuk, V. 163, 193, 224
Fehér, F. 331
Feixiang 99
Feldbrugge, F. 45, 74, 90, 146, 267
fictitious economy 73, 76
Finland 116
first economy 212
  definition 75
'five-anti' campaign 232, 234, 235
Fordism 318
forgery 78, 83, 104–5, 143
Forster, K. 48, 76, 234
'Four Little Dragons/Tigers' 216,
  300–1, 309; *see also* Hong Kong;
  Korea, South; Singapore; Taiwan
'Four Modernisations' 233, 235
France 159, 273, 328
fraud
  definition 82
  examples 101, 171
Friedman, M. 317
Friedrich, C. 65, 90
fubai 76

Fujian 145, 234

Gang of Four 208
Gdlyan, T. 191, 228–31
Georgia x, xi, 4, 51, 146, 147, 159, 160,
  199, 206, 222, 224, 303
German Democratic Republic – *see*
  Germany, East
German Ideology, The 332
Germany 185, 315, 325
Germany, East 17, 53, 160, 194, 197,
  216, 219, 261, 277, 296, 305, 323–4,
  332
  anti-corruption campaigns xii, 8, 154
  attitudes towards pluralism 304
  collapse of communism ix, 1, 293,
    294, 330
  communist party 256, 304, 328, 331
  corruption 98–9, 106–7, 159
  dissidence 297
  economic reform 15, 286
  elections 307, 331
  mass unrest 31, 297
  post-communist problems 300, 306
  transition to post-communism 292,
    293, 300, 303–4
  unification with Federal Republic of
    Germany 300, 330
Germany, West 155, 194, 219, 305
Giddens, A. 62, 331
Gierek, E. 117, 195, 247
Gill, G. 284–5
glasnost x, 6, 22, 59, 138, 148, 155, 182,
  217, 219, 227, 253, 283, 299
Gorbachev, M. x, 1, 3, 16, 17, 21, 22,
  35, 36, 58, 60, 99, 138, 161, 165,
  180, 199, 201, 205, 225–31, 267,
  268, 275, 278, 285, 289, 290, 328
Gradev, D. 249
graft 88
grass-eaters 65, 83
Great Crash of 1929 316
Great Powers 326
Great Proletarian Cultural Revolution
  1, 100, 135, 161, 214, 232, 270, 275,
  298
'Great Terror' 210
'Great Trial' 210
Greece 327
Grossman, G. 73–4
Grósz, K. 281–2